BIG FARMS MAKE BIG FLU

BIG FARMS MAKE BIG FLU

Dispatches on Infectious Disease, Agribusiness,
and the Nature of Science

by ROB WALLACE

MONTHLY REVIEW PRESS
New York

Library of Congress Cataloging-in-Publication Data:
Names: Wallace, Robert G., author.
Title: Big farms make big flu : dispatches on infectious disease,
  agribusiness, and the nature of science / by Rob Wallace.
Description: New York : Monthly Review Press, [2016] | Includes
  bibliographical references and index.
Identifiers: LCCN 2016022329| ISBN 9781583675892 (pbk.) | ISBN 9781583675908
  (hardcover)
Subjects: LCSH: Influenza—Epidemiology. | Epidemics. | Agricultural
  industries—Health aspects.
Classification: LCC RA644.I6 W35 2016 | DDC 614.5/18—dc23 LC record
available at https://lccn.loc.gov/2016022329

Typeset in Minion Pro

MONTHLY REVIEW PRESS, NEW YORK
monthlyreview.org

5 4 3 2 1

Contents

TO VIOLET

When we had no means, we said the end justifies the means. Now that we have no ends, we say the means justify the end.

Neither is immoral.

What is entirely immoral is that there is no longer any contradiction between the two: ends and means have become indifferent to one another. They are quite simply no longer of the same order.

Everything works wonderfully, expanded like polystyrene, driven by the generic flows of the generators: the metastatics of Good.

Everything goes badly, all the circuits diverge, driven by anxiety and driven to anxiety: the erratics of Evil.

—JEAN BAUDRILLARD (1995)

"Eventually? Is that all? Eventually?" Hoock Seng scowls at him. "I don't care about 'eventually.' I care about this month. If this factory fails to produce, we won't have a chance to worry about this 'eventually' you speak of. You'll be back in Thonburi, picking through chicken guts and hoping you aren't hit with flu, and I'll be back in a yellow card tower. Don't worry about tomorrow. Worry about whether Mr. Lake throws us all out on the street today. Use your imagination. Find a way to make this gaiside *algae breed."*

—PAOLO BACIGALUPI (2009)

Introduction

I AM TO GIVE A TALK ON EBOLA at Harvard tomorrow. But as
I am unemployed and in Boston on my own dime, I find myself at
the Milner Hotel. It happens to be where Mohamed Atta, Marwan
al-Shehhi, Fayez Banihammad, and Mohand al-Sheri stayed before
hijacking American Airlines Flight 11 and United Airlines Flight 175
on September 11.[1]

The hotel is serviceable enough, its reputation now more at the
mercy of online reviews than of a terrorist plot fifteen years ago. I can't
help, however, but feel an undertow of recognition. I have no affinity
for Al Qaeda and its descendents whatsoever, or, for that matter, for
our Saudi allies who funded the attack.[2] I was in New York City that
day and when in town still studiously avoid Ground Zero as much
as for the painful memories as for its gift shop of overpriced cheese
boards and plush rescue dogs commemorating a mass murder.[3]

There is, though, in my present accommodations, if by their history alone, a sense of shared fate, symmetrically reversed in the dingy
room's mirror. While once I had a promising career as an evolutionary biologist studying influenza, consulting for the UN's Food and
Agriculture Organization and the Centers for Disease Control and
Prevention, I now find myself professionally ostracized, indeed on the
precipice of earning the moniker of an enemy of the state.

It isn't a matter of the quality of my work—I continue to pub-
lish—or even the dubiousness of my loyalties to a neoliberal empire
attacked in 2001 for reasons with which I disagree. The blacklisting
stems instead from the decisions I have made about the nature of
science.

In the course of producing a statistical phylogeography of bird flu H5N1, making a map of the virus's migration using genetic sequences collected across multiple outbreak zones, evolutionary biologist Walter Fitch and I confirmed the strain emerged out of Guangdong, a southeastern province in China across from Hong Kong.[4] The fallout of that work sent me off in two directions a more careerist mindset would have avoided, well, like the plague.

First, Guangdong officials denounced our paper before it was even published (more of this in the pages within). Although I had already been hardened by a dissertation studying HIV/AIDS in New York City, I was surprised any such work would end up fodder for international intrigue. So I apprenticed myself to learning the dark arts of the political economy of pandemic research. Ostensibly such practice aims at honing self-defense, but taking the initiative on such matters, instead of pinging dumbly from grant to grant like a good little researcher, makes one more the target (more of this too inside).

While I pursued additional phylogeography, and have more in the works, in the end I was deflected in a second direction by my curiosity rather than my self-interest, although one hopes the best of science aligns the two, at least in the direction of the former to the latter. No matter how I looked at them, the genetic sequences I was compiling of influenza couldn't tell me *why* H5N1 emerged in Guangdong in the mid-1990s. So I began to look into the area's economic geography, particularly the ways a shifting agricultural sector changes pathogen trajectories. Many of my evolution colleagues didn't have the foggiest notion what I was up to and the social scientists who became interested were repulsed by the positivist empiricism to which I continue to hew. I found myself stuck in a gulch between epistemologies, with the professional fortunes to show for it. And Boston so expensive this time of year!

There was the additional complication that both paths I struck routinely crossed. I repeatedly discovered that political power shapes both infectious diseases and the sciences that study them. And yet I found myself unprepared for the nature and extent of the depravities attached. In the name of the populace they claim to serve, companies and governments alike are willing and able to risk the very end of humanity as we know it. Perhaps old news to readers of Herodotus, Montaigne, and Melle Mel, but the manifold forms such an observation takes should *always* be in at least some corner of ourselves a surprise. Otherwise our cynicism flatters us into inaction.

On my beat, evolutionary epidemiology, I came to the realization that Big Food has entered a strategic alliance with influenza, a virus that took a newly dangerous turn in an ongoing and wholly avoidable industrial accident of multinational agribusiness's own undoing. That is, so as to leave no doubt of my contention, agribusiness, backed by state power home and abroad, is now working as much *with* influenza as against it. Clearly beyond the realm of respectable discourse. And yet, despite my professional travails, here we are introducing many a report to that effect.

The logistics by which I arrived at such a collection are in comparison straightforward. In 2009, as part of the family business, I co-authored a book with my parents, Rodrick Wallace and Deborah Wallace, on ecological resilience and the evolution of human pathogens.[5] As customary these days, I set up a blog to accompany the book's release.[6]

Farming Pathogens took on a life of its own. I used the blog as a public notebook in which to review and make new discoveries, new to me anyway, including those that led to the shock of agrifood's "Viral Vichy," a regime that collaborates with a virus. This book collects some of the better of the commentaries, lightly edited here; a number of longer peer-reviewed articles I wrote for *Antipode, Human Geography, Social Science & Medicine,* and the *International Journal of Health Services;* and four new dispatches published nowhere else.

Some of the pieces were written with a public audience in mind. Some were mere notes dashed to myself. Two were given as speeches to professional audiences, covering key ideas from which a larger audience would greatly benefit. As these essays develop lines of inquiry across nearly a decade, there are slight overlaps and shameless repetitions here and there. I ask the reader's patience, if only because the pieces present an active struggle to build an understanding of what were, at one and the same time, swiftly moving circumstances arising from deep out of the core of our mode of civilization.

The pieces focus largely on influenza, as biocultural object and sociopolitical antagonist, but also delve into agriculture, other infectious diseases, evolution, ecological resilience, dialectical biology, the practice of science, and, back in the news, revolution. While I followed my muse, perhaps even off the map, the topics inform one another in often surprising and at times critically necessary ways.

Why surprising? For many researchers the limits of the universe are defined by the boundaries of their discipline. By a Platonic fallacy, others mistake their methodologies for how the world works. The possibilities needn't be so limited, of course. Successful multidisciplinarity marries what appears to be at first glance incompatible thinking. Those who bother to negotiate a strange synergism of ideas often strike upon serendipitous discoveries their work would never have caught upon otherwise.

The shocks I've received—Viral Vichy!—have convinced me of the importance of reconfiguring the very guts of the study of evolutionary epidemiology. Pathogens, a great and terrible global threat to human and many a non-human alike, as much a Sword of Damocles hovering above civilization as climate change, respect little of disciplinarity.

Pathogen dynamics often arise from a multitude of causes interacting at multiple scales of time and space and across biocultural domains. I learned in the course of my study of the evolution of HIV's life history, for instance, that the virus uses processes at one level of organization to defend itself against impediments directed at it at a second level.[7] Interventions, it follows, must be based on a multidimensionality that medical and public health problems themselves manifest. Otherwise many epizootics remain intractable no matter what innovative drugs or vaccines are deployed.

It is in this context that I have dedicated my career so far to applying my training in evolutionary ecology to studying how infectious diseases operate in what over human history developed into an intricately socialized world. Humans have built physical and social environments, on land and in the sea, that have radically altered the pathways along which pathogens evolve and disperse.

Pathogens, however, are no mere protagonists, battered to and fro by the tides of human history. They also act of their own volition, if you'll excuse the anthropomorphism. They display agency. And they have by virtue of their evolutionary changes forced agribusiness to the bargaining table, a place where that ilk, given their successes, *think* they excel. The resulting agreement is written as no treaty or contract nor even in anything we would recognize as communication. It is found instead in a form of xenospecific convergence. The two parties have maneuvered into an agriculture of mutual interests, at times reacting forcefully within each's own domain in the other's favor. One thinks perhaps such convergence could be at best unconscious. An emergent epiphenomenon, maybe. I discovered otherwise, and that's the shock. No virus engineered in a lab, no plan to purposely spread influenza, but a conspiracy of man and microbe nonetheless, with humanity and many a wildlife population at stake.

That wild notion is mine alone. But to my co-authors on some of the pieces here, my sincerest appreciation for your generosity and good works: Katie Atkins, Luke Bergmann, Marius Gilbert, Lenny Hogerwerf, Mollie Holmberg, Richard Kock, Raffaele Mattioli, Claudia Pittiglio, Deborah Wallace, and Rodrick Wallace. Special thanks to other collaborators past and present, including Robyn Alders, Dudley Bonsal, William Boto, Noah Ebner, Walter Fitch, Alison Galvani, Kris Hall, Gary Hayward, Rolph Houben, Vincent Martin, Joachim Otte, Jan Slingenbergh, and Thomas Van Boeckel.

Thanks as well to Mike Davis, who wrote a book on influenza that made me remark aloud in the shop I found it, "Whew, that's covered—done!"[8] Of course, that wasn't quite right. Some of the best books continue to speak to us long after we close them. So much so, in fact, that subconsciously much of the work described here followed up many of the points Mike made and questions he raised.

Profound thanks to Michael Yates, Martin Paddio, and Susie Day at Monthly Review Press, and to Erin Clermont, for their exemplar of conscientious publication. And to Peter Cury, my gratitude for designing the cover.

For their support and feedback, I thank friends, neighbors, and supporters Jason Andors, Tamara Awerbuch, Kazembe Balagun, Adia Benton, Terrence Blackman, Sarah Burgess Herbert, Valentine Cadieux, Jahi Chappell, Luis Fernando Chaves, Justin Cheatham,

John Choe, Susan Craddock, Leah Danoff, Shoshana Danoff Fanizza, Nicoline De Haan, Michael Dorgan, Belén Fernández, Mindy Fullilove, Tamara Giles-Vernick, Columba Gonzalez, Veronica Gorodetskaya, Carlos Grijalva-Eternod, Chris Gunderson, Larry Hanley, Tamara Harris, Steve Hinchliffe, Megan Hustad, Julie Jefferson, Tammi Jonas, Katrina Karkazis, John Kim, Colin Kloecker, Mukul Kumar, Jonathan Latham, Ruby Lawrence, Richard Levins, Adrienne Logsdon, Alexis Logsdon, Dave Logsdon, Juliette Majot, Melissa Mathes, and Shanai Matteson.

Another round of applause for Heather McGray, Felicity Mungovan, Scott Newman, Mike Noreen, Eric Odell, Luba Ostashevsky, Patrick Otto, Raj Patel, Richard Peet, Dirk Pfeiffer, Tom Philpott, Jessica Raymond, Robert Rockwell, Ilana Rudnik, Mary Shepherd, Brad Sigal, Janie Webster Sohmer, Matt Sparke, Jeffrey St. Clair, Elisabeth Stoddard, Jayelinda Suridge, John Takekawa, Keeanga-Yamahtta Taylor, Peter Taylor, Jeanine Webster, Kirstin Weigmann, Dale Wiehoff, Kim Williams-Guillen, Chris Wright, Xiangming Xiao, all the commenters on *Farming Pathogens* and its Facebook page, the Brecht Forum in New York City, Works Progress in Minneapolis, the Institute for Global Studies at the University of Minnesota, the Institute for Agriculture and Trade Policy, the Simpson Center for the Humanities at the University of Washington, and the Spirit of 1848.

Finally, to Violet, expeditioner extraordinaire, to whom I dedicate this book, my deepest love and affection.

In the face of such heartfelt appreciation, I claim all errors here— and the backlash from all things accurate—as mine alone.

I can see here in the Milner Hotel's bathroom mirror the threads of Moirai, the three fates, growing rapidly from stubble to beard. The kind of imperium that double-tapped Waziristan wedding parties, undermined its own war efforts to protect agribusiness monopolies, and killed 1.3 million in Iraq, Afghanistan, and Pakistan since September 11 bears little patience for insults upon its prime directives.[9] I am ready to face the consequences.

—ROB WALLACE, BOSTON, MAY 2015

PART ONE

"Yes, my dear fellow. It is my suspicion that the Spire has been tolerating the drone until now—lulling us, if you will, into a false sense of security. Yet now the Spire has decreed that we must discard that particular mental crutch. It will no longer permit us to gain any knowledge of the contents of a room until one of us steps into it. And at that moment it will prevent any of us leaving until we have solved that problem."

"You mean it's changing the rules as it goes along?" Hirz asked.

The Doctor turned his exquisite silver mask towards her. "Which rules did you have in mind, Hirz?"

—ALASTAIR REYNOLDS (2002)

The Great Bird Flu Blame Game

A rose may retain its fragrance under all vicissitudes of human taxonomy, but never doubt the power of a name to shape and direct our thoughts.

—STEPHEN JAY GOULD (2002)

You give each other names you give everything names to assert your place. But we have names too. We take the form of what brought us here—and we take the name of what we killed to stay.

—ADAM HINES (2010)

THE WORLD HEALTH ORGANIZATION HAS proposed new nomenclature for the various strains of influenza A (H5N1), the bird flu virus circulating in Eurasia and Africa.[10] The strains would now be enumerated rather than named after their countries or regions of origin.

WHO declares the change necessary because of the confusion caused by disparate naming systems presently used in the scientific literature. A unified system of nomenclature would facilitate the interpretation of genetic and surveillance data generated by different labs. It would also provide a framework for revising strain names based on viral characteristics. The new system would at the same time bring an end to the stigmatization caused when flu strains are named after their places of origin.

I am a public health phylogeographer. I use the genetic sequences of viruses and bacteria, including H5N1, to make discoveries about pathogen geographic spread and evolution. The proposed nomenclature has direct impact on the work I do.

On the one hand, the proposed changes seem reasonable enough. The new system would offer H5N1 taxonomy room to grow. For instance, the Qinghai-like strain of H5N1 that has spread west from Lake Qinghai in northwestern China across Eurasia and into Africa has undergone subsequent diversification.[11] The new groups must somehow be designated something beyond "Qinghai-like."

On the other hand, including geography in the strain names allows easier recognition than the open-ended enumeration WHO proposes. "Fujian-like" is more readily identifiable than "Clade 2.2.4." Perhaps more fundamentally, as defined by variation in the virus's hemagglutinin and neuraminidase surface proteins, many H5N1 strains are geographically associated, either by their current distribution or place of origin. Clade 2.1 is currently limited to Indonesia. Clade 2.2, the Qinghai-like strain, spread west from Lake Qinghai (although the strain has since been traced a step back to Lake Poyang in Jiangxi).[12]

On its face, this appears a technical problem, one for the scientists and bureaucrats to hash out. But there may be more at stake. The proposed changes represent an epidemiological approach that may threaten our ability to impute bird flu's causes, to implement appropriate interventions, and to name the names of those responsible for controlling local outbreaks.

If a strain of bird flu appears to newly emerge out of a specific province or state of an affected country, that country is responsible for intervening in a way that the outbreak and any sequelae are controlled. Labeling a strain by its probable locale of origin reminds us which countries are responsible and where attention must be directed. Even if the strains subsequently spread, their geographic origins are integral to learning more about the virus's molecular and epidemiological characteristics, as well as preventing the emergence of similar strains.

Cause and blame, then, appear to be the crux of the matter. The terminology WHO characterizes as "stigmatizing" may be viewed instead as solely definitional, a part of pinpointing causality.

Unfortunately, on first appraisal WHO's stance has history in its favor. Epidemiological nomenclature has long been a minefield. Diseases have been tagged with baseless labels often inspired by xenophobia. The French disease, Spanish influenza, illnesses imputed to the "Yellow Peril"—all wrongly affixed or associated. Here, though, WHO's explanation seems a stretch. "Bird flu" has no geographic tag and the origins of those strains that do are established by scientific investigation rather than knee-jerk bigotry.

WHO's terminological umbrella also seems overly protective. Should national governments whose policies contribute to the rise of a disease be treated as if they are defenseless minorities discriminated against because of an ill-conceived notion of disease etiology? Should health and agricultural ministries be regarded as if they have been targeted with the groundless prejudice Haitians suffered in the early days of the AIDS epidemic?

Something more than sensitivity on WHO's part to past injustices seems in play. An exploration of the recent political economy of bird flu research will show the proposed nomenclature part of an effort by WHO to placate member countries that are currently apparent sources for many of the new bird flu strains. Without these members' cooperation, WHO would have no or little access to H5N1 isolates from which genetic sequences and possible vaccines can be derived.

We need ask, however, at what price such appeasement comes. Do we lose the very means by which to maneuver recalcitrant countries into intervening into local epidemics that may threaten the welfare of the rest of the world?

The proposed nomenclature seems emblematic of larger efforts on the part of WHO and many of the world's governments to stage-manage an influenza pandemic. For the conspiracy nuts out there, this isn't to say WHO or any lab or agency of any government started bird flu. Influenza viruses have long circulated among migratory birds and within the last few hundred years have become adapted to humanity's industrial way of life.[13] Nor is WHO out-and-out negligent. I believe WHO genuinely focused on fighting bird flu.

Still, like many institutions, WHO is maneuvering to protect itself. The bird flu train may have already left the epidemiological station and a pandemic may now be all but inevitable. In what would be a catastrophic failure on the part of governments and health ministries worldwide, millions may die.

Who, then, if not the affected countries, will take the blame? International institutions entrusted with preventing catastrophe are often made scapegoats for their members' failures. The Second World War destroyed the League of Nations. A pandemic could do the same to WHO. The new nomenclature may represent one means by which the organization is attempting to extricate itself out of the political line of fire.

ADVERSE REACTIONS

In late 2006 virologist Guan Yi and his colleagues at the University of Hong Kong reported on a previously uncharacterized H5N1 lineage they named "Fujian-like," after the putative Chinese province of origin.[14] They ascribed the emergence of the strain as a viral evolutionary reaction to the government's campaign to vaccinate poultry. The virus appeared to evolve from underneath the vaccine coverage.

Chinese officials went ballistic, rejecting the findings.

"The data cited in the article was unauthentic, and the research methodology was not based on science," Jia Youling, China's chief veterinary officer, told a news conference.[15]

"In fact, there is no such thing as a new 'Fujian-like' virus variant at all," said Jia.

The University of Hong Kong report appeared to deeply embarrass the Chinese government. As WHO officials pointed out, if the government, which has a parallel surveillance effort, didn't know of the emergent strain the new strain would in some minds betray governmental incompetence. If officials did know of the Fujian-like strain, their refusal to inform the international community would imply a cover-up along the lines of SARS.[16]

Even without maps of local H5N1 spread, the Chinese surely recognized their southern provinces were ground zero for the first, and many subsequent, H5N1 outbreaks.

On the other hand, we should appreciate that bird flu is a difficult problem and would be for any national government. Imagine rolling outbreaks across twenty-six U.S. states—Hurricane Katrina writ large. Would CDC, USDA and Fish and Wildlife, currently staffed with unqualified Bush political appointees, be capable of reacting any differently to such a viral onslaught? I do not excuse the Chinese government, but offer the acknowledgment as a preemptive response to what will likely be attempts to paint bird flu as another case of Chinese exceptionalism. Governments worldwide are unprepared.

The pressure on Chinese health officials must be enormous and a tone of hysteria is hard to miss. But even as we recognize the source of the government's reaction, must we accept the claims imparted in its manifestation?

"It is utterly groundless to assert that the outbreak of bird flu in Southeast Asian countries was caused by avian influenza in China and there would be a new outbreak wave in the world," said Jia. Not true.

"Since 2004, China has been keeping a close eye on the bird flu situation in its southern regions," said Foreign Ministry spokesman Liu Jianchao.[17] "Gene sequence analysis shows that all the variants of the virus found in southern China share high uniformity, meaning they all belong to the same gene type." Also not true.

"No distinctive change was found in their biological characteristics," Liu continued. Again not true.

With colleagues at the University of California I published a report in March 2007 that identified the geographic source of multiple strains of highly pathogenic influenza A (H5N1).[18] Our analysis of H5N1 genetic sequences collected through 2005 across twenty Eurasian localities showed Guangdong, another southeastern province, the likely source of H5N1 strains spreading regionally within China and in other countries, including Indonesia, Japan, Thailand, and Vietnam.

While our paper did not address the Fujian-like variant, the results refuted the assertion that China had nothing to do with repeated regional and international outbreaks of H5N1. It is clear that multiple strains have evolved in and dispersed from southern China and, as other work shows, continue to do so. Indeed, scientists from Guangdong's own South China Agricultural University contributed to a 2005 report showing that a new H5N1 genotype arose in western Guangdong in 2003–4.[19]

Official reaction to our work was nearly identical in its virulence to that directed at the Hong Kong scientists. Yu Yedong, head of the Guangdong Animal Epidemic Prevention Institute and the Guangdong Bird Flu Prevention Center called our work "unscientific" and "ridiculous."[20]

He Xia, a spokesperson for the Guangdong Provincial Agricultural Department, told *China Daily* the study was flawed and lacked credibility.[21] "Actually, Guangdong did not witness any bird flu cases in 1996. As a result, the findings are not based on facts," He Xia said.

He's statements are curious given that samples of highly pathogenic H5N1 were isolated by Chinese scientists from a 1996 outbreak on a goose farm in Guangdong.[22] News reports during the initial H5N1 outbreak in Hong Kong in 1997 also detailed local health officials' decision to ban poultry imports from Guangdong where several batches of infected chickens originated.[23]

MULTILATERAL MANIPULATION

The Chinese government isn't the sole source of official denials and delay.

Indonesia's health minister, Siti Fadilah Supari, claimed that findings by a University of Washington team showing that a cluster of infections among members of a Sumatran family were spread by human-to-human infection had "misled the public."[24]

"It's pure logic. . . . If there had been human-to-human transmission, it would have already swept the country and killed thousands," Supari told a news conference.[25] Evidence of human-to-human infection, however, does not require an ensuing pandemic. Chains of transmission may burn out by chance alone.

Supari serves at WHO as well. She was elected a vice president of the World Health Assembly in 2006 and this year unanimously elected a member of the WHO executive board. The executive board has its share of problems, particularly its nettle of competing interests.[26] But one can imagine the impact on the morale of WHO scientists when a member of the organization's leadership rejects scientific findings in favor of nationalist expediency.

Indeed, WHO staff have openly criticized Supari. On another matter—Indonesia's refusal to share H5N1 samples—David Heymann, WHO's assistant director-general for communicable diseases, said of Supari that "she has always said she doesn't trust WHO, and she's finding new reasons not to trust us."[27] Although WHO may have helped bring that distrust about on its own.

The sublimation of scientific practice by political directives cannot be laid at China's or Indonesia's feet alone. Perverting science for political gain is itself in a pandemic phase. Here in the United States, apparatchiks in the Bush administration have revised the content of myriad scientific reports—the bedrock of reality upon which governmental action need take place—for political points. Climate change, deforestation, pollution, stem cells, AIDS and condoms, evolution, the Surgeon General's office, and the Centers for Disease Control and Prevention have all been misrepresented or interfered with by Bush appointees, many scions of corporate lobbies, or the religious right.[28]

Although President Bush has paid greater attention to the possibility of an influenza pandemic than, say, to Katrina and its aftermath—reading John Barry's book about the 1918 pandemic will do that to you[29]—the United States has also pursued an agenda that protects pharmaceutical multinationals at the expense of global health.

The latest maneuver involves blocking efforts to reform the world's influenza vaccine system. Under the Global Influenza Surveillance Network (GISN), countries have for the past fifty-five years annually forwarded samples of prevalent influenza strains to the World Health Organization.[30] WHO offers the samples at no cost to pharmaceutical companies willing to make vaccines. The companies subsequently sell the vaccines at profit. The vaccines are thereby made available only to those populations able to afford them, namely people living in highly industrialized countries.

Indonesia has now refused to forward its H5N1 samples in an effort to force changes in the system, to make vaccines available to its own people. Indonesia, a primary epicenter for H5N1 outbreaks, has suffered considerable condemnation for its decision, including, as Heymann's comment makes clear, from WHO itself. Indonesia, in essence, is holding global health hostage, by refusing scientists around the world access to local samples of bird flu.

As immediately frustrating as the refusal is to scientists, phylogeographers included, Indonesia's protest is a just one in principle. People who cannot afford the latest medicine deserve to be protected from deadly diseases. Detractors have argued back that time is a-wastin' and an outbreak that begins undeterred in Indonesia helps no one, including, or especially, the poor there. But I think the impasse can be quickly resolved once international aid is provided for vaccine factories in poorer countries.

The problem is, of course, that such a solution would undermine profit-driven medicine, a violation of the neoliberal globalization idealized by WHO's wealthiest supporters. At a recent international conference convened in Geneva to resolve the impasse, the United States and the European Union stonewalled efforts to reform GISN. As reported by Ed Hammond on the *Effect Measure* blog, the interference included an attempt to insert language from the World Health Assembly's International Health Regulations that would have forced countries to transfer disease samples to WHO (even as the United States has cited national sovereignty in refusing to return Indonesian influenza samples back to Indonesia).[31]

The impasse could still very well be resolved—let's hope so for all our sakes—but the role of U.S. intransigence in the matter, unlike Indonesia's, has been underreported.

EARLIER WARNINGS

The attacks upon our work on the phylogeography of bird flu arrived via provincial governmental officials in China, even before the paper was available. Beijing, on the other hand, remained curiously silent.

Perhaps the accumulating work showing southern China's role in H5N1 spread gave the central government pause. Perhaps Beijing would have the good taste to criticize the work only after it was published. Perhaps the government learned from the SARS episode, during which it erroneously harangued foreign scientists that no danger existed. Or perhaps officials discovered that Walter Fitch, head of the team that produced our report, gave a presentation on the methods used in the study to an audience that included members of the Chinese Academy of Sciences in Shanghai in December 2005. The work wasn't completely out of left field. Officials may have also recognized a broader denunciation might attract greater attention to China's long history with influenza. A variety of subtypes have been discovered emanating from southern China, Guangdong included, for decades.[32] In the early 1980s, University of Hong Kong microbiologist Kennedy Shortridge identified 46 of the 108 different possible combinations of hemagglutinin and neuraminidase subtypes circulating worldwide at that time in a single Hong Kong poultry factory.[33]

In WHO's own bulletin, Shortridge, writing in 1982, detailed the likely reasons southern China would serve as ground zero for the next influenza pandemic:

- Southern China hosts mass production of ducks on innumerable ponds, facilitating fecal-oral transmission of multiple influenza subtypes.
- The greater mix of influenza serotypes in southern China increases the possibility the correct combination of gene segments would arise by genetic reassortment, selecting for a newly emergent human strain.
- Influenza circulates year-round there, surviving the inter-epidemic period by transmitting through the fecal-oral mode of infection.
- The proximity of human habitation in southern China provides an ideal interface across which a human-specific strain may emerge.

The conditions Shortridge outlined have since only intensified with China's liberalizing economy. Millions of people have moved into Guangdong in the past decade, a part of one of the greatest migration events in human history, from rural China into cities of the coastal provinces.[34] Concomitant changes in agricultural technology and ownership structure have put hundreds of millions more poultry into production.[35] Duck meat in China, for instance, tripled through the 1990s.

In 1995, two years before the first H5N1 outbreak in Hong Kong, Shortridge, in close contact with mainland colleagues, again warned that the next pandemic strain would arise in southern China.[36] "Every effort should be made to improve diagnostic capabilities in China and lines of communication to provincial and municipal health and epidemic prevention centres and then to the National Influenza Centre, Beijing," Shortridge advised.

China is a country of a billion people and it would be absurd to expect anything other than a variety of responses to the research. Dismissal has hardly been the sole reaction.

In April 1982, Shortridge and colleagues convened a meeting of Hong Kong and Chinese virologists and animal health officials to discuss the possible emergence of a human-specific infection from influenzas circulating in the region.[37] Attendees included Yuanji Guo of the Chinese Academy of Medical Sciences' Institute of Virology, F.A. Liu and S.C. Au from South China Agricultural College's Department of Animal Husbandry and Veterinary Medicine, situated in Guangzhou, the capital of Guangdong, and G. Z. Shen of the Health and Anti-Epidemic Station in Guangzhou. Good faith efforts at scientific collaboration have long been practiced.

I received email from scientists from institutions across China after our paper on the phylogeography of bird flu was published. The emails were filled with fascinating insights, questions about methodology, and serious-minded critique. One scientist from the China Animal Health and Epidemiology Center in Qingdao asked about sampling and estimate errors in our analysis and raised the issue whether Hong Kong and Guangdong should be clustered into a single epidemiological unit.

In short, many Chinese scientists have been—and continue to be—addressing bird flu in a dedicated and serious manner. Indeed, a fair amount of the work cited here has been conducted by mainland Chinese. Their efforts to discover the nature of what is occurring in their own country, and elsewhere, should be applauded. That's different, though, from offering the Chinese government *prima facie* exculpation for the responsibilities it holds in allowing conditions that have led to a gathering epidemiological disaster.

Blame Is a Good Thing

The scuffle over the Fujian-like strain seemed part and parcel of an ongoing dispute between the Chinese government and Guan Yi, the Hong Kong–based scientist and leader of the team that produced the report on the new viral variant.

In 2003, when SARS first emerged in Guangdong, Guan smuggled out samples from patients suffering the mysterious new pneumonia.[38] Guan took out the samples underneath an embargo imposed by Beijing when few samples were available for analysis anywhere. Guan has since repeatedly called out the government on its inaction on bird flu.[39] In 2005, the government threatened to close down Guan's Shantou lab in retaliation.

The dispute appears conjoined with chief vet Jia Youling's objections to a case of stolen credit. In early 2006, Jia complained that Western scientists claimed sole authorship on a paper that included samples provided by Chinese government scientists.[40]

In an effort to maintain access to a flow of Chinese H5N1 samples, the World Health Organization apologized for the fleeced credit. But in a clear case of appeasement little related to the original offense, China also won WHO's admonition that no bird flu strain should be identified with any single area, sixteen months before the proposed revisions in H5N1 nomenclature.

"It's very important that naming of viruses is done in a way that doesn't stigmatize countries, that doesn't stigmatize regions and doesn't stigmatize individual people," said David Heymann, WHO's assistant director-general for communicable diseases. Perhaps abject cynicism is unwarranted. Heymann, after all, had expressed similar sentiments during the SARS outbreak.[41] The horse-trading here, though, is obvious.

Another tack is to admit the geographic origins but to shift attention to present circumstances. In response to our work showing southern China to be a source of multiple H5N1 strains, WHO spokesman Gregory Hartl observed that the mainland origins were already known and that "what is most important for us and anyone who works in the field of surveillance and trying to contain and combat H5N1 . . . is knowing where the virus is now, what it is doing and which strains are circulating more widely."[42]

Never mind that strains of H5N1 continue to emerge from southern China. Never mind that bird flu's present course is inextricably interwoven with its origins—the virus's history matters. H5N1's origins provide us more than an epidemiological context. There are fundamentally pragmatic matters involved in identifying strain sources, including discovering the mechanisms of influenza's spread and evolution.

Never mind too that the call for a more forgiving nomenclature hasn't kept the Chinese government from placing blame upon other countries. Beijing News quoted Vice Minister of Agriculture Yin Chengjie to the effect that China needed to strengthen its monitoring and response systems nationwide because of recent outbreaks in "surrounding countries," an apparent reference to Vietnam and other parts of Indochina.[43]

"The disease has continued to spread in neighboring countries. This poses a big danger to our prevention and control work," said Yin. That's absolutely correct. But what is good for the sick goose is good for the sick gander. China cannot extract a free pass from bird flu blame while placing the same upon its neighbors.

Vietnam, in turn, has since reported that the Fujian-like strain has shown up in several of its provinces north and south. In describing the outbreaks Vietnamese officials tellingly used the F-word, as Crawford Kilian of the "H5N1" blog has coined it.

All in all, though, WHO does have a point. Since 1580, influenza outbreaks sweeping across Eurasia have been ascribed to—and named after—foreign lands, often on the basis of precarious evidence.[44] Influenza names have been as much signifiers of scapegoat xenophobia as for any other disease, including, infamously, STDs. The "Spanish" influenza of 1918 did not first emerge in Spain but was instead first reported there by one of Europe's few free presses allowed to operate uncensored during the First World War. WHO, then, isn't incorrect in its efforts to destigmatize bird flu strains, if only by way of its good intentions.

History shows that the Chinese have particular cause for concern. The Third Plague Pandemic began in the Yunnan province in 1855 before infecting millions worldwide over the next hundred years. The disease was essentialized by Sinophobes as a marker of the country's people and a reason for turning back the migration of the "Yellow Peril"—racist grotesqueries deployed for nativist gain.

The awful irony, however, is that the next influenza pandemic will be the first for which scientists will be able to pinpoint a locality of origin, even, if sampling continues to improve, to the very farm of origin or by Global Positioning Systems coordinate.[45] And that is likely a reason the Chinese government and those of other affected countries support or push for the new nomenclature. Scientific investigation may show one or more of these governments culpable for any human pandemic that emerges.

Locality has meaning beyond where the pathogen happened to originate. Local conditions imposed by public policy and social practice shape viral evolution. Other crises and conditions, in contrast, are less freighted with such immediate causality. Sweden, for instance, hasn't registered protest with the U.N. over "Stockholm Syndrome," nor Germany over the Marburg virus.

That all said, the origins of highly pathogenic H5N1 are multifactorial, with many countries and industries at fault. Can we then place blame on the country, say, Indonesia or Vietnam or Nigeria, from which a human-to-human pandemic might first emerge? Should we blame China for repeatedly seeding outbreaks regionally and internationally? Or should we blame the United States, where the industrial model of vertically integrated poultry first originated, with thousands of birds packed in as so much food for flu?[46] The answers are yes, yes, and yes.

Blame, much as the problem itself, must be distributed about its multiple levels of social and ecological organization, and yes, localities. Attempts at placating member countries with politically correct taxonomy may otherwise dissipate honest efforts to identify the epidemic's causes. Each source—country, region, people, to use Heymann's list—must suck up its responsibility and, most important, turn fault into serious concerted and broad-based action.

In the short term, small farmers must be fairly compensated for poultry culled in an effort to control outbreaks. Poultry trade must

be better regulated at international borders.[47] The world's poor
be provided epidemiological assistance, as well as vaccine and antiviral at no cost.[48] Structural adjustment programs that degrade animal
health infrastructure in the poorest countries must be terminated.[49]

For the long term, we must end the poultry industry as we know
it. Bird flu now emerges by way of a globalized network of corporate
poultry production and trade, wherever specific strains first evolve.
We must devolve much of the production to smaller, locally owned
farms.[50] Genetic monocultures of domesticated birds must be diversified back into heirloom varieties, as immunological firebreaks.
Migratory birds, which serve as a fount of influenza strains, must be
weaned off agricultural land where they cross-infect poultry.[51] To do
so, wetlands worldwide, wildfowl's natural habitat, must be restored.

Global public health capacity must also be rebuilt.[52] That capacity
is only the most immediate remediation for the poverty, malnutrition, and other manifestations of structural violence that promote the
emergence and mortality of infectious diseases, including influenza.[53]
Pandemic and inter-pandemic flu have the greatest impact on the
poorest.[54] And, as for any infection, a threat to one is a threat to all.

Only once these objectives are fulfilled will we be able to cover
ourselves against H5N1 and the other influenza serotypes—H5N2,
H6N1, H7N2, H7N7, H9N2—now lining up across factory farms like
tropical depressions in the ocean.

No Generic Labels

Along with the broad plan outlined here, the nature of the World
Health Organization's interactions with China must change.

During the SARS epidemic the Chinese government played WHO
for fools. The government took extraordinary measures in blocking
WHO scientists from visiting Guangdong, the original source of the
outbreak.[55] In a jaw-dropping escapade, WHO scientists were sent
on a wild-goose chase around Beijing. For weeks the Chinese health
ministry had denied that Beijing suffered any more than a few SARS
cases. As WHO scientists visited local hospitals, the Beijing municipal health service offloaded dozens of deadly-sick SARS patients into

ambulances that drove about the city until WHO representatives left each hospital.

Once the ruse was exposed, the health minister was fired and Hu Jianto, China's new leader, sent the Chinese government on an about-face. The government made SARS a key priority and imposed a virtual lockdown on affected areas.

The ability of the Chinese government to impose such drastic public health measures might be taken as the unfortunate upside of a dictatorship. Except, of course, China's treatment of public health data as state secrets helped bring about the crisis in the first place. Doctors in newly infected provinces were kept long in the dark as to the nature of the mysterious pathogen, delaying appropriate treatment and spreading SARS to its next town.

Since SARS, WHO has apparently arrived at a better, though still tenuous, working relationship with the Chinese government.[56] Greater access to samples and sites appears the norm for a number of pathogens. That's good. But if there is one thing I have learned in the reaction to our research report, that cooperation comes at a price.

WHO willfully participates in China's propaganda efforts to minimize, even deny, the government's responsibilities for the outbreaks. Time and again, even as Chinese officials drag their feet releasing samples, WHO officials are called upon to deflect external criticism and praise China's epidemiological openness (sunshine other countries must uphold as standard international practice). It is a self-brinksmanship that nearly blew up in WHO's face during the SARS outbreak.

WHO may view running over the work of a few independent scientists as an appropriate price. China's government, after all, is one of the organization's principal clients, and access to samples is imperative. What happens, though, when the interests of governments come into conflict with the health of the people of the world? How does coddling China's government project my wife, my barber, the Shanghai medical student who emailed me, Peter and Kate and their son Julian, Felipe Pichardo, Auntie Adrienne? When and where are their interests represented? Diplomat-scientists often confuse the great game with how the world works. Certainly negotiations among countries and institutions are a part of the world, but they are n be-all end-all. An evolving H5N1 threatens millions of people along the way. They count.

WHO officials might respond that in coaxing enough cooperation out of China we can stop the next pandemic and save your family and friends. But with H5N1 now percolating across Eurasia and Africa that strategy should be considered a failure. WHO's ill-qualified cooperation may instead give cover to agricultural and public health practices that have placed the world on the precipice of its next pandemic.

WHO needs to stop running interference for China's government (and for the United States, for that matter). If nothing else, WHO should avoid placing Chinese-brand strains of bird flu under generic labels. "Qinghai-like," "Fujian-like," such names should remain intact, if anything as reminders that bird flu has specific origins. The best way the Chinese or any other government can avoid the sting of nomenclature is to devise and enact means by which to keep the next strains from emerging in the first place. There would then be no virus to name.

China could reasonably argue that a finer taxonomy is preferable. Once the factories that have served up the latest virulent outbreaks have been identified, new strains can be rebranded after their corporate sources: the Bernard Matthews strain, the Charoen/Pokphand virus, the Tyson cluster.

By either nomenclature, reputations will be tarnished, yes, not by bigotry or unfairness, but by the infamy governments and companies have brought upon themselves in placing many millions of people in danger.

—*H5N1* BLOG, 27 DECEMBER 2007

The NAFTA Flu

CASES OF THE NEW SWINE FLU H1N1 are now reported in Honduras, Costa Rica, Brazil, Argentina, Austria, Thailand, Israel, etc. Can't keep up at this point.

H1N1 is making its way across the world by *hierarchical diffusion*.[57] By the world's transportation network it is bouncing down a hierarchy of cities defined by their size and economic power and their interconnectedness to Mexico City, the international city closest to the initial outbreak. It's no coincidence that New York and San Diego were among the first cities hit.

The virus is also engaged in *contagious diffusion*, spreading out within each new country hit.

For the most part only a few cases have been reported in countries other than Mexico. But as influenza, unlike SARS, can transmit before symptoms show, there may be no way to stop H1N1 now. New York now reports hundreds infected.

What is clear is that the more countries affected, the more likely the virus will find chinks in the world's epidemiological armor. The new strain may develop the right epidemiological momentum once it reaches those countries whose public health infrastructures are underdeveloped or undermined by structural adjustment programs. On the other hand, that may have happened from the start. Since the early 1980s Mexico has been subjected to IMF-specified truncations in animal and health infrastructure.

Unchecked transmission in vulnerable areas increases the genetic variation with which the new H1N1 can evolve characteristics that accelerate transmission and increase virulence.[58] In spreading over such a great geographic extent, fast-evolving H1N1 also contacts an increasing variety of socioecological environments, including locale-specific combinations of prevalent transportation infrastructure, vaccine and antiviral coverage, and host genetics. In this way, by a type of escalating *demic selection* or natural selection across local populations, the new H1N1 can better explore its evolutionary options. A series of fit variants, each more transmissible than the next, can evolve in response to local conditions and subsequently spread. For the H5N1 subtype, until last week influenza's superstar, the Z reassortant, the Qinghai-like strain, and the Fujian-like strain all outcompeted other local H5N1 strains to emerge to regional and, for the Qinghai-like strain, continental dominance.[59] The more genetic and physical variation produced across geographic space, the more compressed the time until the most transmissible infection evolves. H1N1 is likely fine-tuning itself as it spreads.

H1N1's variation may accumulate from point mutations along its genome. But genetic variation can also arise by what's called *reassortment.*

Influenza's genome is segmented. When two influenza strains infect the same host, the strains can trade segments, like card players on a Saturday night. Most resulting genomic "hands" are piss-poor, but every once in a while the virological equivalent of a royal flush emerges and trumps all other hands. That virus outcompetes all the others.

Early reports have identified the sources of the new H1N1's genome as strains that have infected human, bird, and pig populations from both North America and Europe. In an important way, then, "swine flu" is a misnomer. This influenza is a "swine-bird-human" reassortant. The extraordinarily complex origins of the new influenza—across so many host types and geographic regions—is telling us something about influenza's present ability to cross host species and bridge great spatial distances between livestock populations.

First, we know that agribusinesses are moving their companies into the Global South to take advantage of cheap labor and cheap land (something to which we will return). But companies are also engaging in sophisticated corporate strategy. Agribusinesses are spreading their entire production line across the world.[60] For example, the Thailand-based CP Group, now the world's fourth-largest poultry producer, operates poultry facilities in Turkey, China, Malaysia, Indonesia, and the United States. It has feed operations across India, China, Indonesia and Vietnam. Trade in live animals is also expanding in geographic extent.

These new configurations act as a cushion against the market's putative ability to correct corporate inefficiencies. For instance, the CP Group operates joint-venture poultry facilities across China, producing 600 million of China's 2.2 billion chickens annually sold. When an outbreak of bird flu occurred in a farm operated by the CP Group in the province of Heilongjiang, Japan banned poultry from China. CP factories in Thailand were able to take up the slack and increase exports to Japan. In short, the CP Group profited from an outbreak of its own making. It suffered no ill effects from its own mistakes.

There is, then, another reason why the "swine flu" tag fails. It detracts from an obvious point: pigs have very little to do with how influenza emerges. They didn't organize themselves into cities of thousands of immuno-compromised pigs. They didn't artificially select out the genetic variation that could have helped reduce the transmission rates at which the most virulent influenza strains spread. They weren't organized into livestock ghettos alongside thousands of industrial poultry. They don't ship themselves thousands of miles by truck, train, or air. Pigs do not naturally fly.

The onus must be placed on the decisions *we humans* made to organize them this way. And when we say "we," let's be clear, we're talking how agribusinesses have organized pigs and poultry.

Although considerable attention is being paid to the role of a particular company in the emergence of the new influenza, and rightfully so, we might better focus on the deregulation that allowed such porcinopolises to grow to the point that whole human communities are pushed off the land pigs now occupy.[61]

So if we are to impart responsibility where it should lie, North America's new influenza would be better called the NAFTA flu.

The North American Free Trade Agreement, pushed by Bill Clinton in 1993 and approved by a bipartisan Congress, reduced trade barriers across the United States, Canada, and Mexico. Products could now be marketed across the three countries without levies that favored domestic industries. The agreement also allowed companies to purchase and consolidate businesses in other member countries. Granjas Carroll, the Veracruz-based company under present scrutiny for the present outbreak, is a subsidiary of U.S.-based Smithfield Foods. NAFTA had a fundamental effect on North American agriculture, including Mexico's hog industry. As Batres-Marquez and her colleagues reported in 2006:

> Among the changes that have occurred since NAFTA, many small commercial producers have exited the industry because of their inability to both produce animals more efficiently and meet the quality standards required by their buyers. As a result of the exit of smaller producers, the scale of production has increased and the industry has become more highly integrated. This reduction in small commercial production and expansion of technologically advanced production has taken place alongside continued production using traditional backyard methods. [62]

Batres-Marquez et al., trade boosters, go on to praise the sanitary conditions of large commercial operations at the expense of those of smallholders, but their censure misses an obvious point. Smallholders may be individually less able to control outbreaks, but how do the most virulent strains emerge in the first place? Can we blame small farmers for their failure to control pathogens that first evolved in factory farms? In short, why did the veritable zoo of newly evolved human-specific influenzas arise only with deregulation and once vertically integrated livestock spread across the globe? Is this nothing more than a coincidence?

As Mike Davis notes:

> Six years ago, *Science* dedicated a major story (reported by the admirable Bernice Wuethrich) to evidence that "after years of stability, the North American swine flu virus has jumped onto an evolutionary fast track."

its identification at the beginning of the Depression, wine flu had only drifted slightly from its original genome. n 1998, all hell broke loose.

A nighly pathogenic strain began to decimate sows on a factory hog farm in North Carolina, and new, more virulent versions began to appear almost yearly, including a weird variant of H1N1 that contained the internal genes of H3N2 (the other type-A flu circulating among humans). [63]

The newly porous borders raise another question. Could the new influenza have percolated first in the United States before crossing Mexico's border? The blame game is already under way.[64]

Mexican Health Secretary José Angel Cordova said no one knows where the outbreak began, and implied it may have started in the United States.

"I think it is very risky to say, or want to say, what the point of origin or dissemination of it is, given that there had already been cases reported in southern California and Texas," Cordova told a press conference.

Fascinating that a nationalist ethos reemerges once free trade appears implicated in a disease that could kill millions of people worldwide. The cross-border fisticuffs have the additional effect of detracting from core causes. Will the business nomenklatura who pushed NAFTA across all three countries be held to account for their decisions?

Whereas the housing bubble and banking collapse mark the aftermath of financial deregulation, H1N1 is only one of several pathogens that now track neoliberalism's effects on global health.

—*Farming Pathogens*, 28 April 2009

The Hog Industry Strikes Back

SWINE FLU H1N1 APPEARS AT ONE and the same time moving "full-boar" and on its cloven heels. The World Health Organization reports 15,510 official cases in fifty-three countries, with new countries regularly reporting in.[65] An order of magnitude or two more cases are likely unreported and together represent an atypical spring surge for influenza. At the same time, the strain's virulence appears presently no more than along the lines of a bad seasonal influenza.

One of the mistakes we need avoid is to assume we've been victimized by a media-fueled hysteria. Given the mortality rates reported at the beginning of the outbreak in Mexico—exceeding that of the 1918 pandemic—it looked like we were in for it. Previous pandemics teach us that preparing for the worst is the prudent option. Imagine the reaction if only feeble preparations were made in the face of a truly deadly pandemic. The cost of a Type II error, thinking no pandemic possible with one imminent, is catastrophically greater than that of its Type I sibling, thinking a pandemic imminent with none in the offering.

A second mistake is to accept any "all-clear" at face value. Swine flu H1N1 may be for most of those infected a relatively mild influenza now, but we're still not sure how it all will play out. The virus is undoubtedly evolving as it spreads and may reassort enough with other strains to eventually produce a strain infectious *and* deadly. In other words, whether the new H1N1 continues to mimic the effects of seasonal influenza as it diffuses remains very much an open question.

History offers a warning written in bloody spittle. The 1918 pandemic proved mild in its spring incarnation and apocalyptic the following fall.[66] But even then there remained great variation in the pathogen's effects across the population: some people were exposed but not infected, some were infected but suffered only a seasonal-like flu, and then, of course, there were those whose viscera melted from the inside out. A case fatality rate clocking in at 5 percent—a comfort only to the most perverse of today's naysayers—killed 50–100 million people worldwide.

We are far from the clear for another reason, one finely stitched into the fabric of modern life. There now circulates a veritable zoo of influenza subtypes that have proven themselves capable of infecting humans: H5N1, H7N1, H7N3, H7N7, H9N2, in all likelihood H5N2, and perhaps some of the H6 series.[67] Think hurricanes. We may have dodged one here and yet even now an Influenza Katrina may be gathering its skirts in the epidemiological queue.

A burgeoning variety of new influenza subtypes capable of infecting humans appears the result of a concomitant globalization of the industrial model of poultry and pig production. Since the 1970s, vertically integrated stockbreeding has spread out from its origins in the southeastern United States across the globe. Our world is encircled by cities of millions of monoculture pig and poultry pressed alongside each other, an ecology nigh perfect for the evolution of multiple virulent strains of influenza.[68]

Not a pleasant picture, indeed grounds for ending the bizarre cultural practice of stuffing thousands of inbred animals under the same roof. But unraveling the globalization of vertical agribusiness already more than fifty years in the making will take more than realizing it was a bad idea. Big Food likes making big bucks and aims to protect a racket it took so long to corner. Efforts to test for ties between agribusiness and protopandemic influenza are a threat to such a hard-won competitive advantage.

SO THE HOG INDUSTRY HAS struck back. It successfully lobbied the World Health Organization to rename the swine flu by a scientific name, H1N1, with its confusing connotations of seasonal H1N1.

This isn't the first time WHO has caved to political pressure over nomenclature.[69] In 2007, WHO implemented a new naming system for the various strains of influenza A (H5N1), the bird flu virus circulating through Eurasia, Africa, and Oceania. The H5N1 strains are now enumerated rather than labeled after their countries or regions of origin. The "Fujian-like" strain, first named after its southern Chinese province of origin, is now called "Clade 2.2.4."

WHO declared the new H5N1 names necessary because of the confusion caused by disparate systems used in the scientific literature. A unified system of nomenclature would facilitate the interpretation of genetic and surveillance data generated by different labs. It would also provide a framework for revising strain names based on viral characteristics. The new system would at the same time bring an end to the "stigmatization" caused when flu strains are named after their places of origin.

The changes also represented an attempt on the part of WHO to placate member countries that are currently sources for many of the new bird flu strains. Without these members' cooperation, WHO would have no or little access to H5N1 isolates from which genetic sequences and possible vaccines can be derived. WHO's appeasement, however, never stopped China, H5N1's place of birth, from laying a veritable quarantine around scientific information about bird flu there. Only a few genetic sequences from Chinese H5N1 have been made publicly available since 2006.

The new names also peel back causality to the biomedical. Influenza can indeed be defined by its molecular structure, genetics, virology, pathogenesis, host biology, clinical course, treatment, modes of transmission, and phylogenetics. Such work is, of course, essential. But limiting investigation to these topics misses critical mechanisms that are operating at other broader levels of socio-ecological organization. These mechanisms include how livestock are owned and organized across time and space. In other words, we need to get at the specific decisions specific governments and companies make that promote the emergence of virulent influenza. Thinking virological alone disappears such explanations, very much in the hog industry's favor.

For swine flu H1N1, industrial hogs *are* to blame, even if the full story eventually proves to be more complex. As reported by the CDC, multiple genomic segments of the new influenza are derived from hog influenzas:

> The majority of their genes, including the hemagglutinin (HA) gene, are similar to those of swine influenza viruses that have circulated among U.S. pigs since approximately 1999; however, two genes coding for the neuraminidase (NA) and matrix (M) proteins are similar to corresponding genes of swine influenza viruses of the Eurasian lineage. . . . This particular genetic combination of swine influenza virus segments has not been recognized previously among swine or human isolates in the United States, or elsewhere based on analyses of influenza genomic sequences available on GenBank.[70]

A recent *Science* report makes an even stronger claim, "The closest ancestral gene for each of the eight gene segments is of swine origin."[71]

No small farmer has the industrial capacity necessary to export live livestock of any consequence across countries, nor the market *entrée* livestock influenza needs to spread through an international commodity chain. And yet the hypothesis that the hog industry is responsible has been treated as nigh-paranormal. An April 30 Reuters report grouped the possibility with the wackiest conspiracy theories that could be plucked from the internet:

> Dead pigs in China, evil factory farms in Mexico and an Al Qaeda plot involving Mexican drug cartels are a few wild theories seeking to explain a deadly swine flu outbreak that has killed up to 176 people.
>
> Nobody knows for sure but scientists say the origins are in fact far less sinister and are likely explained by the ability of viruses to mutate and jump from species to species as animals and people increasingly live closer to each other.[72]

The report begs the question by what means animals and people find themselves increasingly living together. The reporters don't bother. At some point, however, the abstract must be instantiated in the acts of particular people in particular localities. Those "evil" factory farms arrayed along rural and periurban bands encircling Mexico City, one of the world's largest cities, may very well have something to do with the start of this particular pandemic and warrant serious investigation. The Reuters report continues:

> In Mexico reports in at least two newspapers focused on a factory farm run by a subsidiary of global food giant Smithfield Foods. Some of the rumors mentioned noxious fumes from pig manure and flies—neither a known vector for flu viruses.
>
> Those reports brought a swift reply from the biggest U.S. hog producer.
>
> "Based on available recent information, Smithfield has no reason to believe that the virus is in any way connected to its operations in Mexico," the company said in a statement.

A lawyer's careful answer. Funny, though, that at the time of the initial outbreak in Veracruz Smithfield dismissed local residents' concerns about illnesses from the company's pollution at its Granjas Carroll subsidy outside Perote, near a major highway and only a half-day's ride from Mexico City, as likely the outcome of "flu." One wonders what Smithfield now blames those illnesses on now that it's taken flu off the table.

WE NAMED THIS STRAIN of influenza after NAFTA to address the broader neoliberalism directed at forcing vertically integrated husbandry onto Mexico at the expense of small farmers.[73] No one company need be blamed in full. But what if this particular influenza strain arose on Smithfield's lots? Contrary to Reuters' attempts to submarine a genuine possibility based on material facts on the ground—rather than conspiracies spun wholesale out of naught but paranoiac fantasy—the Food and Agriculture Organization is taking Smithfield's putative role seriously enough to dispatch a team to Mexico to investigate.

In a preemptive strike, Smithfield CEO Larry Pope announced the company's Veracruz pigs clean of H1N1:

I am pleased to report that the results of the testing process conducted by the Mexican government have confirmed that no virus, including the human strain of A(H1N1) influenza, is present in the pig herd at Granjas Carroll de Mexico (GCM), our joint venture farm in Veracruz, Mexico. These findings, which are consistent with our earlier communications to you, validate what we believed from the very beginning: that the recent subtype of H1N1 influenza virus affecting humans did not originate from GCM.[74]

The Mexican government went so far as to claim *no* disease *anywhere* in Mexico, "Following repeated investigations, Mexico's 15 million pigs are all healthy and ready to eat, according to Agriculture Minister Alberto Cárdenas."

But such certification, to which we will return, is often a political football, with accreditation and rejection dependent on the state of this week's trade battle. As recently as this past December, Cárdenas blocked imports from Smithfield and other U.S. agribusinesses:

Mexico, a major buyer of U.S. meat, suspended shipments from 30 U.S. beef, lamb, pork and poultry plants as of Dec. 23, citing factors like packaging, labeling and transport conditions. It cleared 20 of them on Monday after the USDA reported corrective actions had been taken. . . .

Mexican Agriculture Minister Alberto Cárdenas told reporters the government was stepping up sanitary controls to keep contaminated meat out of Mexico. . . .

U.S. analysts have said the bans were likely because of Mexico's opposition to a recently enacted meat labeling law. Mexico and the U.S. Agriculture Department have both denied the retaliation charge.

Plants owned by Tyson Foods Inc (TSN.N), Smithfield Foods Inc (SFD.N), JBS (JBSS3.SA) and privately owned Cargill Inc are among the plants cleared for export to Mexico, including Smithfield's Tar Heel, North Carolina, pork plant, the world's largest, according to a USDA report. . . .

Mexico is the top export market by volume for U.S. beef, veal and turkey, the second largest for pork, and the third largest for chicken, according to U.S. government statistics.[75]

Smithfield's latest health certification begs a number of questions. Was H1N1 absent in all Veracruz pigs several months ago, as far back as early February when locals began to become ill? How to account for Edgar Hernandes, the Xaltepec four-year-old, the first confirmed H1N1 case in Mexico? Hernandes appeared no anomaly. Mexico's General Directorate of Epidemiology reported an early April outbreak of influenza-like illness in Veracruz weeks before the virus spread outward. How did an influenza with a variety of swine-source genomic segments from around the world originate other than via the swine trade? Is Smithfield instead prepared to blame other companies? Smithfield owns eight large swine farms in the area in which the pathogen appeared to have emerged as a human infection. Could this all be coincidence alone?

According to Smithfield, yes. As a Smithfield manager put it, "What happened in La Gloria was an unfortunate coincidence with a big and serious problem that is happening now with this new flu virus." That's no explanation whatsoever. The company, channeling Jean Baudrillard, appears perfectly comfortable with erasing the connection between cause and effect.

Now it may turn out that Smithfield isn't to blame for this particular outbreak after all. Swine flu H1N1's origins may extend far beyond any one country's borders. Ruben Donis, CDC's chief of molecular virology and vaccines, suggested that the virus

> may have originated in a U.S. pig that traveled to Asia as part of the hog trade. The virus may have infected a human there, who then traveled back to North America, where the virus perfected human-to-human spread, maybe even moving from the United States to Mexico.[76]

It's a logically plausible possibility, consistent with the hypothesis that the geographic extent of influenza's multiple reassortants now extends across the globe. But such a possibility doesn't preclude investigation of the simplest explanation—that the final viral phenotype from a series of reassortment events emerged in the locality where it caused the first human cases. Moreover, it's a reasonable hypothesis that accelerated reassortment may have been promoted by a fundamental shift in the ownership structure of area farms.

Smithfield entered Mexico in 1994, the year NAFTA went into effect. The company consolidated small farms outside Perote, opening Carroll Ranches through a new subsidiary corporation, Agroindustrias de México. In Mexico Smithfield avoided the regulation to which the company has been increasingly subjected in the United States. In 1997 Smithfield was fined $12.6 million for violating the U.S.'s Clean Water Act. Missouri residents are now suing Smithfield for pollution. The feds are now investigating a Smithfield farm in Pennsylvania for releasing pig sewage into local waters in 2007. In contrast, according to *La Jornada*, Carroll Ranches, processing 800,000 pigs annually, is presently under no obligation to subject its swines' feces, tons produced daily, to sewage treatment.[77]

Smithfield has globalized such practices. In something of an instant classic, the *New York Times'* Doreen Carvajal and Stephen Castle wrote of Smithfield's East European campaign and its epidemiological effects:

> Smithfield's global approach is clear; its chairman, Joseph Luter III, has described it as moving in a "very, very big way, very, very fast." In less than five years, Smithfield enlisted politicians in Poland and Romania, tapped into hefty European Union farm subsidies and fended off local opposition groups to create a conglomerate of feed mills, slaughterhouses and climate-controlled barns housing thousands of hogs.
>
> It moved with such speed that sometimes it failed to secure environmental permits or inform the authorities about pig deaths —lapses that emerged after swine fever swept through three Romanian hog compounds in 2007, two of which were operating without permits. Some 67,000 hogs died or were destroyed, with infected and healthy pigs shot to stanch the spread....

"For them, it's like dealing with primitive people in the bush, where only power and strength is important," said Emilia Niemyt, the mayor of Wierzchkowo, a Polish village of 331 people that has pressed complaints about odors. "They fulfill the idea of conquering the East with the methods of the Wild West."[78]

The article, required reading, offers a blow-by-blow account of the regional exercise of Smithfield's political power.

That power extends into the politics of a pandemic above and beyond the name of the virus. Mexico exonerated Smithfield's Veracruz operations on the basis of thirty swine samples chosen by Smithfield itself.[79] A few samples volunteered by the very company under scrutiny do not serve as the basis of the rigorous and unbiased testing one would expect for a worldwide pandemic. As put by blogger Tom Philpott, who has been terrific debunking agribusiness flack around the outbreak:

> For a lobbyist working the Hill on behalf of an industry, the gold standard is self-regulation. No need to send in inspectors—we'll test our process to ensure that it doesn't pollute. Trust us!
>
> Astonishingly, pork giant Smithfield Foods has evidently managed to arrange just such a testing regime with regard to its hog-rearing operations in Vera Cruz, Mexico—some of which lie just a few miles from the village where the swine flu outbreak first manifested itself.[80]

Despite hosting billions of pigs and poultry, the governments around the world offer no systematic testing and regulation. In the United States, no system is in place beyond that offered on the drawing board. According to the CDC:

> [No] formal national surveillance system exists to determine what viruses are prevalent in the U.S. swine population. Recent collaboration between the U.S. Department of Agriculture and CDC has led to development of a pilot swine influenza virus surveillance program to better understand the epidemiology

and ecology of swine influenza virus infections in swine and humans.[81]

Contrast the hysteria over bioterrorism since 9/11 with the millions of influenza suitcase bombs crapping themselves as they're trucked uninspected across borders.

THE HOG INDUSTRY'S MOST BRAZEN gambit is to blame people for threatening pigs with flu:

> "That is the biggest concern, that your herd could somehow contract this illness from an infected person," said Kansas hog farmer Ron Suther, who is banning visitors from his sow barns and requiring maintenance workers, delivery men and other strangers to report on recent travels and any illness before they step foot on his property. . . .
> "There is no evidence of this new strain being in our pig populations in the United States. And our concern very much is we don't want a sick human to come into our barns and transmit this new virus to our pigs," said National Pork Producers chief veterinarian Jennifer Greiner.
> "If humans give it to pigs, we don't have things like Tamiflu for pigs. We don't have antivirals. We have no treatment other than to give them aspirin," said Greiner.[82]

For now let's set aside Greiner's attempt to bury the evidence that several of the new strain's genomic segments originated from a recombinant H3N2/H1N1 influenza that has circulated among U.S. swine since 1998. The evidence for human-to-pig infection is at best circumstantial. *Canadian Press* medical reporter Helen Branswell writes:

> There is no smoking gun in the case of the H1N1 infected pigs— and authorities investigating the first known infections of pigs with this new swine flu virus may not be able to unearth one, a senior Canadian Food Inspection Agency official admits.

Testing of people on the farm—some of which was done too late, some of which may not have used the best technique to get an answer—has turned up no solid proof people brought the virus to the pigs. And it remains to be seen whether blood testing will be able to fill the evidence gap.[83]

So the industry's ploy has little leg to stand on. But even if the bald assertion proves true, it acts only as a damning admission of the nature of influenza traffic between host types. For now, the assertion stands as a monument to the hubris of an industry shameless enough to blame the victims of its own standard practices.

With public health officials, reporters, and PR flacks burying leads and manufacturing diversions in their stead, the rationale for investigating the roles confined animal feedlot operations play in the emergence of pandemic influenzas may—poof!—disappear. The next few months may very well demonstrate that being a well-connected global conglomerate means never having to say you're sorry no matter the damage caused. It is, after all, the kind of protection for which the hog industry has paid.

The infrastructure of such political influence requires both time and care (and enough cash) to build. As Carvajal and Castle report:

> Smithfield fine-tuned its approach in the depressed tobacco country of eastern North Carolina in the 1990s. In 2000, money started flowing from a Smithfield political action committee in that state and around the United States. Ultimately, more than $1 million went to candidates in state and federal elections. North Carolina lawmakers helped fast-track permits for Smithfield and exempted pig farms from zoning laws.[84]

With increasing restrictions in the United States, Smithfield

> took its North Carolina game plan to Poland and Romania, where the company moved nimbly through weak economies and political and regulatory systems. . . .
> Once the top leaders in Romania showed their support for Smithfield, developments fell into place; about a dozen Smithfield

farms were designed by an architectural firm owned by Gheorghe Seculici, a former deputy prime minister with close ties to President Traian Basescu of Romania, who is godfather to his daughter.

Further help came from a familiar front: Smithfield's lobbyist, the Virginia firm McGuireWoods, set up a Bucharest office in 2007 to liaise between Smithfield and the Romanian government. In many ways McGuireWoods was the perfect choice; it had also represented Romania for three years to press its NATO-membership campaign.

The connections in the upper reaches of government meant that Smithfield could weather protests from local communities.

Attempts to proactively change poultry and livestock production in the interests of stopping pathogen outbreaks can be met with severe resistance by governments beholden to their corporate sponsors. In effect, influenza, by virtue of its association with agribusiness, has some of the most powerful representatives available defending its interests in the halls of government. In covering up or downplaying outbreaks in an effort to protect quarterly profits, these institutions contribute to the viruses' evolutionary fortunes. The very biology of influenza is enmeshed with the political economy of the business of food.

If multinational agribusinesses can parlay the geography of production into huge profits, regardless of the outbreaks that may accrue, who pays the costs? The costs of factory farms are routinely externalized. As Peter Singer explains, the state has long been forced to pick up the tab for the problems these farms cause; among them, health problems for their workers, pollution released into the surrounding land, food poisoning, and damage to transportation infrastructure.[85] A breach in a poultry lagoon, releasing tons of feces into a Cape Fear tributary, causing a massive fish kill, is left to local governments to clean up.

With the specter of influenza the state is again prepared to pick up the bill so that factory farms can continue to operate without interruption, this time in the face of worldwide pandemics agribusiness helps cause in the first place. The economics are startling. The world's governments are prepared to subsidize agribusiness billions upon billions for damage control in the form of animal and human vaccines, Tamiflu, culling operations, and body bags. Even an appeal to preserving global greed is apparently insufficient. Along with the lives of a billion people, the establishment appears willing to gamble much of the world's economic productivity, which stands to suffer catastrophically if a more severe pandemic were to erupt. Criminally negligent and politically protected myopia pays, until it doesn't. Then someone else picks up the bill. It is perhaps cliché to evoke the fates of lost empires. And yet Edward Gibbon's eulogy encapsulates our moment in both its spirit and its particulars:

> The forum of the Roman people, where they assembled to enact their laws and elect their magistrates, is now enclosed for the cultivation of pot-herbs, or thrown open for the reception of swine.[86]

In our case, however, pastoral infestation appears the means to a ruins and not its aftermath.

—*Farming Pathogens*, 1 June 2009

UPDATE. H1N1 (2009) turned out to be less widespread and virulent than initially expected. Global accumulative incidence clocked in no more than 20 percent, far less than the expected 50 percent (although school-age children ranged up to 43 percent).[87] American children were no more likely to be hospitalized than during years of seasonal flu infection.[88] However, globally as many as 579,000 people may have died from the virus and its complications appeared fifteen times greater in incidence than initially projected by lab tests.[89] H1N1 (2009) meanwhile continues to circulate and reassort with other influenza strains human, wildlife, and livestock.[90]

The Political Virology of Offshore Farming

HONG KONG, MARCH 1997. An outbreak of deadly bird flu sweeps through poultry on two farms. The outbreak fizzles out, but two months later a three-year-old boy dies of the same strain, identified as a highly pathogenic version of influenza A (H5N1). Officials are shocked. This appears the first time such a strain has jumped the species barrier and killed a human. Shocking as well, the outbreak proves persistent. In November a six-year-old is infected, recovering. Two weeks later, a teenager and two adults are infected. Two of the three die. Fourteen additional infections rapidly follow.

The deaths spur panic in the city and, with the onset of the regular flu season, send many patients to the hospital worried their symptoms might be those of the new flu. By mid-December poultry begin to die in droves in the city's markets, and it now seems most humans infected had handled birds. Hong Kong acts decisively on that information. Authorities order the destruction of all of Hong Kong's 1.5 million poultry and block new imports from Guangdong, the mainland province across the Shenzhen River from which some of the infected birds had been transported. Despite another human death in January, the outbreak is broken.

The poultry infected with this version of the virus suffer more than the gastrointestinal condition typical of avian influenza. The clinical manifestations include swelling of the wattles and infraorbital sinuses, congestion and blood spots on the skin of the hocks and shanks, and a blue discoloration of the comb and legs.[91] The latter is characteristic of the cyanosis and oxygen deprivation suffered by many human victims of the 1918 pandemic. Internally, infected poultry are marked by lesions and hemorrhaging in the intestinal tract and the trachea, with blood discharge from the beak and cloaca. Many birds also suffer infection in other organs, including the liver, spleen, kidney, and the brain, the last infection leading to ataxia and convulsion.

Most worrisome for human health is this strain's capacity for broad xenospecific transmission. The Hong Kong outbreak, first alerting the world to H5N1, infected humans with an influenza much more pathogenic than the relatively mild infections of other avian outbreaks that have intermittently crossed over into human populations. These patients presented with high fever, later developing some combination of acute pneumonia, influenza-like illness, upper respiratory infections, conjunctivitis, pharyngitis, and a gastrointestinal syndrome that included diarrhea, vomiting, vomiting blood, and intestinal pain.[92] Patients also suffered multiple-organ dysfunction, including that of the liver, kidney, and bone marrow. The respiratory attacks involved extensive infiltration of both lungs, diffuse consolidation of multiple infected loci, and lung collapse. If much of H5N1's morbidity is distressing, its associated mortality is alarming. Once infected, the lungs' vasculature becomes porous, and fibrinogen—a protein involved in blood clotting—leaks into the lungs.[93] The resulting fibroblast exudates clog the lungs' alveolar sacs, where gas exchange takes place, and an acute respiratory disease syndrome results. In a desperate effort to save its charge, the immune system recruits such a storm of cytokines that the lungs suffer oedema. In effect, patients drown in their own fluid only days after infection.

After its first strike in Hong Kong, H5N1 slipped underground with outbreaks largely limited to birds in southern China. The virus underwent the first of a series of reassortment events, in which several genomic segments were replaced with those from other serotypes, before reemerging as a human infection in Hong Kong in 2002.[94] The following year H5N1 again reemerged, this time with a vengeance. The Z genotype that surfaced as the dominant recombinant spread across China, into Vietnam, Thailand, Indonesia, Cambodia, Laos, Korea, Japan, and Malaysia. Two additional strains would subsequently materialize. Since 2005 the Qinghai-like strain (H5N1 hemagglutinin clade 2.2) has spread across Eurasia, as far west as England, and into Africa.[95] The Fujian-like strain (clade 2.3), emerging from its eponymous southern China province, has spread regionally across Southeast Asia and, more recently, into Korea and Japan.[96] Since 2003 H5N1 has infected 440 people, killing 262 (WHO, August 2009). Most of these infections have been poultry-related, often striking the children of small farmers playing with a favorite bird. But documented cases of human-to-human transmission have accumulated—in Hong Kong, Thailand, Vietnam, Indonesia, Egypt, China, Turkey, Iraq, India, and Pakistan.[97] The short chains of transmission have largely consisted of relatives living with or tending a patient. The worry, well publicized, is that H5N1 will improve upon these first infections, evolving a human-to-human phenotype that ignites a worldwide pandemic along the lines of this year's swine flu but deadlier in its manifestation.

The geographic diffusion of the virus is intimately related to the emergence of such a phenotype. As are other pathogens, H5N1 is finding the regions of the world where animal health surveillance remains underdeveloped or degraded by structural adjustment programs associated with international loans or neoliberal trade agreements.[98] There is now, in addition, greater integration of stockbreeding, aquaculture, and horticulture, a burgeoning live-bird market system, and widespread proximity to poultry.[99] Rural landscapes of many of the poorest countries are now characterized by unregulated agribusiness pressed against periurban slums.[100] Unchecked transmission in vulnerable areas increases the genetic variation with which H5N1 can evolve human-specific characteristics. In spreading over three continents fast-evolving H5N1 also contacts an increasing variety of socioecological environments, including locale-specific combinations of prevalent host types, modes of poultry farming, and animal health measures.

In this way, by a type of escalating demic selection, H5N1 can better explore its evolutionary options.[101] A series of fit variants, each more transmissible than the next, can evolve in response to local conditions and subsequently spread. The Z reassortant, the Qinghai-like strain, and the Fujian-like strain all outcompeted other local H5N1 strains to emerge to regional and, for the Qinghai-like strain, continental dominance. The more genetic and phenotypic variation produced across geographic space, the more compressed the time until a human infection evolves.

How did we get into this fix? Why this deadly disease now? In a torrent rivaling the research conducted on the central mystery of Stanislaw Lem's *Solaris*, that mysterious planet, thousands of reports have been published on the virus's molecular structure, genetics, virology, pathogenesis, host biology, clinical course, treatment, modes of transmission, phylogenetics, and geographic spread. That body of work, much of it riveting, appears predicated on a molecular narrative that portrays disease largely in terms of a conflict between virion and immunity, between viral evolution and humanity's capacity to produce adequate vaccines and antivirals, between nature red in glycoprotein and nurture white in lab coat.[102] Paradigms compete and in investing in one narrative—perhaps because of its political, commercial, or institutional benefits—other explanations suffer. Some of the most basic questions about bird flu's nature appear lost in the blizzard of micrographs, sequence alignments, tertiary solution structures, SIR models, antigenic cartograms, and phylogenetic dendrograms. What of the virus's greater context?

Noel Castree recently reviewed a new literature aimed at addressing just such a context.[103] The literature, at this point largely a loose affiliation of case studies, tracks the ways the present class of models of globalized finance and production, which structure so much of humanity's daily life, are embodied in the control and exploitation of nonhuman systems. The work traces the means by which nature is "neoliberalized." To Castree's examples—water management, fisheries, logging, mining, plant and animal genomics, and greenhouse gas emissions—we can add agriculture, breeding programs, and pharmaceutical excavation. This article represents another example, although it travels along in something of an orthogonal direction. I review influenza as a case study of the inadvertent biotic fallout of efforts aimed at steering animal ontogeny and ecology to multinational profitability.[104]

Here I will explore the social origins of highly pathogenic influenza A (H5N1) and, as best as one can, given the present literature, connect these with the evolution and spread of the virus. I will first review key concepts in pathogen virulence and diversification. I will hypothesize the means by which influenza's present virulence and diversity arose out of the Livestock Revolution. In the context of a now-globalized poultry, I will next explore a fundamental question so far ill-addressed, surprisingly so given the amount of work dedicated to characterizing the virus: Why did pathogenic H5N1 evolve in southern China? Moreover, why did it do so in 1997? Locating bird flu virulence in China's poultry intensification efforts is one matter. Outbreak persistence there and elsewhere, however, is another: I will also review complications in influenza epidemiology apparent beyond the factory gate. Finally, I will propose a broad albeit preliminary program of intervention that extends beyond the provisional fiddling typically operationalized during each outbreak season. Along the way I will pursue epistemological aspirations. In bridging disciplines, I aim for an evolutionary virology that integrates humanity's impact on pathogen evolution from the very start of any investigation.

To begin, I explore bird flu's deadliness beyond listing molecular mechanisms by which the virus transforms cells into progeny, as important as these are.

GROWING DEADLY INFLUENZA

Despite its epidemiological and psychological impacts, Hong Kong's H5N1 represented no first outbreak of bird flu. In fact, within the United States alone, where highly pathogenic H5N1 has not yet spread, a series of outbreaks have accrued over the past decade.[105] These outbreaks were typically low pathogenic, causing lesser damage to poultry. There was, however, an outbreak of highly pathogenic H5N2 in Texas in 2002. A low pathogenic H6N2 outbreak in California, beginning in large farms outside San Diego, evolved with greater virulence as it spread through California's Central Valley. Another outbreak worthy of note is that of a low pathogenic strain of H5N1 in Michigan in 2002. H5N1, then, has already invaded the United States in a less deadly form, and with different internal genes, telling us that the molecular identity of a strain is insufficient for defining the danger of any single outbreak. Low and high pathogenic strains must be distinguished otherwise. Some mechanism must transform low pathogenic strains into more virulent ones (and, we should hope, back again).

The damage caused by pathogenic influenza may be in part due to an antigenic shift to which susceptible populations presently have no immunity. Humans, for instance, have this past century been infected almost exclusively by H1, H2, and H3 strains to which we eventually developed antibody memory. When many of us are confronted by a seasonal variant of these same types we can slow down the infection. We have partial immunity at the individual level and herd immunity at the population level. But as we have never been exposed to H5 infections *en masse* we have nothing to slow down infection within each person and nothing to keep it dampened down across the population. What cannot be slowed down arrives earlier. It is likely then that, as was the case for the 1957 and 1968 pandemics, the main waves of the next human influenzas will sweep the planet earlier than the typical flu season, with swine flu (2009) as early as August this year or, if another strain, some terrible year in the near future.[106]

But how are we to account for an increase in virulence *within* a particular flu subtype? Recall the low pathogenic strain of H5N1 in Michigan. And in something of the other direction, there is the macabre sight of H5N1-devastated waterfowl, which typically act as the natural (and unharmed) reservoir for multiple H5 strains. Another explanation leans on a large modeling literature that hypothesizes a relationship between the rate of transmission and the evolution of virulence, the amount of damage a strain causes its host.[107] Simply put, to start, there is a cap on pathogen virulence. Pathogens must avoid evolving the capacity to incur such damage to their hosts that they are unable to transmit themselves. If a pathogen kills its host before it infects the next host it destroys its own chain of transmission. But what happens when the pathogen "knows" that the next host is coming along much sooner? The pathogen can get away with being virulent because it can successfully infect the next susceptible in the chain before it kills its host. The faster the transmission rate, the lower the cost of virulence.

A key to the evolution of virulence is the supply of susceptible hosts.[108] As long as there are enough susceptibles to infect, a virulent phenotype can work as an evolutionary strategy. When the supply runs out, it does not matter what virulence a pathogen has evolved. Time is no longer on the particular strain's side. A failed supply of susceptibles, drained by high mortality or rebound immunity, forces all influenza epidemics to ultimately burn out at some point. That is, of course, cold comfort if millions of people are left dead in a pandemic's wake.

Given the explanation, what circumstances changed the relationship between virus and host in such a way as to ramp up H5N1 to breathtaking virulence? Growing circumstantial evidence points to intensive poultry production or, in the more critical lexicon, factory farming.[109] Ilaria Capua and Dennis Alexander, reviewing recent influenza outbreaks worldwide, found no endemic highly pathogenic strains in wild bird populations, the ultimate source reservoir of nearly all influenza subtypes.[110] Instead, multiple low-pathogenic influenza subtypes in such populations developed greater virulence only once they entered populations of domestic birds. Though domestic populations can be divided into backyard and industrial, the former have been raised in one form or another for centuries without the now unprecedented outburst of newly pathogenic influenzas. The conditions for supporting such strains appear best represented in industrial poultry. Graham et al. found significantly greater odds for H5N1 outbreaks in Thailand 2004 in large-scale commercial poultry operations than in backyard flocks.[111] The pattern is repeated across influenza serotypes. In British Columbia in 2004, 5 percent of the province's large farms hosted highly pathogenic H7N3 infections, while 2 percent of its small farms hosted outbreaks.[112] In the Netherlands in 2003, 17 percent of industrial farms hosted H7N7 outbreaks, while 0.1 percent of backyard farms hosted clusters.

Even if these and other such strains first developed on smallholdings, a possibility to which we will return, industrial livestock appear ideal populations for supporting virulent pathogens. Growing genetic monocultures of domestic animals removes whatever immune firebreaks may be available to slow down transmission.[113]

Larger population sizes and densities facilitate greater rates of transmission. Such crowded conditions depress immune response. High throughput, a part of any industrial production, provides a continually renewed supply of susceptibles, the fuel for the evolution of virulence. There are additional pressures on influenza virulence on such farms. As soon as industrial animals reach the right bulk they are killed. Resident influenza infections must reach their transmission threshold quickly in any given animal, before the chicken or duck or pig is sacrificed. The quicker viruses are produced, the greater the damage to the animal. Increasing age-specific mortality in industrial livestock should select for greater virulence. With innovations in production, the age at which chickens are processed has been reduced from sixty to forty days,[114] increasing pressure on viruses to reach their transmission threshold—and virulence load—that much faster. A similar trajectory for the evolution of virulence has been superbly described for efforts at mitigating H5N1 outbreaks by mass culling: the greater the culling, the more pressure on the virus to evolve virulence.[115] The model, however, misses where the virulence of a virus that requires culling arises in the first place. Industrial livestock production comprises little more than continuous culling. The resulting influenzas, expected to transmit out of younger and younger animals, are not only more virulent but able to grow in the face of a host population's more robust immune systems. In short, with a simple host switch, we find here a recipe for the emergence of a deadly pandemic targeting fifteen- to forty-five-year-olds.

Although no smoking guns at present match the emergence of specific strains of deadly H5N1 to specific livestock farms, a growing phylogenetic literature fails to refute the working hypothesis. Duan et al. identified low pathogenic relatives of highly pathogenic H5N1 in migratory birds, lineages dating as far back as the 1970s.[116] None of the recently emergent low-pathogenic H5 relatives became established in aquatic or terrestrial poultry. In contrast, the origins of recent H5 virulence appear characteristic of domestic poultry alone. Vijaykrishna et al. meanwhile showed the source 1996 Guangdong strain entered regional poultry with all eight genomic segments intact.[117] The subsequent diversification into multiple genotypes, including the deadly Z genotype that has dominated outbreaks since 2003, occurred in domestic ducks in China mid-1999 to 2000. Much work, however, remains to be done. The phylogeny work continues apace, focusing on finer geographic scales across better inventoried landscapes. Research now under development tracks the evolution of H5N1 across Eurasia and Africa in niche envelopes defined by combinations of a number of agroecological variables, including levels of poultry intensification.[118] A recent international conference of H5N1 scientists convened in Bangkok laid out a research program aimed at better integrating phylogeographic studies of the virus with geocoded value-chain analyses of agricultural production.

In parallel, a growing number of studies are zeroing in on the sero-epidemiology of poultry-dense regions of southern China, H5N1's putative epicenter, including within specific production plants. Lu et al. showed Guangdong hosted a variety of influenzas.[119] Seasonal influenzas H1N1 and H3N2 composed most of the 1214 human cases discovered. But antibodies for H5N1 (2.5 percent) and H9N2 (4.9 percent) were also found among all tested, with a significantly greater prevalence of H9N2 antibodies (9.5 percent) in those occupationally exposed to birds. Wang, Fu, and Zheng meanwhile detected very few cases of H5 among 2191 Guangzhou workers occupationally exposed to birds.[120] H9, on the other hand, appeared widespread across the poultry commodity chain, especially among poultry market retailers (15.5 percent) and wholesalers (6.6 percent) and workers in large-scale poultry-breeding enterprises (5.6 percent). By way of explanation, H5 are targeted by vaccination campaigns, while H9 are generally not. Retailers handle different poultry species from multiple wholesalers, while wholesalers handle their own lots alone. Finally, Zhang et al. followed H9N2 outbreaks over five years in a single broiler chicken operation in Shanghai.[121] Virus across all outbreaks in the plant appeared related to that of the first outbreak despite vaccination efforts. The H9N2 isolates, with internal loci that arose via local reassortment with H5N1, showed evolution by antigenic drift across the study period. In short, meaningful advances are being made connecting the particulars of human production and influenza's spread and evolution.

Industrial production has already been implicated in increasing the diversity of human-friendly influenza. Over the past fifteen years an unprecedented variety of influenzas capable of infecting humans have emerged across the global archipelago of industrial farms. Along with H5N1 there are now swine flu H1N1, H7N1, H7N3, H7N7, H9N2, in all likelihood H5N2, and perhaps even some of the H6 serotypes.[122] A feedback appears to have emerged in kind: the very efforts pursued to control pathogenic bird flu may in passing increase viral diversification and persistence. In late 2006, virologist Guan Yi and his colleagues at the University of Hong Kong identified the previously uncharacterized Fujian-like H5N1 lineage.[123] The team ascribed the emergence of the strain as a viral evolutionary reaction to the Chinese government's campaign to vaccinate poultry. As in the case of other influenza serotypes, the virus appeared to evolve out from underneath the pressure of vaccine coverage.[124]

Factory practices provide what seems to be an amenable environment for the evolution of a variety of virulent influenzas, including pandemic strains. Swine flu H1N1, the most recent example arising early 2009 and on which we will touch only in passing, appears by definition industrial in origin. The closest ancestor for each of this H1N1's eight genomic segments is of swine origin. The segments have been identified as originating from different parts of the world: neuraminidase and the matrix protein from strains circulating in Eurasia, the other six from North America. No small farmer has the industrial capacity necessary to export livestock of any consequence across such long distances, nor the market entrèe livestock influenzas need to spread through international commodity chains.

If swine H1N1 or any subsequent human-specific influenza proves deadly, the epidemiological pollution threatens the very existence of the livestock industry, embodying James O'Connor's second contradiction of capitalism, in which the system destroys the natural bases of its own reproduction.[125] But it seems to be a risk agribusiness is willing to weather for the immediately cheap manufacture of its products.

EXPORTING THE TYSON MODEL

In Israel, researchers recently selected for a lineage of featherless chickens.[126] At first glance one suffers a Latourian shock at how much the naked birds look like living groceries. Able to survive solely in warm climes, the chickens were developed in the interests of the producer, not the consumer. Consumers have long avoided plucking feathers, a step typically conducted at the factory. A featherless poultry will allow producers, on the other hand, to scratch off plucking from production. The bald bird offers the anatomical equivalent of the factory epidemiology agribusiness is imposing on poultry—generating artificial ecologies that could never persist in nature because of the disease costs they incur, but that allow more poultry to be processed faster. The resulting costs are shifted to the birds, of course, but also consumers, farm workers, taxpayers, local governments, and nearby wildlife.

The lengths to which agribusiness has changed livestock production are remarkable, including, more recently, in the present bird flu zone. Southern China serves as a regional incubator for new methods in poultry breeding.[127] Sun et al., for instance, describe a Guangdong program in which geese were exposed to a counter-seasonal lighting schedule that induced out-of-season egg laying.[128] The innovation helped double profits for local goose production and expanded the market, and Chinese appetite, for goose meat. The resulting market advantages forced smaller farms out of business and led to a consolidation of the province's agribusiness. The structural shift marks a perverse turn back toward the farm collectivization the Chinese government abandoned in 1980, but this time under the control of far fewer hands. As the result of such innovations, to which we will return, millions more birds have been put into production there.

Karl Marx traced many of the fundamentals of such efforts at commoditization. In the first chapter of the first volume of *Capital*, Marx wrote that human-made objects have multiple characteristics.[129] They have use value—a hammer can be used to beat down nails. In many human economies objects also sport an exchange value—how many other objects (say, screwdrivers) can be exchanged with that hammer.

A capitalist economy adds a third characteristic—a fungibility that turns objects, including the labor that produces them, into tradable commodities for sale in the marketplace. The gap between the value added by labor to the commodity as marked by among other measures its price and the wages that capitalists pay in return for the labor embodies a commodity's surplus value, which accrues to capitalists as profit.

This is, of course, a rudimentary presentation of Marx's theory, and others have better elaborated on its applications to organisms and their ecologies.[130] But in these first efforts to better relate influenza's evolution to its social context we will address only the most general of Marx's points, namely that capitalists produce commodities not because commodities are useful—have use value—but because they accrue surplus value, to capitalists the most important characteristic of the object. Changing the color or style of a hammer to attract more consumers may seem negligible in effect, but for other objects changes in use value can have far-reaching, even dangerous, consequences. In this case, agribusiness has changed its commodity— living, breathing organisms—to maximize surplus value. But what does it mean to change the use value of the creatures we eat? What happens when changing use value turns our poultry into plague carriers? Does out-of-season goose production, for instance, allow influenza strains to avoid seasonal extirpation, typically a natural interruption in the evolution of virulence? Are the resulting profits defensible at such a rapidly accruing cost?

Mass commoditization of poultry emerged in what is now called the "Livestock Revolution." Before the shift, poultry was largely a backyard operation. In William Boyd and Michael Watts's map of poultry across the United States in 1929, each dot represents 50,000 chickens.[131] We see wide dispersion across the country—300 million poultry total at an average flock size of only seventy chickens. The production chain of that era shows local hatcheries sold eggs to backyard poultry producers and independent farmers, who in turn contracted independent truckers to bring live poultry to city markets.

That changed after the Second World War. Tyson, Holly Farms, Perdue, and other companies vertically integrated the broiler *filière*, buying up other local producers and putting all nodes of production under each company's roof.[132] Boyd and Watts show by 1992 U.S. poultry production is largely concentrated in the South and parts of a few other states. Each of their map's dots now represents one million broilers, six billion in total, with an average flock size of 30,000 birds. A 2002 map reproduced by Graham et al. shows a similar geographic distribution but ten years later hosting three billion more broilers.[133] U.S. hog and pig populations have similarly exploded in size, particularly over the past fifteen years, and are now largely concentrated in North Carolina, Iowa, Minnesota, and parts of other Midwest states. By the 1970s the new production model was so successful it was producing more poultry than people typically ate. How many roasted chickens were families prepared to eat a week? With the assistance of food science and marketing the poultry industry repackaged chicken in a mind-boggling array of new products, including chicken nuggets, strips of chicken for salads, and cat food. Multiple market shares were developed large enough to absorb the value-added production both domestically and abroad. The United States was for many years the world's leading poultry exporter.

Industrial poultry has since spread geographically. With production widespread, annual world poultry meat increased from 13 million tons in the late 1960s to about 62 million by the late 1990s, with the greatest future growth projected in Asia.[134] In the 1970s, Asia-based companies such as Charoen Pokphand (CP) set up vertical *filières* in Thailand and, soon after, elsewhere in the region. Indeed, CP was the very first foreign company allowed to set up production in Guangdong under Deng Xiaoping's economic reforms. China has since hosted a veritable explosion in annual chickens and ducks produced.[135] Increases in poultry have also occurred throughout Southeast Asia, though not nearly at the magnitude of that of China.

According to political economist David Burch, the shift in the geography of poultry production has some interesting consequences.[136] Yes, agribusinesses are moving company operations to the Global South to take advantage of cheap labor, cheap land, weak regulation, and domestic production hobbled in favor of heavily subsidized agroexporting.[137] But companies are also engaging in sophisticated corporate strategy. Agribusinesses are spreading their production line across much of the world. For example, the CP Group, now the world's fourth-largest poultry producer, has poultry facilities in Turkey, China, Malaysia, Indonesia, and the United States. It has feed operations across India, China, Indonesia, and Vietnam. It owns a variety of fast-food chain restaurants throughout Southeast Asia. Such rearrangements falsify the widely promulgated assumption that the market can correct corporate inefficiencies. On the contrary, vertical multinationalism cushions companies from the consequences of their own mistakes. First, multinationals producing by way of economies of scale can price unprotected local companies out of business—the Walmart effect. Consumers have nowhere else to go to punish subsequent corporate blunders. Second, by threatening to move operations abroad, multinationals can control local labor markets: hobbling unions, blocking organization drives, and setting wages and working conditions. Unions are an important check on production practices that affect not only workers and consumers, but both directly and by proxy the animals involved in production. Third, vertical agribusiness acts as both poultry supplier and retailer. The CP Group, for instance, owns a variety of fast-food chains in countries selling, what else, CP chicken. In short, fewer independent retailers exist to play suppliers off each other in a way that assures demands for better treatment of livestock are met.

In operating factories across multiple countries multinationals can hedge their bets in a variant of David Harvey's spatial fix.[138] The CP Group operates joint-venture poultry facilities across China, producing 600 million of China's 2.2 billion chickens annually sold.[139] As first touched on here in the description of the NAFTA Flu, when an outbreak of bird flu occurred in a farm operated by the CP Group in Heilongjiang Province, Japan banned poultry from China. CP factories in Thailand filled the market gap by increasing exports to Japan. A supply chain arrayed across multiple countries increases the risk of influenza spread even as it allows some companies the means by which to compensate for the resulting interruptions in business.[140]

To protect the interests of agribusiness even as its operations struggle or fail, multinationals also fund politicians or field their own candidates. Telecommunications tycoon Thaksin Shinawatra, the prime minister of Thailand during the country's first bird flu outbreaks, came to power promising to run the country like a business, a promise on which he delivered.[141] Shinawatra's policies were at times hard to distinguish from the business plans of the Thai industries that supported him, including agribusiness. His administration played a prime role in blocking Thai efforts to control bird flu. As Mike Davis describes it, when outbreaks began in Thailand, corporate chicken-processing plants accelerated production.[142] According to trade unionists, processing increased at one factory from 90,000 to 130,000 poultry daily, even as it was obvious many of the chickens were sick. Once the Thai press reported on the illness, Thailand's Deputy Minister of Agriculture made vague allusions to an "avian cholera," and Shinawatra and his ministers publicly ate chicken in a show of confidence.

It later emerged that the CP Group and other large producers were colluding with government officials to pay off contract farmers to keep quiet about their infected flocks. In turn, livestock officials secretly supplied corporate farmers with vaccines. Independent farmers, on the other hand, were kept in the dark about the epidemic, and they and their flocks suffered for it.[143] Once the cover-up was exposed, the Thai government called for a complete modernization of the industry, including requiring all open-air flocks exposed to migratory birds be culled in favor of production in new biosecure buildings only wealthier farmers could afford.

Attempts to proactively change livestock production in the interests of stopping pandemic influenza can be met with severe resistance by governments beholden to corporate sponsors. In effect, influenzas such as H5N1, by virtue of their association with agribusiness, have some of the most powerful representatives available defending their interests in the halls of government. In covering up outbreaks to protect quarterly profits, these institutions contribute to the viruses' evolutionary fortunes. The very biology of influenza is enmeshed with the political economy of the business of food.

If multinational agribusinesses can parlay the geography of production into huge profits, regardless of the outbreaks that may accrue, who pays the costs? The costs of factory farms are routinely externalized. The state has long been forced to pick up the tab for the problems these farms cause, among them, health problems for their workers, pollution released into the surrounding land, food poisoning, and damage to transportation and health infrastructure.[144] A breach in a poultry lagoon, releasing a pool of feces into a Cape Fear tributary that causes a massive fish kill, is left to local governments to clean up.

With the specter of influenza the state is again prepared to pick up the bill so that factory farms can continue to operate without interruption, this time in the face of a worldwide pandemic agribusiness helped cause in the first place. The economics are startling. The world's governments are prepared to subsidize agribusiness billions upon billions for damage control in the form of animal and human vaccines, Tamiflu, and clean-up operations. Along with the lives of millions of people, the establishment appears willing to gamble much of the world's economic productivity, which stands to suffer catastrophically if a deadly pandemic were to erupt, for instance, in southern China.

WHY GUANGDONG? WHY 1997?

In reorganizing its stockbreeding industries under the U.S. model of vertically integrated farming, Chinese farming helped accelerate a phase change in influenza ecology, selecting for strains of greater virulence, wider host range, and greater diversity. For decades a variety of influenza subtypes have been discovered emanating from southern China, Guangdong included.[145] In the early 1980s, with livestock intensification under way, University of Hong Kong microbiologist Kennedy Shortridge identified 46 of the 108 different possible combinations of hemagglutinin and neuraminidase subtypes circulating worldwide in a single Hong Kong poultry factory.[146]

Shortridge detailed the likely reasons southern China has served, and will serve, as ground zero for influenza pandemics:

• Southern China hosts mass production of ducks on innumerable ponds, facilitating fecal–oral transmission of multiple influenza subtypes. Domestic ducks were first moved from rivers to cultivated rice fields at the start of the Qing Dynasty in the middle of the seventeenth century.[147]

• The greater mix of influenza serotypes in southern China increases the possibility the correct combination of gene segments would arise by genetic reassortment, selecting for a newly emergent human strain.

• Influenza circulates year-round there, surviving the inter-epidemic period by transmitting by the fecal-oral mode of infection.

• The proximity of human habitation and a proliferation of live bird markets provide an ideal interface across which a human-specific strain may emerge.

The conditions Shortridge outlined twenty-five years ago have since only intensified with China's liberalizing economy. Millions of people have moved into Guangdong over the past decade, a part of one of the greatest migration events in human history, from rural China into cities of the coastal provinces.[148] Shenzhen, one of Guangdong's Special Economic Zones for open trade, grew from a small city of 337,000 in 1979 to a metropolis of 8.5 million by 2006. As discussed earlier, concomitant changes in agricultural technology and ownership structure have put hundreds of millions more animals into production.[149] Poultry output increased in China from 1.6 million tons in 1985 to nearly 13 million tons by 2000.

As Mike Davis summarizes it, by the onset of pathogenic H5N1, only the latest pathogen to emerge under such socioecological conditions,

> several subtypes of influenza were traveling on the path toward pandemic potential. The industrialization of south China, perhaps, had altered crucial parameters in the already very complex ecological system, exponentially expanding the surface area of contact between avian and nonavian influenzas. As the rate of interspecies transmission of influenza accelerated, so too did the evolution of protopandemic strains.[150]

The hemagglutinin protein of pathogenic H5N1 was first identified by Chinese scientists from a 1996 outbreak on a goose farm in Guangdong.[151] News reports during the initial H5N1 outbreak in Hong Kong detailed local health officials' decision to ban poultry imports from Guangdong from where several batches of infected chickens originated.[152] Phylogeographic analyses of the virus's genetic code have pointed to Guangdong's role in the emergence of the first and subsequent strains of pathogenic H5N1.[153] Scientists from Guangdong's own South China Agricultural University contributed to a 2005 report showing that a new H5N1 genotype arose in western Guangdong in 2003–2004.[154]

Subsequent work has complicated the picture. With additional H5N1 samples from around southern China, Wang et al. showed virus from the first outbreaks in Thailand, Vietnam and Malaysia appeared most related to isolates from Yunnan, another southern Chinese province.[155] Indonesia's outbreaks were likely seeded by strains first isolated from Hunan Province. These are important results, showing the complexity of influenza's phylogeographic landscape. At the same time they need not absolve Guangdong. Even if some H5N1 strains emerged elsewhere in the region, Guangdong's socioeconomic centrality may have acted as an epidemiological attractant, drawing in novel poultry trade-borne strains from around southern China before dispersing them again back across China and beyond.

Meanwhile, Mukhtar et al. traced the origins of the genomic segments from the original 1996 outbreak in Guangdong.[156] The internal proteins (encoding for proteins other than surface proteins hemagglutinin and neuraminidase) appeared phylogenetically closest to those of H3N8 and H7N1 isolates sampled from Nanchang in nearby Jiangxi Province. The 1996 hemagglutinin and neuraminidase appeared closest to those of H5N3 and H1N1 isolates from Japan. In the months before the outbreak in Hong Kong several of the proteins were again replaced by way of reassortment, this time via strains of H9N2 and H6N1.[157] H5N1 strains in the years that followed Hong Kong emerged by still more reassortment.[158] The sociogeographic mechanisms by which the various segments first converged (and were repeatedly shuffled) in Guangdong remain to be better outlined. The results so far do indicate the spatial expanse over which reassortants originate may be greater than Kennedy Shortridge, or anyone else previously imagined. But genomic origins tell us little how this particular complement led to a virus that *locally evolved* such virulence other than showing the genetic variation upon which the virus drew. A closer look at Guangdong's drastically shifting socioeconomic circumstances, then, appears necessary in better illuminating the local conditions that selected for such deadly pathogens so easily spread, not only H5N1, but a diverse viral portfolio, including influenza A (H9N2), H6N1, and SARS.[159] What exactly are the "crucial parameters" for the area's disease ecosystem? What are the mechanisms by which changes in southern China's human–animal composite lead to regular viral pulses emanating out to the rest of China and the world? Why Guangdong? Why 1997 and thereafter?

700 MILLION CHICKENS

We begin with the death of Mao and the rehabilitation of Deng Xiaoping. In the late 1970s, China began to move away from a Cultural Revolution policy of self-sufficiency, in which each province was expected to produce most foods and goods for its own use. In its place the central government began an experiment centered about a reengagement with international trade in Special Economic Zones set up in parts of Guangdong (near Hong Kong), Fujian (across from Taiwan), and later the whole of Hainan Province. In 1984, fourteen coastal cities—including Guangzhou and Zhanjiang in Guangdong—were opened up as well although not to the extent of the economic zones.[160]

By macroeconomic indicators favored by establishment economists, the policy was a success. Between 1978 and 1993 China's trade-to-GNP ratio grew from 9.7 percent to 38.2 percent.[161] Most of this growth stemmed from manufactured goods produced by foreign-funded joint ventures and township and village enterprises (TVE) that were allowed greater autonomy from central control. Starting in 1979, foreign direct investment (FDI) increased from zero to US$45 billion by the late 1990s, with China the second-greatest recipient after the United States. Sixty percent of the FDI was directed to cheap-labor manufacturing. Given the extent of China's smallholder farming, little FDI was initially directed to agriculture.[162]

That soon changed. Through the 1990s poultry production grew at a remarkable 7 percent per year.[163] Processed poultry exports grew from US$6 million in 1992 to US$774 million by 1996.[164] China's Interim Provisions on Guiding Foreign Investment Direction, revised in 1997, aim to encourage FDI across a greater expanse of the country and in specific industries, agriculture included.[165] The government's latest five-year plan sets sights on modernizing agriculture nationwide.[166] Since China joined the World Trade Organization in 2002, with greater obligations to liberalize trade and investment, agricultural FDI has doubled.[167] But much opportunity for AgFDI remains available to a wider array of sources of investment. By the late 1990s Hong Kong and Taiwan's contribution to China's FDI had declined to 50 percent of the total, marking an influx of new European, Japanese, and American investment.

In something of a bellwether, in August 2008, days before the Beijing Olympics, U.S. private equity investment firm Goldman Sachs bought ten poultry farms in Hunan and Fujian for US$300 million.[168] The outright ownership appears a step beyond the joint ventures in which the firm had until then participated. Goldman Sachs already holds a minority stake in Hong Kong–listed China Yurun Food Group, a mainland meat products manufacturer, and 60 percent of Shanghai-listed Shuanghui Investment and Development, another meat packer. Goldman Sachs's new purchase, further up the *filière,* signals a shift in the global fiscal environment. The firm adeptly moved out of high-risk U.S. mortgages and, during a global food crisis, into the brave new world of offshore farming in China.

In October 2008 China's leadership finalized plans to formalize such privatization.[169] Under the rubric of land reform and doubling rural income, peasants will be allowed to engage in unrestricted trade as well as—this is key—to buy and sell land-use contracts. These contracts are, in addition, to be extended from a ceiling of thirty years to seventy years. Contracting permits the government to retain land sovereignty as a political emblem. But as companies domestic and foreign are largely the only entities with the reserves on hand to enter such contracts, now extended to near perpetuity and for the incorporated dirt cheap, China's small farms will soon be open to a great land rush. We have, then, an "accumulation by dispossession" managed by a Communist Party.[170]

Guangdong, as throughout, remains at the cutting edge of these economic shifts. It hosted the central government's first efforts at internationalizing the rural economy.[171] Starting in 1978, Guangdong agricultural production was redirected from domestic grain to Hong Kong's market. Hong Kong businesses invested in equipment in return for new output in vegetables, fruit, fish, flowers, poultry, and pigs. In something of a reprisal of its historical role, Hong Kong (the front of the store) also offered Guangdong (the back of the store) marketing services and access to the international market.[172] In a few short years Guangdong's economy again became entwined with and dependent upon Hong Kong's economic fortunes. And vice versa. As of the Hong Kong outbreak, investment in China comprised four-fifths of Hong Kong's FDI outflow.[173] Much of Hong Kong–funded production is now conducted in Guangdong, with Hong Kong's industrial base increasingly hollowed out as a result.

Eighty-five percent of the agricultural FDI brought into China during the 1990s was funneled into Guangdong and several other coastal provinces.[174] Guangdong was allowed to invest more in its transportation infrastructure, in part as an invitation for further investment. Many of the province's companies were allowed to claim 100 percent duty drawbacks. Guangdong also developed trading arrangements with many of the 51 million Chinese overseas.[175] As a class, the expatriates, nearly two hundred years abroad, control large percentages of regional market capital, including in Indonesia, Thailand, Vietnam, the Philippines, Malaysia, and Singapore. At the time of the first H5N1 outbreaks, overseas Chinese collectively made up the group with the greatest investment in mainland China.[176]

As a result of the area-specific liberalization, Guangdong accounted for 42 percent of China's total 1997 exports and generated China's largest provincial GDP.[177] Of the coastal provinces, Guangdong hosted the greatest concentration of joint-venture export-oriented firms, with the lowest domestic costs for each net dollar of export income.[178] Guangdong's three free economic zones (Shenzhen, Shantou, and

Zhuhai) boasted an export-to-GDP ratio of 67 percent, compared with a national average of 17 percent.

By 1997, and the first H5N1 outbreak in Hong Kong, Guangdong, home to 700 million chickens, was one of China's top three provinces in poultry production.[179] Fourteen percent of China's farms with 10,000 or more broilers were located in Guangdong.[180] Guangdong's poultry operations were by this point technically modernized for breeding, raising, slaughtering, and processing birds, and vertically integrated with feed mills and processing plants. AgFDI helped import grandparent genetic stock, support domestic breeding, and update nutrition feed milling/mixing.[181] Production has been somewhat constrained by access to interprovincial grain and the domestic market's preference for native poultry breeds less efficient at converting feed. Of obvious relevance, production also suffered from inadequate animal health practices.

The magnitude of poultry intensification appears to have combined with the pressures placed on Guangdong wetlands by industry and a burgeoning human population to squeeze a diversifying array of influenza serotypes that circulated year-round through something of a virulence ratchet. The resulting viral crop—for 1997, H5N1 by molecular happenstance—is exported by easy access to international trade facilitated partly by expatriate capital.

Expanding Pathogens' Scope

Guangdong's ascension was not without its detractors, a dynamic with epidemiological consequences. Domestic producers in Hong Kong competed with Hong Kong–Guangdong joint ventures for export licenses.[182] Landlocked provinces meanwhile chafed at the liberalization the central government proffered coastal provinces alone. With so much domestic currency on hand, the coastal provinces could outcompete inland provinces for livestock and grain produced by the inland's own TVEs. The coastal provinces were able to cycle their competitive advantage by turning cheap grain into more profitable poultry or flat-out re-exporting the inland goods, accumulating still greater financial reserves. At one point rivalries became so intense that Hunan and Guangxi imposed trade barriers upon interprovincial trade. The central government's efforts to negotiate interprovincial rivalries included spreading liberalization inland.[183] Provinces other than Guangdong and Fujian began to become entrained in market agriculture, albeit at a magnitude still outpaced by their coastal counterparts. Industrial poultry's expanding extent—by re-exporting and inland development—increases the geographic scope for H5N1's emergence and may explain the roles Yunnan and Hunan appear to have played in serving up H5N1 abroad.

An additional source of conflict, often forgotten in the cacophony of macroeconomic indicators, requires comment—the Chinese people themselves. China's state capitalism has induced such a polarization of wealth that, along with threatening its own economic growth, it impoverishes hundreds of millions of Chinese. In engaging in internally imposed structural adjustment China has largely turned away from its real and ideological investment in the health and well-being of its population.[184] Tens of millions of state industrial workers have been laid off. Labor income as a share of Chinese GDP fell from about 50 percent in the 1980s to under 40 percent by 2000.[185] FDI and private companies—under no obligation to offer housing, health care, or retirement benefits—are used to discipline Chinese workers who were long used to a living wage, basic benefits, and job protection.[186] Discipline, however, does not always take. Protests running now into the tens of thousands, some turning into riots requiring army deployment, have battered provincial governments accused of corruption, land confiscation, expropriating state assets, wage theft, and pollution. In something of an ironic twist, in defending foreign capital against its own people, China's Communist leadership has taken on the role of the comprador class it first defeated in 1949.[187]

Farmers have been particularly hard hit by the government's capitalist turn. While decollectivization of agricultural land to household control propped up by governmental price supports led to a doubling in rural incomes by 1984, rural infrastructure and attendant social support have since deteriorated.[188] In the late 1980s, agricultural incomes stagnated, eaten away by inflation and a decline in price supports. Families began to abandon farming for informal industrial work in the cities. There, many rural migrants are treated as a reviled caste, discrimination codified by levels of officially designated migrant status and with attendant reductions in income.[189] China's macroeconomic growth has been unable to absorb many of the 100 million migrants. Urbanization, meanwhile, has diffused into the rural regions, eating up peasant land. One million hectares have been converted from agriculture to urban use.[190] Remote sensing shows that from 1990 to 1996 13 percent of agricultural land in a ten-county region in Guangdong's Pearl River delta was converted into non-agricultural use, in all likelihood China's most rapid conversion.[191] Rural towns have been transformed into growing industrial cities, some supporting populations tipping a million people.[192]

The termination of the commune system has left hundreds of millions of peasants without access to medical care and health insurance.[193] Universal health coverage has degraded to 21 percent of the rural population insured.[194] The number of affordable doctors has precipitously declined. Infant mortality has risen across many provinces. Rural public health has largely collapsed. Hepatitis and TB are now widespread. HIV incidence has increased in several southeastern provinces, Guangdong included.[195] STI incidence by province is correlated with immigration associated with surplus men from rural regions separated from their families. Multitudes of malnourished and immunologically stressed peasant-factory workers cycle migrating back and forth from what may be the geographic origins of an influenza pandemic would appear to compromise World Health Organization plans for intervening at any new infection's source.

ASIA'S FINANCIAL FLU

It is hard to discuss 1997 without mentioning two events of geopolitical significance. On July 1 that year, Hong Kong, long a British colony, was officially transferred to China as a Special Administrative Region, the first in a series of steps to full integration to be undertaken up through 2047. The next day the Bank of Thailand floated the baht off the U.S. dollar. The baht had been hammered by currency speculation and a crippling foreign debt. International finance fled from the baht and soon, with the economic strength of Thailand's neighbors also under suspicion, from other regional currencies. The FDI-dependent economies of the Philippines, Malaysia, Indonesia, Taiwan, and South Korea suffered in the ensuing wave of devaluation. The rest of the world too felt the effects of the infectious "Asian flu," as the crisis came to be called, with stock markets worldwide free-falling in response. Although Hong Kong's transfer to China and the Asian financial crisis followed the first outbreaks of bird flu in March, the events marked long-brewing shifts in regional political economy with apparent impact on viral evolution and spread.

Hong Kong's role in China's internally imposed structural adjustment, as we explored above, is amply documented. The intensification of Guangdong poultry went hand in hand with the ongoing transformation of the province's border with Hong Kong.[196] The resulting poultry traffic, however, is in no way unidirectional. Hong Kong exports to mainland China large amounts of poultry, fruits, vegetables, nuts, oilseeds, and cotton.[197] There is too a large illegal trade. At the time of the outbreak, Hong Kong chicken parts smuggled into China alone may have amounted to over US$300 million per year.[198] Hong Kong is clearly less a victim of Guangdong's bird flu ecology, as often portrayed, than a willing participant.

The financial crisis meanwhile slowed China's economy. China, however, avoided the worst of the financial flu.[199] By staking billions in public works and loans, the central government kept the country's economic engine primed in the face of slowing exports. Prophetically, four years before, the government introduced fiscal austerity measures to cool off inflation and the possibility of an overheated economy. An associated regulation package was initiated to control the kind of short-term speculation that would soon strain China's regional neighbors. The central state maintains tight control over the macroeconomy, capital flows, and corporate structure even as it cedes much of the day-to-day operations to provincial authorities. Concomitantly, China's economy is more than export driven. Even as austerity leaves millions of Chinese destitute in its wake,[200] up until the past year's global contraction the domestic economy continued to grow, albeit increasingly dependent on luxury goods and real estate speculation. Finally, exports out of China were until the 1997 crisis largely destined for East and Southeast Asia. During the crisis's aftermath China redirected more of its trade to Europe, North America, Africa, Latin America, and Oceania. China, then, was able to maintain a trade surplus, retain foreign investment, and prop the yuan against the fiscal buffet from abroad. Be that as it may, China was something more than a bystander to the crisis. Its economy's growing size and hemispheric reach may have exposed its neighbors to the worst excesses of the neoliberal model.[201] In attracting FDI at rates above and beyond those of its neighbors, China has become the prime exporter in the region for textiles, apparel, household goods, televisions, desktop computers, an increasing array of high-end electronics, etc. The smaller economies were forced to restructure production in such a way as to complement China's increasingly diverse commodity output, in a type of regional division of labor. China's transnational impact on supply lines forces each of the other countries to depend on producing a smaller array of parts to be put together in China for final export.

The resulting economies are more dependent on the few foreign multinationals they are able to attract. The company town becomes the company country. Such economies are more "brittle"—less robust in reacting to and reorienting around downturns in any single industry, a particularly pernicious problem as the United States begins to falter in its role of importer of last resort. Capital flight exposes countries to the temptations of currency speculation. To attract additional investment, establishment economists declare that these countries, once burned by such speculation, must now remove remaining barriers to the movement of money, goods, and capital, leaving domestic production unprotected, the very conditions that brought about the 1997 crisis in the first place.

It would appear bird flu and the financial flu are intimately connected, their relationship extending beyond serendipitous analogy. Although agriculture has been until recently less export dependent than manufacturing, in part from its perishability and now endangered trade protections,[202] there are already a number of epidemiological ramifications. These include a geographically expanding and intensifying poultry production, greater exposure to transnational poultry, wider illegal poultry trade, and a truncation in animal health infrastructure by austerity measures domestically imposed in return for international loans or by ideological imperatives.[203] More acutely, the aftermath of the financial flu may have also provided China a window for expanding regional poultry exports. A hypothesis worth testing is that some of these shipments seeded bird flu outbreaks abroad.

How do we operationalize this model? How do we determine whether transnational companies breed and spread influenza? Identifying poultry crates carrying H5N1 locality-to-locality remains a difficult but important task.[204] Tracing pathogens through commodity chains is increasingly viewed as a critical topic of study and mode of intervention.[205] One difficulty centers about the willingness of government regulators to inspect livestock plants, including conditions under which pathogen virulence may evolve. At the same time, there is a danger such efforts, once successful, may detract from the larger political ecology that shapes influenza evolution. With billions annually at stake, a few unlucky contract farmers or truck drivers may be sacrificed to protect a system stretching across the globe's interlocking markets. We have explored here the possibility that a deadly bird flu is an unintended but not unexpected accessory to multinational efforts to export a growing portfolio of Chinese agricultural commodities. The problem of influenza is more than a police matter. It is systemic, buried deep in political tissue. The virus, moreover, is complicated by a causality that extends beyond the factory gate.

LAYERS OF COMPLICATION

Ending large livestock operations as we know them could make a great difference in Guangdong as elsewhere. Such politically protected operations appear to promote both pathogen virulence and transmission. Graham et al. review a number of proximate environmental pathways by which pathogens can spread across and out of large confined animal feedlot operations, including via animal waste handling and use in aquaculture, workers' occupational exposure,

open transport of animals between farms and processing plants, contamination of shipping containers, non-livestock animals such as rats
and flies, and tunnel ventilation systems that blow animal materials
into the environment.[206] It would appear "biosecure" operations are
not so biosecure.

But there are additional layers of complication. There is no easy
one-to-one relationship between poultry density and H5N1 outbreak
at a variety of spatial scales. Across Asia, some areas where outbreaks
have occurred support comparatively few poultry, while other areas
with millions of chickens so far have been left untouched. There is a
stochastic component to disease spread. Epidemics start somewhere,
in this case in southern China, and take time to wend their way elsewhere, starting with regions nearby and, in part by due cause and
in part by chance, farther abroad. There are, however, demonstrable
causes other than those inside the poultry industry.

Thailand offers one such example. As mapped by ecologist Marius
Gilbert and colleagues, the distributions of both Thai broilers and
backyard poultry appear little associated with H5N1 outbreaks.[207]
Local outbreaks appear better fitted to the densities of ducks that are
allowed to graze freely outside. After harvests these ducks are brought
in to feed on the rice that is left over on the ground. Satellite pic-
tures show rice harvests matching duck densities. The more annual
rice crops the more ducks and the greater the association with H5N1
outbreaks. It seems these ducks, free to graze outdoors, exposed to
migratory birds, and tolerant of a wider range of influenzas, serve
as epidemiological conduits for infecting nearby poultry. Although
a rather ingenious agricultural practice, raising a cohort of ducks on
fallen waste rice may carry serious epidemiological overhead. Double
and even triple cropping are practiced in other bird flu zones, including southeastern China, the final stretches of the Xun Xi River, the
Ganges floodplain, and on the island of Java.[208]

We have, then, an integrated viral ecology with highly complex dependencies. The variety of farming practices, for one, splits
atwain a number of facile dichotomies. There is a panoply of farm
types, beyond the rough polarities of "small" and "large." In Thailand
alone there are closed-off farms, open structures with netting to

block passerine birds, the aforementioned free-grazing ducks, and backyard poultry.[209] Even then, such a taxonomy implies a compartmentalization often absent in the field. On a recent trip to Lake Poyang in Jiangxi Province, China, an international team of experts discovered an astonishing farming ecology in which domesticated free-range ducks fed in fields, bathed in local estuaries, swam in the lake, and intermingled and presumably interbred with wild waterfowl. Some flocks daily commuted across dikes from their sheds to the open water and back again. The epidemiological implications are obvious. Indeed, the facility by which pathogens spread and evolve in the area is of an order that, according to local farmers, chickens cannot be raised around the lake. For some poultry species the region is epidemiologically radioactive.

Absent too from the taxonomy are profound structural changes imposed by economic pressures upon world farming.[210] For the past three decades, the International Monetary Fund and the World Bank have made loans to poorer countries conditioned on removing supports for domestic food markets. Small farmers cannot compete with cheaper corporate imports subsidized by the Global North. Many farmers either give up for a life on peri-urban margins or are forced to contract out their services—their land, their labor—to livestock multinationals now free to move in.[211] The World Trade Organization's Trade-Related Investment Measures permit foreign companies, aiming to reduce production costs, to purchase and consolidate small producers in poorer countries.[212] Under informal contract, small farmers must purchase transnational approved supplies and are not always guaranteed their birds will be bought back by their transnational partner at fair market price or bought back at all.[213] The new arrangements belie the superficial distinction that has been made between industrial farms exercising "biosecurity" on the one hand and small farmers whose flocks are exposed to the epidemiological elements. Factory farms ship day-old chicks to be raised piecework by contracted farmers. Once grown (and exposed to migratory birds), the birds are shipped back to the factory for processing. The violation of biosecurity appears to be built directly into the industrial model.

A third complication is the historical shift in the relationship between nature and farming. Maps by Pasuk Phongpaichit and Chris Baker show that since 1840 Thailand has been transformed from primary wilderness into an agricultural state, a veritable bread basket.[214] Agriculture's new girth comes at the expense of wetlands worldwide, either out-and-out destroyed, polluted, or irrigated dry. The latter abuse serves as another basis for conflicts between agribusiness and small farmers. Socially stratified power struggles over the Chao Phraya basin have wracked Thailand for hundreds of years.[215]

Wetlands have traditionally served as *Anatidae* migration pit stops.[216] A growing literature shows many migratory birds are no sitting ducks and have responded to the destruction of their natural habitat. Geese, for example, display an alarming behavioral plasticity, adopting entirely new migratory patterns and nesting in new types of wintering grounds, moving from deteriorating wetlands to food-filled farms. The shift has for some waterfowl populations substantially *increased* their numbers.[217] The population explosions have initiated a destructive feedback in which the swarms of farm-fed migratory birds overgraze their Arctic breeding grounds to the point the tundra is transformed into a landscape of mud. In the course of colonizing our planet's natural habitats—some 40 percent of the world's usable land now supports agriculture—we may have unintentionally expanded the interface between migratory birds and domestic poultry. Clearly agribusiness, structural adjustment, global finance, environmental destruction, climate change, and the emergence of pathogenic influenzas are more tightly integrated than previously thought. The nest of dependencies requires fuller investigation. But, given the stakes, the connections we have been able to make deserve immediate action.

THE POLITICAL WILL FOR AN EPIDEMIOLOGICAL WAY

Guangdong may only represent the front of a socioecological transformation spreading across much of southern China and now much of the world. The origins of highly pathogenic H5N1 *are* multifactorial, with many countries and industries and environmental sources at fault. Can we then place blame on the country—say, Indonesia or

Vietnam or Nigeria—from which a human-to-human H5N1 infection might first emerge? Should we hold China accountable for
repeatedly seeding outbreaks regionally and internationally? Should
we broach Hong Kong's offshore farming? Or should we castigate
the United States, where the industrial model of vertically integrated
poultry first originated, with thousands of livestock packed in as
so much food for flu? The answers are affirmative across the board.
Responsibility, much as the problem itself, must be distributed about
its multiple levels of social and ecological organization.

To beat back industrial influenza, or at the very least promote
some sort of sustainable epidemiological mitigation, a number of
radically invasive changes are required, changes that challenge core
premises of present political economy, neoliberal and state capitalist alike. Whether there exists the political will to change is an open
question. Denial, jockeying, and obfuscation are presently rampant.
Chinese officials have expended much effort in denying responsibility for bird flu or, in the epidemiological equivalent of the American
practice of paying off the families of collateral damage without
admitting guilt, offered small sums to affected countries.[218] In 2007,
China donated US$500,000 to Nigeria's effort to fight bird flu. Never
mind that Nigeria would never have needed the aid if China had not
infected it—albeit indirectly—with bird flu in the first place. The
Qinghai-like strain Nigeria now hosts first originated in southern
China. Meanwhile, the United States and the European Union, criti-
cizing a stubborn Indonesia unwilling to share H5N1 samples, have
blocked Indonesian efforts to reform a system of worldwide vaccine
production that rewards pharmaceutical companies and the richest
populations at the expense of the poorest.[219]

What must be done to stop panzootic influenza, if the political will
is found by, or forced upon, governments worldwide? In the short
term, small farmers must be fairly compensated for animals culled in
an effort to control outbreaks. Livestock trade must be better regulated at international borders.[220] Livestock disease surveillance, largely
voluntary at this point, must be made mandatory and conducted by
well-funded governmental agencies. Frontline farm workers and
the world's poor more generally must be provided epidemiological

assistance, including vaccine and antiviral at no cost.[221] Structural adjustment programs degrading animal health infrastructure in the poorest countries must be terminated.

For the long term, we must end the livestock industry as we know it. Influenzas now emerge by way of a globalized network of corporate feedlot production and trade, wherever specific strains first evolve. With flocks and herds whisked from region to region—transforming spatial distance into just-in-time expediency[222]—multiple strains of influenza are continually introduced into localities filled with populations of susceptible animals. Such domino exposure may serve as the fuel for the evolution of viral virulence. In overlapping each other along the links of agribusiness's transnational supply chains, strains of influenza also increase the likelihood they can exchange genomic segments to produce a recombinant of pandemic potential. In addition to the petroleum wasted and the loss of local food sovereignty, there are epidemiological costs to the geometric increase in food miles. We might instead consider devolving much of the production to regulated networks of locally owned farms.

While the argument has been made that corporate food supplies the cheap protein many of the poorest need, the millions of small farmers who fed themselves (and many millions more) would never have needed such a supply if they had not been pushed off their lands in the first place. A reversal need not involve ending global trade or an anachronistic turn to the small family farm, but might include domestically protected farming at multiple scales.[223] Farm ownership, infrastructure, working conditions, and animal health are inextricably linked. Once workers have a stake in both input and output—the latter by outright ownership, profit sharing, or the food itself—production can be structured in such a way that respects human welfare, and, as a consequence, animal health. With locale-specific farming, genetic monocultures of domesticated animals which promote the evolution of virulence can be diversified back into heirloom varieties that can serve as immunological firebreaks. The economic losses influenza imposes upon global livestock can be tempered: fewer interruptions, eradication campaigns, price jolts, emergency vaccinations, and wholesale repopulations.[224] Rather than jury-rigged with each outbreak, the capacity for restricting livestock movement is built naturally into the regional farm model. The devil of such a domain shift is in its details. Richard Levins, with decades of experience collaborating with local researchers and practitioners on ecological approaches to Cuban agriculture and public health, summarizes some of the many adjustments a new agriculture anywhere may require:

> Instead of having to decide between large-scale industrial type production and a "small is beautiful" approach *a priori*, we saw the scale of agriculture as dependent on natural and social conditions, with the units of planning embracing many units of production. Different scales of farming would be adjusted to the watershed, climatic zones and topography, population density, distribution of available resources, and the mobility of pests and their enemies.
>
> The random patchwork of peasant agriculture, constrained by land tenure, and the harsh destructive landscapes of industrial farming would both be replaced by a planned mosaic of land uses in which each patch contributes its own products but also assists the production of other patches: forests give lumber, fuel, fruit, nuts, and honey but also regulate the flow of water, modulate the climate to a distance about 10 times the height of the trees, create a special microclimate downwind from the edge, offer shade for livestock and the workers, and provide a home to the natural enemies of pests and the pollinators of crops. There would no longer be specialized farms producing only one thing. Mixed enterprises would allow for recycling, a more diverse diet for the farmers, and a hedge against climatic surprises. It would have a more uniform demand for labor throughout the year.[225]

Rather than to the expectations of an abstract neoclassical model of production, the scale and practice of agriculture can be flexibly tailored to each region's physical, social, and epidemiological landscapes on the ground. At the same time, it needs to be acknowledged that under such an arrangement not all parcels will be routinely profitable.

As Levins points out, whatever reductions in income farms accrue in protecting the rest of the region must be offset by regular redistributive mechanisms. Transforming the business of farming so broadly, as outlined here or otherwise, is likely only one of many large steps necessary to stop influenza and other pathogens. For one, migratory birds, which serve as a fount of influenza strains, must concomitantly be weaned off agricultural land where they cross-infect poultry. To do so, wetlands worldwide, waterfowl's natural habitat, must be restored. Global public health capacity must also be rebuilt.[226] That capacity is only the most immediate bandage for the poverty, malnutrition, and other manifestations of structural violence that promote the emergence and mortality of infectious diseases, including influenza.[227] Pandemic and inter-pandemic flu have the greatest impact on the poorest.[228] As for many pathogens, particularly for such a contagious virus, a threat to one is a threat to all.

In implementing interventions for an industrial pollutant that evolves, we will also be forced to reimagine a virology that extends from underneath the microscope. Disease interventions, at both the individual and population levels, are, with a few bright exceptions, faltering across multiple pathogens. Vaccines, pharmaceuticals, and low-tech solutions, such as bed nets and water filters, though successful in addressing many reductionist diseases, cannot contain pathogens that use interactions at one level of biocultural organization to evolve from underneath interventions directed at them at another. Such holistic diseases, operating across fluctuating swaths of space and time, infect and kill millions annually. HIV, tuberculosis, malaria, along with influenza, confound even the most concerted efforts.

New ways of thinking about basic biology, evolution, and scientific practice are in order. In a world in which viruses and bacteria evolve in response to humanity's multifaceted infrastructure—agricultural, transportation, pharmaceutical, public health, scientific, political—our epistemological and epidemiological intractabilities may in fundamental ways be one and the same. Some pathogens evolve into population states about which we cannot or, worse, refuse to think.[229] None of the broader factors shaping influenza evolution and drug response can be found underneath the microscope, no matter how many more automated microplates can now be loaded or how much industrial computing power becomes available. A geography connecting relationships among living organisms and human production across scale and domain may help us make the mental transitions necessary to excavate those population states in which influenza is able to shield itself. It may be only then that we can better control a pathogen seemingly capable—by distributed epiphenomena—of a chilling premeditation.

—*ANTIPODE*, NOVEMBER 2009

Do Pathogens Time Travel?

In answer to every letter from a creditor, write fifty lines on an extra-terrestrial subject, and you will be saved.

—CHARLES BAUDELAIRE (1856)

EVOLUTION ARISES FROM A WEALTH of failure. Natural selection requires large and variable populations comprised largely of organisms that fail because their designs do not match their present circumstances.[230] And chance destruction occurs at all spatiotemporal scales.[231]

So, clearly, strict optimization does not reside in the designs, contra *religiosos* and radical adaptationists alike. Nor does it reside in the process of selection. Every species eventually dies out—by maladaptation, stochastic extirpation, or an external force (say, a large meteorite in yo' face).

And yet biological life began early on Earth and continues on, four billion years later, and will do so after the present climate state collapses or we nuke ourselves senseless.

By this persistence, then, organismal life can be conceptualized as a locally bounded and frame-shifting Turing process, after Alan Turing's notion of a machine that can simulate the logic of any computer algorithm.[232] Organisms' contingently recursive ontogenies aim to solve just about any and all problems they face during their lifetimes, until the next generation is birthed and reaches reproductive maturity. Just enough push until the baton is passed on.

In this context, natural selection emerges as a search protocol for biological meaning. An organism has meaning if it can survive and reproduce in its present environment. Mortal Keats's ode speaks less to a Grecian pisspot than to life's bright star, its capacity to persist in endless forms most beautiful: *Beauty is truth, truth beauty,—that is all / Ye know on earth, and all ye need to know.* And yet, what of all those other figurines, a litter of forgotten Baupläne, left behind to ashes and to dust or to our imaginations alone? What do they tell us? Phylogenetic and developmental constraints, the idiosyncrasies of all those scale transitions from molecules to ecologies, and the hazards of stochastic chance together embody a taxon-specific syntax that defines the contours of any given population's phenospace—the combinations of physical, biochemical, and behavioral characteristics its members can express.[233] Such historicity introduces a Gödel-like incompleteness: not all phenotypes, whatever their biophysical qualifications, evolve.[234]

Some species, however, may be able to defy the logic of biological incompleteness. High mutation rates, large population sizes both within and among hosts, recombination and reassortment, broad tropism, short generation times, and membership in mutualist guilds render influenza and HIV Turing infections of facultative life histories that simultaneously track an array of fitness maxima. In other words, pathogens specialize in failing across huge tracts of their phenotypic space, to their great success.

As a result, the pathogens—with a loose multicellularity but without the physiognomic overhead—can generate solutions to just about any problem of consequence they confront in their corners of the evolutionary space. The resulting variants that work best can be subsequently dispersed just about anywhere in the world by way of host migration, including, today, by humanity's global travel network.

Such a convergence of pathogenic and sociocultural mechanisms may be so powerful as to represent an evolutionary rocket fuel that permits epidemiological time travel: 1) influenza and HIV infections spread across populations of susceptibles before disease-specific symptoms are detected; and 2) circulating strains of both pathogens have evolved drug resistance to novel therapies long before the drugs are first introduced.[235]

The inversions are so integral to their epidemiologies as to represent a not insubstantial breakdown in causality, wherein effects are expected to follow causes. Simultaneous hyperdimensional exploration of many multiple hills across Sewell Wright's adaptive landscape repeatedly generates the phenotypic results of natural selection before the conditions that select them appear to arise.[236] In a spooky way, the bugs can read our epidemiological minds before we recognize our own intentions.

The less stringent temporality that results loosens the pathogens from biological incompleteness and toward a more ontological existence. They can evolve into mind-boggling variants at just about any and all times. The viruses may very well represent a kind of counterintuitive limit case for Darwin's concept of natural selection by virtue of expressing so much, not so little, variation.

—*FARMING PATHOGENS*, 12 JANUARY 2010

PART TWO

On nights when the King visits the Queen, the bedbugs come out at a much later hour because of the heaving of the mattress, for they are insects who enjoy peace and quiet and prefer to discover their victims asleep. In the King's bed, too, there are yet more bedbugs waiting for their share of blood, for His Majesty's blood tastes no better or worse than that of other inhabitants of the city, whether blue or otherwise.

—JOSÉ SARAMAGO (1982)

We Can Think Ourselves into a Plague

The power of the mind is a New Age staple. But really, can I concentrate enough to levitate myself (much less get my laundry done today)? The materialist answers, funny you mention it, but yes, you can. A few minds thought through the ideas that produced the airplane and perhaps soon enough the personal jet pack with smartphone dock and coffeemaker.

The dialectical materialist would modify science's self-congratulations with the observation that it's taken many generations' labor to produce the surplus permitting a few their deep thinking. Ingenuity is itself a social object.

And yet, despite, or perhaps because of, that backing, we can think ourselves into era-specific traps. Among these include animal and plant diseases that rope-a-dope us into a frustration we feel obliged by our lords and masters to fail to understand.

"It's not only this concrete problem—big companies controlling, through money donations, universities," philosopher Slavoj Žižek complains:

> It's something more fundamental going on. It's a well-organized . . .
> campaign to turn us scientists, human or natural, into "experts."

The idea is, we have a problem—let's say oil spill in Louisiana—oh, we need experts to tell us how to contain it. We have a public disorder, demonstrations; we need psychologists and so on. This is not thinking. What universities should do is not serve as experts to those in power who define the problems. We should redefine and question the problems themselves. Is this the right perception of the problem? Is this really the problem? We should ask much more fundamental questions.[1]

Problematics, much less their solutions, are capital-driven. Beware the questions with which one bothers, scientist.

Given the nature of newly emerging and reemerging pathogens, interdisciplinarity, following pathogens across epistemological domains, shifts front and center.[2] We might otherwise confuse cheap logistical advances against disease for strategic victories.

But interdisciplinarity's pursuit beyond lip service is contradicted by capitalism's prime directives. The puzzle of the pathogens, already a haze, is obscured by the machinations of funding and reputation—the mechanisms by which capital disciplines science.

CAPITAL ALSO ATTEMPTS TO DISCIPLINE pathogens. But the little buggers routinely violate protocol.

To their great credit, vaccines, pharmaceuticals, and modern public health policies have been successful in addressing a wide array of diseases. The smallpox and polio vaccines work and have driven the former to extinction and the latter to widespread extirpation. Clean water marginalizes cholera.

In falling to what are now standard health practices, these pathogens show themselves to embody the very reductionism used to defeat them. Their biologies are indeed the sum of their parts. In understanding the molecular properties of the viruses and their proximate means of transmission, Žižek's experts have been able to deliver stunning epidemiological victories for humans and their livestock alike.

But not all pathogens appear so cooperative. HIV, tuberculosis, malaria, and influenza, among others, killing millions, confound even the most concerted efforts. Lab, field, and modeling efforts, powered now by industrial computing, appear presently inadequate to the task of rolling back these scourges. Interventions are faltering. The more intransient diseases are intrinsically holistic in nature.[3] They are capable of using interactions at one level of biocultural organization to evolve out from underneath interventions directed at them from another. They operate across fluctuating swaths of time and space and host range. So vaccines and pills alone are rarely decisive. Indeed, in some parameter spaces such interventions can exacerbate outbreaks.[4] That is to say, taking a step back, modeling, or scientific epistemology more broadly, may have helped *cause* the evolution of such holistic diseases. We may be guilty of more than a failure of imagination. We may have had a role in selecting for such pathogens in the first place.

AN EXAMPLE. IN UNPUBLISHED WORK Hal Stern and I attempted to use a molecular constraint to predict where a human-specific bird flu might emerge.[5] We used a nucleotide substitution bias in favor of uracil previously shown in the polymerase loci of a variety of influenza serotypes to identify localities that may host strains of influenza A (H5N1) closer to a human-specific infection.[6] The more the uracil, the greater the human specificity. There is a possibility that areas hosting H5N1 polymerase of the greatest uracil may act as sources for more human-specific strains.

The details of the methodology matter little here. What the results might mean, however, is critical to our larger point.

Statistical significance may arise from truly adaptive changes in uracil content in space and time. It may also arise in part from an imbalance in the data imposed by sampling bias toward human cases and/or poultry of economic importance. We focus on what we believe is the pathogen's most important impacts *to us*. Such sampling bias may also arise, however, *from the very nature of epidemiological spread*.

Panzootic dynamics undermine the kinds of factorial design upon which much science depends. Researchers typically aim at making sure there are enough samples across the various combinations of factors potentially impacting the phenomenon they're studying. But many pathogens spread out-of-phase across multiple geographic fronts and, as in the case of H5N1, by way of different host species. The resulting anisotropic distributions, bulging in one place here and then another there, punch holes into the factorial coverage and for some factor combinations reduce statistical power. We may have a lot of geese infected in the Chinese province of Guangxi in 2006, for instance, but none elsewhere.

In addition, sampling resolution producing irregular geographical spacing reduces statistical power by decreasing the effective sample sizes of pairs of localities at a variety of proximities. The irregular spacing arises in part *from H5N1's spatial spread itself.*

We need to recognize, then, that the evolution and spread of the more successful pathogens are defined by uneven spatiotemporal dynamics that in many ways allow them to elude our efforts at discovering the nature of their spread. As a result we are less able to easily propose interventions for control or extirpation.

IN OTHER WORDS, IN A WORLD in which viruses and bacteria evolve in response to humanity's multifaceted infrastructure—including our science—our epistemological and epidemiological intractabilities may be in fundamental ways one and the same. Some pathogens evolve into population states in which we cannot easily think.

Redemption is possible. Behind new efforts is a perspective that attempts to better match the dynamics of the holistic pathogens that bring about mortality and misery in animals and humans alike.

We can model such pathogens across the scales and processes over which they themselves operate. Modeling panzootics must include making large leaps across scale and discipline. New concepts and objects must be defined. Econolandscapes. Cultural virology. Is influenza's demic selection mitigated or facilitated by economies of scale? Do traditional SIR models oversimplify human impact on pathogen evolution by defining sociality in terms of density dependence alone? These kinds of questions emphasize Richard Levins's point that the variables we include in our models are often a social decision.[7] What we choose to make internal or external to these models, including which data to concatenate, can have a significant impact on their success.

It seems a true health interdisciplinarity means moving away from the kinds of expertise the powerful shop for in the marketplace of ideas. Whistling to the Muzak.

—*FARMING PATHOGENS*, 25 OCTOBER 2010

Influenza's Historical Present

I delivered the following speech, co-written with economic geographer Luke Bergmann, at an NIH-FAO–sponsored workshop on avian influenza in Asia, held in Beijing, June 2010.[8] The speech is based on a book chapter published in Influenza and Public Health: Learning from Past Pandemics (London: EarthScan).[9] The text is lightly edited.

THIS IS THE FIRST OF TWO TALKS I'll be giving. Both I believe attempt to address one of the key concerns of our workshop: How do we work together?

And work together we must. Influenzas operate on multiple levels of biocultural organization: molecularly, pathogenically, and clinically; across multiple wildlife biologies, epizoologies, and epidemiologies; evolutionarily, geographically, agroecologically, culturally, and financially.

But it's more than just a complicated story. The expanse of influenza's causes and effects play out to the virus's advantage. As I discussed at last year's workshop, influenza appears to use opportunities it finds in one domain or scale to help it solve problems it faces in other domains and at other scales.

Collaboration, then, is mission-critical, even as the logistics are difficult. How do we get different research disciplines to talk to each other in such a way as to address influenza's full dimensionality?

We should remind ourselves, however, that success isn't merely a matter of concatenating data sets that have long been segregated by disciplinary boundaries. Despite some commonalities, each discipline *thinks* in its own way. Each discipline imagines problems differently.

It is my view, then, that listening to each other, however important, isn't enough. It is when we *assimilate* each other's professional imaginations—whatever the risks we personally take—that we will begin to cleave influenza's Gordian Knot. And figuring out influenza is, after all, why we find ourselves in the same room today.

Although trained as an evolutionary biologist I will in this talk address an albeit rough attempt to assimilate another imagination, in this case, that of human geography, and more specifically economic geography.

LET'S START OUT WITH AN INTERESTING result that requires explanation. Lenny Hogerwerf and her colleagues separated out the world's countries by the agroecological niches they host.[10] In this version of the map, five niches are differentiated on the basis of four agroecological variables: agricultural population density, duck density, chicken production, and purchasing power per capita. Here some niches support more ducks than others, etc.

We will leave the whys and wherefores one niche supports H5N1 over another for another day. But one immediately observes that despite a few exceptions, the niches themselves are clearly structured by geography, with the most H5N1-vulnerable niches arrayed across South and East Asia, especially along the Chinese lowlands into the river basins of Indochina and, farther south, to Indonesia.

Why are countries within each agroecological niche for the most part geographically contiguous? I'll give you a short answer before entering some detail.

First, yes of course shared enviro-climatic conditions may contribute to the spatial autocorrelation in niche geography. There is, however, another possibility. Through history, agricultural innovations have emerged locally and undergone bouts of regional diffusion. And prevalent modes of regional agriculture have influenced subsequent developments.

In China, rice cultivation marked the transition between Mesolithic foragers and the surplus food-producing economies of the Neolithic.

Domestic ducks were deployed in rice paddies for pest control as early as five hundred years ago. And finally, the last layer in our rough cultural sedimentation, Western-style poultry intensification was introduced at scale during the economic liberalization of the past thirty years. We hypothesize that the duck-rice-intensive poultry niche in Asia resulted from a series of changes in agricultural practice—ancient (rice), late imperial (ducks), and present-day (poultry intensification)—melding in such a way as to support in a unique way the evolution and persistence of multiple influenzas.

Now to the details. I will avoid giving a complete history of Chinese agriculture but will hit on some key events and circumstances that I believe can inform our thinking about how to move forward our analyses of influenza in Asia.

FIRST, DOMESTICATED ANIMALS IN CHINA have long been integrated, not merely juxtaposed, with other elements in local agro-ecological systems.

The domestication of ducks has been placed at least 3,000 years ago, with funerary art dating from the Eastern Han Dynasty depicting agricultural scenes with rice fields, and ducks and fish in ponds.

Rice-duck systems—in which flocks of ducks, whether backyard or more nomadic, are allowed to graze on fields after the harvest—have long been in place. By about five hundred years ago, in the middle of the Ming Dynasty, ducks were very popular for pest control in the rice paddies of the Pearl River Delta. From various points in the Ming and Qing dynasties, ducks were also promoted for the control of locusts in Fujian and northern China, a mode of control still in practice today.[11]

Fredrick Simoons reviewed a number of foreign accounts that indicate early husbandry bore markings of high-order poultry intensification.[12] One sixteenth-century account, quoting Simoons,

> described a sophisticated system of Chinese duck husbandry, with thousands of ducks kept in cages on boats at night. In the morning the ducks were permitted to leave, entering the water by means of bamboo bridges, feeding in paddies during the daylight

hours, and returning when their owners, as evening approached, signaled them to return.

Contemporary practices bear similarities. An international team, including several attendees here today, witnessed several years ago a similar permeability, wherein domestic ducks intermixed with wild birds on their daily commute into Lake Poyang in Jiangxi Province. Simoons also summarizes a late-nineteenth century account of a proto-commodity chain that began with hatcheries that, again quoting,

> sold the young ducklings to duck merchants who raised them in enclosures. When sufficiently grown, such ducks were sold by the merchants to itinerant duck vendors who transported them by water, as many as two thousand to a boat. While he kept the ducks, a vendor permitted them to feed twice a day along the river or in nearby fields, thereby saving the cost of feed. . . . Though the itinerant sold ducks retail in communities along the way, most found provision dealers who specialized in salting and drying them.

By early twentieth-century agricultural surveys, ducks and chickens were found in much greater densities in rice-growing regions, especially areas of double-cropping. Densities found nowhere else in the world at that time.

A SECOND OBSERVATION THAT SHOULD inform our thinking: Integrated farming practices in China, layering and interweaving multiple types of farming, were long diverse in their character. Not just duck-rice.

For instance, the origins of rice-fish farming extend back at least 1,700 years and records from over 2,000 years ago describe other aquatic plant-fish systems. Whereas various livestock-crop systems are widespread and relatively well-known, livestock-carp systems are a somewhat more unique contribution less widely understood today but dating in China at least back to the Ming Dynasty.

By about four hundred years ago, fruit tree–fish and mulberry-silk-worm-fish dike-pond integrated systems are documented. Into these, domestic ducks were integrated in the 1860s. The mulberry-silk-fish system is of interest in and of itself because it speaks to two additional observations:

First, the dynamics of integrated farming are locale-specific. A case in point is the southern Chinese province of Guangdong, a contemporary epicenter for multiple influenzas.

We will focus on those processes that have brought humans, livestock, and wild birds together in the Pearl River Delta, at the core of the province, around which contemporary centers of industrial production and population such as Guangzhou, Shenzhen, and Hong Kong were built. Dynamics elsewhere in the region are critical, of course, but we must start somewhere.

Much of the Delta itself emerged over the past two thousand years, some causes of which were, and are, anthropogenic, from conscious acts of reclamation to increased siltation from deforestation upstream. Beginning perhaps in the Song Dynasty about a thousand years ago, Delta wetlands were increasingly converted to ponds divided by soil piled onto dikes, forming the first iterations of what would be known as the dike-pond system. Fish were raised in the ponds, then fruit trees and various crops were planted on the banks, with chickens and ducks potentially integrated.

By the latter half of the sixteenth century, in the middle of the Ming, instead of fruit trees, mulberries were increasingly planted on the banks in order to feed silkworms, helping close a rather efficient nutrient cycle between banks and ponds. By 1581 the mulberry dike-pond system occupied about 30 percent of certain key counties in the Delta. By the early twentieth century almost all the land in a number of parts of the larger area had been converted to this silk-producing system.

The changes to the Pearl River Delta were tied not only to their locales but to their global context, too. In other words—a fourth observation—changes in the kinds of integrated farming have long been related to the state of global and regional economies. Guangdong, for instance, was a key point for foreign trade, and a long-distance international market for silk explicitly drove the development of local land-use and the rise of the dike-pond system.

The effects of globalization have almost always run in multiple directions. Whatever the socioecological virtues of dike-pond ecosystems, in no sense were they simply "sustainable" systems of locally closed loops. The mulberry-dike system was functionally open and at the center of many flows, sustained by products exported internationally and by substantial food and potentially other inputs imported interregionally.

By the middle of the eighteenth century, the Delta and a vast hinterland stretching into neighboring provinces had been functionally integrated within a single differentiated agroecosystem. The whole landscape of the region would then also have been more directly coupled to the dynamics of an emerging global political economy, influenced whether by the expansion of world silk markets or by the emerging crises of capitalism in distant lands.

Within this larger interconnected region, but further away from major population centers and their resources than the dike-pond regions, other agroecosystems were prevalent. For example, the *zheng gao* system is a variant of paddy-rice intercropping requiring less labor and resources to expand output in the Delta peripheral.

Extensive use was made of ducks as well, to eat crab pests in the paddies and to recycle grain waste in the fields after the harvest. The system grew alongside the dike-pond systems from the Ming to the Qing until state initiative in water-management projects to raise yields eliminated *zheng gao* in the early years of the socialist period in the 1950s.

THE CHINESE REVOLUTION ILLUSTRATES ANOTHER observation. The state of agroecology can be reset by broad shifts in the society at large.

The Maoist period brought a number of agrarian reforms, including changes in cropping systems, in land-tenure, in labor conditions, in social relations, and in extra-regional economic linkages. Development was, in theory, aimed at decreasing polarization and dependence on the export markets of the global core, and toward spatial and social parity, focusing on a national economic space. The Pearl River Delta's previous international trade linkages and associated flows of commodities and money were thereby radically reshaped.

A doubling in population required a focus on developing grain production in order to meet the basic caloric needs of the people, a task that met with several setbacks and was only secured in the 1980s after the maturation of the fertilizer industries in which heavy investments were made in the 1970s. During this period integrated farming wavered in the Pearl River Delta. The silk-mulberry economy had already collapsed during the Great Depression and the *zheng gao* cropping system was now replaced, as we alluded to earlier. Rice-fish farming was promoted early in the socialist period, with 700,000 hectares nationally by the late 1950s, but disruptions, whether political, policy, or pesticide in origin, resulted in a sharp decline during the 1960s and 1970s. In Guangdong, rice-fish acreage declined from around 40,000 hectares to a mere 320 by the beginning of the Cultural Revolution in 1966.

By the middle and late 1970s, interest in ecologically integrated farming arose again, with communes establishing farms and conducting research on optimizing combinations of rice, silkworms, chickens, ducks, fish, and pigs. At the same time, other communes were leading the way in something of another direction, in researching and implementing local versions of industrial livestock intensification.

WHICH BRINGS US TO THE RECENT ERA. Economic liberalization changed China's agroecological landscape yet again.[13]

As we described in our political virology of offshore farming, in the late 1970s China began to move away from a Cultural Revolution policy of self-sufficiency, in which regions were expected to produce most foods and goods for their own uses. In its place the central government began an experiment centered about a reengagement with international trade in Special Economic Zones set up in parts of Guangdong, Fujian, and later the whole of what would become Hainan Province. In 1984, fourteen coastal cities were opened up as well, though not to the extent of the economic zones.

Starting in 1979, annual foreign direct investment (FDI) increased from zero to 45 billion U.S. dollars by the late 1990s, with China the second-greatest recipient after the United States. Sixty percent of the FDI was directed to manufacturing. Given the extent of China's smallholder farming, little FDI was initially directed to agriculture. That soon changed. Through the 1990s poultry production grew at a remarkable 7 percent per year. Production for domestic consumption and investments were not confined to chickens, given the longstanding interest in the consumption of duck and goose. Processed poultry exports grew from 6 million U.S. dollars in 1992 to 774 million U.S. dollars by 1996.

The changes were more than merely emergent. They were structured by new legislation and diplomatic efforts. China's Interim Provisions on Guiding Foreign Investment Direction aim to encourage FDI across a greater expanse of the country and in specific industries, agriculture included. The government's 2005 five-year plan set sights on modernizing agriculture nationwide. Since China joined the World Trade Organization in 2002, with greater obligations to liberalize trade and investment, agricultural FDI has doubled. By the late 1990s Hong Kong and Taiwan's contribution to China's FDI had declined to 50 percent of the total, marking an influx of new European, Japanese, and American investment.

Economic liberalization, particularly its changes in ownership structure and its geographic integration within and beyond southern China, has had a fundamental effect on regional husbandry. By 1997, and the first H5N1 outbreak in Hong Kong, Guangdong, home then to 700 million chickens, was one of China's top three provinces in poultry production. Some of Guangdong's poultry operations were by this point technically modernized for breeding, raising, slaughtering, and processing birds, and vertically integrated with feed mills and processing plants.

Foreign direct investment helped import grandparent genetic stock, support domestic breeding, and update feed milling. The majority of breeds used in industrial production were now imported, bred for profit and high rates of capital turnover. At times, production has been somewhat constrained by access to interprovincial grain and the domestic market's preference for native poultry breeds less efficient at converting feed. Of obvious relevance, production also suffered from less-than-adequate animal health practices.

Today, expansion is robust and so-called high-quality chickens, long-standing domestic breeds or hybrids, are increasingly being produced, despite their higher costs and longer turnover times. Guangdong is producing approximately one billion of these broilers a year.

THE PROVINCE'S ECONOMIC ASCENSION was not without its detractors, however, a dynamic with potential consequences for influenza.

Among them, landlocked provinces chafed at the liberalization the central government initially established in coastal provinces alone. With so much domestic currency on hand, the coastal provinces could outcompete inland provinces for livestock and grain produced by the inland's own town and village enterprises.

The coastal provinces were able to cycle their competitive advantage by turning the inland's cheap grain into more profitable poultry or flat-out re-exporting the inland's goods, accumulating still greater financial reserves. At one point rivalries became so intense that Hunan and Guangxi, bordering more prosperous coastal provinces, imposed trade barriers upon interprovincial trade.

The central government's efforts to negotiate interprovincial rivalries included spreading liberalization inland. Provinces other than Guangdong and Fujian were also becoming entrained into market agriculture, albeit, in something of a reprise of pre-Revolution dynamics, at a magnitude still outpaced in certain sectors by their coastal counterparts.

Industrial poultry's expanding extent—by re-exporting and inland development—increases the geographic scope for the emergence of market-oriented influenzas and may explain in part, as shown by the phylogenetic evidence, the roles Yunnan and Hunan appear to have played in serving up H5N1 abroad.[14]

DESPITE THESE DEVELOPMENTS, DIVERSITY remains the order of the day. Numerous forms of ownership, organization, and production coexist. Foreign investment and intensive production have not eliminated all backyard producers. Equally, not all small-scale producers are operating independently. Instead, thick webs of contractual obligations interweave a diverse ecology of economic actors. For instance, Guangdong Wen Foodstuff Group, the largest chicken producer in the province as of early in this decade, drew revenues of 1.6 billion renminbi in 2000, employed about 4,400 employees in the central company and 12,000 household contract farmers, and maintained a close relationship with South China Agricultural University. As of the 1990s, provincial feed mills were operated publicly, by village cooperatives, by joint-ventures, and by private capital all at the same time.

Such developments in the poultry industry, many of them in the greater region around the Pearl River Delta, are not occurring in isolation, but in the midst of a period of extremely rapid urbanization, suburbanization, inward migration, industrial expansion, interregional integration and economic differentiation, and export-led growth.

The greater delta's agroecological landscape mosaic was built, and is being built, on the historical dynamical patterns we described earlier. At the same time, the development represents a historically unprecedented density and juxtaposition of activities, with potentially fundamental consequences for influenza evolution.

In other words, influenza's regional epizoology arises out of a complex interplay of agroecologies past and present, in what the philosopher Louis Althusser called the "historical present."

That mix of past and present is arrayed across the region's geography. Maps from studies of land use in the Pearl River Delta, approximately ten and twenty years after the start of economic liberalization, show in 1989 huge swaths of land are still cropland, cities relatively compact (Guangzhou is spatially the most prominent), and the dike-pond land relatively isolated from concentrated populations.[15] By contrast, in 1997 urbanization is vastly greater, spreading out not only from multiple city cores but also along suburban filaments stretching through the countryside.

Studies indicate that much land-use change in the Pearl River Delta is fragmenting in nature and is directly related to foreign direct investment.[16] The question remains, however, as to the exact relationships livestock industry investments may have with such patterns. Landscape ecological metrics also suggest significant increases in developed land "edge density" over this time period, on the fringes of the major cities in the Pearl River Delta. Cropland in the later time period is almost absent, having been replaced by horticulture, development, and ponds.

THE STORY OF THE GROWTH OF AQUACULTURE is also apparent in the maps. As aquaculture's economic returns were perhaps two to three times those to cropland in the time between these two maps, it is not unexpected that much land would be converted, often by village cooperatives.

Much of what is described as "dike-pond" land in these maps may actually reflect a greater emphasis on "pond" than previously, as the land is converted into aquaculture. However, some observers still suggest that aquacultural ponds are also likely to be used for the production of waterfowl. As ponds have spread out from the traditional core of the dike-pond region in the west section of the area, the amount of built-up land spread across the pond regions appears to have increased greatly, potentially bringing increasing human population densities and aquatic habitat into proximity.

So new layers of export-driven landscape are being superimposed upon those of previous eras. However, as the Delta's export-driven economy develops, diversifies industrially, moves toward more costly technologies, and further urbanizes, there is pressure to move livestock industries farther away from valuable urban land. Other large producers have long been located in smaller urbanized areas in the peripheries of these larger interurban systems.

There appear to be certain similarities between the resulting landscapes and peri-urban regions of other newly industrializing states across Southeast Asia called alternately *desakotas* (city villages) or *Zwishenstadt* (in-between cities). Many may very well share the same agroecological combinations described in the niche modeling of Hogerwerf and her colleagues with which we began.

The sum effect for the Pearl Delta, and farther afield across southern China, may include the possibility that poultry intensification and the pressures placed on agroecological wetlands have squeezed a diversifying array of influenza serotypes circulating year-round through something of a virulence ratchet.

The resulting viral crop—for 1997, H5N1 by molecular happenstance—may have the opportunity to be subsequently exported out by international trade facilitated by Hong Kong and diasporic capital.

ADDITIONAL RESEARCH FOR SUCH AN assertion is required. But we may have found a peg on which to place such work. Namely, history and context matter, as much for pathogens as the humans they infect.[17]

Indeed, at the risk of reifying arbitrary blocks of time, pathogens have their own origins, diasporic migrations, classical eras, Dark Ages, and industrial revolutions. As human pathogens evolve and spread in a world of our own making, these analogous eras are often coupled with our own.

What we find in southern China today for influenza is neither effortlessly remade independent of history nor enslaved to a static past. The region has neither been unconnected from the rest of the world nor had its specificities erased by a wave of recent generic globalization. The socioecological environment in which influenzas are evolving there is the complex and layered product of past and present, of global and local. The causes of emerging influenzas in southern China today are threads that may bind many places, peoples, and times together, though never evenly, and in a place-specific way.

In other words, southern China's role as a primary influenza epicenter is far from inherent, instead arising from a contingent confluence of local and global factors in what the geographer David Harvey would call an "active moment" in spatial configuration.[18] The mechanics of that dynamic configuration as it relates to influenza remains largely a mystery.

For the landscape itself: What are the exact locations and practices of intensive livestock operations across the region? What is their proximity to smallholders practicing duck-fish aquaculture? Is the effect of present-day industrial siting of significance? Are there synergies in the landscape today that were not present in the less spatially heterogeneous rural systems still prevalent thirty years ago?

Efforts at putting numbers on the relations between the historical environments and the evolution of influenzas are correspondingly more challenging—of another order of complexity altogether.

Are these mixed landscapes what produce the aggregate averages of the most epidemiologically vulnerable agroecological niches Hogerwerf *et al.* introduced? Are some molecular phenotypes repeatedly selected for by specific micro-niches? Is influenza's repeated parallel molecular evolution a marker of the virus's ability to evolve in response to the landscape features defined by both past and present together?

In other words, getting back to how we might work together, when we whittle analyses of Southern China's economic geography against its agroecological history we can ask new questions about influenza's evolution. And asking questions no one has yet bothered with is half the battle.

—*FARMING PATHOGENS*, 11 JUNE 2010

Does Influenza Evolve in Multiple Tenses?

This essay follows up on the previous one. It is adapted from our book chapter published in Influenza and Public Health: Learning from Past Pandemics *(London: EarthScan).[19]*

THE PAST MAY POSSESS A POWER greater than prologue. Anyone with a social networking account knows that. All of a sudden you find yourself daily interacting with people long thought boxed away. People mature, yes, but sensibilities remain largely intact and an old year, fine wine or vinegar, pours back up into the bottle.

"The past," as William Faulkner diagnosed it, "is never dead. It's not even the past." Living in multiple tenses, in what we characterized in the previous post as Louis Althusser's "historical present," can be exhilarating or exhausting depending on the day.[20]

That kind of time travel may be influenza's bread-and-butter. Strains of the bug may retain, and strategically exploit, the capacity to evolve molecular characteristics of bygone eras.

To address whether exposure to previous H1N1 strains, as far back as the 1918 pandemic, protected humans from the worst of new influenza swine flu H1N1 (2009), Yasushi Itoh and colleagues exposed the new virus to influenza antibodies circulating in humans of different age groups.[21] Only patients born before 1920 expressed the antibodies that could neutralize the new virus. That is, the new H1N1 appeared to be expressing epitopes similar to those of the 1918 H1N1, antibody targets to which very few living humans could immunologically respond before the latest pandemic.

Although influenzas—with life cycles of only a few days—evolve from infection to infection, the molecular constraints upon, and opportunities for, influenza evolution may extend in this case back nearly a hundred years. That's the viral equivalent of a geological eon. Influenza's evolutionary history is riddled with such parallelisms, arising when independent lineages evolve similar adaptations above and beyond chance alone. The parallelisms may accrue from more than mutational dumb luck, although the numbers involved in influenza infections could very well permit such raw selection in principle. Something other than natural selection? We can hypothesize that in drawing upon the structural constraints that shaped previously evolved responses, the genome engages in a type of cognition.[22] At the risk of anthropomorphizing a virus, a cognitive influenza can choose, depending on its context, among a variety of genomic responses. Unlike most molecular work, assuming that viral evolution algorithmically converges on the same or similar phenotypes via random mutation and raw selection, we hypothesize here that the convergences are context- and path-dependent.

In other words, the effects of the agroecological historical present discussed in the previous essay may be fundamental to the evolution of livestock pathogens such as influenza. The very real presence of an agriculture's past in today's landscape, albeit transmogrified by waves of cultural reappropriation and reemphasis, may offer pathogens a hook on which to draw upon their own histories.

How so? We can hypothesize a variant of Conrad Waddington's "genetic assimilation." In Waddington's assimilation, an organism's behavioral response to the environment is canalized— incorporated— into the genome over a number of generations.[23] The new genotype will thereafter be expressed even when the environment changes. In our version of assimilation, the canalized response is incorporated but hides when environments change, remaining a potentiality even generations later as an open-ended polymorphism.

Again, how so? By what mechanism would such polymorphism be tapped?

The genetic variation within any local population may be greater than what organisms actually express in the field. A local environment may select for characteristics consonant with the expression of only a limited genetic combination from a greater cryptic reservoir.[24]

Once the environment changes, however, that reservoir can be drawn upon. In effect, the hidden potentiality may act as a kind of genetic archive from which to reconstruct relevant adaptations or converge on related ones once they are again needed.

A viral adaptation in the archive associated with a host switch routinely undertaken over hundreds of years—say, duck to human—may be revisited if only by way of the architectural constraints canalized on the genome and on the emergent biochemistry of the proteins produced.[25] Such constraints are embodied by stereochemical relationships among amino acid residues, path-dependent epigenetic and biochemical pathways across genetic loci, and a compensatory evolution wherein changes in one amino acid select for changes in another.[26]

Whenever the pathogen is confronted with elements of a previous era's agroecology, the constraints together channel viral expression to what the virus evolved previously as the "right" amino acid combination. That's the "historical" in the historical present.

At the same time, the evolutionary trajectory through the combinations of possible phenotypic expression may depend on the current mix of agroecological actors and opportunities. The successful virus must step through a unique combination of changes to "solve" the new matrix of agroecological relationships as they are presented across the landscape. That's the "present" in the historical present.

We have here, then, something very different from the algorithmic approaches to influenza's molecular repeats. The virus evolves by more than just mutation-selection to immunological or prophylactic environments "from below" in the immediate time interval.[27] We hypothesize the virus also expresses a genomic cognition that permits a choice in emergently archived host- and niche-specific characteristics asked of it "from above."

Such cognition may help explain influenza's capacity to succeed in agroecological niches defined by shifting geographic mosaics of old and new forms of farming. Although the mechanisms for such a molecular cognition require further elucidation, including its capacity in the face of environmental fluctuation, it appears influenza can straddle past and present.[28]

The duck-human interface virologist Kennedy Shortridge proposed as the means by which influenzas have long seeded human outbreaks across southern China appears to have undergone a fundamental shift once intensively farmed livestock were added.[29] But virulent influenzas selected in such intensive livestock operations may be able to avoid burning out by switching to free-range ducks that have been feeding in local waterways and on waste grain for hundreds of years.

It would appear, then, that across such a landscape everything old for influenza is new again.

—*FARMING PATHOGENS*, 6 OCTOBER 2010

Virus Dumping

It was a lost colony, she said, a handful of sentients eager for
trade. She knew so much and I so little, but now I have buried
her and spat upon her grave and I know the truth of it. If slaves
they were, then bad slaves surely, for their masters set them
upon a hell, beneath the cruel light of the plague star.
—GEORGE R.R. MARTIN (1986)

DUMPING GRAIN ON ANOTHER COUNTRY is a classic maneuver in economic warfare.

When a country's borders are opened by force or by choice, by
structural adjustment or by neoliberal trade agreement, when tariffs
and other forms of protectionism are finally scotched, heavily subsidized multinational agribusiness can flood the new market with
commodities at prices less than their production costs.

That is, these companies are happy to sell their foodstuffs abroad at
a loss. That doesn't make sense, you say. Aren't these guys in business
for profit? They are indeed. The deficits are in actuality a cold-blooded
calculation.

The objective is to drive previously protected domestic sectors,
unable to compete with that kind of pricing, out of business. Once the
mom-and-pop competition is rubbed out, Walmart-style, the multinationals, their competition cleared off the field, can impose what
prices they please across a market they now dominate.[30]

Tuft University's Tim Wise recently reported that when the North
America Free Trade Agreement opened borders to commodity traffic, Farm Bill–backed U.S. agribusiness dumped eight goods on

Mexico: corn, soybeans, wheat, rice, cotton, beef, pork, and poultry.[31] Dumping margins—the gap between the cost of the item and its pricing—ranged from 12 percent to 38 percent, costing Mexican producers billions. Corn proved the harshest:

Average dumping margins of 19% contributed to a 413% increase in U.S. exports and a 66% decline in real producer prices in Mexico from the early 1990s to 2005. The estimated cost to Mexican producers of dumping-level corn prices was $6.6 billion over the nine-year period, an average of $99 per hectare per year, or $38 per ton.

As we explored in the first section with NAFTA flu, our name for swine flu H1N1 (2009), the first new pandemic strain in forty years, Mexico's meat industries, including the hog sector from which H1N1 may have emerged, were similarly marginalized by cheap imports.[32] As Wise describes it:

Meats were exported at below-cost prices because U.S. producers benefited from below-cost soybeans and corn, key components in feed. This so-called implicit subsidy to meat producers resulted in dumping margins of 5–10% on exported meat. This cost Mexican livestock producers who did not use imported feed an estimated $3.2 billion between 1997 and 2005. The largest losses were in beef, at $1.6 billion, or $175 million per year.[33]

Commodity dumping permits more than a competitive advantage. It provides a foothold on the landscape itself. Virginia-based Smithfield Foods, whose Granjas Carroll subsidiary remains a prime suspect for the emergence of H1N1 (2009), was one of several foreign companies able to buy out or contract Mexican farmers who were weakened by the barrage of imports. Those local farmers who escaped the onslaught did so only by consolidating neighbors' failing plots into midsize domestics still able to stand up to their foreign competition.

Such tactics are part and parcel of a strategy aimed at making legality more a matter of expediency than of principle, although that might be argued in its way a principle of sorts. One at best of dubious distinction. When what is illegal at home in the United States is perfectly legal elsewhere, move your operations offshore. In many countries of the Global South, few labor laws and environmental regulations are on the books. For those that are, enforcement is lax or bribed away. On the other hand, when what is legal in the United States is *banned* elsewhere, export U.S. rules. Subject other countries' domestic operations to the kind of discipline of the invisible hand one's own multinationals avoid like the plague. Impose a protectionism in reverse.

Roberto Saviano writes of the duality of the Neapolitan mafia, the Camorra, in similar terms:

> It might seem that the clans, once they've accumulated substantial capital, would stop their criminal activities, unravel their genetic code somehow, and convert to legality. Just like the Kennedy family, who had earned enormous amounts selling liquor during Prohibition and later broke all criminal ties. But the strength of Italian criminal business lies precisely in maintaining a double track, in never renouncing its origins. . . .
>
> Various inquiries by the Naples Anti-Mafia Public Attorney's Office revealed that when the . . . legal track was in crisis, the criminal one was immediately activated. If cash was short, they had counterfeit bills printed. They annihilated the competition through extortions and imported merchandise tax-free. . . . The legal economy means that clients get steady prices, bank credits are always honored, money continues to circulate, and products continue to be consumed . . . reduc[ing] the separation between the law and economic imperative, between what regulations prohibit and what making money demands.[34]

In other words, make whatever works work, whatever the law of the land. In such a framework even grand failures are but new opportunities:

In a kind of bioeconomic warfare, agribusiness can prosper when deadly influenza strains originating from their own operations spread out to their smaller competition. No conspiracy theory need apply. No virus engineered in a laboratory. No conscious acts of espionage or sabotage. Rather we have here an emergent neglect from the moral hazard that arises when the costs of intensive husbandry are externalized.

The financial tab for these outbreaks is routinely picked up by governments and taxpayers worldwide. So why should agribusiness bother with ending practices that repeatedly interrupt economies and will someday produce a virus that kills hundreds of millions of people? Companies are often compelled to invest in livestock vaccination and biosecurity—however incomplete—but if the full costs of outbreaks were placed on their balance sheets larger operations as we know them would cease to exist.

Corporate farms are also able to skirt the economic punishments of the outbreaks they cause by their horizontal integration. They can weather the resulting bad publicity and intermittent breaks in their commodity chains by increasing production in affiliates elsewhere.

Thailand's CP Group operates joint-venture poultry facilities across China, producing as of 2005 600 million of China's 2.2 billion chickens annually sold.[35] When an outbreak of bird flu occurred in a farm operated by the CP Group in Heilongjiang Province, Japan banned poultry from China. CP factories in Thailand filled the market gap by increasing exports to Japan. A supply chain arrayed across multiple countries can compensate for the interruptions in business, even as it also, ironically enough, increases the risk of influenza spread.

In contrast, many small farmers suffer catastrophically from this virus dumping, even when they're under contract to agricultural companies. Smallholders typically can't afford the biosecurity changes needed to protect themselves from such outbreaks in the first place or the wholesale repopulation of their livestock in the aftermath (even when subsidized in part by their government). Living market day to market day, they can't afford the losses incurred upon their already thin margins when their operations are disrupted by the government-imposed quarantines and culling campaigns that follow.

That's nasty. But the insult to injury is in agribusiness's faux-righteous follow-up. And here we see the kind of conscious manipulation at the heart of grain dumping. In an act of evil genius, multinationals support national efforts to institute new biosecurity standards only the largest companies can afford.

Mike Davis offers an example.[36] When H5N1 outbreaks began in Thailand in 2004, corporate chicken-processing plants accelerated production. According to trade unionists, processing increased at one factory from 90,000 to 130,000 poultry daily, even as it was obvious many of the chickens were sick. Once the Thai press reported on the illness, Thailand's Deputy Minister of Agriculture made vague allusions to an "avian cholera" and then–prime minister Thaksin Shinawatra publicly ate chicken in a show of confidence.

It later emerged that the CP Group and other large producers were colluding with government officials to pay off contract farmers to keep quiet about their infected flocks. In turn, livestock officials secretly provided corporate farmers vaccines. Independent farmers, on the other hand, were kept in the dark about the epidemic, and they and their flocks suffered for it.

Once the cover-up was exposed, the Thai government, with industry support, called for a modernization of the industry, including requiring all open-air flocks exposed to migratory birds be culled in favor of production in new biosecure buildings for which only the best-capitalized farmers could pay. Reward those who cause the problem. Punish those who suffer most.

Another example. In an effort to better track animal outbreaks, the USDA has proposed requiring all U.S. livestock be tagged with radio chips. A source of a new disease could then be tracked within a matter of days. A good idea, it seems, given the United States now knows nothing of the whereabouts and movements of its livestock. Except, as Shannon Hayes writes,

> the National Animal Identification System . . . would end up rewarding the factory farms whose practices encourage disease while crippling small farms and the local food movement. . . .

For factory farms, the costs of following the procedures for the system would be negligible. These operations already use computer technology, and under the system, swine and poultry that move through a production chain at the same time could be given a single number. On small, traditional farms like my family's, each animal would require its own number. That means the cost of tracking 1,000 animals moving together through a factory system would be roughly equal to the expense that a small farmer would incur for tracking one animal.[37]

The diseases that wipe out Big Food's smaller competitors also offer an opportunity to cripple them between outbreaks.

—*Farming Pathogens*, 11 November 2010

That's the Thicke

THE LOGISTICS OF A JUST, EQUITABLE, and healthy agricultural landscape here in the United States would remain a problem if Michael Pollan himself, Wendell Berry, or better yet Fred Magdoff were appointed Secretary of Agriculture.

Decades-long efforts pealing back agribusiness both as paradigm and infrastructure, however successful, would require a parallel program. With what would we replace the present landscape?

As a black hole about its horizon, a poverty in imagination orbits the question stateside. The vacuum is most recently felt in the developing animus between public health officials and artisan cheesemakers.[38] What Europe has long streamlined into amicable regulation, the United States has lurched into clumsy opposition: cheese wheels are increasingly treated as suitcase bombs filled with *Listeria*.

After sixty years of industrial production Americans have quite forgotten the logistics of real food.

There are three broad classes of alternatives floating about the small but growing food movement. Prelapsarian fantasies widely prevalent would have us return to the family farm as it never existed. On the other hand, the microgeographic localism now emerging appears as much a victim of diminished expectations, provisional classism, and the constraints imposed by a scarcity of working examples as of agribusiness's stranglehold on the market.[39]

If pursued to their logical, and logistical, conclusions, both options, as geographer David Harvey noted in a recent radio interview, would likely contribute to the kinds of famines that predated industrial development (as opposed to the very different famines that originate in today's global capitalism).[40]

There are, however, visionaries here and abroad who have blocked out broader possibilities tied to both the contours of our historical present and the globalized economy. This third class appears based on real-life experience and some intriguing, albeit often preliminary, experimentation:

1) In his campaign for Iowa Secretary of Agriculture, dairy farmer Francis Thicke (pronounced TICK-ee) described a regionalization encompassing trade policy, energy, farm structure, and environmental regulation:

> Thicke wants to help farmers develop the means to process their own food, which he feels empowers them against increasingly unstable markets. Radiance is one of the few small dairies with on-farm processing equipment, and as a result, Thicke has avoided big processors and distributors who set demand, and prices. When dairy farmers were having record losses last year because of low market prices—and dairy processors were making record profits—Radiance Dairy kept selling at their standard rate, and loyal customers kept buying. "We never changed our prices," Thicke said. "We were fully unaffected." With access to on-farm or local farm-to-farm mobile processing equipment, Thicke feels, "more of the profits can stay with the farmer instead of being taken by middleman corporate monopolies." . . .
>
> "We import 80 to 90 percent of the food we eat. If we can grow more of what we eat in Iowa, we could have fresher, healthier, safer food. We could have more diversity on the landscape. And it would be an economic development—food dollars would stay local and circulate back into the local economy."[41]

2) With the support of the Mexican government, Zapotec Indians have developed a certified-sustainable, community-controlled forestry.[42] Plain pine is sold to the state government and—shades of Thicke—finished goods, including furniture, are produced in

an on-site factory. The Oaxaca cooperative, still a work in progress, plows a third of its profits back into the business, a third into forest preservation, and the rest into its workers and the local community, including pensions, a credit union, and housing for its children studying at university.

3) Dialectical biologist Richard Levins, collaborating with Cuban colleagues on ecological approaches to local agriculture and public health, summarizes some of the many adjustments a new agriculture anywhere may require, an encapsulation I've quoted several times in this book as it bears repeated consideration:

> Instead of having to decide between large-scale industrial type production and a "small is beautiful" approach *a priori,* we saw the scale of agriculture as dependent on natural and social conditions, with the units of planning embracing many units of production. Different scales of farming would be adjusted to the watershed, climatic zones and topography, population density, distribution of available resources, and the mobility of pests and their enemies.
>
> The random patchwork of peasant agriculture, constrained by land tenure, and the harsh destructive landscapes of industrial farming would both be replaced by a planned mosaic of land uses in which each patch contributes its own products but also assists the production of other patches: forests give lumber, fuel, fruit, nuts, and honey but also regulate the flow of water, modulate the climate to a distance about 10 times the height of the trees, create a special microclimate downwind from the edge, offer shade for livestock and the workers, and provide a home to the natural enemies of pests and the pollinators of crops. There would no longer be specialized farms producing only one thing. Mixed enterprises would allow for recycling, a more diverse diet for the farmers, and a hedge against climatic surprises. It would have a more uniform demand for labor throughout the year.[43]

Rather than to the expectations of an abstract neoclassical or all-too-real neoliberal model of production, the scale and practice of agriculture can be flexibly tailored to each region's physical, social, and epidemiological landscapes on the ground, interconnecting ecology and economy. Under such an arrangement not all parcels will be necessarily profitable. As Levins points out, whatever reductions in income farms accrue in protecting the rest of the region must be offset by regular redistributive mechanisms.

Levins's radical practicality is part and parcel of a number of experiments under way, some now ongoing for decades.

Jules Pretty offers a list of practices that are even now already inputs and outputs of more sustainable agroecosystems, including of "sustainable intensification," in some cases producing as much food per acre as clear-cut, chemical agribusiness:

1. *Integrated pest management,* which uses prevention through developing ecosystem resilience and diversity for pest, disease, and weed control, and only uses pesticides when other options are ineffective.
2. *Integrated nutrient management,* which seeks both to balance the need to fix nitrogen within farm systems with the need to import inorganic and organic sources of nutrients and to reduce nutrient losses through control of runoff and erosion.
3. *Conservation tillage,* which reduces the amount of tillage, sometimes to zero, so that soil can be conserved through reduced erosion, and available moisture is used more efficiently.
4. *Cover crops,* which grow in the off-season or along with main crops, help protect soil from erosion, manage nutrients and pests, maintain healthy soil, enhance water infiltration and storage in soil.
5. *Agroforestry,* which incorporates multifunctional trees into agricultural systems and collectively manages nearby forest resources.
6. *Aquaculture,* which incorporates fish, shrimp, and other aquatic resources into farm systems, such as irrigated rice fields and fish ponds, and so leads to increases in protein production.
7. *Water harvesting in dryland areas,* which can mean that formerly abandoned and degraded lands can be cultivated and additional

crops can be grown on small patches of irrigated land, owing to better rainfall retention.

8. *Livestock reintegration into farming systems*, such as the raising of dairy cattle, pigs, and poultry, including using both grazing and zero-grazing cut-and-carry systems. Mixed crop-livestock systems provide many synergies that enhance production and allow for better nutrient cycling on farms.[44]

An ecological agriculture, responsive to people's needs rather than offshore margins, should, Pretty proposes, be able to feed the world's growing population.

A number of books published in the last year speak not only to this growing sophistication but to a new *confidence* in the food movement.[45] There is a dawning realization that Big Ag, whatever its power and infrastructure, is, to use an ironic Texasism, all hat and no cattle.

Propping up the empire is little else but a raw greed and political power turning biology—human and animal—into cash at any and all costs. The paradigm behind the *food* and *farming*—ostensibly the industry's *raison d'être*—is bankrupt to its core.[46]

When the use value of *food*, of all things, is traded in for surplus value, humanity's survival is nothing less than threatened (and the integral pleasures of eating abandoned). When most commercial-grade poultry feed is purposely laced with arsenic to keep bird flesh pink over shipment and sale, there is a seriously sociopathic denialism at work.[47]

When U.S. livestock are stuffed with up to 28 million pounds of antibiotics annually solely to accelerate growth to a finishing weight, providing stock enough protection only until their industrial diet kills them, perversity verges on perversion.[48] When livestock monopolies manipulate already cheap and highly subsidized prices by forcing farmers to sell their animals all at the same time, a criminality masquerades as the law of the land.[49]

And yet even in the face of such unprecedented power and a relentless propaganda a swelling number of Americans are coming around. Siena Chrisman's recent dispatch from a DOJ-USDA joint national listening tour on corporate consolidation in food and agriculture markets offers a sense of the breadth of antipathy.[50] It cuts across occupations, region, race, religion, politics, and agricultural sector:

> In Iowa, the crowd chanting "bust up big ag!" was full of white farmers in their 50s wearing feed caps and faded jeans. In Colorado, it was ranchers in cowboy hats, pressed checked shirts, and big belt buckles who were on their feet calling for change. Around the country this year, it has been almost quarter of a million citizens who have signed petitions calling on DOJ and USDA to take swift action in this investigation. Similarly, in Brooklyn, New York, last month, it was a diverse crowd of hundreds of mostly African-American urban and rural farmers strategizing and organizing at the first Black Farmers and Urban Gardeners Conference—just as in cities and small towns around the country, communities of all colors, ages, and experiences are joining together to create a more just and fair food system.

Agribusiness, bringing Americans together.

It would appear, to put it wildly mildly, we live in interesting times, with all the idiom's conflicting connotations, an era characterized by agribusiness's dominance and, as Chrisman describes, a sharpening resistance to its excesses. We find ourselves at a true historic juncture cut in two directions. Along one path, fear and exploitation. On the other, the wonders of the possible, with the chance to literally make a new landscape.

Francis Thicke lost his race, he did. But in a state beholden to agribusiness across multiple sectors he managed 37 percent of the vote, a marker of a deepening, and increasingly acted upon, dissatisfaction.

Expect much more along these lines, including, and here is where it will get really interesting, seismic shifts in the food paradigm, found not only in plans on paper, but out there, on and in and across large swaths of American soil.

—*Farming Pathogens*, 16 December 2010

PART THREE

I can conceive of no nightmare as terrifying as establishing such communication with a so-called superior, or, if you wish, advanced technology in outer space.

—GEORGE WALD (1972)

What is amazing—and also terrifying about tigers—is their facility for what can only be described as abstract thinking. Very quickly, a tiger can assimilate new information—evidence, if you will—ascribe it to a source, and even a motive, and react accordingly....

"I've tried tiger.... It's quite unusual—slightly sweet, but I don't care for it anymore—not since I saw a tiger eat a rotten cow in 2000. He ate the meat with worms and everything."

—JOHN VAILLANT (2010)

Alien vs. Predator

Dallas: (looks at a pen being dissolved by alien's body fluid)
I haven't seen anything like that except, uh, molecular acid.

Brett: It must be using it for blood.

Parker: It's got a wonderful defense mechanism. You don't dare
kill it.

—DAN O'BANNON, *ALIEN* (1979)

NASA ANNOUNCED EARLIER THIS MONTH one of its research teams discovered an "alien" bacterium at the bottom of California's Mono Lake.[1] Call off the men in black, it's strictly still a matter for the nerds in white.

The bacterium isn't really from another planet, even as we all are a kind of astronaut wherever and whenever we find ourselves spinning through space and time. Rather, this earthly bug showed that under the kinds of stringent conditions found on other planets it could assimilate arsenic into its very cellular fabric in place of what was until now thought mission-critical phosphorous.

Arsenic and phosphorous share a similar electric charge and atomic radius. Arsenate—arsenic bound with four oxygen molecules—is for the most part poisonous to most Earthling species because it mimics phosphorate, the biologically useful form of phosphorous.

The team, led by Felisa Wolfe-Simon, inoculated *in vitro* colonies of the *Halomonadaceae* family of Gammaproteobacteria with a series of highly alkaline sediments from Mono Lake differentiated only in their ratios of arsenate-to-phosphorate. In effect, Wolfe-Simon and her colleagues increasingly starved sequential generations of the bacterium of phosphorous, in the meantime offering arsenic hors d'oeuvres in phosphorate's stead.

The team found that the free-floating arsenate it radio-labeled became associated with the proteins, metabolites, lipids, and nucleic acids of the GFAJ-1 strain of the bacterium, consistent with the arsenate's incorporation into the newly evolved strain's proteins and DNA.

Despite its publication in *Science*, one of the world's most respected peer-reviewed journals, the work has been subjected to scurrilous attack.[2] Critics, burned by NASA's 1996 announcement of bacterial tracings in a Martian meteorite, objected to, among other things:[3]

- The failure of the Wolfe-Simon group to wash GFAJ-1's DNA of contaminants and loose arsenic before testing for the latter's biological presence—basic microbiology 101.
- The small concentrations of arsenic found, consistent with contamination rather than incorporation.
- The failure to rule out the possibility the alleged arsenate-based bacteria survived the high arsenate-low phosphorate environment by scavenging phosphorate off dead comrades.
- The premise that arsenic bonds in a DNA backbone would be stable enough.
- The premise that a transition phenotype with both arsenate and phosphorate could survive, as multiple enzymes must interact with DNA with great precision, or that it would emerge in such short order.

Some of the criticisms appear on their face pointed, others seem founded on the self-referential presumption that surely evolution can't do that because our models tell us otherwise.

Whatever its ultimate fate, NASA's announcement has as much to do with life on Earth as with extraterrestrial biological entities. If not phosphorus-starved bacteria switching to an arsenic-based life form, then those thriving in the deepest layer of the oceanic crust in the face of caustic heat and crushing pressure, eating methane and benzene, show the extent to which our planet's microbes can adapt.[4]

For agriculture that should mean kaput for a propagandistic reification. Contrary to the term's connotations of Level 4 protection, there is no such thing as total "biosecurity," blocking any and all pathogens from inside a confined animal feedlot or other intensive operation. If bacteria can survive in the face of arsenic or benzene, what can livestock operations possibly do in their own defense?

Even ignoring the routine violations in biosecurity and biocontainment built into the industrial livestock model,[5] we must now assimilate the impediment that eliminating the conditions under which many a microbe, influenza included, thrives only establishes niches for new and at times strange strains. If fastidiously sterile First World hospitals are routinely assaulted by drug-resistant pathogens, then feedlots turfed in shit, run by predatory agribusinesses minimizing margins in offshore hovels, stand no chance.[6]

Indeed, the problem of livestock pathogens was already locked in to a Nietzschean syllogism from the get-go. What kills many pathogens makes those left over stronger. The few with the weirdo mutation that lets the virus or bacterium survive a new threat now emerge to thrive. Even the very notion of causality appears threatened, with cause and effect effectively reversed.[7] How do we protect ourselves against influenzas and other pathogens that have evolved a counter-response several times over only the past week to any prophylaxis we could ever imagine?

Influenza's phenotypic variation, generated at mind-boggling mutation rates (2.0×10^{-6} mutations per site per infectious cycle), embodies the choices with which the virus—if you'll excuse the anthropomorphism—can naturally select a solution to the problems it faces, including those it has yet to even encounter.[8] Along with producing new viral functions, including molecular exaptations, the mutations permit escape from learned immune T- and B-cell responses fixated on previous epitopes.

By reassortment, that variation is multiplied at the broader genome level: influenza can trade whole genomic segments like card players on a Friday night. Both H5N1 and last year's H1N1 emerged as multiple reassortants from across many serotypes.

There are other tricks in influenza's bag:[9]

- Transformations beyond point and double-point mutations, including partial, complete, and flanking deletions, can induce changes in viral protein conformation.

- A polybasic site in the glycoprotein hemagglutinin expands the range of host proteases able to cleave the hemagglutinin precursor, increasing the range of host tissue that supports infection and diversifying modes of transmission. Poultry infected with the worst H5N1, their insides liquefying, suffered both bloody coughs and diarrhea.

- Amino acid replacement E627K in polymerase protein PB2 increases the efficiency of viral replication in mammalian cases, as does the SR polymorphism in poultry. Other polymerase markers for mammalian adaptation include PB1 P13 and PA R615.

- Several influenza proteins block or down-regulate the immune response. The alternate reading frame PB1-F2 protein, found in several pandemic strains, induces apoptosis in macrophages. H5N1 NS1 protein with glutamic acid at position 92 acts as an antagonist to host interferon. NS1 with carboxyl terminus motif EPEV can also disrupt human regulatory pathways.

- H5N1 proved viable across hosts of a diversity of animal orders traditionally thought to be one another's epizootic barriers.

- Several years ago virologist Robert Webster reported H5N1 samples were becoming increasingly viable at warm temperatures, at which they are expected to degrade. If the result still holds, the implications are fundamental to the virus's persistence in equatorial estuaries and perhaps even sewage systems.

The outlandishness may transcend individual virions, infections, and strains. By virtue of infecting multiple-million hosts, in which a multitude of molecular and epizootic problems are simultaneously addressed, the virus engages in an emergent unconscious cognition the discoveries from which are traded among strains by reassortment. We find ourselves confronted with a distributed intelligence arrayed across whole continents. The truly unworldly here on Earth.

And yet this is no counsel of despair, no lost regret to be discovered by the outraged survivors of an oncoming apocalypse. We should be able to better corral pathogens once we reimagine disease control—and agriculture more generally—across levels of biocultural organization.

An integrated pathogen management might depress capitalist surplus value over the short term—frankly no bad thing—but it should multiply the dimensions of the problems our world's little green men must solve in the course of stalking poultry, pigs, and people alike. And what could be more important, even for monomaniacal economists concerned with little else than macroeconomic indicators? Along with much of humanity, a bad pandemic would destroy global economies.

At the cost of next quarter's shortsighted returns, a fully applied IPM would put us in a better position to save a billion people from a deadly pandemic. In contrast, the present agricultural model is *farming* tomorrow's deadliest pathogens alongside its meat monocultures.

That is, despite their apparent antagonism, today's influenzas increasingly feed on agribusiness to little punishment. Indeed, Big Ag has gone so far as to use the new diseases to its own advantage, rubbing out smaller competitors that can't afford biosecurity upgrades.[10]

The new spate of virulent strains and of those of a variety of other pathogens, to reference Ridley Scott's cult flick, are bursting out of the Livestock Revolution's belly, bloody-mawed and shrieking. And in perhaps their greatest trick, in the most sadistic of ironies, they are being allowed free range.

To control the alien we must kill the predator.

—*Farming Pathogens*, 31 December 2010

UPDATE. In 2011, A Binghamton University team discovered bacteria and algae still living inside 150,000-year-old salt halite from California's Saline Valley.[11]

Four years later Lee Kerkhof's group showed a betaproteobacterium at a contaminated ore mill in Colorado reducing uranium into a terminal electron acceptor for respiration.[12] A bacterium "breathing" uranium! The species "picked up a genetic element that's now allowing it to detoxify uranium, to actually grow on uranium," said Kerkhof.[13]

The Scientific American

Science is the business right now. If the science works, the business works, and vice versa.

— CRAIG VENTER (2010)

BIRD FLU MARINATES A CHICKEN in its own juices, a satay best avoided whatever the menu special. In short order, rapid service better for the bistro than the barn, infected birds bleed from the inside out. What to do about this bit of bad news?

Broilers and layers are as much commodities as they are birds. As much engineering problems as living organisms. So ask research-and-development for a solution comes the answer.

It was, after all, by virtue of its open morphogenesis and behavioral flexibility that the chicken was first domesticated multiple times from red and grey junglefowl distributed across South and Southeast Asia, artificially selected for the backyard, then scaled up in size and population to its factory model.[14]

Bred for what the market and the industrial *filière* demand—big breasts in six weeks tops—many a Single Comb White Leghorn now stumbles about on its spindly, underdeveloped legs. Too much weight grown too fast atop too little leg. It's often hard to differentiate agribusiness birds on a regular day from those struck by a bird flu–induced ataxia.

It's been a long, strange trip from those early days in the jungle village.

In this framework, influenza becomes merely an industrial glitch to be Taylorized out, rather than an intrinsic flaw stitched into the very fabric of the business model. We can just filter out the virus with a level of biosecurity, at a frequency of vaccination, that can't possibly be implemented given the financial margins on which just-in-time intensive operations teeter. Or else—smacking our foreheads—we can just breed-in resistance. At the cost of temporarily adding to the roundaboutness of production, scotch the problem from the start. Laurence Tiley's group, funded by Tyson Foods' Cobb-Vantress, the chicken-breeding conglomerate, recently made an important step in that direction.[15] The team didn't genetically engineer flu resistance out-and-out, but was able to turn chickens into transmission dead ends. Transgenic birds could be infected, but in producing short-hairpin RNA decoys that hooked influenza polymerase they could keep the virus from replicating enough to spread to the next susceptible.

Beyond the issue of the affordability of the new frankenchicken, especially for the poorest countries, influenza's success arises in part from its capacity to outwit and outlast such silver bullets.[16] Hypotheses tied to a lucrative model of biology are routinely mistaken for expectations about material reality, expectations are mistaken for projections, and projections for predictions.

One source of vexation is the dimensionality of the problem. Even among mainstream scholars there is a dawning realization that influenza is more than mere virion or infection; that it respects little of disciplinary boundaries (and business plans) in both their form and content. Pathogens regularly use processes accumulating at one level of biocultural organization to solve problems they face at other levels, including the molecular.

IN THE JANUARY *SCIENTIFIC AMERICAN,* Helen Branswell, a Canadian, one of the world's best influenza reporters, offers an instance of such clarity.[17] She addresses the role pig husbandry plays in the emergence of pandemic influenza. Much as with their poultry counterparts, how hog are organized into economic units influences the evolution of the pathogens with which they are infected.

Though Branswell's is a good review, well-aimed at a time when the problem of livestock influenza has dropped off the media radar, the article is a startling example of the conversion syndrome reporters and scholars suffer when reconciling two masters, in this case epidemiology and commerce. Even the basic facts of the former can be colored by one's willingness (or reluctance) to address the latter on terms outside those imposed by industry.

To start, Branswell gives us a nice round-up of pig influenza's evolutionary history. Modern strains originated as a spillover of humanity's 1918 H1N1 monster, steadily accumulating their own host-specific mutations over the decades that followed. Their evolution suddenly lurched forward in the 1990s when "for unknown reasons, influenza viruses in pigs began to evolve at a dizzying rate in North America, where enormous numbers of pigs are raised."

The reasons *are* known, however, if not yet in all their detail. The emergence of multiple reassortants, new mixes and matches of genomic segments across influenza strains, went hoof-in-hoof with the reorganization of the hog industry.

Three years before the emergence of the new H1N1 in 2009, Gregory Gray's group conducted controlled, cross-sectional tests for swine influenza among pig wranglers, veterinarians, and meat processors, finding seroprevalence greatest among the wranglers, but widespread through the commodity chain.[18]

The team, quoted here extensively, placed their results in this context:

> During the past 60 years, the US swine industry has changed in composition from primarily small herds on family farms to include immense herds in large, corporate facilities. The US pork industry now generates $11 billion annually and employs an estimated 575,000 persons (2002 figures). Although pork production facilities today are larger, fewer, and more efficient and require fewer workers, it is estimated that, nationwide, at least 100,000 workers work in swine barns with live pigs.
>
> Iowa is the leading swine-producing state in the United States, with 9,300 farms (2004 figure), raising 25 million hogs per year (a rate of 8.6 swine per human resident). Today's large herds are maintained through the frequent introduction of young swine into swine-producing facilities. This constant influx of potentially pathogen-susceptible animals makes swine pathogen eradication

difficult to achieve. Therefore, swine influenza infections, which were formerly seasonal (like human influenza infections), now have become enzootic, and swine influenza transmission occurs year-round in much of the U.S. swine industry. Although these influenza virus infections among pigs are generally thought to be mild, they provide a constant opportunity for zoonotic influenza virus infections among humans who are occupationally exposed. Continual swine influenza transmission in U.S. swine herds also provides the opportunity for human influenza viruses to mix with swine or avian influenza viruses and generate novel progeny viruses.

The potential for animal-to-animal transmission (reflected in the basic reproductive number, R_0) among pigs in a swine confinement operation will be much greater than on a traditional farm because of the pigs' crowding (resulting in prolonged and more frequent contact). In addition, virus-laden secretions from pigs may be more concentrated, and reductions in ventilation and sunshine exposure may prolong viral viability. Thus, a confinement operation worker's probability of acquiring influenza virus infection may be increased, compared with that of a traditional swine worker, and certainly increased when compared with the risk among non-swine workers exposed only to human-to-human influenza activity. This risk is even greater if the virus does not kill pig hosts and if new susceptible animals are frequently introduced to the farm, sustaining transmission.

Swine workers may initiate epidemics by enhancing the mixing of viral strains that may lead to reassortment and novel progeny influenza viruses of pandemic potential. They may serve as a conduit for a novel virus to move from swine to man or from man to swine. One might envision that, once a novel virus is introduced into a densely populated swine barn, the viral loads swine workers would experience could overwhelm any partial immunity they might possess. After work, they may readily communicate that virus to their family members and neighbors.

As we've described in other posts, the Livestock Revolution, infiltrating the hog industry with any force only in the 1990s, was with the North American Free Trade Agreement exported into Mexico, where H1N1 (2009) first emerged, and with cheaper transportation and more liberal trade policy across the world.[19] In short, again, we do know something about the swine industry and influenza. But you can smell the fear in Branswell's article, which takes great pains to tread across a false middle ground. On the one hand, Branswell offers some excellent detail as to the craven powerlessness the CDC, USDA, and U.S. universities display in the course of failing to regulate the hog industry:

Farmers have historically had their pigs tested for flu, often at the diagnostic laboratories of the National Animal Health Laboratory Network (NAHLN). And companies that make flu vaccine for hogs need to know what flu threats the animals face so that they can tailor their vaccines accordingly. But the information that is gathered by the animal health sector is rarely shared with the researchers and officials who safeguard human health. In fact, in the wake of the 2009 outbreak, testing for flu on pig farms screeched to a halt.

The disconnect, the failure of the industry's privatized self-regulation, is a corrupt one, although Branswell refuses to put it in such explicit terms:

The priorities of these labs and companies are shaped by what is best for pigs and their owners. The NAHLN labs—often housed in universities, such as the University of Minnesota and the Iowa State University—work for the farmers, their clients. Any findings, positive or not, are kept confidential, explains Montse Torremorell, who holds a chair in swine health and productivity at the University of Minnesota. "There is a lot of actual [genetic] sequencing surveillance, if you will, but the information is fed back to the people who have submitted the samples."

And not fed back to the virologists, epidemiologists, and phylogeographers with the scientific expertise needed to best protect livestock and humans alike. The broad sweep of animal and human health, manifest at the system level, is confined to the myopic dictates of local commercial transactions.

The reporting system, now broken completely, bears replacement. But what CDC and the USDA are implementing in its stead is if not stillborn then irrevocably damaged:

> [The] program . . . cannot work without the cooperation of pork producers, who have to date been reluctant to support what many see as a bid by government to meddle in their affairs. "The pigs are owned by the farmer. And what happens to their pigs is the farmer's business, not the government's business, as long as the infection that is going on in those pigs is not what's termed a program disease that is considered to be a risk to the national herd," says Paul Sundberg, vice president for science and technology for the National Pork Board.

We're back to the premises that produced the failures of the previous system.

To solicit cooperation from the industry, the CDC and USDA have built-in anonymity. Any viruses found, including data describing on which farm or even in which county an outbreak has occurred, will be made available to a larger network of scientists only with the affected producer's permission. Researchers will be allowed only the state in which the virus is found, an insulting triviality.

In other words, a federal government of a major industrial country won't allow itself the information needed to determine where an outbreak of pandemic influenza emerges within its own borders. Even if a person is subsequently infected by pigs the government would still require approval from the owner before the source pigs could be tested.

The hog industry favors the new system, obviously, particularly as the threat is, in its characterization, overblown at the expense of its farmers. According to Branswell, the National Pork Board's Sundberg argues:

Millions of pigs come in contact with people every day, yet human cases of infection from pigs are rare. Farmers saw what happened to Arnold Van Ginkel, the Canadian producer whose herd was the first in the world to test positive for pandemic H1N1. Van Ginkel's pigs recovered, but he had to put down the animals because no one would buy them.

We have here back-to-back syllogistic fallacies. First, as if the emergence of a pandemic influenza out of American industrial swine didn't happen *just two years ago*, a highly unlikely event with nearly infinite opportunities will inevitably occur again.

Second, the economics that brought about a pandemic virus, the next time perhaps with a deadlier phenotype, cannot be excused with an appeal to economics. The industry has survived only by long externalizing the costs of disease, pollution, and labor violations.[20] Governments and consumers the world over have had to pick up the check. It's high time those costs showed up instead on the industry's balance sheets or at the very least in addition.

If Van Ginkel and his fellow contract farmers have anyone to blame, it's the industry that produced the virus in the first place. So go sue them. Or they should help push the government into protecting their hogs first thing, including instituting a real reporting system.

That is to say, it's *not* the Kafkaesque bureaucratic conundrum Branswell sketches. Perhaps more obvious in the podcast that accompanies the article, she appears to trap herself into confusing the premises underlying the very real reality of the system—how the damn thing works—for their soundness.[21]

The state universities are land grant institutions and recipients of millions in federal funds, as is the Farm Bill–dependent agriculture sector.[22] With the rule of law and political legitimacy behind it, the U.S. government could force the players into a federally run and industry-subsidized surveillance system that, in the end, would restore confidence in an industry that presently responds to criticism by circumventing it.

It's not a matter of logistics, but power, plain and simple. So let's stop talking about it as if it's really about something else.

THIS IS NO *AD HOMINEM* ATTACK. We make no effort here to rob Branswell or anyone else with good intentions of their diligence or expertise, from which we can learn much.

But capitalism so sets the bounds within which a free and critical inquiry is allowed, including or especially for work on threats to humanity's very existence, that scholars and reporters, brilliant as they may be, are trapped into limited and limiting tranches of thought. The philosopher István Mészáros sketches out the trap's dimensions:

> According to all available evidence the insurmountable problem is that the major intellectual representatives of capital's epoch which we are concerned with, no matter how great they might be as thinkers, take for granted the fundamental practical premises of the given social order in their combined totality, as a set of deeply interconnected determinations.[23]

Labor's divorce from the means of production, assigning any and all collective decisions to capital's portfolio, folding the fundamental mediation between humans and nature squarely inside capitalism's idiosyncratic dynamics, and the power accorded the capitalist state together embody the precepts upon which intellectual work is produced or—when push comes to shove—permitted.

For Mészáros, by virtue of dependence on capital much intellectual activity becomes a kung fu aimed at passing off an era-particular social organization as a naturalized abstraction of universal validity. Capital's premises are what the world has always known (and has been and will be). It is based on nature's core mechanics. It is an eternalized truth, which by virtue of its self-evident certainty must now disappear from our view. That is, its presumptions need no examination (and so no critique). In other words, we must blind ourselves and pull out our own teeth to allow the world to be as it has always been and will always remain.

That's a bad place to start for efforts, however well intended, aimed at characterizing influenza's economic roots.

Could such a context get any worse? It could. When we can no longer suppress the extent to which we deceive ourselves in this way, we can rationalize our weakness by celebrating such untruths as best for the common good. Slavoj Žižek, writing in the context of the war on WikiLeaks, asks us to

> consider . . . the renewed popularity of Leo Strauss: the aspect of his political thought that is so relevant today is his elitist notion of democracy, the idea of the "necessary lie." Elites should rule, aware of the actual state of things (the materialist logic of power), and feed the people fables to keep them happy in their blessed ignorance. For Strauss, Socrates was guilty as charged: philosophy is a threat to society. Questioning the gods and the ethos of the city undermines the citizens' loyalty, and thus the basis of normal social life. Yet philosophy is also the highest, the worthiest, of human endeavours. The solution proposed was that philosophers keep their teachings secret, as in fact they did, passing them on by writing "between the lines." The true, hidden message contained in the "great tradition" of philosophy from Plato to Hobbes and Locke is that there are no gods, that morality is merely prejudice, and that society is not grounded in nature.[24]

Setting aside what Žižek describes as liberal democracy's compulsive disgust for its own pronouncements, the self-deception becomes a mite more difficult a path when the fables told become confused for the actual state of things.

Who can keep score when the best way to tell a lie is found in believing it? It's a conundrum that extends to the scientist, directly employed under or on the hook to corporations or a government beholden to said corporations for funding and access.

With research increasingly proletarianized, its objectives confounded with capital's, whatever his or her country of origin the "Scientific American" becomes as subjected to an artificial selection as any chicken he or she studies. A top-heavy bird with its beak snipped off. A protoplasmic commodity in tweed or white coat, clucking at request for proposals for a little seed money.

—*Farming Pathogens*, 18 January 2011

The Axis of Viral

THE ENEMY OF MY ENEMY is my friend. We might accept that viruses and bacteria at best instantiate the coincidental nature of such an alliance. The success of one bug might pave the way for another. But we'd be hard-pressed to imagine that pathogens would whittle the syllogism to a sharper point and actively pursue our sorry asses in tandem or even in triplicate.

Kaposi's sarcoma-associated herpesvirus (KSHV or human herpesvirus 8) and the human immunodeficiency virus (HIV) appear to engage in just such a collaboration.

Kaposi's sarcoma (KS) and AIDS, the diseases the two cause, have long been associated in the scientific literature. Indeed, KS lesions were important markers identifying AIDS as a novel syndrome in the first place.[25] KS proved one of a multitude of "opportunistic infections" that arise only when the immune response collapses, as it does during an HIV infection.

KS dynamics, however, may be more than opportunistic. A preponderance of circumstantial evidence tying KSHV and HIV together and several newly discovered mechanisms by which the two pathogens partake in *reciprocal activation* suggest the pathogens have a more functionally integrated relationship. That is, KSHV and HIV appear marked by a mutualism that on further analysis may explain several little understood aspects of the two viruses' origins and pathogenesis.

The ecological and epidemiological circumstances KSHV and HIV share appear on their face coincidental. KSHV and HIV-1 share common xenospecific origins—chimpanzees.[26] Both appear to have evolutionarily radiated out of the same general geographic region in

Sub-Saharan Africa. Both are chronic infections of immune cells. HIV is capable of infecting B cells KSHV typically infects.[27] Conversely, KSHV is capable of infecting the dendritic cells and macrophages HIV infects.[28] KSHV and HIV appear to share overlapping modes of infection, including sexual transmission.

Indeed, coinfection may cause a convergence of modes of infection. Anne-Geneviève Marcelin and colleagues show KSHV load increases in circulating blood cells when a patient is infected with HIV and expresses active KS, suggesting coinfection broadens KSHV's cell range.[29] Hmmm. In that vein, Henke-Gendo and Schultz reviewed accumulating evidence for a KSHV infection spread by reused needles.[30]

But it's in the molecular work where the relationship starts to get downright conspiratorial.

Li-Min Huang and colleagues review evidence that KSHV and HIV regulate each other's expression beyond the diffuse effects of immune suppression.[31] HIV-1–induced cytokines can induce lysis, the virus-producing stage of KSHV's life cycle. HIV-1's Tat protein can activate epithelial growth factor KDR in endothelial cells KSHV infects, helping bring on KS tumor growth.

Huang et al. offer additional evidence that KSHV and HIV undergo reciprocal transcriptional activation. KSHV's ORF45 KIE2 protein can activate HIV's regulatory Long Terminal Repeat (LTR). In turn, HIV's Vpr and Tat proteins appear to activate KSHV intracellular expression, including of the major capsid protein.

Sun and colleagues meanwhile show that KSHV K13 protein vFLIP, involved in blocking programmed cell death in KS lesions, also regulates HIV expression by way of nuclear transcription NF-kB.[32] K13 and HIV-1 Tat synergistically activate HIV LTR. Guo and co-workers showed KSHV chemokine receptor vGPCR (ORF74) also synergistically activates NF-kB and NF-AT with HIV-1 Tat, generating KS tumors.[33]

There appear other pathways for KSHV-HIV crosstalk. Several researchers have reported that KSHV-encoded cytokine interleukin-6 (vIL-6), along with inducing vascular endothelial growth factor, increases HIV replication.[34] In turn, HIV-infected cells produce elevated huIL-6, contributing to KSHV activation.

Fc gamma receptors for immunoglobulin receptor IgG on the surfaces of effector immune cells mediate phagocytosis, antibody-dependent cell-mediated cytotoxicity, and activation of cytokine pathways. Lehrnbecher et al. showed polymorphic forms of Fc gamma R to be associated with differing KS outcomes in HIV-infected individuals.[35] The FcgRIIIA receptor effects antibody-dependent cell-mediated cytotoxicity and the lysis of infected cells. Lehrnbecher and colleagues suggest the FF genotype is protective because it reduces the kinds of inflammatory responses that induce KS pathogenesis.

We might be able to relate these activation mechanisms back to our seemingly coincidental transmission dynamics.

Gandhi and colleagues showed CD4 cell count in KSHV-HIV co-infected individuals to be the strongest predictor for KSHV salivary shedding.[36] Greater CD4 cell counts were associated with greater shedding. The results suggest KSHV loads should be higher early in the HIV-1 infection, during primary infection when CD4 cells counts are still relatively high.

In other words, the results imply KSHV piggybacks on HIV's acute and epidemiologically-predominant first stage, within the first two months of infection. That stage, when few patients know they are infected, largely drives HIV's epidemiological spread.

Elsewhere I have described HIV infection as a dual life history.[37] In an outbreak's epidemic phase, when many new susceptible hosts are available, HIV acts much like a precocious semelparous organism, using an initial burst of viral reproduction in each infection to rapidly infect the large pool of available susceptibles. In an endemic phase, when available susceptibles are comparatively rare, HIV uses its iteroparous nature, depending on multiple exposures over a long asymptomatic stage to wait out a new cohort of potential hosts.

It stands to reason that in a mutualism with HIV, KSHV's life history may shift in turn, in such a way as to co-express an acute phase, with epidemiological dividends.

In perhaps a related phenomenon, HIV may better "prep" KSHV for transmission by hobbling the immune response. Jacobson and co-workers showed males infected with KSHV after HIV infection were more likely to develop KS.[38] Even if KS lesions themselves prove little involved in generating subsequent KSHV infection, although Krishnan and colleagues suggest that very possibility, a full exploration of its life cycle—from latent through lytic infection—may better permit KSHV infections greater pathogenic and epidemiological flexibility.[39]

Such mutual amplification may explain in part the geographic distribution of Africa's HIV strains. Cohen describes several hypotheses for subtype C's recent geographic expansion:[40]

- Subtype C quasispecies rarely make the switch from coreceptors CCR5 and CXCR4. Those patients infected with subtype C virus will likely have more copies of the CCR5 virus that are typically involved in establishing subsequent infections.

- Individuals infected with multiple venereal pathogens produce more proinflammatory cytokine tumor necrosis factor (TNF)α, boosting HIV replication, particularly for subtype C.

- A third possibility that Cohen misses involves the socioeconomic conditions of many of the countries where subtype C is prevalent.[41] Central Africa has been devastated by war and structural adjustment programs and undergone resulting changes in behavior regimens, including behaviors that spread HIV. Such top-down increases in the number of susceptibles may select for more infectious variants that can burn through the supply of hosts at little cost to their epidemiological persistence.

- The KSHV-HIV mutualism offers a fourth, mutually inclusive, possibility. The HIV-1 LTR activation by KSHV protein K13 described above appears to be subtype-specific and dependent on the number of NF-κB sites. So KSHV prevalence—in some African populations as high as 87 percent—may help select for HIV subtypes. HIV subtype C, with three NF-κB sites, may use KSHV as an epidemiological amplifier in Central and East Africa.

A follow-up phylogeographic study, tracking how genes change over geographic space, could test whether the natural distributions of KSHV K13 and HIV LTR, including the clinical outcomes of both infections, are co-determined.

Such microscopic mutualisms may be more common than first thought. Indeed, HIV and the tuberculosis bacterium have long been shown to amplify each other's transmission. Steve Lawn reviews other relationships HIV shares in Africa, including with malaria, schistosomiasis, and a number of STDs.[42] Lawn catalogs some specifics. "Cytokine-mediated activation of the HIV-1 LTR," for one,

is the main mechanism by which bacterial coinfections enhance proviral transcription. However, certain DNA virus coinfections such as human T lymphotropic virus type 1 (HTLV-1), herpes simplex virus type 2 (HSV-2) and cytomegalovirus (CMV) may also more directly enhance proviral transcription by encoding proteins that themselves transactivate the HIV-1 LTR via other specific receptors. By this mechanism, these chronic viral infections may exert a more direct and prolonged co-factor effect on HIV-1 replication.

The scope of possible combinations across circulating pathogens boggles the mind.

When a good friend of mine was a child he thought people who spoke other languages hadn't as rich of an emotional life as those who spoke his native tongue. It isn't just a kid's miscue. We routinely confuse our failures in comprehension with the state of a system's complexity. We think what we don't see (or hear) can't be there.

The bias appears to extend to our view of the lives of pathogens. Infectious agents must routinely learn new tricks with old tools. Their kit may include a shock of shocks. Disparate viruses and bacteria, mixed and matched by historical happenstance humans have helped impose, may farm each other as assiduously as we do corn and cattle.

—*Farming Pathogens*, 14 September 2010

Are Our Microbiomes Racial?

Imagine . . . that all human bodies which exist looked alike, that on the other hand, different sets of characteristics seemed, as it were, to change their habitation among these bodies. Such a set of characteristics might be, say, mildness, together with a high pitched voice, and slow movements, or a choleric temperament, a deep voice, and jerky movements, and such like. Under such circumstances, although it would be possible to give the bodies names, we should perhaps be as little inclined to do so as we are to give names to the chairs of our dining-room set. On the other hand, it might be useful to give names to the sets of characteristics, and the use of these names would now roughly correspond to the personal names in our present language.

—LUDWIG WITTGENSTEIN (1933–34)

FROM ANYWHERE BETWEEN AN ORDER of magnitude—10 to 1—to a one-to-one match, many of the cells in our bodies aren't even our own.[43] We handle the indignity by assuming ourselves the ecological stage across which "our" microorganismal visitors must mindlessly interact. As if we were gods looking down upon subjects so puny they didn't know we existed.

As if our consciousness was synonymous with control. As if the quorum effects routinely documented in microbes couldn't possibly include a distributed if insentient cognition, or, perhaps more disturbingly, in an ironic reversal, a sentience so unearthly we wouldn't recognize it if it were staring us in the face.

Maybe the animists have it right after all, material mechanisms aside. Whether we sense it or not, perhaps we are routinely and multiply possessed. And when we are sickened by infection, our ill at ease arises in part out of a sinking feeling we are momentarily inhabited by a diffuse and alien being.

The nastier visitors live a lifetime folded inside our own: birth upon infection, kids by transmission, and death on immunal clearance or—bummer—our own passing (although some outlive their hosts, making it to the next susceptible *by virtue of* killing us).[44]

Within hosts and across populations, disparate pathogens can converge on locale-specific disease guilds, a possession by committee, with each member cutting ground for the other. HIV, KSHV, and TB, for instance, arrived at a passing Sub-Saharan detente, producing an epidemiological mutualism scientists have found embodied by specific molecular mechanisms.[45] In reciprocal activation, two bugs' proteins set off molecular pathways in the other.

New work by Peer Bork's group shows a trinity of such communities among humanity's natural gut fauna, the microbes that live inside us, aiding our digestion and producing vitamins.[46] With twenty-two new fecal metagenomes added to those already in the literature, sequencing every microbial gene found in the gut, the team identified by cluster and principle components analyses three basic enterotypes—"gut types"—across our species' microbiomes.

Type 1 is largely dominated by *Bacteroides* bacteria, type 2 by *Prevotella*, and type 3 by Ruminococcus. Each major actor is accompanied by a unique entourage at the exclusion of other taxa. The *Bacteroides* of type 1, for instance, is positively associated with *Clostridiales* and *Parabacteroides*, and negatively associated with six others.

The three enterotypes, however, aren't stratified by country or continent, nor by host sex, health, age, or, as previously shown, weight.[47] They do differ in the mix of enzymes they produce. Enterotypes 1 and 2, for instance, generate energy by way of enzyme clusters involved in fermenting carbohydrates and proteins and degrading mucin glycoproteins, respectively. Fascinating differences in their divisions of labor. Some of these individual protein clusters evidently differ by a number of demographics. Enzymes involved in starch degradation, such as glycosidases and glucan phosphorylases, increase with age.

As the study's subjects were entirely drawn from industrial countries, the work is incomplete. Other enterotypes may yet segregate by food regimen or locale, for instance.

Recent work by Eric Alm's group shows microbiomes generally group more by ecological niche than host genotype and locality, and do so even across host species.[48] With dumbfounding implications, the team showed livestock- and human-associated bacteria that recently shared forty-two antibiotic-resistance genes. In some profoundly fundamental ways, industrial pigs and people are becoming more closely related to each other than either of us is to our indigenous cousins.

THE BORK GROUP RAISES THE POSSIBILITY that some as of yet unidentified mix of host and environmental differences causes the variation in enterotype. That may be a matter of putting the cart before the horse. While enterotyping's *applications* are apparent—in everything from diet to drug intake to disease diagnostics—*explanations* for such ecological assemblages need not be founded solely on the adaptationist program's search for organismal purpose.

The Bork work, for one, doesn't clarify whether the enterotypes are inherited. Setting aside for now the problem of horizontal gene transfer, at the population level the propagation of one enterotype over another may be from our perspective near-random. The enterotypes may crisscross human families in lineages outside the scope of their hosts' genetic inheritance. Familial correlation may be more a matter of environmental proximity than host genetics or even local vicinity.

The assembling itself, on the other hand, is most certainly functionally locked in, a taxon here and there notwithstanding given the inevitable differences in individual host guts and the occasional stochastic burps across enteric environments. Once one key bacterium taxon colonizes a newborn gut by chance, even if those odds are weighted by some familial factor, including exposure at birth, the pioneer prepares the gut for its enterotypic successors.

What we're getting at here is that we need to offer the concepts of *contingency* and *historical constraint* the kind of room in our explanation that natural selection is oft afforded.[49] And if enterotypes move from person to person with little or no reference to their host's identity, turning people, at least in this domain, into Wittgenstein's nameless, or into races defined by the content of their gut rather than the color of their skin, then causality, and our sense of self, must be situated as much in the field as it is in the object.

Indeed, as we are co-dependent on these microbes for survival, perhaps we are as much their visitors as they ours. Each newborn must meet and greet its group of commensurate bacteria. And these unicellular confederates in turn emerge out of a historical trajectory that microbe and human mold off-and-on together.

CUTTING-EDGE WORK, HOWEVER, is by definition in flux. Conclusions are routinely overturned (only to be overturned again). Work published just this past month by the Human Microbiome Project documenting the microbiome over a larger population and across multiple body parts, including the gut, indicates that, well, in fact, at least in this new study, the human microbiome *is* racially segregated.[50]

The project screened the microbial genomes of nearly 5,000 specimens from 242 healthy Americans. Samples were drawn from across eighteen body habitats: oral cavity and oropharynx, saliva, inside cheek, gums, palate, tonsils, throat, tongue, tooth biofilm above and below the gum line, behind the ears, inner elbows, a nostril, a stool sample, and for the lucky ladies, three vaginal specimens. For 131 individuals a second sample was taken from each part at a subsequent time point to test the stability of microbial community structure.

The consortium isolated and sequenced sections of all 16S ribosomal RNA (rRNA) it detected in each sample. Species across the tree of life can be differentiated by their 16S, which consist of highly conserved regions alternating with variable sequences.

By a second protocol the genomes of the entire microbial community were profiled by whole-genome shotgun sequencing, within specified limits in detection, sequencing depth, and statistical power. Community membership was identified by comparing the resulting reads against reference sequences available for bacteria, archaea, viruses, and microeukaryotes. Finally, the genes identified were assigned as best as possible to protein families and annotated for gene function.

Ostensibly the aim of the project to this point was to produce reference microbial profiles of "healthy" individuals against which eventually to compare those of sick people. Do specific illnesses correlate with shifts in microbial taxonomic and functional profiles in any particular body part or across parts as smaller studies so far suggest? A fascinating and fundamental question indeed. But what the Human Microbiome Project did find in these reference individuals is in and of itself illuminating.

Oral and stool microbial communities were particularly diverse in community taxonomy. Body parts, however, differed in their alpha and beta diversities. Individual saliva samples, for one, displayed great diversity in their taxonomy but differed little among individual subjects.

Variation *within individuals* over time differed less than between subjects in both taxonomy and function. That is, albeit over only two time points, individual microbial communities appear to remain relatively stable. More sampling across longer periods is likely to capture profile shifts, even in individual hosts who remain in good health. *Across individuals,* depending on the body part, the study showed microbial configurations either locked into discrete blocks or varying continuously.

No microbial taxa were observed present in *all* body parts or in *all* individual subjects. In other words, the Human Microbiome Project found strong niche differentiation within and among subjects. Some metabolic pathways, however, were universally present, indicating multiple taxa functionally converging on core housekeeping tasks, including, in the gut, spermidine biosynthesis, methionine degradation, and hydrogen sulphide production.

Although no ubiquitous taxa were apparent, each body part hosted primary signature species. Lots of *Streptococcus* across body parts, for instance. *Haemophilus* in the inside cheek. *Actinomyces* in the tooth biofilm above the gum. Even so, within this methodological context microbiome profiles proved deeply personalized, particularly in the makeup of less abundant species. In other words, microbial succession isn't wholly deterministic. Within specific taxa, across individuals, there also appeared considerable genetic variation, perhaps, as the consortium surmises, a result of host selection pressures and the functional trade-offs across taxa, but perhaps also, as discussed above, from contingent founder events. Cholera, TB, and salmonella and other NIAID class A-C pathogens weren't detected in the study population. On the other hand, genes from the Computation Institute's PATRIC bacterial disease database were found in relative abundance across hosts and habitats. The result suggests the health/disease divide may depend on the state of the microbial community rather than the mere presence of an etiological agent, including shifts in the relative abundance and functional interactions among the community's constituents. The Project hypothesizes that if suppressor taxa shift, then a "recessive" disease agent may become suddenly microecologically active.

AND RACE? DO OUR MICROBIAL communities differ by particular host characteristics? Do age, body mass index, ethnicity, and other clinical metadata correlate with microbial taxonomy and metabolism?

As with Bork's group, the consortium found most of the relationships, for instance with body mass index, weak. The Human Microbiome Project hypothesizes that other factors as yet unstudied may be important, including short- and long-term diet, daily metabolic cycles, and, as we discussed, founder effects such as mode of transmission and individual host genetics.

A small number did stand out, however. As previous research has showed, vaginal pH appeared correlated with microbial shifts, including at higher pH a drop in *Lactobacillus* and an increase in overall diversity. Increasing age appeared associated with greater diversity in metabolic pathways on the skin.

Finally, the big reveal, unlike the Bork work subject ethnicity strongly dropped out across body habitats. Ethnicity showed 266 associations with various microbiome data, more than any other demographic/clinical factor. Asians, Mexicans, and whites, for instance, showed large relative abundances in ornithine and histidine biosynthesis in the tongue and small abundances in Proteobacteria and Gammaproteobacteria clades in the nares and inner elbow. Blacks and Puerto Ricans showed the reverse.

Perhaps with good sense, the Project offered nary a word about why. But it's clear, depending on the resulting applications, we find ourselves on the eve of the next battle over the meaning of racial differences in biomedical outcomes.

Ten years ago the essentialist typology underlying race-based drugs such as BiDil set off a firestorm. As Troy Duster described it early on:

> In what has been touted as "the first ethnic drug," the biotech firm NitroMed received a green light from the Food and Drug Administration in March 2001 to proceed with a full-scale clinical trial, "the first prospective trial conducted exclusively in black men and women suffering from heart failure." . . .
>
> BiDil is a drug designed to restore low or depleted nitric oxide levels to the blood to treat or prevent cases of congestive heart failure. It was originally designed for a wide population base, and race was irrelevant. But the early clinical studies revealed no compelling results, and an FDA advisory panel voted 9 to 3 against approval.
>
> In a remarkable turn of fate, however, BiDil was suddenly born again as a racialized intervention. . . .
>
> [NitroMed claimed] that BiDil has a special effect greater on African Americans than whites. The clinical trials now under way are not designed to test that hypothesis. Rather, by concentrating only on blacks, the study can have little or nothing compelling to say about comparative results, by race.[51]

Developmental biologist Armand Leroi retroactively certified such expediency.[52] As race can affect medical treatment, "many new drugs are now labeled with warnings that they may not work in some ethnic or racial groups." That such effects need not be predominantly biological in origin—or even exist—mattered little.

Leroi cagily conceded that differences among races arise from population averages alone. But as we are unlikely to sequence individuals' genomes at scale any time soon and presumably won't be able to individualize medical treatment that way, he argued, we'll just have to accept a racialized medical genetics.

Even many among those who have accepted racial genomics as biologically real have since rejected such crass calculation:

> In the case of BiDil, [geneticist Craig Venter and his colleagues] note, the manufacturer "is voluntarily financing a study to investigate the genetic basis for the response to the drug." But in general, "Once a race-based drug has been developed, there is a possibility that a drug company may terminate its research and not pursue follow-up studies into the underlying cause. This could stunt medical care with race-based medicine, rather than personalized medicine."[53]

Venter's position here puts him at odds with his own creed that "science is the business right now. If the science works, the business works, and vice versa."[54] Accordingly, NitroMed's quarterly margins would sanctify the science behind the drug, even as the science here was found more in the marketing than the biology. As Jonathan Khan discovered:

> [No] firm evidence exists that BiDil actually works better or differently in African-Americans than in anyone else. . . . So how did BiDil become tagged as an ethnic drug and the harbinger of a new age of medicine? The story of the drug's development is a tangled tale of inconclusive studies, regulatory hurdles and commercial motives.[55]

The drug's effects were more financial than biological. "Why the mistake, and what is at stake?" Duster asked:

> Part of the answer lies in the role of prospective markets for biotech products. While the new mantra of biotechnology is to claim that pharmaceuticals will someday soon be marketed to individuals based upon their DNA, the fundamental truth is that selling drugs is about markets. These markets are not about individual designer drugs, but about groups and population aggregates that become the target market.

In a classical piece of epidemiological research, Michael Klag and his associates showed a decade ago that, in general, the darker the skin color, the higher the rate of hypertension for American blacks, even inside the African American community. Klag indicated that the issue was not biological or genetic in origin, but biological in effect due to stress-related outcomes of reduced access to valued social goods such as employment, promotion, housing stock, etc. The effect was biological, not the origins.[56]

NitroMed repackaged a failed drug as racially based. And Leroi used NitroMed's marketing to confirm race's biological reality.

The problem extends beyond racial drugs to medical genomics itself, which has largely fallen flat delivering on its prospectuses. However amenable they are to commoditization, our genomes aren't our health destinies. Yet there remains considerable impetus to such an ideological imperative. And so given science's present economics—increasingly capital-financed—method and interpretation alike appear now turning to the new metagenomics for recourse.

"Research into the nature of the human microbiome has yielded many surprises," writes Jennifer Ackerman,

> no two people share the same microbial makeup, for instance—even identical twins. This finding may help unravel a mystery presented by the Human Genome Project, which confirmed that the human DNA of all the people the world over is 99.9 percent alike. Our individual fates, health and perhaps even some of our actions may have more to do with the variation in the genes found in our microbiome than in our own genes.[57]

Capitalism's ingenuity can be found in repeatedly packaging epigenetic biology into preformationist precepts. With dividends in systemic legitimization. Nature is made capitalist in nature, making capitalism natural. Health disparities arise out of our genes or our guts rather than systems of apartheid.

NEW EPISTEMOLOGICAL BOSS SAME as old epistemological boss. Such essentialisms deserve continued rebuke, in whatever forms they transmogrify. There may be, however, a more positive, if not also positivist, response. We *do* risk letting metagenomics change the topic. By way of their emotional and material deprivations, racism and other sources of population-level stress have definitional effect on individuals as early as conception, as well as on the populations of which they are a part. Racism shapes ontogeny, our individual development, regardless of allelic frequencies. And it's to that relationship and its overdetermination of health outcomes by race where research and social action need to be directed.

But it may be worth the risk reappropriating the terms of the debate. By a true social science of the microbiome we can investigate host determinants under a more sophisticated rubric than clunky clinical metadata.

For instance, how is microbiome diversity geographically distributed? Are microbiomes racially segregated more in racially segregated neighborhoods, cities, or countries than in integrated ones? Or from block to block? Does racial oppression, and its material and sociopsychological stresses and deprivations, select for particular microbial profiles over others?

Do microbiomes display a class structure? Is there such a thing as a Great Recession microbiome? Do the discrete blocks vs. continuous diversity that the Human Microbiome Project study found map to different parts of this social multispace? Do profiles from body part to body part depend on the kinds of environmental insults found locally? And if so, across which aspects of the social and physical environment? What is the shape and nature of the population social network across which commensal microbes are transmitted?

All such questions would require rethinking people less as clinical subjects from which to tap samples—a Gray's Physiology—and more as socially active beings, part and parcel of particular populations at particular localities, shaped by an idiosyncratic history, and differentially exposed in time and space to the greater world.

As a result, each of our microbiomes may indeed deserve a personal name, representing more than a single person but in addition the histories each of us shares with whom and with where we live. I've taken to greeting mine as Ludwig St. Paul. What it may call me in return is beyond our present understanding.

—*FARMING PATHOGENS*, 2 JULY 2012

UPDATE. Imagine my surprise and delight nearly four years after I called for a true social science of the microbiome beyond clinical metadata when someone tweeted me exactly such a study.[58]

Gregory Miller and colleagues geocoded colonic microbiota, finding lower gut diversity in Chicago zip codes of lower socioeconomic status:

> In unadjusted analyses, neighborhood socioeconomic-status explained 12–18 percent of the variability in alpha-diversity of colonic microbiota. The direction of these associations was positive, meaning that as neighborhood socioeconomic-status increased, so did alpha-diversity of both the colonic sigmoid mucosa and fecal microbiota. The strength of these associations persisted when models were expanded to include covariates reflecting potential demographic (age, gender, race/ethnicity) and lifestyle (adiposity, alcohol use, smoking) confounds. In these models neighborhood socioeconomic-status continued to explain 11–22 percent of the variability in diversity indicators.

Stunning results with profound implications for chronic population health. The dawn of a social microbiome.

The X-Men

The organism becomes a Chinese nest of boxes of qualities, and there is now seen to be no necessity for explaining change as change. . . . Biology can then proceed to its real task, that of discovering the determined, material sequence of qualities, in each step of which organism and environment are involved as warp and woof.

—CHRISTOPHER CAUDWELL (1936/1986)

MY VIEWS ARE MUTATING. I'm beginning to think that when evolutionary biologists characterize the source of variation on which natural selection operates as "random," it is an attempt to impose on biologies the syllogism underlying Darwin's ingenuous contribution: 1) heritible variation, 2) with effects on reproductive success, 3) produces natural selection.

Mutations, however, are, generally speaking, gamma-distributed across genetic sequences, including non-coding loci.[59] That is, regardless of the final distribution eventually inferred, their substitution rates vary across sites and do so in particular directions (for example, by transitions or transversions) and in domain-specific ways.[60]

Take hemagglutinin, the influenza glycoprotein, characterized by a hypervariable head resistant to host antibody memory surrounding a conserved core used to help key the virus into target cells. Ostensibly selection operates in favor of surface hypervariability at the level of the phenotype. But we might ask whether it does so in such a way that imprints upon the mutation process itself.

Perhaps we have here a generalization of directed mutagenesis — mutations generated "on purpose" here and there—but really more an epiphenomenon arising from the very fabric of biological reality, however stochastic its short-term rhythm.

The classic counterargument is that there *are* influenza quasi-species that originate expressing *little* variation in the hypervariable region and/or with *lots* of variation in the conserved region. They just don't make it through the selection filter. They do not become part of the population of sequences that characterize the gamma distribution. Shades of Nassim Taleb on the nature of silent evidence.[61] But I think this misses the point or, better yet, in a roundabout way *makes* the point. Assuming the source of variation precedes selection and not also the other way around misses a causal interpenetration at the heart of our biologies. Selection can shape the stereochemical drama by which mutations arise.

That is, mutation—or recombination or reassortment—isn't just a statistical feature, emerging as a kind of Platonic orphan. It is also a bloody biochemical event embedded in the real-world push-and-pull of molecules forming and breaking and in the path-dependent evolutionary trajectories shaped by passing historical circumstance. The latter include, given our interests here, the agricultural regimes humanity imposes.[62]

—*FarmingPathogens* blog, 31 January 2014

UPDATE. Something's in the air. I only recently came across evolutionary geneticist Arlin Stotlzfus's 2012 piece on constructive neutral evolution which he has since followed up with some historical background.[63] Building on Force et al., H. Allen Orr, and some evo-devo, Stotlzfus unpacks the Neo-Darwinian Synthesis as an unjustifiably narrow attempt to reconcile natural selection and Mendelian genetics.[64]

In fact, the Modern Synthesis integrating Darwin and Mendel suspiciously fails to assimilate the full extent of the revolutions in evolutionary genetics apparent even as far back as William Bateson:

In Darwin's original theory, and in the later Fisherian view, individual differences are properly a raw material, like the sand used to make a sand-castle: each individual grain of sand may be unique in size and shape, but its individual nature hardly matters, because it is infinitesimal in relation to the whole that is built by selection. By contrast, if an episode of evolution reflects the individual nature of a significant mutation—a developmental macromutation, a gene or genome duplication, an event of lateral transfer or endosymbiogenesis, etc.—then the infinitesimal assumption no longer applies, and [Darwin's] verbal theory fails: when variation supplies form (not just substance), it is no longer properly a raw material, and selection is no longer the creator that shapes raw materials into products.

Stoltzfus describes a number of mechanisms by which patterns of mutation are shaped at the level of genetic architecture, extending beyond neutral evolution, as we discussed above. Their cause is a

bias in the introduction of variants, and its lack of concordance with the classical forces theory arises because it is not based on the "shifting gene frequencies" view of the [Modern Synthesis], which assumes abundant variation as a pre-condition for "evolution," but on the mutationist conception of evolution as a 2-step proposal-and-acceptance process.

Computational biologist Eugene Koonin, one of Stotlzfus's reviewers, adds:

The contribution of mutations to evolution does not stop at biases. It is clear now that a variety of mechanisms exist for directing mutations to specific targets that are relevant for adaptation under the given conditions. This results in a plethora of Lamarckian and pseudo-Lamarckian processes that substantially contribute to evolution.

PART FOUR

Capitalism is just paid slavery. It's the same set-up as slavery, only difference was slaves wasn't getting paid. But it's the same set-up. I own this plantation. You are at the bottom. I've got some managers right here that oversee the field. They get paid a little more than you, but they ain't that much better off than you. They feel better because they're on top of you. The manager at McDonald's feeling a little better than the dude on fries. But it's like, you ain't that guy. That guy is milking everybody.

—J. Cole (2014)

Two Gentlemen of Verona

*As they combed through [German agent] Kühlenthal's message
to Berlin, the British code breakers noticed something rather
odd. [Double agent] Garbo's [faked] intelligence was already
sensational enough, but Kühlenthal was spicing it up still further,
to lend extra weight. He was not above inventing his own
subagents and adding them to the pot. . . . The British watched
with pleasure as Kühlenthal grew steadily dependent on Garbo
and his stock rose in Berlin.*

—BEN MACINTYRE (2010)

FOR A CUP OF COFFEE I FOUND myself allowed inside world
health, conducting contract research for the Food and Agriculture
Organization on influenza A (H5N1).

During that stint I was invited to a joint scientific consultation of
influenza and other zoonotic diseases held outside Verona by FAO, the
Organization for Animal Health, and the World Health Organization.[1]
Over two days seventy academics and intergovernmental officials,
primarily from Europe and the United States, discussed and debated
the nature of emerging pathogens and their control. Some of the talk
was stellar, some—for fascinating reasons—dubious.

Getting the Big Three health agencies to work together is quite an
accomplishment. Each had long ruled its own fiefdom, standing little
interference. A deadly bird flu outbreak forces cooperation if only out
of fear and panic. With influenza presently ebbing, however, WHO
has since pulled back.

The conference begins with a long announcement from WHO
describing Dutch molecular biologist Albert Osterhaus's conflicts of

interest. Osterhaus has financial interests in multiple pharm firms, including Viroclinics BV, Coronovative BV, and Isoconova AB, from which he claims to be divesting.

In the first break-out session, Osterhaus misrepresents his own reductionist ideas as those of our group, despite what had been a heated discussion. I move to the other side of the room for the rest of the conference.

In a classic opening, molecular biologists first dominate the discussion. But over the two days ecologists and their numbered veterinarian allies, primarily centered around FAO, push back. To his credit, by conference's end even Osterhaus comes around, professing interest in integrating molecular and ecological approaches. A good sign.

FAO's Jan Slingenbergh, with whom I worked, offers a brilliant rubric on the conflicts among the disciplines. Each field addresses a different part of a new pathogen's epicurve. Typically animal ecologists react to an emergent pathogen pre-celebrity, as the pathogen circulates in wild species in real and proverbial forests. Once the pathogen makes its way into sentinel livestock, the vets address the new bug. With human spillover and a typical expansion in geographic extent, molecular biologists, medical doctors, and epidemiologists step in.

It's not that any one domain of study is more important than the others so much as that each covers a different stage of the outbreak, skeins only collaboration can integrate.

Kansas State's Juergen Richt acts the boar. He misdirects an ad hominem attack on an Osterhaus query on a different matter, that at least *he* doesn't suffer a conflict of interest. At dinner that night, Richt gets drunk, boasting about his institute's eight-million-dollar budget and that on this very night he was going to score a few million more over the phone.

I ask Ouafaa Fassi Fihri, one of only two epidemiological vets in all of Morocco, what *she* would do with eight million dollars. She laughs low and slow.

Slingenbergh sets me straight: the conference is displaying a laudable tolerance for people's personalities, in the interest of larger goals. I am at times a bristly one myself. But still. Richt appears an exemplar of a research system that selects for donation magnets at the expense of just about everything else. Indeed, more damning than any drunken obnoxiousness I find none of Richt's many comments at the conference novel or incisive. Even Osterhaus makes a few good contributions.

Virologist Ilaria Capua surprises me. A heroine who in 2007 forced WHO into releasing privatized genetic sequences, here she defends a WHO proposal she apparently helped craft.[2] The group proposes reorganizing influenza around the *gene pool concept*. The approach treats the influenza population as a cloud of genomic segments that the virus swaps pell-mell by reassortment.

But it's clear the proposal is presented with diplomatic rather than scientific aims in mind. Under this formula, countries couldn't be blamed for, nor serve as the source name of, the next new influenza strain. Influenzas are not *panmictic*, however. Not all segments mix with all other segments everywhere. Indeed, some countries host multiple reassortment events, leading to the routine emergence of new strains there. Whatever its good intentions, disputable as those may be, the gene pool concept as applied here erases causality at the level of the agroecological niche.

Capua replies that I must then prefer genetic sequences locked away. I say she's confounding two issues. How we scientifically characterize influenza should have nothing to do with, nor be held hostage to, efforts aimed at convincing countries to release their data.

Herve Zeller describes how West Nile Virus became entrained into an anthropogenic cycle. John Mackenzie shows how Nipah virus emerged in Malaysia once hog husbandry turned intensive. Pierre Formenty speaks of unintended consequences. Following an outbreak of Rift Valley Fever, which had escaped its home range, subsistence farmers resort to bushmeat, exposing themselves to monkey pox.

The talks together ask us, Is the writing on the wall or what? We are farming our own pathogens. Or put another way, pathogens are acting like early dogs, increasingly nibbling at our trash piles leading to a domesticated—but not necessarily friendly—life inside our huts. At times, as H5N1 demonstrated, our new housemates blow back out, killing the wild animals from which they initially emerged fairly harmless.

During a break David Swayne, who has made fundamental contributions to our understanding of the molecular biology and transmission of influenza, disses Johns Hopkins's Jessica Leibler as an ideologue for calling out agribusiness's role in influenza emergence. I tell him anyone—ahem—accepting Big Ag research dollars is as much in danger of violating scientific principles. If agribusiness *was* involved in influenza emergence, speaking strictly hypothetically of course, such a scientist would somehow some way never think to ask the question.

On another break William Karesh of World Conservation Society, one of bestseller David Quammen's rangers,[3] admits his group takes Cargill money. I like Billy personally, and he has many interesting things to say, making yeoman efforts at getting wildlife folded into epidemiological studies, but all of a sudden he's acting the walking—or here sitting—advertisement, talking points on Cargill's improved practices. I reply that Cargill is heavily involved in a neoliberal approach to farming. They're in the Global South for cheap land, cheap labor, and little regulation. "Interesting," he replies, as if he hadn't thought of it, and invites me to visit when next in New York.

Peter Daszak, of Wildlife Trust, now EcoHealth Alliance, and the editor of the excellent journal *Ecohealth*, leads another break-out group tasked with devising interventions.

I offer the group the idea that early detection does not begin with identifying a new pathogen. That's way late in the game. Instead we need to focus on characterizing landscapes that are likely to promote disease emergence. It's no coincidence H5N1 and SARS emerged in Guangdong at a time the Chinese province was undergoing fundamental shifts in its agroeconomic geography.

We should be able to identify those areas by jolts in the times series of validated indices, then reverse-engineer the pathogens that are most likely to emerge given the specific changes in the environment and the pathogens already circulating in local wildlife.

Daszak immediately recognizes the idea's implications—"You're trying to maneuver the molecular biologists right out of the picture"—but bad-mouths the concept to the larger group as "Project Utopia," with no chance of implementation.

Search "Daszak" through the program of the One Health conference held ten months later in Melbourne, however, and you'll see the idea no less than four times.[4] Straight out of *Dilbert*, but I suppose it's nice to see someone following up. It'd be nice if my ideas could pay bills other than someone else's. Unfortunately that's the kind of truculence that conveniently serves any community's critic as "just deserts."

All in all, human nature on full display in its fire and folly, mine included.

Many of us might feel a touch self-righteous in the face of the behavior of Osterhaus and Richt, our two gentlemen of Verona. But Frederic Keck, a social anthropologist, was the only person in the room with the integrity to raise the prospect that the "c" word—and it ain't "cancer"—had something to do with the emergence of new disease threats.

During the breaks everyone else lobbied each other to make one emerging virus or another pay off. Which has its place, right? Diseases need to be fought. People gotta eat. Except few there seemed food-insecure across the many sumptuous meals served.

Science itself—our albeit flawed attempt at rationality—isn't so much the problem here as its practitioners' acrobatic accommodations for all things lord and master.

This is, however, no character assassination (as I am more than willing to eviscerate myself as anyone else). And I believe the folk who attended the meeting are genuinely interested in stopping influenza and other deadly pathogens, dedicating thousands of hours in humanity's service in countries the world over. They are, however, also prone to induction's path of least resistance, and the pull of the lizard parts of their brains, melding scientific hypotheses and gut desires in a game long rigged off-site.

Not an excuse, but a description of the circumstances under which scientific judgment is presently exercised.

—9 JUNE 2011

UPDATE. Against Osterhaus's depiction here, it would be unwise to underestimate his wiles and wherewithal. EcoHealth practitioners

I've spoken with since are concerned that among others he is co-opting One Health, the study of health across species, into a narrow program organized around a reductionist medical model conducive to greenwashing corporate reputations.

With Curtin University's John Mackenzie, who up until 2010 was also invested in pharm companies, Osterhaus now offers this solicitation:

> The One Health Platform actively develops synergies with companies that share our mission to improve the health of humans, animals and their environments. If you are developing and/or producing vaccines, antiviral medicines, antibiotics, diagnostic tools, anti-parasitic agents or any other product or service that contributes to One Health, you are cordially invited to become a corporate supporter. Partner with the One Health Platform now to play a pioneering role in the fast-growing One Health movement.
>
> Every institution or company is unique, so we work closely with our partners to tailor lasting partnerships that deliver the best results.[5]

This is not a matter of a bad apple, however. At a time of declining state outlays for science, there is much money to be made reappropriating the tools by which researchers might investigate how agribusiness produces novel diseases in the first place. What was once an awkward whiff of opportunism has become standard stock-in-trade.

The program for the Cargill– and Gold'n Plump–sponsored "The Science Behind One Health" conference held in 2014 here in Minnesota included respected researchers and governmental health officials, but in addition included a panel of speakers from Pepsi and Cargill and a litigator who, tellingly, "represents food processors, distributors and retailers in foodborne illness and contamination cases, defending them against labeling and class action consumer fraud claims, and representing them in complex commercial litigation and supply chain disputes."[6]

Only weeks after Greenpeace called out personal care giant Colgate-Palmolive in March 2016 for its refusal to trace its palm oil back to source plantations, the EcoHealth Alliance, as we learned one of the major proponents of the One Health concept, gave an award to Colgate, one of its financial backers, for "the leadership Colgate-Palmolive has shown in addressing sustainability and environmental issues."[7]

"We are thrilled," announced Alliance president Peter Daszak, "to honor our first Fortune 500 Company that aligns with EcoHealth Alliance's innovative programs aimed at improving the health of people, animals and ecosystems. Colgate-Palmolive's sustainability practices are forward-thinking, and socially responsible. We are excited to honor that good work."

Food and Pharm WikiLeaks

To these provincial autocrats, before whom the peaceable
population of all classes had been accustomed to tremble, the
reserve of that English-looking engineer caused an uneasiness
which swung to and fro between cringing and truculence.
Gradually all of them discovered that no matter what party was
in power, that man remained in most effective touch with the
higher authorities in Santa Marta.

—JOSEPH CONRAD (1904)

EACH OF THE HEADY, AND NOW increasingly bloody and co-opted, revolts across the Middle East, reverberating as far as Wisconsin and China, were long brewing reactions to dictatorship. In extolling Facebook and Twitter, lazy American commentators mistook superficial means for fundamental causes, a high-tech update on the canard that the poor and the oppressed experience no history and are never agents of their own change. That is, the very hubris now bringing down one regime after another.

We shouldn't, however, underestimate the role of the Internet, a neutral net Wild West as much Tortuga as Thames—Tahrir Square as Tiananmen—a place where global neoliberalism *can* be subverted even while by other means enforced. Tunisia's rebellion, setting off the dominoes, appears in part precipitated by Net-leaked U.S. diplomatic cables coming clean to the extent of ally Ben Ali's corruption. In some way, in some venue, empire must level with itself, however much even its own apparatus must be kept in the dark.

But too much light and oxygen are typically poisonous to the more secretive taxa. So the U.S. security nexus, its imperial initiative temporarily untracked, maneuvers for Julian Assange's extradition even as it remains unsure whether the WikiLeaks are damaging.[8] The conflicting impulses arise in part because the revelations are, first, as destructive to other countries as they are to the United States, and, second, largely back in the box. Once pissed on by bipartisan indignity—a splash too bitter for their cocktails—editors at the *Guardian* and the *New York Times*, who published exclusives based on the leaks, cleaned up their messes, soft-pedaling their own stories, and undertaking vicious ad hominem attacks on Assange, their source.[9] Indeed, the *Guardian* has now published more on Assange and his legal problems than the cables themselves.

SEVERAL COMMENTATORS HAVE FOUND the WikiLeaks cables' significance less in what exactly they reveal than in their exposure of the immense apparatus of secrecy.[10] The details do matter, however, as they concretize the crass extent to which the U.S. government works for American commercial interests abroad and, by turns, the inanity and paucity of that work's rationale.

The cables show U.S. embassies addressing all manner of events and circumstances. At the same time, many an individual embassy appears to focus on particular topics. Energy in Azerbaijan. Terrorism supported by Syria. War, terror, and lots of high-level U.S. diplomatic traffic in Pakistan. Or even particular companies: BP in Azerbaijan, Blackwater in Djibouti, and Visa and Mastercard in Russia.

Some topics, say Cuba and Venezuela, are deranged obsessions across embassies, including, I found, in Spain, Chile and, of all places, Iceland. Some embassies are vehemently more ideological in bent than others, responding to what are perceived as uncooperative host regimes. If the cables are any indication, leftish Bolivia and Venezuela, for instance, host particularly truculent diplomatic corps.

Some cables speak to an enemies list back home. During the George W. Bush era a New Zealand minister *almost* sponsored a screening of a Michael Moore film.[11] The crisis was averted, however, Jack Bauer breaking that dirty Kiwi's fingers, one for every Moore release.

At first gander the cables give the impression that though the State Department is concerned about security and diplomatic issues, the embassies are tasked with immediate commercial interests. Clearly State is very much organized around the specifics of trade, tariffs, and even contractual outcomes, but it's fascinating the way the agendas dance together, converging and diverging in both tone and content, within even the same cable. High-minded rhetoric is routinely undercut by the very expediency it condemns, a particular American double-talk that the rest of the world, if my experience is any indication, despises.

U.S. personnel, in one Embassy Abuja cable, matter-of-factly relay a dirty trick drug company Pfizer played on a Nigerian official, as told by Enrico Liggeri, Pfizer's country manager.[12] In an attempt to pressure Federal Attorney General Michael Aondoakaa into dropping two multimillion-dollar lawsuits around oral antibiotic trials on children that Pfizer mishandled during a meningitis outbreak, including failing to obtain parental consent, Pfizer passed on evidence of the AG's corruption in other matters to local newspapers.

By way of a justification, Liggeri characterized the Nigerian suits as a shakedown that would discourage pharmaceutical companies from helping out should another such outbreak occur. That is to say, one, Nigeria endangers its children in attempting to secure damages for tests on children Pfizer botched. Two, looking for evidence of corruption on the part of the local official you are trying to corrupt is good business practice.

The U.S. Embassy's concluding commentary speaks neither to the lawsuits nor the dirty trick, but, without a mote of self-consciousness, and noting Nigeria a Pfizer growth market, offers support for the company's efforts to secure "transparency" in the settlement's $75 million payout. Breathtaking.

THE PUSH FOR GENETICALLY MODIFIED foods follows a similar script if on a global scale.

A search through WikiLeaks finds by my count 472 cables across ninety-six countries with "genetically modified" in their text. Although some describe other countries' own efforts, cable after cable shows that the premises of an aggressive business model favoring American agribusiness are assimilated into diplomatic policy, as if transmogrified into a matter of international law or even as an inalienable human right.

One short U.S. Embassy Warsaw cable describes a meeting with an official at the Polish Ministry of the Environment, on the unlikely potentiality Poland would vote to approve EU permits for Pioneer and Syngenta GMO corn hybrids.[13] The cable ends with this horse head left at the end of the bed:

> Post will follow up to obtain information on Poland's decision and details of a law on cultivating genetically modified crops now being drafted. However, Poland's established policy to vote against approval of all GMO varieties remains in effect, and we expect it to follow that policy and vote against the approvals during this vote as well. Nevertheless, Director Dalbiak's comment that Poland might abstain shows Poland at least is having an internal debate on biotech. Decision makers have a greater appreciation that their actions have consequences after facing a large retaliation sanction in the WTO beef hormone case.

Are these offers-they-couldn't-refuse scut work embassy staff must schedule, paying back one PAC campaign contributor at a time? Or, in addition, like China in Africa, are they a part of a grander design around imperial infrastructure?

Much attention has been paid to GMOs' health, ecological, and social costs. Agribusiness externalizes these to governments, workers, wildlife, and consumers. Someone else picks up the bill. But there may be a second-order game here. GMOs appear the focus of a stunning program: to privatize biology itself, turning sovereign soils and the very act of farming, as much as its produce, into commodities. "Cargill is engaged in the commercialization of photosynthesis," CEO Gregory Page said in a 2008 speech, "That is at the root of what we do."[14]

Consider the power a country would wield should whole swaths of the world's agriculture—crop on crop, input on input—be locked into production pathways copyrighted by monopolies incorporated back home. If fully realized, such a project would maneuver the world's populations one by one into that country's command, if only as a matter of survival. Soft world domination. Occupation by suits in suites rather than by boots on the ground.

WITH THESE STAKES THE UNITED STATES' GMO operation appears elephantine in extent and intrigue: from Armenia to Zimbabwe, from busting local activists to jacking international confabs, from the most marginal outposts to the richest markets. France offers an illustrative example. In 2006, the U.S. Embassy Paris wrote approvingly of two French judicial rulings.[15] The first upheld the convictions of "Faucheurs Volontaires" (Voluntary Cutters), a group of anti-GMO activists who had destroyed Monsanto test plots of the only GMO seed approved in France, MON810, near Orléans. The second ruling ordered Greenpeace to remove online maps of GMO corn across France and lists of French GMO growers.

The cable describes anti-GMO protests and field raids that to this point were discouraging to GMO farmers and researchers alike:

On April 13, fifty people from Faucheurs Volontaires and Greenpeace stormed a Monsanto site in southwestern France (Aude area), demonstrated against GMOs and hung a banner stating "from the field to the plate, no GMO." Demonstrators were arrested at the site.

In June, another group of Faucheurs Volontaires, associated with the activist farmers' union, Confederation Paysanne, sent approximately forty anti-biotech activists to sow organic corn seeds in a GM test field in southern Paris (Loiret area). The group claimed responsibility for "sowing life" in contrast to their position that biotech companies "sow death."

In July, Monsanto announced that three of its test plots were damaged and Limagrain, the leading French seed company, and its genetics subsidiary, Biogemma, also announced it had had test plots destroyed by a group from "Voluntary Cutters." Also in July, the "Voluntary Cutters" announced they would expand their destruction from experimental test plots to commercial production fields for the first time this summer.

In contrast, the cable approvingly relays PR efforts GMO farmers and their industry had launched in favor of their corn crops, the great majority of which are exported to Spain as feed:

> [At] the annual French corn producers meeting in June, a farmer publicly discussed his justifications for planting Bt corn. He listed the advantages of reduced pesticide use, higher production of high-quality corn not weakened by European corn borer attacks, and the benefits of staggering corn harvests. . . . And further, *Cultivar* magazine, a French technical publication, published an interview in its July issue with a farmer growing biotech corn for commercial sale in which he described the different management steps he took from planting, to coexistence with non-biotech corn, through harvesting.

The cable fails to note the pests' pesticide resistance, concomitant *increases* in pesticide use, and contamination of non-GMO crops that routinely result. The Manichean instinct is found also in the cable's characterization of French legislative efforts. On the one hand, bills aimed to permit GMOs are "reasonable," while those aimed to block them are "political."

In a 2007 update Embassy Paris worried the campaign was faltering.[16] Whereas the 2007 GMO acreage registered four times 2006's, GMO crops still represented only 0.75 percent of French corn, trailing crop forecasts as

> farmers' spring planting decisions were negatively influenced by the anti-biotech positions of several leading presidential candidates and the new requirement [right out of Greenpeace's playbook] that biotech field locations, which must be made to the Ministry of Agriculture, be made public.

The embassy's frustration here is palpable and it is hard to conclude that the United States is attempting to organize anything less than an invasion of France by diplomatic and economic means. Several losing fronts are described:

In France, lack of consumer acceptance of agricultural biotechnology in products for human consumption continues to be very strong. Food products labeled as containing or derived from biotech are generally not available on the French market. . . . Anti-biotech activists (mainly Greenpeace, Faucheurs Volontaires, ATTAC, Friends of the Earth, CRI-GEN and Confederation Paysanne farmers union) are well organized, highly visible and work consistently to discourage progress for biotech acceptance. During the summer of 2006, activists destroyed two thirds of the open-field test plots. Farm groups fumed at the immunity that anti-biotech groups have been afforded in these acts of destruction. . . .

FNSEA, the largest farmers union in France, usually quiet on the biotech issue, publicly decried the fact that biotech farmers are growing their crops under almost clandestine circumstances to avoid being targeted. . . .

Biotech farmers are also facing attacks from traditional farmers. A beekeeper is alleging that pollen from a biotech corn field has ruined his honey harvest and is suing the biotech farmer for damages. . . .

Less visible to the public, but still very effective, is the pressure imposed by anti-biotech groups on the feed and food industries. For example, the Greenpeace website has a "blacklist" containing the name of any biotech food product marketed in France. Experience has shown that the negative publicity generated by offering a biotech product in a French supermarket is usually so detrimental that the retailer or distributor removes the product from the shelf. . . .

French biotech farmers have found little governmental support for their efforts. Nathalie Kosciusco-Morizet, the new Minister of State for Ecology, advocates a strong precautionary approach and only supports biotech research. . . .

Farmers are also frustrated that the police, in general, observe and tolerate the crop destructions, and the judicial system metes out moderate punishment to the activists who are prosecuted. In one case, the activists were found not guilty by reason of necessity, basically allowing them a self-defense argument that biotech development could be harmful to public health. The French legislature has also failed to pass any substantive measures on behalf of the biotech farmers.

France—government, labor, farmer, environmentalist, consumer, retailer, police, judge—appears here a multi-frontal *L'armée des ombres*, à la Jean-Pierre Melville's Resistance flick, against GMO occupation. The following year France went nuclear on the GMO efforts, suspending MON810 cultivation.[17] Monsanto claims Greenpeace/ Friends of the Earth reached a de facto agreement with the government. In return for the government acting against GMOs, joining Austria, Hungary, Greece, Luxembourg, and later Germany, environmentalists, according to Monsanto, would turn a blind eye to President Sarkozy's nuclear energy initiatives.

France turned next to stirring trouble elsewhere, urging member states to review EU renewal of MON810. By such external pressure and indigenous resistance, a rollback appeared imminent in what had been a MON810 stronghold—Spain next door. Catalonia, Basque Country, and the Canary Islands legislated themselves GMO-free or with strict biotech coexistence clauses, with Catalonia a particular problem as it is a center for GMO corn production. As was the case in France, the central government is under increasing pressure to ban MON810 production and imports:

> Agricultural factions against agricultural biotechnology include the environmental side of [the Ministry of the Environment and Rural and Marine Affairs] and organic farmers. Increasingly, consumers are also expressing negative attitudes toward genetically modified crops. On April 18th, the newspaper "El Pas" conducted a survey on whether or not GM food should be prohibited. The following results were obtained after a one month period: 85 percent voted "Yes, they can be dangerous" and 15 percent voted "No, they are absolutely safe."

Given these complications, U.S. Embassy Madrid, acting on the behalf of GMO proponents, requested Washington take action, and sought advice from other posts, crystallizing the continental extent of the United States' GMO campaign and its claim to the scientific mantel:

> In response to recent urgent requests by MARM State Secretary Josep Puxeu and Monsanto, post requests renewed USG support of Spain's science-based agricultural biotechnology position through high-level USG intervention in support of the [European Food Safety Authority] findings. Post also requests USG support for a non-USG science fellow to meet with influential Spanish interlocutors on this issue and assistance with developing an agricultural biotechnology action plan for Spain. Post would also welcome any comments from other posts concerning the anti-GMO campaign.

As if there couldn't possibly be scientific objections to GMOs' health, ecological, and economic impacts.[18]

INDEED, EVEN THE PAPACY, LORD KNOWS culpable for a global crime or two, gets served a wafer of condescension:

> When individual Church leaders, for ideological reasons or ignorance, speak out against GMOs, the Vatican does not—at least not yet—feel that it is its duty to challenge them. Post will continue to lobby the Vatican to speak up in favor of GMOs, in the hope that a louder voice in Rome will encourage individual Church leaders elsewhere to reconsider their critical views.[19]

The EU, however, is by no means the sole market on which American GMOs are marching. WikiLeaks details the extent to which U.S. embassies act as agribusiness subsidiaries in the Global South.

In a 2009 cable, to pick one out of the pile, the embassy in Nairobi gives the impression of a much smoother GMO introduction in

Kenya.[20] Kenya was the first African country to sign off on the Cartagena Protocol on Biosafety but took until February 2009 to establish a legal framework for the use of and trade in genetically modified organisms, joining South Africa, Tanzania, Uganda, Malawi, Mali, Zimbabwe, Nigeria, and Ghana:

> Following the demise of Kenya's cotton industry and renewed fears of widespread hunger and famine, biotechnology proponents, pointing to the success of GMO agriculture in South Africa, made the case before Parliament last fall that the technology could help revive Kenyan cotton and address the country's chronic food insecurity . . . Previously some were unduly concerned about the potential risks posed by the technology. Their anxieties blocked potential corn imports by requiring that imported corn not exceed a two percent adventitious presence for biotechnology-produced corn. This provision led to unnecessary corn supply constraints resulting in food deficits and artificially high corn prices.

The cable presumes a convenient causality without substantiation. Widespread hunger in Kenya, for one, arises in part from the kind of land grabbing biotechnology serves to legitimize.[21] Whatever its practical merits, technology is often used as a Trojan horse by which to smuggle in new social relations, in this case enriching Kenya's elite and its multinational beneficiaries at the expense of small farmers. Corn, for another, is a global commodity, its price controlled in part by commodity markets and the grain dumping undertaken by heavily subsidized multinationals.[22]

The U.S. government offered Kenyan GMO proponents more than mere liaison support via the local embassy:[23]

> [The] USAID-funded Program for Biosafety Systems created linkages among key [Kenyan] national institutions, thus building support for the bill among policymakers and biosafety regulatory agencies. The program also provided technical regulatory support to facilitate confined field trials of genetically modified cotton and corn.

The results have proven transformative, helping commercialize biotech crops:

> Genetically modified products that have been approved for contained and confined field trials include insect-resistant maize and cotton, tissue culture bananas, GM sweet potato, virus-resistant cassava, and rinderpest vaccine. Confined field trials of genetically modified insect-resistant cotton and maize are already underway in Kenya. The Kenya Agricultural Research Institute intends to begin open field trials of transgenic cotton Bt in October 2009.

Contrary to the cable's characterization of a polite and loyal opposition, Kenyans are deeply divided by GMOs' introduction in the field, now scheduled for maize by 2017. According to Paige Aarhus:

> Farmers here are skeptical of risking everything for a few seasons of higher yields. In Kangundo, [smallholder Fred] Kiambaa said he would try GM technology if it was a matter of life or death—but he is wary.
>
> Kiambaa uses the Katumani breed of maize, a widely available seed that is reasonably drought-tolerant and affordable. Higher yields are tempting, of course, but Kiambaa said he doesn't want to chance his livelihood on a foreign corporation. While his family has been on the land for decades now, Kiambaa said they didn't get to farm it until British colonialists returned it to local farmers. He pointed out trees that line the steep hillside, planted by the British.
>
> "It's because of Mzungus that we have charcoal," he said, smiling wryly.[24]

No review in Kenya has been directed at the potential socioecological costs of GMOs, both in-country and abroad, notably India: crop failures, pesticide resistance, superpests, farmer debt and suicide, production spirals trapping locals into purchasing an expanding series of company inputs. Indeed, such failure is agribusiness's own reward as it takes advantage of widespread collapse by buying up land smallholders are forced to abandon.

The research gap is no accident, as several of Kenya's institutes are wholly in Monsanto's pocket. Writes Aarhus:

> At the African Agricultural Technology Foundation (AATF), a massive NGO working on GM research and development in partnership with [the Kenya Agricultural Research Institute], Regulatory Affairs Manager Dr. Francis Nang'ayo says GM crops are "substantially equivalent" to non-genetically modified foods and should be embraced as a solution to persistent drought and hunger.
>
> In 2008, the AATF received a $47 million grant from the Bill and Melinda Gates Foundation. This partnership involved the Howard G. Buffett Foundation and American seed giant Monsanto [in which the Gates Foundation holds $23.1 million in shares].

The gap reproduces one found at American land grant universities, where farmer-instigated investigations and public varieties have been abandoned in favor of a research agenda for which agribusiness pays. Many Kenyans object to the dereliction, including Anne Maina, advocacy coordinator for the African Biodiversity Network, a coalition of sixty-five Kenyan farming organizations:

> "Our public research institutions must shift their focus back to farmers' needs," she told *The Indypendent*, "rather than support the agenda of agribusiness, which is to colonize our food and seed chain. We believe that the patenting of seed is deeply unethical and dangerous."

Yet the only skeptic the embassy's cable acknowledges is Dr. Willy Tonui, a researcher then at the Kenya Medical Research Institute and the African Biological Safety Association, who asked that the Biosafety Act be amended to "capture bio-safety concerns":

> But for the vast majority of professionals in the field, biotechnology holds the promise of improved food security in Kenya.[25]

Even Tonui, now CEO at the National Biosafety Authority, is no opponent, however. Three years later we find that

> Tonui claims media hysteria and inaccurate reporting are to blame for resistance to GM technology, arguing the NBA maintains stringent guidelines about GM seeds in Kenya.[26]

PRIVATE CHELSEA MANNING, WHO ALLEGEDLY released the U.S. cables to WikiLeaks and the world, suffered sexual humiliation and solitary confinement while eight months in a Marine brig in Quantico, Virginia.[27] She better embodies what we should hope the rest of the world can draw from the United States than anything in the documents.

We can honor Manning's act of conscience by investigating and publicizing (and funding) WikiLeaked finds. What I covered here represents only a minuscule fraction of food and pharmaceutical items in the cables. Some of it *was* reported in the early days of the cables' release, including Pfizer's dirty trick and France's MON810 rejection, but I discovered that only in reading the cables directly could I grasp all the plot points and subtleties in tone and context that many of the articles missed.

Much more, however, has gone unreported. I came across whole batches dedicated to the Brazilian landless movement, Russian deforestation, anti-HIV generics, whaling off Japan and Iceland, and over 3,000 cables on influenza alone. All of these and more are now open to scholars, journalists, activists and anyone else looking for and sharing insight on the logistics of empire, typically conducted under the veil of secrecy, and, surprisingly given the clout on hand, over many a bad meal:

> Over rubbery fish at an Adenauer Stiftung affair on April 27, External Relations Commissioner Chris Patten touched briefly on why the EU will never be a "real power," the dubious backgrounds of some of the leaders of the EU's new members, next steps on Cyprus/Turkey, the differences between a union and an alliance, and Russian President Putin's "killer's eyes." . . .

Cautioning that "I'm not saying that genes are determinant," Patten then reviewed Putin family history: grandfather part of Lenin's special protection team, father a Communist Party apparatchik, and Putin himself decided at a young age to pursue a career in the KGB. "He seems a completely reasonable man when discussing the Middle East or energy policy, but when the conversation shifts to Chechnya or Islamic extremism, Putin's eyes turn to those of a killer."[28]

—*JACOBIN*, 5 SEPTEMBER 2012

Synchronize Your Barns

I gave the following speech on pathogen virulence I co-wrote with Katie Atkins, now of the London School of Hygiene and Tropical Medicine, to the Food and Agriculture Organization's Animal Production and Health Division. The speech, edited for the page, asks which livestock production landscapes produce the deadliest influenzas.

HIGHLY PATHOGENIC INFLUENZA H5N1—bird flu—surprised us on two accounts. First, there was its direct transmission from birds to humans. Second, it proved deadly to birds and humans alike. Today we'll be addressing the latter: Why so deadly?

There are a number of proximate explanations:[29]

- The polybasic site in hemagglutinin expands the virus's tissue range.
- The lysine replacement at position 627 in the PB2 protein increases viral replication in mammals. The SR polymorphism does the same in birds.
- An alternate reading frame for the PB1 protein causes greater cell death and an attenuated immune response.

These, among other molecular mechanisms, are important insights. They help us characterize the nature of the virus's pathogenesis, its modes of infection, as well as vaccine and drug targets. But causality extends beyond such mechanisms.

For a pathogen pool that dynamically spreads and contracts across multiple host species and over a large geographic range, we need to investigate the circumstances under which such molecular adaptations are selected. Why evolve a particular characteristic then and there? It seems any explanation for influenza's evolution that omits such context is by definition incomplete.[30]

CONSIDERABLE MODELING HAS BEEN CONDUCTED around the relationship between pathogen epidemiology and virulence,[31] but little of such work has been conducted within an agricultural context. Is one agricultural production system more likely to select for a virulent strain over others? Would backyard or intensive farming be more likely to do so? What of live bird markets? Is it the mix of farms that matters? Is there a spatial or functional configuration of farms across the landscape that most likely selects for virulence?

There has been a recent radiation of new livestock influenzas, concurrent with the spreading Livestock Revolution—the accelerated growth in demand for meat and the expansion, vertical integration, and consolidation of the meat sector.[32] A growing number of novel H5 and H7 highly pathogenic infections are shown to be unrelated to any previous high pathogenic presence, including evidence of on-site transitions from low to high pathogenicity.[33]

The very nature of stockbreeding has dramatically shifted the broiler *filière* in space and time, extending supply lines and compressing product turnaround. The shifts are apparent at the global scale and within individual countries. It is a reasonable question to ask if such changes are responsible for, or at the very least related to, the new virulence: increased population sizes, increased densities, declining genetic diversity, increasing throughput speed, ever-younger livestock, increasing geographic concentrations, overlapping geographies of different livestock species, more extensive transport, and an increasing encroachment on forest and wetlands expanding the interface between livestock and wildlife.

Certainly suggestive, if anything. There is now more "food" for the virus to eat and the more voracious strains should outcompete the rest.

WHAT EVIDENCE IS THERE THAT LIVESTOCK ecologies support such evolution?

Dhanasekaran Vijaykrishna and colleagues show that H5N1 underwent a population increase—and an attendant cladogenetic burst, a burst in diversity—only when the virus entered populations of domestic ducks and geese in China.[34] At the genome level, the series of reassortment events that amped up virulence occurred only when H5N1 entered domestic populations.

In a broader review, Capua and Alexander, reviewing influenza outbreaks worldwide up to 2004, before the goose outbreaks at Lake Qinghai, found no endemic highly pathogenic strains in wild bird populations, the ultimate reservoir of nearly all influenza subtypes.[35] Instead, multiple low-pathogenic influenza subtypes in such populations developed greater virulence only once they entered populations of domestic birds.

A series of seroepidemiological studies show multiple influenza types widespread across China's poultry chain. Wang and colleagues showed H9 widespread, especially among poultry market retailers and wholesalers, and workers in large-scale poultry-breeding enterprises.[36] Zhang and colleagues meanwhile followed H9N2 outbreaks over five years in a single broiler chicken operation in Shanghai.[37] Virus across all outbreaks in the plant appeared related to that of the first outbreak despite repeated vaccination and other biosecurity efforts.

Graham's group found significantly greater odds for H5N1 outbreaks in Thailand in 2004 in large-scale commercial poultry operations than in backyard flocks.[38] The pattern is repeated across influenza serotypes.[39] In British Columbia in 2004, 5 percent of large farms and 2 percent of small farms hosted outbreaks of highly pathogenic H7N3. In the Netherlands in 2003, 17 percent of industrial farms and 0.1 percent of backyard farms hosted H7N7 outbreaks. Of the twenty outbreaks we found in the influenza literature undergoing shifts from low to high pathogenicity, all except one appeared in large-scale commercial enterprises.

Many examples and sources of data. But can a virulent influenza first evolve and succeed in such context from first principles? And what is the mechanism by which a production system might select for virulence?

BEFORE ANSWERING, WE NEED to back up a bit and review some key concepts in modeling virulence. Virulence is most generally defined as the amount of damage a pathogen causes its host.[40] Some pathogens newly introduced to a host species can cause serious damage—think Ebola—but the virulence there results from no evolutionary interplay between host and pathogen that any tenable evolutionary theory of virulence would require. We're instead interested in the ways changes in host population dynamics might affect viral characteristics over the course of their coevolution.

Several key concepts have emerged over the past thirty years of modeling.

First, there appears a relationship between *virulence* and *transmission*.[41] Pathogens must typically replicate enough to reach a quorum at which they can transmit to the next host. The faster and/or more extensive that replication, the greater the damage to the host. Replicate too fast and you kill your host before getting a chance to infect the next susceptible. As a result, you break your chain of transmission. In other words, the amount of damage a pathogen inflicts on a host must track the rate of susceptibles encountered and successfully infected.

Second, there's a relationship between *virulence* and *immune clearance*.[42] An immune system that clears a pathogen faster also selects for a pathogen that can better replicate in the face of that clearance.

Third, *coinfection* matters.[43] How related competing strains are to each other should help determine virulence. Unrelated strains compete with each other for the limited resources in each host.

Fourth, no matter how fast or slow transmission occurs, ultimately it is the *supply of susceptibles* that determines virulence.[44] Local host population growth alone can determine that supply. As long as there is food to be eaten, the most voracious strains can continue to outcompete other strains, whatever the transmission rates, and without cutting off their own transmission chains.

I'VE ENCAPSULATED THREE DECADES of modeling in short order. There's more to it, but that's enough for our purposes. Little of this kind of modeling has been conducted within an agroepizoological context, though that is starting to change. Eunha Shim and Alison Galvani, for instance, modeled the effects of post-outbreak culling and vaccination on the evolution of influenza virulence.[45] They showed that culling, depopulating an infected herd or barn, a primary course of intervention in livestock disease control, selects for *greater* virulence in influenza and *lesser* natural host resistance. The time needed for resistance to reach threshold levels in a host population, levels at which a virus can't invade, is minimized for culling rates that are about equal only to the background poultry mortality. In other words, with natural resistance in mind, better to cull not at all.

Rapid culling can eliminate influenza but at the cost of failing to select for host resistance to the circulating strain. As a result, the system fails to engage in self-correction and repeated culling events are required if the virus proves persistent or re-invades. Indeed, in delaying or even denying host resistance, culling—and to a lesser extent vaccination—may upon cessation cause *greater* livestock mortality in the longterm.

In some sense, though, Shim and Galvani get ahead of themselves. Yes, culling post-outbreak may affect virulence, but what about *before* the outbreak? Aren't the day-to-day operations of raising and slaughtering poultry and livestock culling by another name? Does the *filière* itself select for virulence? What kinds of production are more likely to select for virulence?

We can reorder Shim and Galvani's model to look at pre-outbreak selection for virulence. The new model follows the usual method for quantifying virulence selection by assuming a trade-off between transmission rate and virulence rate; that is, there is a cost to the strain when its virulence outpaces a certain transmission rate.

We assume constant population size. R_0, the reproductive number, is a fitness metric of the expected secondary infections produced by a single case in a fully susceptible population. The long-term stable strategy, the one that wins out, can be found in the viral phenotype whose virulence maximizes this fitness. That is, the virus that tunes its evolved deadliness in such a way as to maximize its infection across the host population.

R_0 can be written as a function of harvesting rate and genetic susceptibility, both of which can help show how agricultural production systems can shape the long-term virulence observed. We maximize R_0 when the transmission matches infectiousness (the latter modified by disease mortality, background mortality, the harvesting rate, and the clearance rate).

THE MODEL SHOWS, FIRST, that the harvesting rate indeed can select for a greater virulence rate.

Second, genetic susceptibility, acting to slow the clearance rate inside the host, doesn't affect virulence, as we have defined it. Although, if increasing genetic susceptibility manifests as an increasing recovery time, it may act to increase the damage the host feels, but that's unrelated to the direct evolutionary dynamics between host and pathogen.

We can look at cohort duration or finishing time as well—how long the birds are allowed to live before sacrifice. Strain fitness here is only a function of cohort duration when the cohort duration is less than the infectiousness. Rearranging the terms of our model, we find that there is a *critical value of virulence* above which the reproductive number does *not* depend on the cohort duration.

When we set these variables to values from the field—infectious period (1–7 days), natural mortality rate (0.0005) and cohort duration (30–70 days)—the critical virulence value is less than zero, implying the host's recovery time and the expected fitness of a strain are *independent* of the duration of the cohort, even under industrial conditions.[46]

That's a surprise. We expected that a shorter cohort duration would put pressure on the virus to increase its viral load, causing greater damage to the host, in order to leave its hosts faster before the shorter harvest takes place. But the problem here is that the infectious period is too short even for industrial finishing time.

The result appears marred by a technical glitch we'll need to fix. R_0 maximization determines the long-term preferred evolutionary strategy for the trait, in this case virulence. But R_0 may not be consistent with the cohort (and bounded) nature of harvesting, and so may offer an inappropriate metric for strain fitness.

Secondly, and this is more interesting, the model here focuses on the *individual* infectious period. Influenza's infectious period (no more than a week) will likely never approach industrial finishing time, even under the most rapid throughput speed (presently forty days). Selection occurring at another level of organization—namely *across the poultry or livestock cohort*—may better bear down on the relationship between finishing time and virulence.

Even as individual infections die off, the outbreak continues to propagate on the farm over several continuous viral generations until a strain can infect enough birds to threaten violating biocontainment and spreading to the next barn or farm. If that's the case, the time it takes to successfully propagate to such a threshold of infected birds may approach finishing time. From this perspective, it's the final number of birds infected that is the key variable, and *not* the individual infectious period.

If so, reducing finishing time could affect the evolution of virulence. A shortened finishing time may select for strains able to reach the propagation threshold faster (before the cohort is slaughtered).

IF VIRULENCE INCREASES AS A RESULT, and symptoms become more obvious, the farmer may be alerted to the outbreak and kill off the cohort before the pathogen can reach the next barn. We need ask if such culling, shortening finishing time still further, would only select for still greater virulence or, as appears the case in some influenzas, select against such noisy symptoms but not against the virus's deadliness.[47] The farmer's intentions—biosecurity or market day—matter little from the virus's perspective, except, perhaps, as something to solve.

A practical consideration, however, comes to mind. If we are intent on running large-scale farms, we might be able to reduce a highly pathogenic strain's access to susceptibles by *synchronizing* harvesting and repopulation across barns. In that way virulent strains would be unable to find a nearby population in an early stockbreeding stage, one in which the next round of propagation can be successfully conducted. The strategy mimics the birthing bursts undertaken by prey populations. No predator can possibly prey upon all the neonates, allowing a large proportion of the offspring to reach their size refuge unscathed.

Such a strategy flies in the face of industrial practice. Barns of livestock, even all-in all-out, are raised out of phase to permit the market a continual supply of mature animals. Out-of-phase slaughter also permits using a small labor force to move and cull across a large farming operation.

Influenza apparently never received the memo that it is expected to cooperate with industry standards.

OUR FIRST MODEL OFFERED ONLY an analysis of *asymptotic* fitness: Which strain wins out in the end once population equilibrium is arrived upon? But in the past week we came to understand that we should also ask about the *transient* dynamics. Under what conditions in the short term, from initial introduction, would a high-path strain win out? What kind of agricultural system is likely to permit a single low-pathogenic infection to ramp up in virulence? That remains work to be done.

In the meantime, we tried another approach, one that assumed a low-path infection already present. Could a high-path strain successfully invade and replace resident low-path strains? In the interest of time I will skip much of the formalism, save to say that we can distinguish the reproductive value for the high-path strain under different culling regimens, either when only those birds that are infectious are culled or when all are culled.

A reminder that only when the high-path's reproductive value is greater than 1 can it invade the resident low-path population. Our preliminary results show that, one, increasing the harvesting rate increases the chance of high-path emergence.

Two, increasing low-path prevalence *decreases* the chance of high-path emergence—by decreasing the susceptible population via a kind of natural vaccination, as it were.

Three, wild bird-to-domestic bird transmissibility at the same time reduces the chance of high-path emergence by natural vaccination even as it also increases such a chance by increasing the variation on which selection for a high-path strain can draw.

Finally, post-outbreak culling (without repopulating farms) *decreases* the chance of the high-path strain successfully invading by culling out infected birds (sources of new infections) as well as susceptibles (sinks for any new infection).

AS TO THE QUESTION OF THE MIX of landscapes, we haven't started modeling that, sorry. It's in the pipeline. Specifically, we'll be looking at industrial farm/live bird market dynamics as they affect virulence across time and space. We'll also be looking at the different types of production systems as they are related to each other across the landscape.

But allow us here some observations to hint at where we are going with this.

Under the kind of non-spatial trade-off between transmission and virulence with which we began today, the pool of susceptibles is shared across all variants everywhere. A new literature dedicated to *spatial models* of virulence shows that in a spatially structured population this need not be the case.[48] One variant can overexploit its pool of susceptibles driving itself into extinction in one area, without driving all other variants extinct elsewhere. High-path and low-path strains can coexist.

A number of factors appear key to producing a landscape in which low-path strains can persist. Low *host reproduction* and highly localized *host interaction* together produce such a landscape. Different pathogen strains are hereby exposed to their own pools of susceptibles. Restrained *host dispersal*, where hosts move, amplifies the effect. Such structure permits selection on virulence to act according to the constraints of a competition-persistence trade-off—you shouldn't kill off your limited local source of hosts.

There exists, then, a *critical connectivity*—say, within a network of Vietnamese farm communes and the live bird markets they supply—that would allow the more virulent strains to break out of their local cages and invade distal low-path reservoirs.[49] In other words, a growing connectivity changes the rules under which the evolution of virulence takes place.

Indeed, increasing access to susceptibles across the landscape could in and of itself select for greater virulence regardless of the transmission rate. Invasion alone changes the evolution of the virus.

HOW MIGHT ALL THAT WE HAVE discussed today play out in our landscapes of small and large livestock and poultry producers? We showed previously that continuous harvesting of longer duration permits low-pathogenic strains to circulate among smallholder populations, locking out high-path by a natural vaccination (conditional on the right molecular cross-reactivity and wide-enough low-path dispersal).

In contrast, industrial stockbreeding, by short-term discrete harvesting and at the level of among-barns and among-farms a mix-age mosaic of cohorts in close proximity, keeps a steady supply of susceptibles at peak epidemic levels, at which pathogenicity appears best selected.

The real perversity may arise at the landscape level.

At a first approximation, at the level of individual farms, virulence may be selected against in backyard birds or, with enough biosecurity, in industrial birds. But when less-regulated industrial farms are embedded in the peri-urban landscapes of the emerging economies, a critical connectivity may be reached and the evolutionary game changes.

From out of the surrounding landscape, low-path influenza may be sucked into the intensive farms, where the evolution of virulence, fed by the variety of low-pathogenic strains, can be ramped up. Once high-path is selected for there, it may blow back into the greater landscape, into wildlife and backyard livestock by way of porous ecological interfaces and along commodity networks.

Secondly, as the spatial modeling of virulence informs us, increasing host reproduction, expanding the extent of host interactions, and increasing host dispersal by regionalizing the commodity network—all as intensive husbandry aims for—may permit highly pathogenic strains to both evolve greater virulence and invade low-path populations.

So the decision to introduce intensive farming on the industrial model into smallholder landscapes may offer a transformative effect on virulence. The effect may not necessarily arise from the farms in and of themselves, though that is clearly still on the table, but from their relationship with the local landscape, including indigenous production systems and local wildlife.

—22 OCTOBER 2010

The Dirty Dozen

You have total control over nearly every aspect of your egg laying and egg processing operations. From rearing, feeding and housing birds to processing and marketing eggs, your job requires you to manage just about everything. You don't need insurance added to the list.

— NATIONWIDE INSURANCE WEBSITE (2016)

THE CHICKEN OR THE EGG? Scientists from Sheffield and Warwick recently claimed the chicken came first.[50] A species-specific protein, ovocleidin-17, must be present in the mother's ovary if the eggshell is to grow.

But evolutionary arguments trump appeals to molecular pathways, says biologist PZ Meyers.[51] Ovocleidins, one of a large family of C-type lectin-like proteins often involved in binding calcium, didn't evolve upon chicken's speciation, but were already long in use, including in cell signaling and cell adhesion.[52] The presence of this specific protein speaks little to the transition to the modern chicken, whose ancestors, duh, laid eggs themselves. Indeed, we have little idea when the ovocleidin-17 evolved. It could have happened long *after* the first chicken.

Team Egg claims instead that a series of meiotic mutations and cross-hybridizations were required before the jungle chicken could speciate from its ancestral stock.[53] Something else may have laid the first minted chicken, if anyone took notice in the Indochinese jungle, but it's *that* egg that grew up into the first modern chicken.

Under the Livestock Revolution we have, characteristically, a reversal in causality. Layers had to be bred away from broilers and the production line vertically integrated from fertilization to freezer before the first fully Big Ag egg spun free out from underneath its mum's bum. The turnabout extends from origins to operations. Evolution generates biodiversity aplenty, although losing it in bouts of stochastic extirpation or—guano happens—during catastrophic extinction. Industrial agriculture aims instead at *reducing* the diversity of poultry breeds, as much as a matter of principle as practice.

IN 1940 HENRY B. WALLACE DEVELOPED the first breed of industrially hybridized chicken at what would become Hy-line International, a spin-off of the agricultural company his father, former U.S. Secretary of Agriculture, Vice President, and presidential candidate Henry A. Wallace, founded in 1936.[54] Within a decade, nearly all commercial poultry breeders worldwide multiplied stock from these Hy-line hybrids, which by 1960 numbered 70 million. Broilers would eventually grow three times faster on less than half the feed. The growth, brought about in part by selecting against the pituitary-regulated cap on appetite, would come at the cost of the kind of skeletal morbidity and stress mortality—including tibial dyschondroplasia—associated with growing so much meat on so many birds bunched together atop spindly legs.[55] Hy-line layers were meanwhile selected for producing one egg a day, up from 250 eggs a year.

Today, as a result of a wave of consolidation, nearly three-quarters of the world's poultry production is in the hands of a few multinationals.[56] The primary breeders, who engineer the first three generations of broiler lines commercial multipliers market, declined from eleven companies in 1989 to four in 2006. The ten companies producing layer lines in 1989 were consolidated to two by 2006.

The Erich Wesjohann Group, which now controls Hy-Line International USA, Lohmann Tierzucht, H&N International, and Aviagen, services multipliers across eighty-five countries with 68 percent of the industry's white egg production and 17 percent of brown egg production. Hendrix Genetics, producing ISA, Babcock , Shaver, Hisex, Bovans, and Dekalb layers across one hundred countries, controls 80 percent of brown egg and 32 percent of white egg production.

Hendrix holds a 50 percent stake in Nutreco Holding, which breeds broilers, turkeys, pigs, and day-olds and eggs under its Hybro, Hybrid, Hypor, and Plumex subsidiaries. The Grimaud Group is the second-largest company in avian genetics and specializes in specialty markets (colored chickens, ducklings, guinea fowls, rabbits, and pigeons). Cobb-Vantress, finally, is owned by Tyson Foods, the world's largest processor and marketer of chicken meat.

The value of the products these primary breeders provide is biologically "locked" by offering multiplier companies only the males of the male lines and females of the female line.[57] As a result batches of hybrid chickens—trade secrets—must, in the poultry equivalent of Monsanto seed, be continuously purchased. By this industrial cascade, a single-source male chicken can generate *millions* of broiler progeny.

Any unplanned diversity is controlled for in production. In 2009, Mercy for Animals, a Chicago-based animal rights group, released undercover video of a conveyer belt at Hy-Line's North American hatchery in Spenser, Iowa, shuttling live male chicks into an automated meat grinder.[58] The video shows birds on the factory floor, some of whom are apparently hurt falling off the belt. While Hy-Line issued a statement that the video "appears to show an inappropriate action and violation of our animal welfare policies," in reference to the chicks found on the floor, the practice of grinding layer male chicks, who by definition can't lay eggs, is industry standard:

> "There is, unfortunately, no way to breed eggs that only produce female hens," said [United Egg Producers] spokesman [Mitch] Head. "If someone has a need for 200 million male chicks [annually], we're happy to provide them to anyone who wants them. But we can find no market, no need."

Head's argument, an attempt to affirm a consequence, is fallacious in the extreme. Yes, we can't breed only female hens, but what's at issue here are the premises of an industry that by market imperatives of its own making must grind alive half its product. There *are* other ways of running hatcheries, without such waste and without such cruelty.

The production practices and the industry's consolidation dramatically reduces the size and number of breeding populations under selection, and, ironically, the number of geneticists working on them, the consequences of which, as Ilse Koehler-Rollefson points out, are raising even insiders' alarms.[59] James Arthur and Gerard Albers of Hy-Line and Nutreco, respectively, put it:

> There is also concern about the narrowness of the base of the genetic stock now being marketed. There is danger in this situation due to the potential susceptibility of "monocultures" to new diseases that could destroy or damage a genetically uniform population, as happened with maize in the southern corn leaf blight epidemic in the US in 1970.[60]

So there was a reason for all that hot chicken sex in the jungle. Meiotic recombination offers eukaryotes the means of responding in near real time to rapid pathogen evolution. Cladogenesis—ever producing new variants—protected against annihilation at higher taxonomic levels. Funny, then, that America's hostility to evolution as a concept extends to its scientific stockbreeding, from where the rest of the world's industrial poultry practices originated, as Darwin's good book so depended on the conceit of bird breeding and artificial selection.

At least, then, the industry now recognizes its responsibilities in conserving the diversity it destroys. Not at all, writes Janet Fulton of Hy-Line:

> It has been suggested that industry should be maintaining poultry genetic resources, as industry has gained the most from the use of this variation, and they can afford to maintain it. However, the poultry breeding industry consists of a very small number of highly competitive companies. They have very tight financial responsibilities. Lines not performing at required economic levels will be eliminated. Every merger between breeding companies results in elimination of lines with lesser economic efficiency. Industry is not the location for preservation of genetic variation of limited value today, but with potential value tomorrow.[61]

FULTON ARGUES THAT THE PRICE FOR industrial practices must instead be borne by the public. Governments must cover the costs of preserving animal germplasm.

The money backing such a dangerous operation—building billions of birds incapable of evolving their own immune protection—also blocks efforts at controlling the resulting danger. Over the past decade a group of U.S. egg farmers attempted to institute epizootic controls on their own but bore the brunt of the competition Fulton treats as first and foremost the natural order of things.[62] Those operations that didn't bother spending money on such prevention grew at their more conscientious competitors' expense. When an agricultural sector "self-regulates," it almost invariably favors the refusal to act.

When in 2000 the egg industry finally agreed to being regulated, the United States, across administrations, somehow failed over the next nine years to devise and implement the rules to which many in the industry were prepared to agree. The power of money—crippling regulation in Congress and the federal agencies—is so absolute as to poison a sector's own efforts to save itself.

Even positive momentum in the face of such inertia is diverted. A report from the Cornucopia Institute shows factory farms are skirting USDA rules on organic labeling.[63] Some operations are offering penned birds limited access to enclosed porches or stocking mass numbers in movable henhouses, as if a peek of daylight or a new patch of dirt constituted parole enough.

More sincere efforts within the sector, embodied in some advances in biosecurity—absurdly heroic efforts more indictment than solution—fail to paper over inherent flaws in the chosen industrial model.[64] Namely, in the end, a sharp epidemiological potential, ultimately held back only by a chronically defective dam of pharmaceuticals, will always be present when thousands of monoculture poultry are packed together.

The irony, then, is that bad eggs, if you'll excuse the pun, are rewarded with the kinds of investment needed to expand unsafe production and the distribution that transports pathogens across state lines. The *New York Times* places one, Wright County Egg owner Austin J. DeCoster, at the scene of just about every U.S. salmonella outbreak since the late 1970s.[65] Why, then, was his company, the source of a 2010 outbreak of enteritidis that sickened thousands of Americans and led to a recall of a half-billion eggs, allowed to operate so long?

While the geography of production and distribution is national, and increasingly international, the geography of food regulation in the United States largely runs state-to-state. Despite state pleas, the feds, under industry pressure, kept hands-off on egg safety for twenty years, with the expected uneven enforcement (and widespread illness) a result. Although Maryland and Maine imposed stringent testing on DeCoster farms—and New York banned DeCoster eggs altogether—Iowa, where the 2010 outbreak originated, did not. As a result, outbreaks have typically run far beyond any one local government's grasp, which means food-borne pathogens can routinely find holes in the United States' regulatory fabric. Even states with excellent farm enforcement in place can suffer outbreaks from animal products shipped in from more susceptible areas.

The best of states can themselves, in turn, serve as sources when local regulation of *production*, however excellent, fails to keep up with the range, complexity, and speed of *distribution*. In 2012 Minnesota-based Michael Foods recalled hard-cooked eggs—used in deviled eggs, Cobb salad, deli potato salad—from across thirty-four states when *Listeria* was discovered in the company's Wakefield, Nebraska, plant.[66] The same strain had hit Michael Foods' brown potatoes three years previously.

Agribusiness sees a lesson here, indeed, but it's not the one you'd think. The industry views the globalization spreading poultry and livestock disease as the very means of protecting the industry, appearing as much against efforts to control diseases as, if you'll allow the anthropomorphism, the diseases themselves.[67] Again, Fulton of Hy-Line:

> Protection of the elite commercial lines against various natural disasters is of great concern. Housing of pedigree lines at remote locations is security against losses caused by fire, tornado, or other physical disaster. Also, disease outbreaks can kill or

reproductively damage valuable breeding stocks. Multiple locations are insurance against these types of losses. . . .

This has become a very important issue within the past 3 yrs. Outbreaks of disease, such as avian influenza, exotic Newcastle Disease, and lymphoid leucosis have resulted in importation restriction for hatching eggs or chicks by some countries. These embargoes are frequently politically based, as disease-affected flocks may be hundreds of miles away from the source of the hatching eggs or chicks to be exported. These embargoes can completely halt the export of breeding stock, effectively closing down all international business. The embargo boundaries are politically defined. Thus, these additional flocks must be located in different countries.[68]

A second irony is that heavy biosecurity may at times make matters demonstratively worse. In eliminating low-pathogenic salmonella, industrial operations may have opened up a niche for more dangerous strains:

One theory, by Andreas J. Bäumler, a microbiologist at the University of California, Davis, ties the bacterium's emergence to the virtual eradication of two related strains of salmonella that make chickens sick. Once those strains were stamped out, through culling of infected birds, the theory goes, immunity to similar strains of salmonella decreased. That opened up a niche for enteritidis to thrive.[69]

Low-pathogenic strains, as discussed in the preceding essay, may very well act as a kind of natural inoculation under certain circumstances. These include the kinds of technical and economic support of which many village-based, free-range poultry production systems in the developing world have been largely expropriated.[70] How one might go about organizing production around such a possibility—integrating socially cognizant ecohealth approaches across the landscape—is utterly outside the present industrial paradigm. It's as if a bunch of extraterrestrials extended us a limb we couldn't recognize.

Do we shake it, risking our civilization's existence at such a diplomatic offense?

We have so little understanding of what an integrated agriculture might look like, if only because at present even for the greenest among us, our most rudimentary thinking is bound by capital's premises, repeatedly putting the cash before the crop. As if by some strange alchemy money were more real than flesh and feathers and flu.

—8 JUNE 2012

UPDATE 1. In June 2014, Quality Egg LLC, the umbrella company for Wright County Egg, pled guilty to charges of bribing a USDA inspector to approve sales of suspect eggs, selling misbranded eggs, and introducing adulterated food to interstate commerce.[71] It also agreed to pay $6.8 million in fines. In a rare instance in which executives are held personally responsible for corporate malfeasance, Quality owner Austin DeCoster and chief operating officer Peter DeCoster, Austin's son, pled to misdemeanors for the adulterated food, each paying a $100,000 fine and facing a sentence to range from probation to a year in jail. The DeCosters, who have left the industry, could still face paying restitution to salmonella victims.

The plea bargain included new details about the DeCosters' operation. Government investigators found no evidence that the DeCosters knew of the contamination, but did uncover a Quality manager's scheme to deliberately mislabel eggs to fool regulators and consumers, including in states such as California and Arizona where state law requires eggs be sold within a month of their processing date. Eggs were also shipped without expiration dates that wholesalers later added. Both practices permitted Quality—*nomen est omen*—to circumvent selling the eggs half-price to breaker facilities that liquidize "distressed eggs."

UPDATE 2. United Egg Producers has joined the Humane Society in supporting a bipartisan bill in Congress that would amend the Eggs Products Inspection Act and nationalize new layer standards.[72] Over the next fifteen years egg farmers would be expected to provide double the cage space and include perches, scratching areas, and nesting boxes. The bill also requires egg cartons be labeled by the sources' living conditions: caged, cage-free, or free-range. The Farm Bureau, the National Pork Producers Council, and the National Cattlemen's Beef Association, fearing precedence, oppose the bill.

In October 2014, a United States District Court judge threw out a lawsuit six states filed against a new California law barring the sale of eggs produced by chickens raised in cramped conditions.[73] Alabama, Kentucky, Iowa, Missouri, Nebraska, and Oklahoma produce 20 billion eggs a year, 2 billion of which are sold in California.

"It is patently clear plaintiffs are bringing this action on behalf of a subset of each state's eggs farmers, not on behalf of each state's population generally," Judge Kimberly Mueller commented.

UPDATE 3. By 2015, even the CDC had caught up to the notion that the ownership structure of the food sector can drive both the geographic extent of outbreaks of food-borne pathogens and their virulence.[74]

The *Washington Post* summarized the CDC report:

> Major foodborne outbreaks in the United States have more than tripled in the last 20 years, and the germs most frequently implicated are familiar to most Americans: Salmonella, E. coli, and Listeria.
>
> In the most recent five-year period—from 2010 to 2014—these multistate outbreaks were bigger and deadlier than in years past, causing more than half of all deaths related to contaminated food outbreaks, public health officials said Tuesday.[75]

"Food industry consolidation," the Associated Press quoted anonymous health officials, "means companies ship to wider networks of grocery stores and restaurants than in the past, so a tainted product can appear in more states now."[76]

What, then, did the CDC recommend on the record?[77] Everything but matters of ownership. Food industries can:

- Keep records to trace foods from source to destination.
- Use store loyalty card and distribution records to help investigators identify what made people sick.
- Recall products linked to an outbreak and notify customers.
- Choose only suppliers that use food safety best practices.
- Share proven food safety solutions with others in industry.
- Make food safety a core part of company culture.
- Meet or exceed new food safety laws and regulations.

The Red Swan

The following is an excerpt of a longer piece on Nassim Taleb's "Black Swan," available online.[78] The full version adds explorations of Taleb's animosity toward science, his anti-theoretical theory of history, his assumptions about human nature, and, for good and for ill, applications of Black Swan thinking to disease modeling, with guest appearances by Bernard Baars, Bruno Bosteels, Paul Davies, Mike Davis, Jodi Dean, Philip K Dick, Terry Eagleton, William Faulkner, Richard Fortey, Errol Morris, Richard Nisbett, Raúl Ruiz, Salman Rushdie, and Nate Silver.

Taleb since has turned into more of a frenemy. There's still much with which I disagree, but he continues to thrash academic economists, who richly deserve it, as well as, as I describe in an update to the piece online, Steven Pinker on war and J. Craig Venter on GMOs.

PERHAPS BY CHANCE ALONE Nassim Nicholas Taleb's best-selling *The Black Swan: The Impact of the Highly Improbable*, followed up by the just released *Antifragile*, captures the zeitgeist of 9/11 and the foreclosure collapse: if something of a paradox, bad things unexpectedly happen routinely.[79]

For better and for worse, *Black Swan* caustically dismisses academic economics, which serve, more I must admit in my view than Taleb's, as capitalist rationalization rather than as a science of discovery. Taleb crushes statistical finance, but fails as spectacularly on a number of accounts. To the powerful's advantage at one and the same time he mathematicizes Francis Fukuyama's end of history and claims epistemological impossibilities where others, who have been systemically marginalized by the kleptocratic program, predicted precisely to dead silence.[80]

Power, after all, is the capacity to avoid addressing counternarratives.

A "BLACK SWAN" IS AN UNEXPECTED event of great impact that many an observer rationalizes after the fact. Taleb's swan, while related, differs from Karl Popper's, who proposed the search for a black swan as the proper means of testing the proposition that all swans are white.[81] To Popper, falsification offered a workaround for the problem of induction, whereby we mistakenly generalize conclusions on the basis of a few observations.

Taleb is more concerned with the reasons for, and consequences of, the failure on the part of academics and financial analysts to assimilate unexpected events into their models. According to Taleb, many researchers confuse the frequency of events with their likely effect. They confound low frequency and low impact. Anomalies, then, can be ignored. Practitioners transform the fallacy into a mathematical given. The Gaussian measures of risk most researchers use exclude Black Swans as out beyond the distributions they assume beforehand.

Taleb, for instance, sticks it to Robert Merton Jr., Nobel Laureate, father of learning portfolio theory and Long-Term Capital Management founding partner, whose Gaussian risk models, Taleb says, ruled out large deviations, leading LTCM to take on the monstrous risk that sank the firm.[82] Models—however elegant their formalism—rarely fit reality when built on false premises.

The details are worth exploration. Under the Gaussian (or normal or bell curve) distribution, the mean stabilizes as the population increases. Most of the population is distributed about the mean, with only a small fraction found in the extreme tails. As we can effectively ignore these infrequent "outliers," the population becomes characterized by particular boundaries of known dispersion.

Take a "population" of coin flips. The Gaussian emerges by two effects Taleb shines in explaining. First, if the outcomes—heads or tails—have an equal and, on each flip, independent chance, it would be highly unlikely we would end up with many of the same kind in a row the more flips we make. The unlikelihood explains why the tails of the distribution are so small, and why these extreme deviations precipitously decline in frequency the more flips we add. What, after all, are the chances we hit 32 heads in a row? Or 320?

In the second effect, the various combinations by which half (or near-half) heads/half tails can be produced increase the frequencies for the more mixed outcomes. The combinatorial explains why the frequencies around the mean are so large. There are a lot of ways of producing half heads/half tails: for four flips, for instance, HHTT, HTHT, TTHH, THTH, HTTH, and THHT. For forty flips, many, many more.

The Gaussian arbitrarily sets the standard deviation, the range $-1s$ to $1s$ straddling the mean, as containing 68.27 percent of the population. From one arbitrary metric another is derived: the variance of the population is set at s^2. The more standard deviations added, that is, the more we move away from the hump of the curve toward the tails, the more the number of observations added exponentially declines. The second and third deviations, for instance, hold 95.45 percent and 99.73 percent of values, respectively. The sharp drop-off emphasizes how much the observations are concentrated about the mean and the great unlikelihood of outliers or, at the most extreme, Black Swans.

Populations differ in their specifics, of course. The curve itself is defined by the equation

$$f(x) \ -ae^{-(x-b)^2/2c^2}$$

with a the curve's amplitude, b its position along the x-axis, and c the width of the curve. The curve's characteristic kurtosis and skew are dependent in part on the population's inherent variation and, if constructed by sampling, the size of the sample taken.

THERE ARE A NUMBER OF IRONIES in Taleb's treatment of the bell curve. He identifies an essentialism in the Gaussian view, which treats what it views as the utter unlikelihood of Black Swans as something real. The thinking of the biometricians behind the modern statistical derivation of the curve was in fact in direct opposition. As Ernst Mayer describes it, Darwinism switched biologists out of an essentialist thinking, which saw the mean organismal form as the real archetype and any deviations counterfeit to viewing reality in the variation of a population and the mean as a construct.[83]

Without explanation Taleb says he accepts the application Darwin's half-cousin Francis Galton and the latter's colleagues made of the Gaussian to genetics and heredity, probably because, if we must attach a reason, biological measurements often approximate the distribution. However, he sees in its application to social systems a sham. Human societies are inherently uncertain, Taleb says, subject neither to the law of large numbers, which underlies the Gaussian. On what grounds he frames biological systems as tidier than their social counterparts is unclear. Biological systems are routinely lurching through regime shifts that stretch out and pop normal distributions.[84]

At the same time, his assertion about human societies fails inspection. By the very statistical physics Taleb claims can circumvent Gaussian gaffes, Rodrick Wallace and Robert Fullilove show regression models explain violence and other risk behaviors at multiple geographic scales across the United States.[85] Wallace and Fullilove conclude that racial and economic apartheids stateside constrain behavioral dynamics across population and place.

In other words, social systems can *impose* the kind of structure that turns populations Gaussian in nature, even through the country's various demographic shifts, perhaps back to the founding of the Republic. Manhattan's Lower East Side, for instance, has been home to impoverished populations of black slaves, immigrant Jews, and, even now, the Latinos of Loisada.

In a third irony, Taleb sets the social origins of Gaussian statistics in the aspirations of the eighteenth-century European middle class, a sheeple, in Taleb's characterization, that bet on a future of mediocre outcomes against its fear of divergent outcomes. He attaches Saint-Simon, Proudhon, and Marx to the political hope of a statistical *aurea mediocritas*. He spins Marx, the revolutionary punctuated equilibrist, into a straw man who champions a fallacy of the average man—average in everything he does—as well as the glorification of mediocrity as found in *la loi des erreurs*, wherein even the standard deviation was thought an error.[86]

"No wonder Marx fell for Adolphe Quetelet's ideas," Taleb concludes QED, as if industrial countries with the highest Gini scores don't also suffer some of the worst indices in every social and health category.[87] As if rich people are by definition also brilliant, etc., a recapitulation of the fallacy of the average man in reverse. As if copious wealth doesn't also select for sloppy thinking, which is Taleb's own complaint elsewhere in the book.

TALEB DIVIDES INFERENCE INTO QUADRANTS of risk defined by the distribution of outcomes along one axis and the complexity of those outcomes on another.[88] Gaussian models work when normally distributed outcomes are clear and final (for example, true vs. false). Even under such outcomes, however, modeling can turn tenuous for systems of deeper uncertainty. In a third quadrant—simple payoffs under large deviations—failure is a respectable option if only because frequency and impact are disconnected. It's the Fourth Quadrant in which all hell breaks loose. Complex, unexpected, and accumulative outcomes under fat tailed uncertainty turn statistical modeling Gaussian and other otherwise into putty.

Taleb confuses things a jot by claiming elsewhere—cake and eat it too—this last quadrant can indeed be captured by statistics. He spins Benoît Mandelbrot's fractal—repeating patterns across scales—as the geometry of (some) Black Swans.[89] The Mandelbrotian or fractal rejects the notion of a quantifiable dispersion of known and "standard" deviations on which Gaussian statistics, including correlation and regression, depend. Even the latter's notion of statistical significance is, to Taleb, reified. How can a sample be significant when compared to a distribution that isn't real? While Gaussian probabilities collapse toward the tails, fractals (somewhat) preserve probabilities across scales—even toward the tails—better conserving the possibility of extreme events. In other words, the fractal is, unlike the Gaussian, invariant to scale.

Taleb claims the fractal as how nature works, as Platonic a notion as the geometry he condemns. Yes, snails, leaves, snowflakes, shorelines, lightning, and peacocks, among many examples, exhibit fractal patterns, but not all of nature need fold in on itself that way. Scale effects abound. As ecologist Simon Levin describes, some characteristics are specific to one scale and not others.[90] Taleb concedes fractality has its limits. He also concedes we are unable to say where to draw the line. Even as we can scale the fractal with non-ordinal exponents, say 1.5 or 3.2, the fractal isn't something we observe, but something we can only guess or infer from the data we collect. In other words, despite Taleb's efforts to naturalize fractals—and by extension Black Swans— they are as ideational as Gaussian "mediocrity." So we are back to the Fourth Quadrant's dark matter. It isn't that we can predict Black Swans, fractal or no, but, Taleb continues, that we should acknowledge they exist and should budget or, in the case of the stock market, bet accordingly. By Taleb's tautology, if we can predict it, it isn't a Black Swan.

There have long existed alternatives apparently off Taleb's radar, however. We could ask, for instance, if he's such an empiricist, why not let the data he repeatedly refers to speak for themselves? Nonparametric multi-chain Monte Carlo analyses of millions of trials can produce the distribution under which the system as a whole is generated and against which we can contrast our sample set, including for so-called Grey Swan systems we might actually be able to predict.[91] Indeed, there are nonparametric analogs to ANOVA, regression, and correlation: Kruskal-Wallis, ANOSIM, kernel regression, Spearman's rank correlation, etc.[92] The Popperian nulls Taleb champions are in the meantime increasingly abandoned for a Bayesian structure, whereby probabilities are assigned (and reassigned with each new datum) to a *series* of hypotheses.[93]

Clearly all these alternatives have their own problems. Computing power can't solve incomplete data. Multi-chain Monte Carlo analyses still need enough representative sampling to get the chains to converge. The point is, however, as we'll discuss further along, all is not lost. Not everything is Black Swan or White. Even Taleb's central dichotomy smells. Within the Wallace and Fullilove counterexample alone, we see ourselves in a regression structure operating at multiple scales. A fractal series of Gaussian distributions.[94]

OUR OBJECTIONS TO TALEB'S TREATMENT needn't be confined to technicalities. If we follow Taleb's lead and historicize his own line of thought we discover a particular *political* logic.

Taleb, channeling Allen Ginsberg's Moloch, appears to exist in an acosmos in which his metaphysics are affirmed only by the money he can make off it.[95] He says he came to abandon the notion that we can discover the market's laws of history. He knows only that bad things happen regularly, if rarely, and with devastating impact. Half of the market's earnings over the past fifty years accrued across ten separate days of trading. So over the long haul Taleb shorts the market even if he doesn't know the reasons why it intermittently (and catastrophically) collapses.

He does identify the brokers' premise of a steady rate of return as one such self-fulfilling cause, producing events that happen precisely because they weren't expected to. Conversely, he claims, what we already know doesn't happen because we make ready for it.

That is, Taleb makes a mash of the political economy of knowledge. *Who* knows? At my end of the pool, in epidemiology, many of us know, for instance, that turning poultry and livestock into monocultural widgets helps produce deadly epizootics, a conclusion suppressed here in the United States of Agribusiness with Lysynkoist ferocity.[96]

Because treating the market as a black box has paid off for him, Taleb, putting his money where his brain is, characterizes reality for all practices and purposes as random. But surely just because something doesn't go according to plan doesn't mean no cause exists. This Taleb acknowledges, but defines the failure of prediction—of appropriating information—as an estemic opacity, as equivalent to physical randomness.

Taleb derides utopianists who by a Platonic fallacy confuse the narrative map for the territory:

> So I disagree with the followers of Marx and those of Adam Smith: the reason free markets work is because they allow people to be lucky, thanks to aggressive trial and error, not by giving rewards or "incentives" for skill. The strategy is, then, to tinker as much as possible and try to collect as many Black Swan opportunities as you can.

But can we conclude his own treatment here as doing otherwise? With every commercial on TV, and every business book, capitalists immanentize the eschaton, promising transcendental fulfillment with every bar of soap and financial model sold.

We need ask again, free markets are free (and generously random) *for whom?* Capital parlays stealing the majority's degrees of freedom—its capacity to organize the means of production on its own terms—into wealth for a few. Everyone else without capital pays the price. On a $1 a day there is little room for trial and error without the severest punishment. Taleb repeatedly shows himself throughout the book unable to think outside his own class, which includes the academic enemies against whom he rails. I find this telling.

There is too the inconvenience that the market has little to do with innovation. Doug Henwood proposes IPOs raise little, if any, capital.[97] The largest firms, which regularly retire hundreds of billions of dollars more in stock than they issue, finance research and production by way of in-house funding streams. Stock is instead a means by which the wealthy negotiate ownership and attendant claims on societal power.

In that case, then, Taleb's conclusion about trial and error resonates for all the wrong reasons. "I then realized that the great strength of the free-market system is the fact that company executives don't need to know what's going on," he writes. That's as much a rationale for incompetence as indemnifying executives of the responsibilities of an economic Maxwell's Demon.[98]

Flippant stochasticity "works" well if there exist mechanisms for self-correction. Almost all such corrections, however, are presently externalized. Consumer, worker, nature, governments—always someone else—must pick up the cost of rentier bad judgment or willful malfeasance. The "freer" economies are—that is, the more deregulated—the *more* executives *should* know what they are doing, from the prole viewpoint anyway. Otherwise, contrary to Taleb's core argument in *Antifragile*, the greater the impact of executive failures felt by the larger society.

TALEB INVESTIGATES THE SOURCE of our innumeracy:

> We do not spontaneously learn that we don't learn that we don't
> learn. The problem lies in the structure of our minds: we don't
> learn rules, just facts, and only facts. Metarules (such as the rule
> that we have a tendency to not learn rules) we don't seem to be
> good at getting. We scorn the abstract; we scorn it with passion.

Perhaps metarules aren't rules either, however. Indeed, Taleb's
complaint appears directed at a particular Anglo-American cultural moment, integral to the kind of technicist capitalism Taleb
embraces.

We know rare events aren't synonymous with uncertainty. There are
any number of astronomical events we can predict: comets, simultaneous planetary transits, reversals in Earth's axial tilt, etc. In the other
direction, randomness can happen at many temporal scales, including, when continuously, as stochastic noise. What Taleb is trying to
get at here, however, is that rare *and* random events surprise us worst,
particularly because they are camouflaged by the workaday. We can't
or refuse to get our minds wrapped around that failure.

Taleb sees in the Gaussian approaches an attempt to quantify what
is in actuality unknowable risk. Such efforts typically suffer the *ludic
fallacy*, whereby the odds of an event are defined by games of chance
with known denominators. We know, for instance, that any side of a
fair die has 1/6 a chance upon a throw. Can we really prescribe risk for
something much more complex—for which we can't describe—such
as a pandemic or collapse in the housing market?

In this way Taleb repeatedly positions himself as a hero among
Gaussian dragons. His braggadocio appeals to this transplanted New
Yorker of childhood heroes Giorgio Chinaglia and Reggie Jackson,
but whatever their pose and style, scientists, like athletes, are, as
Joseph Campbell quotes Oswald Sprengler, integral parts of their his-
torical moments:

> "Supposing . . . that Napoleon himself, as 'empirical person' had
> fallen at Marengo—then that which he *signified* would have been

actualized in some other form." The hero [Campbell continues], who in this sense and to this degree has become depersonalized, incarnates, during the period of his epochal action, the dynamism of the culture process. . . . And insofar as the hero's act coincides with that for which his society is ready, he seems to ride on the great rhythm of the historical process.[99]

Where does Taleb's ride take him? He diagnoses a triplet of opacity predictions suffer. Many, perhaps Campbell himself, fill in what history refuses to divulge, producing an illusion of understanding, in which specific events stand in for historical circumstance. Or they produce a retrospective distortion that imports wishful revisionism. Or an overvaluation of factual interaction, from which grand schema are inflated puff by Platonic puff.

Taleb's "novel" focus on revolutionary outcomes, abandoning essentialist quasi-equilibria, is dialecticalism's old hat. And yet it's also the latter's diametric opposition, for Taleb has turned humanity's struggle with itself into no history at all. In Taleb's world, regimes—economic and otherwise—aren't overturned by due cause but by chance alone.

By virtue of excising causality—and blame and responsibility—Taleb, even as he assures us he wishes he wouldn't have to, reframes the nature of the world in an essentialist stochasticity. The world is beyond our capacity to act on it. Despite rejecting determinism, if only as something we can act on, Taleb channels his Wall Street colleagues' contempt. The world matters only as it is filtered through the market, which, like God, is both necessary and unfathomable. And everybody else must act as a means to its ends.

The key point here is that the Black Swan isn't merely a statistical phenomenon. It can be bent to serve its masters, including, as we shall see, financial, but others very much as well.

TALEB TOOK HIS DOCTORATE IN DERIVATIVES, but ended up betting against them as they precipitate negative Black Swans whose mathematical errors compound losses. At first, Taleb traded against the instruments' technical inefficiencies—one instrument against another—before abandoning the horse race approach for a more insurance-like stance against the entire class of models, along the lines of the financial freaks of Michael Lewis's sideshow.[100] The October 1987 market collapse left Taleb a very rich man, with enough fuck-you money to quit the trading floor but remain in the quant world of data that he says "thinkers" can't see.[101] He became a café flâneur, a self-styled limousine philosopher who, in his middle-brow way, could both bash middlebrow academics and intellectualize capitalist greed. The latter emerges as if by entelechy, rather than—with 662 American bases in countries around the world—by primitive accumulation.

"There is more money," Taleb waxes, echoing William Gibson's Hubertus Bigend,

> in designing a shoe than in actually making it: Nike, Dell and Boeing can get paid for just thinking, organizing, and leveraging their know-how and ideas while subcontracted factories in developing countries do the grunt work and engineers in cultured and mathematical states do the noncreative technical grind. The American economy has leveraged itself heavily on the idea generation, which explains why losing manufacturing jobs can be coupled with a rising standard of living.[102]

Whatever we may say of Taleb, he *is* efficient, packing in many an absurdity in so few lines.

It isn't intellectual property that's parlayed into capital, for one. In 2005 industrial designer Dan Brown patented a new wrench whose prongs encircle a screw like a camera shutter.[103] Sears, which first sold Brown's wrench, offshored the design, Walmart-style, to a Chinese manufacturer, and now, daring Brown to sue, sells the knockoff under the Craftsman brand at a more competitive price. "I'm in favor of free trade," Brown told the *New York Times*, and "the person who's out-innovated loses." What Brown missed is that the *theft*, not the patent, is now the intellectual innovation.

Brown isn't an anomaly. His expropriation is emblematic of a systemic deformity. As Giovanni Arrighi explains it, capitalism entered one long but metamorphosing crisis in the early 1970s.[104] For the first decade, intensive competition induced falling rates of profit.

Organized labor could still at this point put up a good fight against capital's attempts to shift such losses onto workers via productivity gains and other givebacks. In the Anglo-American sphere, Margaret Thatcher and Ronald Reagan broke what remained of labor's national reach, with the aim of expanding the industrial reserve army and depressing wages and benefits by more direct means.

Capitalism, now less bound by such annoying overhead as labor rights and environmental standards, Arrighi continues, switched into an overproduction crisis. When income is concentrated into the hands of the few, effective demand collapses. This crisis was mitigated—and ultimately exacerbated—two ways. Finance's not-so-fictitious speculation stumbled drunkenly from bubble to bubble, spreading surplus capital and producing booms—and inequality—that covered up the economy's underlying ill-health. Demand meanwhile was itself turned into a market for new financial instruments. Workers were extended comical lines of credit, their debts themselves speculated on, a bubble popped by the housing collapse, severely degrading the economy and leaving millions penurious.

Keynesian intervention—for anyone other than the biggest banks—was viewed by an albeit divided capital class as too much a political risk. It would open the door to reversing labor's fortunes. In other words, at least until the Occupy movement took off, the kleptocrats were perfectly comfortable with, and some maniacal about, a pauperized population. Better to rule a banana republic of "right-to-work" than share what remains of a declining empire.

David Harvey describes how capital spatially parlayed its structural risk.[105] Reintegrating the Soviet Bloc into circuits of capital; the economic liberalization of China (and just about every other country); interlinking the world's financial markets; and innovations in transportation and communication, including containerization, eased capital flows, extended lines of production and distribution, and press-ganged millions more into the global industrial reserve army. Once such conditions are in place, the globe becomes a toy:

> Why invest in low-profit production when you can borrow in Japan at a zero rate of interest and invest in London at 7 percent

while hedging your bets on a possible deleterious shift in the yen-sterling exchange rate?

The more capital surplus produced as a result, however, and the larger the extent across which it is produced, the greater (and faster) the reinvestment required, the fewer the relative opportunities to do so, and the greater the risks to somehow somewhere recapitalize—privatizing fire departments, marketing credit cards to prepubescents—increasing the precariousness of the entire apparatus.

The rot, then, isn't found merely in the schemes of desk scalpers such as Nicholas Leeson and Kareem Serageldin covering up bad bets, in the likes of higher-ups Jeffrey Skilling and Jon Corzine, or even in the infrastructural corruption of Libor and Timothy Geithner's New York Federal Reserve.[106] The *system* is the rot.

TALEB ARGUES THAT HUMANITY IS MOVING increasingly into a world defined by Black Swans rather than by centroidal gravity. Winner-takes-all tournaments in politics and economics, yes, but in the "harder" version he omits, socialism for the rich. Cumulative advantages—whether it be finance or academic reputation—are politically protected. Those without such initial capital drop out. Precocity and genius matter little. Social resources, whether or not won by merit, do. Conversely, those who have lost continue to mount losses in a ratchet downward.

So the dynamics of inequality feed on their own momentum. Any Marxist could tell you that. But despite all the evidence to the contrary, the details available even in more mainstream outlets than Arrighi and Harvey, Taleb rejects it as an outcome of the system itself. After all,

> one had only to look around to see that these large corporate monsters dropped like flies. Take a cross-section of dominant corporation at any particular time; many of them will be out of business a few decades later, while firms nobody ever heard of will have popped onto the scene from some garage in California or from some college dorm. . . . Almost all [the] large corporations

were located in the most capitalist country on earth, the United States. The more socialist a country's orientation, the easier it was for the large [failing] corporate monsters to stick around.

Taleb transubstantiates luck into an equalitarianism that destroys even the largest company in favor of the smallest "little guys." A system *structured* around the most vicious exploitation, with Gini scores in the stratosphere, is now the most equalitarian. It's the legend of Microsoft and Facebook—frogs kissed by Lady Luck into princes.

But the system remains, whatever the turnover. Capital and governmental subsidies are rolled over from one technological regime to the next. Exxon, BP, and GE, paying no taxes, have a stranglehold on the political economy, whatever Valdez or Gulf spill may come. Diseconomies of scale, inherent to capital accumulation, are politically protected. Cumulative advantage is a class prerogative continually financed by expropriating working labor, who, in Taleb's world, don't even qualify as the "little guys" to whom he repeatedly alludes.

In other words, Taleb suffers his own case of epistemic opacity, imparting to chance well-documented processes of which he knows nothing or to which he turns a blind eye.

To Taleb, capitalism's problems emerge by stupid thinking or by chance. True enough on both accounts, but there is as well primitive accumulation, corruption, political expediency, and intrinsic structural contradictions, the costs of which are externalized to workers, consumers, governments and the environment. It's always someone else who picks up the bill, permitting bad economics to masquerade as bad luck, off of which Taleb himself wins big by betting against. Taleb, it would appear, has a vested interest in letting systemic failure off the hook.

WILLFUL IGNORANCE OF THE MARKET'S historical context— after all we can't track history—colors more than Taleb's statistical, and by extension political, assumptions. His behavioral proclivities are nigh on pronoid. Taleb, adding insult to injury, writes in parable of a regular "compassionate" prank. He'd give a taxi driver a $100 bill as a tip, and

I'd watch him unfold the bill and look at it with some degree of consternation ($1 million certainly would have been better but it was not within my means). It was also a simple hedonistic experiment: it felt elevating to make someone's day with the trifle of $100.

As if his ilk hadn't already structurally punked the immigrant into a hemorrhoid driving sixteen hours a day. I'm sure the driver appreciated the fare, but the self-aggrandizement—at the heart of every $10,000-tip-for-the-waitress story—speaks to a mélange of guilt, fear, and contempt. Tithes to the gods of fate.

Tellingly Taleb ends the tips, "We all become stingy and calculating when our wealth grows and we start taking money seriously." We do, do we? Even such ineffectual redistribution, a contemptuous tease, becomes anathema the greater the inequality. For those increasingly in the know about how utterly preposterous their prosperity, tithing apparently only alerts angry gods where to strike.

To his credit, Taleb destroys conservative ideologues, who are none too conservative, "just phenomenally skilled at self-deception by burying the possibility of a large, devastating loss under the rug." On the other hand, one can't help but think oneself conservative when the whole system is dedicated to protecting them against losses, "When 'conservative' bankers make profits, they get the benefits; when they are hurt, we pay the costs," producing, as I've described elsewhere, moral hazards of apocalyptic proportions.[107]

Indeed, the whole notion of compensation is out-of-whack, even within the confines of a capitalist economy dedicated to theft. Bankers are paid annual bonuses for short-term profits they lose once a Black Swan hits:

> The tragedy of capitalism is that since the quality of the returns is not observable from past data, owners of companies, namely shareholders, can be taken for a ride by the managers who show returns and cosmetic profitability but in fact might be taking hidden risks.[108]

Of course, while Taleb's point is worth salvaging—capitalism incentivizes cons—the rest of us, the poisoned and dispossessed, the billions who literally don't know how they are to survive the month, can only snigger low and slow at Taleb's view of "tragedy."

Is it any wonder Taleb and Big Tobacco shill and fellow *New York Times* bestselling author Malcolm Gladwell profile each other?[109] Each stakes the claim that our social problems are nothing of the sort and are in actuality mathematical perversions dumb innumerates can't see. Gladwell's classic prison guard solution—fire the few abusive guards—is a neoliberal apologetics for a system that by percent imprisons five times more blacks than the greater population. Abusing the poorest is that system's natural order, and prison its rationalization, with enough "bad apple" deniability to indemnify itself. Gladwell's pragmatic technocrat, aiming to run the police state more efficiently, is an ideologue by another name.

Even the most thoughtful of allies will find it hard to blind themselves to the breadth of Taleb's myopia. He misses that the money he makes off shorting these conservatives—his second-order gains—is also folded into the system's protection. It begs whether armed communist revolutionaries, among them hemorrhoidal cab drivers, *their* Swans spotted with blood, would bother to parse the difference.

IS THERE, THEN, AN ALTERNATIVE? How would a Red Swan that assimilates chance's political context change our perspective (and our capacity for action)?

By all appearances dialectical biologists Richard Levins and Richard Lewontin, who for five decades have applied their approaches to biological systems, take Taleb head on:

> Randomness has been associated with lack of causality, and with unpredictability and thus of irrationality, a lack of purpose, and the existence of free will. It has been invoked as the negation of lawfulness and therefore of any scientific understanding of society. It then becomes a justification for a reactionary passivity. As the bumper sticker says, "Shit happens." So stop complaining. For the

most part, however, randomness and causation, chance and necessity, are not mutually exclusive opposites but interpenetrate.[110]

A car crash, for instance, involves two drivers whose trips were determinate and even planned. The crash is "random" only as the two cars' trajectories were independent. So, contra Taleb, the quantum notion of randomness isn't synonymous with causal independence. The latter point is particularly acute for mesoscale, heterogeneous systems, such as ecosystems and societies, which Levins and Lewontin describe as characterized by "a very large number of individually weak forces . . . essentially independent" with respect to one another.

Randomness, then, should always be defined in terms of its scale or to other objects. In Levins and Lewontin's example, Franklin Roosevelt's death was no accident as to the state of his body but was random as to his day's international politics.

Determinacy, meanwhile, can arise out of randomness. All the molecules of a chair need not shift together—causing the chair to jump in Taleb's example—for the sum total to produce Newtonian objects. If we can't predict every mutation, we can still infer that exposing organisms to radiation and toxic chemicals will produce more mutations.

Levins and Lewontin offer a third example. Months before the Chernobyl accident, the plant's director assured an interviewer of only 1-in-10,000-years odds of an accident. Sounds crazy, given what followed. But at the level of Europe's 1,000 reactors, an accident at those odds should happen once every ten years. "A chance event with low probability," they write, "becomes a determinate certainty when there are a large number of opportunities."

Causality can be found in the aggregate. And the Black Swan can turn deterministic.

Conversely, Levins and Lewontin continue, randomness can arise out of determinacy. Computers, in their example, can generate random numbers. But these are more accurately pseudo-random as their generative rule is deterministic (and their sequence repeatable). But they are random in relation to the simulation for which one is using them.

Finally, random processes are bounded. Not everything goes. Randomness in real life is constrained by states of origin. In contradiction to Taleb's sweeping pronouncements, boundaries as they apply to social processes are the focus of fruitful research. So while humanity, and society more generally, is no machine—and here Levins and Lewontin strike at the core—"The error is to take the individual as causally prior to the whole and not to appreciate that the social has causal properties within which individual consciousness and action are framed."

Indeed, one can apply their observation to *The Black Swan* itself:

> While the consciousness of an individual is not determined by his or her class position but is influenced by idiosyncratic factors that appear as random, those random factors operate within a domain and with probabilities that are constrained and directed by social forces.[111]

In other words, Taleb's books stand as their own refutation.

—*Farming Pathogens*, 28 January 2013

Social Meadicine

IT WASN'T ALL DRAGON EGGS and codpieces at the local Renaissance Faire. A plague doctor, *il medico della peste*, stalked the town (when not queuing for the mermaids and sipping forest fruit mead through a straw).

These "community doctors" wore beak masks, *maschera dello speziale*, filled with flower petals, burning incense or aromatic herbs, to protect against the miasmas or "bad air" thought to cause infection.[112] The eyes of the masks were made of glass to block face-to-face contact. Some wore coats covered in wax.

The municipal doctors, contracted out from town to town and quarantined when not on the job, bloodlet their patients, although one, Nostradamus, discouraged the practice. Others placed frogs and leeches on the bubonic buboes "to rebalance the humors." Still others, denied tenure and kicked off their research grants, recommended isolating the sick, imposing a broad cordon sanitaire, and exterminating rats.

Historian Sheldon Watts, channeling Foucault, described the new public health as a means of social control, but noted several Carnival-like reversals:

> Yet in their rush to save themselves by flight, Florentine magistrates worried that the common people left behind would seize control of the city; the fear was perhaps justified. In the summer of 1378 when factional disputes temporarily immobilized the Florentine elite, rebellious woolworkers won control of the government and remained in power for several months.[113]

—*FARMING PATHOGENS*, 23 SEPTEMBER 2013

PART FIVE

As we know, revolution is in this year. So Chipotle puts out this bag.... There's a little pig on it. And it says, ¡Viva la Revolución! ... What fucking Uncle Pig is this that's telling other pigs, "We want equality!" Yeah, dope, we gonna get rid of the farmer! "No, no, I was thinking of something a little different." Oh, we're gonna march for our rights? "No, bigger pens. We're building bigger pens. Because if that plane is going down, we're going down in first class." Wait—wha—Wilbur, this is ridiculous! This is all you have planned? We are all going to die! "Well, I mean, uh, not all." Wilbur we haven't seen you in a while, where are you? "I, well, I sleep in the house with the farmer..."

—HARI KONDABOLU (2011)

Pale Mushy Wing

*Owing to this struggle for life, any variation, however slight and
from whatever cause proceeding, if it be in any degree profitable to
an individual of any species, in its infinitely complex relationship
to other organic beings and to external nature, will tend to the
preservation of that individual, and will generally be inherited by
its offspring.*

— CHARLES DARWIN (1859)

AGRIBUSINESS LAB-BREEDS ITS FEW poultry lineages at the
level of grandparent stock before shipping out the product to clientele
around the world.[1]

The practice in effect removes natural selection as a self-correcting
(and free) ecological service. Any culling upon an outbreak or by
farmers in reaction to an outbreak has no bearing on the development of immune resistance to the pathogens identified, as these birds,
broilers and layers alike, are unable to evolve in response.

In other words, the failure to accumulate natural resistance to circulating pathogens is built into the industrial model before a single
outbreak occurs. There exists no room for a real-time, ecologically
responsive, and self-organized immune resistance.

From a world away, human breeders and vaccines must somehow
track microscopic molecular trajectories across dynamic mixes of

myriad local pathogen variants, a Sisyphean task. It's a system that appears able to repel pathogens only under the kind of biosecurity and biocontainment that often can't be implemented in developing countries and even in some developed countries.

No ecologically selected resistance surrounded by a fence. The image of a broken arm, pale and mushy in a cast, comes to mind. Or perhaps more appropriately, a pale mushy wing.

Setting aside barn architectures, reifying capitalism's angry fight against nature, and the resulting effects on flavor and nutritional fitness of the food produced, Fortress *Filière* should be subjected to an additional query. Does it even work?

In increasing the rate of livestock turnover, blocking entry by low-pathogenic strains, and restricting selection to grandparent stock, intensive farming is forced to increase the precision of its biosecurity efforts if only in order to keep deadlier pathogen variants from emerging in a context of no or little new natural host resistance.[2]

We can ask if there are combinations of harvesting rate and finishing time selecting for virulence and/or transmissibility that supersede the precision of which the industry is capable or is willing to pay for. At what point does the nature of the problem supersede the margins dedicated to its solution?

That last is perhaps a silly question, as how could we possibly assume companies are responsible for the dangers that originate on their property? Sarcasm aside, it offers an explanation for the lengths to which agribusiness goes to externalize the integral environmental, social, and health costs of their operations to any and every passerby—governments, consumers, workers, livestock, and the environment. Agribusiness, some of the largest companies in the world, can't afford them otherwise.

—21 JUNE 2011

Whose Food Footprint?

I co-authored the following, slightly edited here, with Richard Kock for Human Geography.

SCIENTISTS ACROSS DISCIPLINES AGREE that humanity is on an environmental precipice. Climate change, ocean acidification, water and air pollution, nitrate and phosphate loading, and disruptions in thermohaline circulation have either surged across ecological tipping points or are rapidly approaching them.[3]

The crisis has been brought about largely by exponential increases in resource extraction and per capita consumption. We are dipping deeply into many of Earth's assets, with profound implications for humanity's existence as we know it. In a blink of a geological eye, habitat destruction, biodiversity loss, ecosystem dysfunction, disease emergence, resource depletion, eutrophication, soil degradation, oceanic collapse, environmental toxicity, peak energy, and climate shifts have hit home together, threatening many of the plant and animal populations upon which our very species' survival depends.

The resulting environmental damage, accruing across biomes and at the global scale, is impinging upon our capacity to feed a world population growing in both its size and rates of consumption. The Food and Agriculture Organization estimates a record 1.2 billion people the world over suffered from chronic hunger or undernourishment in 2009, with the greatest morbidity and mortality in the Global South.[4] Of the 925 million undernourished people FAO estimated in 2010, 906 million live in developing countries.

Humanity has so far "resolved" one famine after another by shifting food surpluses, with millions left dead in the wake of these successes. As recent and looming famines in the Horn of Africa and the Sahel illustrate, the crises continue to multiply nonetheless and the options for resolving them are dwindling in number and scope. Ecosystem resilience continues to decline and food availability is threatened by the very models of production presently used to feed the world. As food prices spike, in part spurred by equity speculation,[5] the poorest are closed out of the commodity markets through which food staples are increasingly distributed.

A veritable army of researchers, policymakers, and advocates of a variety of stripes has articulated the problem. But a clear course of action has yet to be agreed upon, much less acted on. There are, however, a number of efforts making the attempt.

In a recent *Nature* opinion Jason Clay, senior vice president for market transformation at World Wildlife Foundation, one of the world's leading environmental NGOs, describes one such program,

> In the past 18 months, members of non-governmental organizations (NGOs), academia and the private sector have come together to develop ways to reform the global food system by increasing food production without damaging biodiversity. Groups such as Global Harvest Initiative . . . and the Sustainable Agriculture Initiative . . . are working to freeze the footprint of food.[6]

Clay offers a variety of strategies around which efforts aimed at reducing the impact of agriculture on the environment should be organized, paying particular attention to Sub-Saharan Africa. According to Clay, we must cut consumption, eliminate food waste, rehabilitate degraded lands, double the efficiency of agricultural inputs, codify property rights for farmers, increase the productivity of neglected crops through genetics and cutting-edge technologies, and protect soil carbon by growing trees and root grasses and introducing a carbon market for agriculture.

Clay's program appears a mix of sound advice and objectives other teams have also presented.[7] Any effort aimed at alleviating food crises across locales would seriously consider many of his technical suggestions. However, the larger argument in which Clay situates his advice essentially posits the solutions to the food and environmental crises lie in more of the same. In other words, Clay, in terms rarely found so explicitly, proposes that any successful effort to feed humanity sustainably must pivot about handing corporate agribusiness, the progenitors of energy-intensive monocropping, greater control of the world's food regimen.[8]

We review Clay's position here, unpacking the line of argument that the responsibility for food security should devolve to a small cartel of agricultural conglomerates. We address its appeal to political expediency, its narrow view of production efficiency and economies of scale, and its marketing of agribusiness's magnanimity despite historical evidence to the contrary. Along the way we enlarge upon key omissions in the argument, notably its treatment of capitalism as a force of nature, the declensionist narrative that justifies expropriating smallholdings, and the socioeconomic, health, and environmental consequences already arising from just such a food program.

Finally, we offer examples of alternate paradigms for feeding the planet as it converges on its environmental limits. Communally directed efforts in conservation agriculture, minimizing input costs and ecological subsidies, embody living refutations of the agribusiness model. Their specifics offer concrete evidence that such projects, some feeding millions, are means enough for sustainably feeding and employing local populations, supporting responsive food sovereignty, and protecting wildlife, health, and the environment for generations to come. A food revolution is underway and growing, even in, or especially in, developing countries that agribusiness views as its path of least resistance for commoditizing what land and resources remain.

PRESS-GANGING CONSTITUENCIES

To support a global population projected to grow to as large as eleven billion by 2050, FAO estimates the world must bring six million additional hectares into cultivation every year for the next thirty years.[9]

These numbers appear to put a premium on the kind of rapid expansion in large-scale production of which multinational agribusiness alone seems capable. It is an assumption Jason Clay and many of his colleagues appear to accept and promote. Their project, then, can be construed as much a political program as technical advice, aimed first and foremost at justifying, and consolidating support behind, the corporate model.

In a 2010 TED Talk, Clay describes what any successful effort to simultaneously save and feed the planet must look like:

> We've got thirty-five [biodiversity hotspots]. We've got fifteen priority commodities [with the greatest impact on biodiversity]. . . . Who do we work with to change the way those commodities are produced? . . . Three hundred to five hundred companies control 70% or more of the trade of each of the fifteen commodities that we've identified as the most significant. If we work with those, if we change those companies and the way they do business, then the rest will happen automatically.[10]

Even that group appears too large a one with which to collaborate:

> One hundred [of those companies] control 25% of the trade of all fifteen of the most [ecologically] significant commodities on the planet. We can get our arms around 100 companies. . . . Why is 25% important? Because if these companies demand sustainable products they'll pull 40–50% of production. Companies can push producers faster than consumers can. By companies asking for this we can leverage production so much faster than by waiting for consumers to do it. After forty years the global organic movement has achieved .7 of 1% of global food. We can't wait that long. We don't have that kind of time.

Working with individual companies is not enough, however:

> We need to begin to work with industries. So we've started roundtables where we bring together the entire value chain, from

producers all the way to retailers and brands . . . to figure out what
are the key impacts of these products, what is a global benchmark,
what's an acceptable impact, and design standards around that.

Why are these companies participating? Two reasons:

For the big companies it's reputational risk, but more importantly
they don't care what the price of the commodities is. If they don't
have commodities they don't have a business. They care about
availability. So the big risk for them is not having product at all.
For the producers if a buyer wants to buy something produced a
certain way, that's what brings them to the table. It's the demand
that brings them to the table.

To his credit Clay puts on a polished presentation. But his TED line
of reasoning is rooted in a number of dubious assumptions and stray
inferences. For one, why should the top 100 companies be allowed
to retain—and expand—control over the fifteen ecologically significant products Clay identifies when their practices helped produce the
environmental crises to begin with?

In passing over the question, Clay's argument effectively corners
the environmental and food movements into catering to these companies' needs. It presents naked expediency as reason enough. It is
too hard for "us" to organize consumers and small producers, who,
after all, hold too small a market share to make a difference. As if
these very companies weren't engaged in all-out campaigns against
alternate models of food production.

The appeal to this kind of economy of scale press-gangs myriad
constituencies, false premise by false premise. Throughout his talk
Clay repeatedly alludes to a nebulous "we," who, if *really* interested
in saving the world, should work with agribusiness. He addresses the
possibility that millions of small farmers and their communities can
make major contributions to local and regional food production in
equal terms by omission and dismissal.

The Jevons Trap

During his TED Talk Clay offered veritable prospectuses for two companies with which he works, confounding collaboration and boosterism.[11] First, Cargill, the food conglomerate, which has

> funded research that shows that we can double global palm oil production without cutting a single tree in the next twenty years and do it all in Borneo alone by planting on land that's already degraded. . . . They're also undertaking a study to look at all of their supplies of palm oil to see if they could be certified, and what they would need to change in order to become third-party certified under a credible certification program. Why is Cargill important? Because Cargill has 20 to 25% of global palm oil. If Cargill makes a decision, then the entire palm oil industry moves.

Clay skips here what Cargill did to win such a large proportion of palm oil production. The World Rainforest Network points out the industry-dominated Roundtable for Sustainable Palm Oil, to which Clay refers, partakes in the same omission.[12] The Roundtable has absolved its members, Cargill included, of their sordid pasts deforesting the land and dispossessing its inhabitants. The sustainability clock would now be set starting at 2005, which, according to WRN,

> means that all deforestation prior to that date will not be taken into account, and that plantations where such deforestation occurred will still receive the RSPO seal of approval. Given that oil palms can be harvested for up to 30 years, this implies that much of the palm oil traded with the RSPO "sustainable" seal in the next 10–20 years will be harvested from plantations that have "replaced primary forest."

The certification process is itself voluntary, in effect allowing the industry to sanction its own bad practices. To WRN, to pretend that a product obtained from large-scale monocultures of mostly alien palm trees can be certified as "sustainable" is— to say the least—a misleading statement, especially for oil palm plantations, with their history of tropical deforestation and wide-spread human rights abuses. . . . RSPO certification is a fraud.

Clay next endorses M&M Mars, the candy company:

Mars has made sustainability pledges to buy only certifiable prod-uct for all of its seafood. Turns out that Mars buys more seafood than Walmart, because of pet food. But they're doing some really interesting things around chocolate. And it all comes from the fact that Mars wants to be in business in the future. And what they see is that they need to improve chocolate production. . . . [Mars is] sequencing the genome of the cocoa plant. They're doing it with IBM and the USDA. And they're putting it in the public domain because they want everybody to have access to this data. Because they want everybody to help them make cocoa more pro-ductive and more sustainable. What they've realized is that if they can identify the traits on productivity and on drought tolerance, they can produce 320% as much cocoa on 40% of the land. The rest of the land can be used for something else. It's more with less and less again. That's what the future's got to be.[13]

"Everybody" includes none of the tens of thousands of children Mars suppliers enslave to cultivate monoculture cocoa in Ghana and Côte d'Ivoire, or the thousands of contract farmers, living there in abject poverty, to which the company refuses to offer Fair Trade prices.[14]

In championing Cargill and Mars, Clay makes the claim that agribusiness is in the best position to improve on the kinds of pro-duction efficiencies needed to reduce resource depletion, the key article of faith underlying green capitalism. The contention is at best ahistorical, omitting the wholesale destruction that produced these monocultures. Efficiencies found in producing commodities are often traded in for deficiencies elsewhere, including such cloying "overhead" as human rights, health, wages, and, to use a reductionist term, ecosystem services.

But even as a logical premise, production efficiencies as deployed by "sustainable" capitalism have long been contradicted by the Jevons paradox.[15] In researching coal, William Stanley Jevons observed that increasing efficiency in extracting a resource in the long term led to an *increased* use of the resource. Runaway fossil fuel consumption proves Jevons's case well enough, but the idea also has been supported spectacularly with respect to food. The Green Revolution doubled food production per hectare but also drove widespread malnourishment.[16]

In an economic system dedicated to 3 percent compound growth, better—and cheaper—extraction, increasing efficiency per unit currency invested, actually selects for *greater* exploitation, often until a resource is exhausted. Under the present economic model the paradox is "solved" only by exploiting an alternate resource once the original is depleted, wiping out the natural base species by species, mineral by mineral, and region by region, a practice from which Cargill and Mars, among others, until now profited to a superlative degree.

If history is any guide, agribusinesses have rarely let worrying about losing a commodity's resource base change anything more than their operational *tactics* from one annual report to the next. Green marketing, for instance, presently sells best in upscale markets in the United States, the European Union, and Asia, even as these host greater per-capita consumption across products than much of the rest of the world.[17] The companies' core *strategies*, however, structured by competitive advantages they are unlikely to give up voluntarily, remain largely intact.

Turning other people's resources into enormous private profit (and blaming somebody else for the resulting damage) remains the order of the day. As Luke Bergmann's calculations show, much of the carbon emissions, market cropland, and forestry in the Global South originate, or result, depending on one's perspective, largely in capital accumulation and consumption in the United States, Europe, and Japan.[18] Becky Mansfield and her colleagues meanwhile refute the influential Forest Transition Theory linking economic growth and forest regrowth.[19] The team shows that the direct relationship is no intrinsic universal but is dependent on the Global North's capacity to import forest and agricultural products—and export the attendant environmental impact—when its economies are flush. In this context, green marketing in the wealthier regions appears a means of transubstantiating responsibility for the damage incurred by and along the circuits of capital into the moralism of individual consumer choice.

There is, however, a fly in the sector's ointment. As Jason Moore describes it, the globalizing crises of land loss and environmental damage may signal a tipping point in neoliberalism's capacity to deliver continuing declines in systemwide production costs, or, perhaps more grandly, may even mark the end of capitalism's *"longue durée* regime of 'cheap ecology'"*:* cheap energy, labor, raw materials, and food.[20] Either scenario, to foreshadow our argument, could explain the urgency with which agribusiness is pushing a narrative of dystopic rescue.

A CONVENIENT OMISSION

It is on this background that the character of Clay's ostensibly benign recommendations changes, however free his *Nature* article may be of references to specific brands.[21] If enacted, his recommendations would bring about underlying shifts in Africa's agrifood context that would work to the multinationals' strategic advantage.

Clearly, as Clay suggests, local populations should consider an array of labor-saving and green technologies when devising new agricultures. On this point we have no objections, but agribusiness, only one source of such measures, is not in the business of handing out such solutions for free. Technologies often serve as Trojan horses by which to smuggle in new social relations, in this case letting foreign capital cheaply buy up or lease what until now was sovereign land worked by subsistence farmers, or locking small farmers into fiercely copyright-protected, biotech production spirals.

Improving the performance of the "worst" producers—which Clay discusses only in terms of absolute productivity rather than nutrition, sustainability, or community—would indeed require offering such smallholders support and expertise. "Conventionally, such extension systems have been run by governments, but it is not clear if they are up to the task in Africa," writes Clay.[22] It is an observation that elides at one and the same time the support many African countries—much like their European counterparts—have successfully provided their farmers and the structural adjustment programs that stripped out such assistance in agribusiness's favor elsewhere on the continent.[23] If privatized support is predicated on turning land and labor over to agribusiness, such assistance would unlikely be offered on anywhere near equitable terms.

Clay's recommendation that farmers' property rights be individually granted requires elaboration. Though there well may be merits in shifting such rights from governments to specific communities of smallholders, agribusiness appears to support such a change only in its own interests. Companies favor producing a legal framework under which they may purchase land out from underneath the smallest farmers, many of whom, impoverished by export economies bereft of price supports, would sell cheaply. Similar campaigns took place in post-Soviet Russia and appear underway in China.[24] The agroecological and social degradation that results from such land rushes are already undercutting the demonstrable economic and ecological efficiencies African pastoral and transhumant communities have until now enjoyed for centuries.[25]

Setting up food regimes under which agribusinesses, as opposed to local populations, best prosper can take other forms. For instance, the soil carbon markets Clay promotes, expanding nature's neoliberalization, would likely permit companies that are able to pay for the kinds of offsets smaller operations can ill-afford to continue to produce and pollute unimpeded.[26] The offsets become another green barrier to smallholders, who, on their own, when not being forced by dispossession into the forest, contribute relatively insignificantly to the problem.

These kinds of economies of scale, green or otherwise, are, however, in no way guaranteed. Large operations are more productive than smaller units if and only if their scale economies persist with growth, and diseconomies—labor costs, exhaustion of resources, etc.—are postponed.[27] Smaller production models, many of which have evolved over millennia and assimilate the inherently biological (and social) nature of agriculture, can, and often do, succeed in the face of multinational competition, particularly those cooperatives that can negotiate the costs of managing production across many small farms.

But the primary fallacy in Clay's argument pivots about an omission common to many programs in ecological modernization.[28] Clay treats present-day neoliberal capitalism as a force of nature along the lines of the planet's rotation and gravity. In this way capitalism's political and economic premises, whatever any of us think of them, are left outside the bounds of analysis and action.[29] We must work with agribusinesses not just because they produce and distribute much of the world's food supply, but because they *are* and *will continue to be,* by dint of declaration, the world of food as we know it.

If history is any indication, however, capitalism as we know it is as much a conditional—and likely passing—form of social organization as the pharaohs and feudalism; dominant one day, subject to collapse, modification, or rejection the next. The political and financial rewards found in assuming otherwise drive such greenwashing efforts. For once we assume capitalism to be a part of the natural order, an accommodation itself greenwashed as "ecopragmatism," we find ourselves tied into a series of subsidiary presumptions, which together lock all subsequent discussion in agribusiness's favor.

Clay, for instance, confounds capitalist efficiencies in turning natural resources into commodities with the efficiencies needed in conserving resources and feeding the world. Multinationals may be able to transform vast landscapes into billions of packaged products, often of dubious nutritional value, but this speaks little to whether they can, or frankly are willing to, feed the world's population, even as a matter of rapacious expediency. The billion hungry worldwide own few of the assets needed to participate in the capitalist markets in which agribusiness prospers, and so, by virtue of their poverty, are treated on the demand end as if they do not even exist.

On the supply end, the largest agribusinesses and the rural and urban poor who farm are placed fundamentally at odds. The industry's growth is dependent on dispossessing millions of subsistence farmers of the lands it needs to grow export crops and livestock for more lucrative markets.[30] As Clay himself put it, agribusiness cares about availability. The collateral damage that results—the unfed and increasingly restive masses left unabsorbed by the new labor markets that arise in place of indigenous food systems—long has been left to local governments and NGOs to clean up or control.[31]

THE KEYS TO THE PLANET

If agribusiness is to save the world, it needs a free hand to do what it pleases, or so says the sector. Clay concurs, in essence arguing that self-regulation, by which companies operate outside governmental interference, provides the means by which the companies can save themselves from the environmental destruction they have wrought. If we are lucky enough, the argument suggests, these companies will, in passing, if their margins provide, save the planet too.

This is as dubious a proposition as it is self-serving. Multinational agribusinesses become and remain as large as they are by virtue of translating capital accumulation into political power. That power, in turn, secures the very laissez-faire economic environment that allows agribusiness to continue to decimate the environment with impunity. Indeed, political power permits agribusiness its bottom line in the first place, allowing it to externalize its costs elsewhere: to indigenous peoples, governments, farm workers, taxpayers, consumers, livestock, and nearby wildlife.[32] If anything goes wrong—a spill, unemployment, a disease outbreak, price fluctuations—someone else picks up the bill, introducing moral hazards of apocalyptic proportions.

Only by socializing such costs and moving these off their balance sheets have agribusinesses survived as incorporated entities. Despite depending on the public for their very survival, multinationals, with the aid of many of the foundations they fund, are now trying to position themselves as the only recourse to which the world can turn.

Consider that another eminently arguable proposition, but the effort's primary objective is something else entirely. The notion that only agribusiness can save the world serves as the packaging in which the companies are delivering a chilling demand. In exchange for access to enough food in the future—a fraught possibility as it is—humanity must hand over control of what is left of virgin land and resources to a small, highly remunerated minority. Corporate expropriation has been underway for centuries, but its justification within an environmental narrative, as a means of further cementing material control over the world's resources, is something new altogether. One does find similar appeals in other sectors. On a background of slower growth, megabanks embraced high-risk financial instruments, gambling whole sectors of the world's real economy under the guise that the new packages would ensure cost benefits to consumers.[33] The results we know well enough.

The demand for the keys to the planet is itself a product of another capitalist conundrum. Lauderdale's paradox has been on the books for over two hundred years.[34] It arises out of the inverse relationship between, on the one hand, public wealth, including what were for most of human history our environmental commons, and, on the other, private riches. The environment was long defined by its availability to humanity at large, and so embodied little exchange value. We cannot bottle and sell air (or until recently water) if it is freely available. In contrast, the value of private riches emerges out of extracting scarce resources—or, more precisely, rolling over enough capital to pay someone else to do the work.

The paradox emerged post–Industrial Revolution with a shift in the relationship between public wealth and private riches. By destroying the natural environment, capitalists *added* exchange value to what they had yet despoiled, transforming our commons into valuables scarce enough to commoditize.

A decaying resource base, then, is no due cause for agribusiness turning into good global citizens, as Clay argues. On the contrary, agribusiness seeks securing exclusive access to our now fiscally appreciating, if ecologically declining, landscapes. It is, again, all about availability. As a consequence, the industry is maneuvering to rub out alternatives operating on what were until now economic peripheries. As an alternate farm economy, subsistence farmers, comprising in some locales 80 percent of the population, must effectively be removed, marginalized, or turned into laborers so that agricultural capital can geographically spread as it pleases unopposed.[35]

LAND GRABBING BY ANOTHER NAME

It is in this context that the race for Africa, Clay's beat, where 60 percent of the planet's undeveloped farmland remains, is intensifying.[36] The Oakland Institute, an independent policy think tank in California, recently reported that agribusinesses are collaborating on African projects with a number of American universities, including Harvard, Vanderbilt, and Spelman.[37] The universities are investing their endowments through European hedge funds and speculators to buy or lease vast swaths of African farmland that the schools' private partners subsequently develop. The Institute estimates US$500 million from all sources invested in African farmland, with expectations of 25 percent returns from production and land price appreciation on leases running tax-free for as long as ninety-nine years.[38] McKinsey consultants estimate Africa's agricultural output could treble as a result, to US$880 billion a year by 2030.[39]

One such land grab in Tanzania is spearheaded by AgriSol Energy, Iowa-based agribusiness Summit Group, and the Global Agriculture Fund of the Pharos Financial Group, in partnership with Iowa State University's College of Agriculture and Life Sciences.[40] The site, according to the Oakland Institute,

> encompasses three "abandoned refugee camps"—Lugufu in Kigoma province (25,000 ha), Katumba (80,317 ha), and Mishamo (219,800 ha), both in Rukwa province . . . [with] negotiations . . . . underway with the Tanzanian government involving . . . award of strategic investor status to assure availability of incentives (tax holidays, repatriation of dollars out of the country, waiver of duties on diesel, agricultural and industrial equipment and supplies, etc.); and commitment and timetable for construction of a rail link for Mishamo.

Together the three tracts will host agricultural developments in large-scale, genetically modified crops, beef and poultry production, and biofuels, contingent on shuttling out thousands of resident smallholders in favor of labor crews led by expatriate managers.

A spokesman for Emergent Asset Management, handling one of the largest land acquisition funds, defended the university-associated efforts this way:

Yes, university endowment funds and pension funds are long-term investors. . . . We are investing in African agriculture and setting up businesses and employing people. We are doing it in a responsible way. . . . The amounts are large. They can be hundreds of millions of dollars. This is not land grabbing. We want to make the land more valuable. Being big makes an impact, economies of scale can be more productive.[41]

The facts refute the assurances, which on their own are damning enough. Much of the new farming appears focused on export agricultures, and many thousands of indigenous farmers are being forced off their land. The memorandum of understanding for AgriSol's Tanzania project

stipulates that the two main locations—Katumba and Mishamo—for their project are refugee settlements holding as many as 162,000 people that will have to be closed before the $700m project can start. The refugees have been farming this land for 40 years.[42]

Tanzania is no exception. Accumulation by dispossession, North to South, is underway across Africa:

A 2010 study showed that Awash Valley pastoral production produced returns per hectare equal to or greater than those from subsidized irrigated cotton and sugar farming.[43] Yet the Ethiopian government is presently forcing tens of thousands of farmers and pastoralists off traditional lands into new villages, its obligation under a number of international land deals.

A forty-nine-year lease of 600,000 hectares in South Sudan's Central Equatoria, at a dirt-cheap US$25,000, with an option for 400,000 more hectares, gives Dallas-based Nile Trading and Development full rights to oil and timber there.[44]

Seventy percent of Kenyan grantees awarded by the Alliance for a Green Revolution in Africa (AGRA), the Gates Foundation's "Africa face," work directly with Monsanto.[45] The Gates Foundation holds 500,000 shares of Monsanto stock worth an estimated US$23.1 million. In turn, the Foundation effort is staffed by ex-Monsanto executives.

In Rwanda, the tiny plots of refugees who returned from Tanzania after the genocide are on degazetted national park land and is being expropriated by the politically connected raising livestock or bought up by beer and biofuel companies for export production.[46]

To round out our examples, Madagascar leased an area the size of Connecticut to Korean conglomerate Daewoo; Mozambique put seven million hectares, 27,000 square miles, up for sale; and South African companies are collaborating with European hedge funds to bring in the investment needed to buy up forest and farmland.[47]

Primitive accumulation, however clothed in neoliberal or NGO garb, has its privileges, of course. But even on their own terms, land grabs trade one set of contradictions for another. As Giovanni Arrighi warned as far back as his 1966 study of Rhodesia,[48] fully proletarianizing peasants by driving them off their land and into the labor market can, in an example of the diseconomies of scale, ultimately produce more problems for agribusiness than advantages:

> [The] process of extreme dispossession was contradictory. Initially it created the conditions for the peasantry to subsidize capitalist agriculture, mining, manufacturing and so on. But increasingly it created difficulties in exploiting, mobilizing, controlling the proletariat that was being created. . . . Fully proletarianized labour could be exploited only if it was paid a full living wage.[49]

Arrighi and colleagues inferred political control could be better exercised by only partially proletarianizing, forcing peasants to feed themselves by off-seasonal subsistence in the home village, as is now routine today in Africa and elsewhere.[50] Ironically, the strategy runs up against agribusiness's appetite for farmland and accessible labor, as peasants have transformed the pluriactivity forced on them into an albeit precarious means by which to survive increasingly informal and inequitable economic conditions.[51]

Land grabs, breaking up historically mediated, indigenous agrofood complexes, offer little in the way of the "green" efficiencies proponents claim.

THE DECLENSIONIST DIET

The increasing divide between rich and poor that results from such dispossession is itself now treated as a rationale for an agribusiness Earth, even as greater inequality typically produces worse environmental damage.[52] Egypt offers a telling example.[53]

During the Mubarak regime Egyptian horticulture and livestock underwent massive consolidation, deserting millions of smallholders on the peri-urban margins. Over the regime's final five years many of the poorest communities were further impoverished by public health interventions ostensibly undertaken to protect them. In an effort to staunch rolling outbreaks of highly pathogenic influenza A (H5N1) (bird flu) and H1N1 2009 (swine flu), authorities destroyed forty million poultry and the entire swine population, respectively. The greatest impact fell on backyard and small-scale operations despite precarious evidence that extensive poultry or wild birds were *driving* influenza's emergence.

Considerable evidence favors the contention that intensive poultry and livestock instead serve as the crucible in which many of the newly virulent animal pathogens are now evolving.[54] These pathogens, including the influenzas, are routinely introduced into other countries by way of the geographic reach of the sector's commodity chains, which stretch across continents to extents no smallholder can match.

At no stage, however, were industrial poultry systems seriously investigated as a possible cause of the H5N1 outbreaks in Egypt, or elsewhere for that matter. Nor was the destruction of industrial poultry and livestock undertaken at the scale pursued among smallholder animals. The industry's biosecurity, its capacity to technically respond to a disease of its own making at the expense of its smallholding rivals, serves as the industry's own rationale.

In the case of Egypt the consequences of such an approach extended beyond its epidemiology and agriculture to the country's political core. The technicist interventions into endemic H5N1 appeared to exasperate Egypt's deepening poverty beyond anecdotal evidence of stunting in children under five. Poultry loss alone may not have been the primary cause of the revolution that followed, but its impacts on food prices, food availability, and the Egyptian people's desire to decide their own destiny—including whether they kept chickens— played its part.

Despite these connections, the literature around the influenza outbreaks in Egypt, as well as those elsewhere, at one and the same time embodies the premises of and offers tautological arguments for the transition into highly capitalized farming. That is, the system's failures serve as its justification. Under the prevalent model of offshore agriculture, agribusiness effectively dispossesses indigenous farmers, producing hunger and disease and destroying environments directly and by proxy. The resulting crises are then treated as due cause for expanding dispossession.

Diana Davis describes such a "humanitarian" framework as part and parcel of

> a declensionist colonial environmental narrative, appropriated to help justify and implement the neoliberal goals of land privatization and the intensification of agricultural production in the name of environmental protection.[55]

The narrative appears to be this season's Malthusian tragedy of the commons, wherein a rabble competing for a shared resource destroys it, a straw man for fencing off the commons for the very few to ruin instead.[56] In reality, even when and where nature has provided enough for nearly everyone, commons routinely have been regulated by local councils of a variety of social organization.[57] Interestingly, the objection is embraced as much by some on the right who favor blocking out federal and international intervention as those on the left who favor community control.[58] Such councils are never a guarantee against history—populations do collapse—but the notion of the commons' intrinsic dysfunction is more ideology than data.

DISEASE BY COMMODITY

To what end are such "humanitarian" narratives directed? Of what are corporate production efficiencies really composed? Wealthier societies showcase the best of what nomadic capital offers the poorest regions.

Cheap food is mass produced and homogenized, enabling centralized control from source to fork and massive profits for a few. Cleverly packaged and marketed, highly processed, calorific and addictive, nutritionally deficient foodstuffs have created a new suite of epidemic chronic diseases, from diabetes to morbid obesity.[59]

Agricultural diseases meanwhile evolve at increasing speed in industrialized, genetically limited domestic animal and crop communities.[60] Such ills are often managed in comparatively sterile, though at such densities still pathogen-conducive, conditions, requiring continuous applications of vaccine and pharmaceutics in livestock to reduce now endemic diarrheas and respiratory diseases. Pesticides are applied to crops largely engineered for withstanding still greater petrochemical application, selecting for superweeds and pests.[61]

The resulting waste runoff carries highly evolved cassettes of drug resistance genes, joined by increasing concentrations of hormone mimics and other ecotoxins seeping into local soils, groundwater, and river systems, and even recycled as fertilizer.[62] Even pharmaceuticals are becoming detectable in biologically active concentrations in the environment with increasing evidence of ecological, physiological, and pathological impacts.[63] Despite their passing contributions to animal and public health, live-attenuated virus vaccines have selected for new strains evolving from underneath immune coverage and can themselves turn into pollutants of a sort by recombining with circulating strains and returning to field virulence.[64]

Pollution and pathogens have become an integral part of the risk frame of the industrialized food system.[65] The science of food safety is daily called upon to mop up disease spills throughout a global system of shipments of breeding or neonatal stock and potentially contaminated food products. The eleven tons of Egyptian fenugreek sprouts that sickened 4,100 Germans with *E. coli* O104 in 2011, for instance, were repackaged by a German distributor and resold to seventy companies across twelve European countries.[66] Agribusiness's economies of scale extend to the evolution and spread of the pathogens the sector selects, in the biological sense of the word. A wildlife squeezed by encroaching livestock populations in turn dumps its own pathogen community back into wet markets, bushmeat butcheries, farmland, and urban environments, producing risky natural experiments in disease transmission and pathogen evolution across multiple animal orders.[67]

The short-term gains in agribusiness's production and supply efficiencies have been developed only by way of a series of perverse subsidies from and costs to local peoples and the environment—costs kept off company balance sheets. Occupational hazards, pollution, food poisoning, antibiotic resistance, price spikes, climate change, monopolistic consolidation, declining nutritional content, flooding, export economics, farmland bubbles, grain dumping, farm dispossession, forced migration, research gaps, and damage to transportation and health infrastructure are routinely externalized to governments, the indigenous, workers, consumers, taxpayers, livestock, and wildlife.[68]

Once removed from the protection of such creative accounting, the agribusiness model turns unsustainably expensive (and given its capacity for catastrophe, nigh on sociopathic). What to do, then? All parties to such debates, agribusiness included, routinely cite human ingenuity as the means by which we can solve the ecological crises. But as soon as something other than agribusiness is suggested, tax-deductible consultants, Clay included, object with "That's impossible!"[69] The ideological cover agribusiness enjoys is itself a marginal cost we are asked to subsidize.

CONSERVATION AGRICULTURE

Another agriculture, however, *is* possible and in fact is, at various stages of development, already underway.[70] Alternate approaches propose lower input costs—minimizing ecological subsidies to be floated by governments, consumers, and wildlife alike—using organic, naturally renewable production methods and cutting-edge conservation cultivation.

A number of practices even now cultivate sustainable agroecosystems, including of "sustainable intensification," which where best developed are producing as much food per acre as petrochemical agribusiness.[71] Integrated pest management, integrated nutrient management, conservation tillage, cover crops, trap crops, contour cropping, agroforestry, aquaculture, water harvesting, and mixed crop-livestock systems are all already in play.[72]

Underlying such efforts is the presumption that humanity is still part of the ecology from which we emerged. As much as human civilization has been organized around segregating our welfare from nature red in tooth and claw, we cannot *escape* the ecologies in which we are embedded, however much we modify them. Nor, however, should we fall into prelapsarian fantasies of agriculture as it never was. Farmers are daily devising and applying new innovations in organic agriculture to solve today's problems in growing plants and raising livestock, and in climatic and economic contexts of a particular historical moment.

The work still required in developing such theoretical and practical applications cannot be overstated. Many such nascent efforts have been financially and infrastructurally starved. However, even now examples abound across orders of industrial integration and community organization:

With the support of the Mexican government, Zapotec Indians developed a certified-sustainable, community-controlled forestry.[73] Plain pine is sold to the state government, and finished goods, including furniture, are produced in an on-site factory. The Oaxaca cooperative, still a work in progress, plows a third of its profits back into the business, a third into forest preservation, and the rest into its workers and the local community, including pensions, a credit union, and housing for its children studying at university.

The Federation of Unions of Farmers' Groups of Niger (FUGPN-Mooriben)—with over 62,000 members, 60+ percent women—offers its members training, grain banking, input shops, credit lines, savings services, liaison consultation, advocacy, and community radio.[74] Previously, on the dismantling of state cooperatives, farmers could only consume their harvests or sell them to traders to whom they owed massive debt. The poorest cut trees for sale or housing, causing a silted Niger River to flood and worsening already bad conditions. The grain banks cut out usurious traders and improved food coverage during lean seasons. Mooriben shops meanwhile permit farmers informed access to quality farm inputs and rental machinery. The federation's credit cooperatives allow farmers to turn excess grain into cheap liquidity for non-farm economic activity.

In the face of national policy aimed at subsidizing conventional irrigated crop agriculture and livestock ranching, community trusts in Northern Kenya have established viable integrated land management, diversifying livelihoods while benefiting natural resources and livestock production alike.[75] Using conservation of selected key resources, including grass banks, the environment and wildlife is recovering from a previously degraded state, while the economy and income of the people has increased threefold.

Tarun Bharat Sangh, a local voluntary organization in Jaipur, India, initiated a watershed restoration program that grew to a thousand villages.[76] The organization rebuilt *johads*, traditional mud barriers for collecting water that recharge groundwater, improve forest growth, and conserve water for irrigation and wildlife, livestock, and domestic use. The efforts, coordinated by village councils, restored the Avari River—dry since the 1940s—as well as native bird populations.

Some agricultural innovations are informal to the extreme but no less fundamental. A social network of women farmers across neighboring villages in Mozambique copied farmers participating in more formal agricultural projects in the area.[77] To cushion the risk of increasingly variable weather the women adopted short-maturing varieties of cassava and sweet potatoes, which could be grown on marginal sandy soils during increasingly frequent droughts. Their effort speaks both to the power organized women can exert and the marginalization they must routinely overcome.

As the examples illustrate, many such efforts work only because local populations take executive initiative beyond the "community-led" market-oriented pathways promoted by neoliberal natural resource management.[78] Sustainability arises in part from communal ownership of the problem of integrating food and ecology, including recycling physical and social resources for the next season, year, or generation. Such communities are almost by definition unlikely—even unable—to engage in the kinds of "spatial fixes" routinely undertaken by agribusinesses, which, with little compulsion otherwise, are able to move their operations out of a region they've environmentally ruined or even geographically "surf" their own wave of destruction.[79] Indeed, as far back as the 1850s German chemist Justus von Liebig framed chemically driven intensification in and of itself, destroying soils for generations, as an act of theft.[80]

The success of community alternatives is never guaranteed and is contingently dependent upon 1) routinely reconceptualizing responses; 2) accumulating natural and social buffers to global environmental and economic processes that can swamp or contradict local efforts; and 3) state support in material and morale. The details are critical and, as described here by Richard Levins, require constant place- and time-specific adjustment:

> Instead of having to decide between large-scale industrial type production and a "small is beautiful" approach *a priori*, we saw the scale of agriculture as dependent on natural and social conditions, with the units of planning embracing many units of production. Different scales of farming would be adjusted to the watershed, climatic zones and topography, population density, distribution of available resources, and the mobility of pests and their enemies.
>
> The random patchwork of peasant agriculture, constrained by land tenure, and the harsh destructive landscapes of industrial farming would both be replaced by a planned mosaic of land uses in which each patch contributes its own products but also assists the production of other patches: forests give lumber, fuel, fruit, nuts, and honey but also regulate the flow of water, modulate the climate to a distance about ten times the height of the trees, create a special microclimate downwind from the edge, offer shade for

livestock and the workers, and provide a home to the natural enemies of pests and the pollinators of crops. There would no longer
be specialized farms producing only one thing. Mixed enterprises
would allow for recycling, a more diverse diet for the farmers, and
a hedge against climatic surprises. It would have a more uniform
demand for labor throughout the year.[81]

If a community's source of wealth is found in its landscape, rather
than solely in wages from externally sourced capital or a small plot's
seasonal output, taking care of the land and local wildlife turns into a
prime directive even—or especially—in a global marketplace. Wealth
in a commons a population shares turns back into the kind of value
neoclassical economics has long abandoned. Lauderdale's paradox,
by which the market rewards efforts to destroy Earth's remaining
resources, is resolved in favor of populations that conserve the environments they consume.

FOOD REVOLUTION

Current concerns about global food security are certainly justified,
but long-term resolution requires more than pursuing a second Green
Revolution, whatever heavily capitalized transgenics, chemicals, and
dispossession such a thing might entail. Refuting agribusiness's bedrock assumptions, even if at first by example alone, opens up space for
alternate models aimed at assuring food's long-term viability.

In the end, however, the power of example must be consolidated
into a paradigm shift that transcends the agrifood sector. The larger
world needs to assimilate the already detrimental consequences
should unfettered human growth and consumption continue as
presently, or as green (or greenwashing) neoliberalism effectively proposes anew. If the likelihood can be conceptually absorbed, there is a
chance policy, behaviors, and practices around reducing "growth" and
resource consumption, even to a negative rate, can be accepted globally as both the norm and beneficial. Wealth and wages can be newly
conceived in our efforts to restore landscape regenerative capacity
and to better calibrate community production and consumption.

The resulting "breathing room" should permit ecosystems and biodiversity time enough to recover, highly sophisticated integrative agricultures to develop, and the quality and sustainability of human life to improve. The rapid growth of interest in steady-state economics is cause for hope, as is the development of the "One Health" approach, wherein the health of humans, livestock, crops, wildlife, and wild plants are treated as inextricably linked in integrated ecosystems.[82] Both are good albeit insufficient starts. Each largely leaves out the central roles expropriation and material alienation play in reordering ecologies and epidemiologies alike. Contrary to charges of Luddism,[83] attempts at devising a sustainable commons that feeds a growing global population are conceptually orders of magnitude more difficult than keeping the agricultural regime on its present— and disastrous—course. The science around moving out of the trap into which we maneuvered ourselves and toward a sovereign conservation agriculture is exceedingly difficult if also at this point our sole option for a future both fed and fair.

A key to such a revolution—and there can be no other word for it—will be its governance. To give credit where due, many institutions have shifted their policy thinking around food security toward more sustainable and equitable solutions, however much these still remain highly dependent on present global and local governance. Unfortunately, such good faith has been repeatedly cracked with enough lobbying. The political pressure multinational agribusiness exerts in local arenas extends to global institutions.[84] As a result, to date the progress has been found more in rhetoric and less so, if at times at all, in the field. Change, if still only in principle, is nominally accepted during macroeconomically prosperous fiscal quarters, but is soon abandoned in a panic as economies fail by way of the very models used to justify continuing current production practices.

If such contradictory impulses continue to manifest in weak governance and an inability to boldly take on sustainable food security, the political will may be supplied from elsewhere instead, namely by popular movements outside the present political infrastructure. For some, including Clay, the present revolts across North Africa and the Middle East, correlated with food crises,[85] serve as fair warning. For much of the world, on the other hand, the more populist revolts symbolize the very hope of the future.

As our species' history has repeatedly shown—a series of radical shifts born as much out of desperation as innovation[86]—a food revolution is not only a good idea but, as we look across our planet, a precarious necessity. Precarious, as its outcome is no sure thing. History offers us an illusion of inevitable existence. Humanity has repeatedly overcome dire food limitations, even as archeological strata are also littered with dead civilizations. These near-misses, however, can offer us no sample sufficiently representative for guaranteeing a future. So the direction we next choose may literally mean the world.[87] Agribusiness, on the one hand, treating Earth's ecological collapses as an investment prospectus, machinates at holding the globe at ransom: food for those who can afford it in return for food's control and command.

Millions the world over, on the other hand, see another way. There's plenty of capacity for food production even with a growing population if we treat food as first a source of ecologically integrated nutrition rather than of commodities alone, as a use value before a surplus value, as a renewable and locally tended if globally connected source of income, as well as, lest we forget one of life's pleasures, a tasty delight. In this way, albeit with all the details still open to discovery, we can sidestep the very consumption spirals that commodities putatively aim to plug. Our wealth is found in our soil's—and water and air's—self-regeneration. It is found in the work put into preserving those capacities in the course of exploiting them for our own needs.

A conservation agriculture in more than name alone, in a plurality of forms that from place to place sustainably aligns people and their ecologies, marrying food security with food sovereignty, can be brought about in time, but only by prying capital's grip off policy and power. In liberating ourselves we can save our planet and feed its people, as beautiful an act of redemption as it is now by Earth's present damage compulsory.

—*Human Geography*, November 2012

A Probiotic Ecology

"There is no fucking prefix," Kalb said . . . There are certain songs that provoked such responses in certain people, and one learned to avoid them, or in the case of a very clever bird like Bruno, to choose one's moments . . . Because Kalb seemed to want so badly to hear the train song, Bruno was careful now only to sing it when the man was asleep, with instinctive and deliberate perversity that was among the virtues most highly prized by his kind. The sound of the train song, arising in the middle of the night, would jar the man from his slumber, send him scrabbling for his pencil and pad. When at last he was awake, sitting in a circle of light from the lamp with pencil clutched in his fingers, then— of course—Bruno would leave off singing. Night after night, this performance was repeated. Bruno had seen men driven mad. . . . He knew how it was done.

—MICHAEL CHABON (2004)

CONTEXT ISN'T MERELY THE FIELD on which causal relationships play out. Nor is it some fail-safe when our model—in math or mind—goes bust. Context *is* causality.

The philosopher Ludwig Wittgenstein offered this deceptively simple example: →←.[88] Clearly two arrows pointing in opposite directions, you say. In actuality, that all depends. A mirror between means the two face the same way. I'll leave you the transitive to work out on your own.

There are epidemiological corollaries. Ecologist Felicia Keesing and colleagues show that the state of an ecosystem's biodiversity and the connections among its populations have a definitional effect on the emergence of epizootics, pathogens circulating among wild animals and livestock and in danger of spilling over to humans.[89] The direction of the effect depends on that context. Biodiversity and the ecological relationships connecting populations under different conditions can staunch *or* promote outbreaks:

> For initial invasion, biodiversity may act as a source pool. . . . [Most emerging diseases in humans] are zoonotic—jumping to humans from other vertebrate animals. In one recent analysis, the probability of emergence of pathogens from wildlife to humans was positively correlated with mammalian wildlife species richness when data were corrected for reporting bias.

By the world's latitudinal gradient in species diversity we broadly expect a greater diversity of pathogens toward the Equator, where exists a greater diversity of plants and animals. But such a host substrate is hardly enough:

> Other environmental and socioeconomic factors that bring humans into closer contact with potentially new pathogens (for example, forest clearing for agriculture, wildlife hunting) may also contribute to this pattern. Indeed, almost half of the zoonotic diseases that have emerged in humans since 1940 resulted from changes in land use, from changes in agricultural or other food production practices, or from wildlife hunting. These human activities increase rates of contact between humans and animals, which may be a critical factor underlying spillover.

Even then, pathogens have long spilled over into human populations, although perhaps not to today's extent and frequency. The question remains what gives intermittent zoonoses their epidemiological momentum once in their new surroundings. Here, the collapse of biodiversity plays its role:

> High densities of . . . host species may facilitate establishment and transmission within a new host. For example, Nipah virus

spilled over from wild fruit bats to domestic pigs in Malaysia; high densities of pigs in local farms appear to have facilitated establishment of pig-to-pig transmission, and the pathogen then spilled over from pigs to humans. Such high densities of domesticated species are almost always associated with low biodiversity.

By email a colleague, in many ways as consistent a champion of the key concept behind my work, a better conscience than my own, found the argument at best an approximation and weaker than the one that could have been made:

> To a large extent, [the review] reads as if the lack of biodiversity is the problem, whilst the main problem is intensive farming here. . . . I find that the "farming pathogen" concept is truly what should receive large attention when we talk about these diseases. . . . Biodiversity should be protected for what it is, not for what it brings us.

True and much appreciated on a number of accounts. Drafting pathogens into the conservation fight, despite the desperate odds, might be in some frameworks a touch overkill. That said, I found the Keesing review helped better order in my mind the mechanisms by which ecological interactions translate into outbreaks, something with which our own group was having some trouble in our work on influenza and agroecological resilience.[90]

SHIFTS IN THE HOST GUILD

Keesing et al. review several studies on the epizoological effects of host community diversity. Communities with low avian diversity, for one, tend to be dominated by bird species that happen to amplify West Nile Virus in mosquito vectors and people. Similarly, reductions in the diversity of small mammal species increase the prevalence of hantavirus in its host species and as a result the number of human spillover events.

The mechanism appears predicated on a loss in the complexity of weak ecological ties, which previously separated functionally distal populations across a biome. The relationship is, however, something of a double-edged sword. When the species lost are *not* typically infected, the encounter rates, and by extension the transmission rates, between the pathogen and the host species should increase. On the other hand, if the host species itself is lost, then obviously transmission should decline. Even that complication is an oversimplification. Keesing et al. point out that the loss of a major host species might lead to the emergence of one or more minor host species in its stead, with no loss in overall transmission, and only a rearrangement in the pathogen's transmission patterns. At the same time, transmission need not depend on host densities and encounter rates alone. Keesing's group describes the effects of the *quality* of hosts. A suboptimal host, for instance, can absorb pathogens without subsequently transmitting them.

Agroecological Tiling

What happens to the pathogen as absorbing or amplifying host species are lost (or gained)? I would coin such shifts "ecological tiling": the effects of adding and subtracting species (and agricultural practices) in a particular order and spatial array on the resulting disease patterns.

Keesing et al. describe tiling's effects on Lyme disease in North America. As the forest contracts, the more environmentally resilient, tic-prone white-footed mouse grows or is sustained at the expense of the more deforestation-susceptible, tic-resistant Virginia opossum. In other words, the opossum's buffering effect disappears, allowing tics, and Lyme disease, to spread.

The example inspires new questions. When intensive farming moves in, what exactly happens to the local agroecosystems in sequence (in time and in space)? How do different spatiotemporal trajectories affect epizootic dangers? We've discussed one method of detecting such changes: jolts in time series prefiguring shifts in epizootic regime.[91]

Tiling and ecological resilience are clearly related, as each involves changes in the functional relationships among populations, including livestock. In other words, changes in resilience can be operationalized by decisions about land use. What we do with the landscape when and where, shaping ecological tiling, will determine the course of interconnections among community populations and, as a result, their resilience, including in the face of new pathogens.

In the case of intensive livestock, however, resilience is as much economic as it is ecological. By their evolved life histories intensive livestock offer the flexible morphogenesis and behavior amenable to market demands and agricultural Taylorization. In exchange, the livestock are provided ecological protection by way of 1) medical interventions; and 2) by deforestation and declining smallholder production, reducing interspecific and even conspecific competition. In other words, their ecological resilience is profoundly and inextricably anthropogenic in origin, much in the way some species of fungus depend entirely on leaf-cutter ants.

Domestication is a two-way street, with great mutual obligations— and deceptions—asked of the crop or livestock and their handlers alike. As we have discussed elsewhere, livestock epizootic dynamics are as a result dependent on the agricultural economics shaping husbandry, including capital flows, commodity networks, technological innovations, market dynamics, labor costs, and spatial fixes, wherein companies move operations to places better suited to their production needs and margins.[92]

A Probiotic Ecology

Keesing et al. also discuss community diversity *within* hosts. Individual animals, humans included, with *greater* microbial diversity in their bodies are now repeatedly shown *more* resistant to infection and illness. Probiotics are gaining a prominence in the medical literature.

The team makes the analogy to ecosystem-level dynamics explicit. Ecologies, including livestock systems, with a microbiome of greater diversity should be better protected from invasion. They cite a 2009 report[93] showing piglets raised in natural environments supporting a high diversity of microbes were more resistant to invasion by pathogenic gut microbes than those raised in more sterile environments.

In that vein, then, our own group's virulence modeling,[94] arguing along similar lines that low-pathogenic strains may act as natural vaccines, need no longer appear pie-in-the-sky, even to many of our skeptical colleagues. There are real-world applications to be followed up, including for livestock influenzas. The details, only touched on in passing in our initial report, require follow-up. What does a probiotic livestock system look like? Can one model niche, resilience, and virulence together in such a way as to better project disease dynamics? In other words, can we make a science of sustainable husbandry?

In important ways the applications of such work are already well underway elsewhere. Resilience, shaping the network of ecological relationships in such a way as to control emergence and invasion, is an idea at the heart of *integrated pest management*.

Plant scientists, long interested in increasing yields with minimal or no pesticide, are decades ahead in this line of research and application. The Plant Production and Protection Division at the UN's Food and Agriculture Organization has considerable experience in IPM, including its power and problems. A number of case studies, dealing with the nitty-gritty details, turning theory to practice on the ground, are also available on the FAO website.[95]

A new world appears before us: applying IPM to livestock pathogens.

Resistance Is Fissile

It isn't just that an integrated agriculture may in some circumstances be ecologically better cushioned from epizoological emergence. Such an agriculture may keep itself open to evolution's useful side.

Disease resistance genes flow from wild birds into backyard poultry and livestock in ways unavailable to more intensive operations, which box in their pigs and chickens.[96] The phenomenon remains an empirical question from place to place: Do China's Lake Poyang wildfowl and domestic birds—an uneasy distinction there—trade in resistance genes in addition to the disease agents to be resisted? Conversely, does biosecurity filter out such alleles?

In restricting selection to grandparent stock, intensive husbandry removes natural selection as a real-time and free ecological service the industry must substitute with expensive breeding and pharmaceuticals. We see here now that even if livestock *were* bred on-site, intensive operations would still block out the benefits of evolution, even if all the hard work—including the suffering associated with selection's excess mortality—were done elsewhere, in another population off the balance sheets entirely.

An integrated agriculture, then, is fundamental not only to conservation and epizootic control but to any economic criteria beyond next quarter's margins, that maddening numeric string sung by a very clever bird. Whatever smoke and mirrors (and plucked feathers) are deployed by Big Food, confounding obfuscation and divination, all the arrows still point in the same direction.

—14 JUNE 2011

Strange Cotton

"Odious resource" though it might be, as Merivale called it, slavery was an economic institution of the first importance. It had been the basis of Greek economy and had built up the Roman Empire. In modern times it provided the sugar for the tea and the coffee cups of the Western world. It produced the cotton to serve as a base for modern capitalism. It made the American South and the Caribbean islands. Seen in historical perspective, it forms a part of that general picture of the harsh treatment of the underprivileged classes, the unsympathetic poor laws and severe feudal laws, and the indifference with which the rising capitalist class was "beginning to reckon prosperity in terms of pounds sterling, and . . . becoming used to the idea of sacrificing human life to the deity of increased production."

—ERIC WILLIAMS (1944)

OUR POLITICAL CONSCIOUSNESS GESTATES early enough, perhaps in a rudimentary fashion as far back as the womb, but certainly on the playground and at the dinner table, Daddy or Mommy haranguing some politico. On the other hand, we also never really make it there. A ninety-something I know, nodding out her window, copped to asking herself, Am I ever gonna figure that out?

Along the way there are revelations, some more trap doors than epiphanies. We learn history is both contingent and unexpectedly accumulative—shit happens in a growing pile—even as the pathways along which any set of circumstances converge aren't always clear.[97]

How, for instance, did agribusiness become so powerful and in quite that way? It is as if one day we wake to find the industry just there—like Old Man of the Mountain, a granite formation on Cannon Mountain—jutting its stone chin out daring any punch or poke.[98]

HOW FAR BACK, THEN, DO WE need to go for a beginning? Craig McCalin takes us back 100 million years ago to the Cretaceous.[99] A tropical sea covered much of what is now the southern United States. The sea's coastline proved rich in plankton, whose carbonate skeletons accumulated as alkaline and porous chalk, enriching soils across what later became the most productive cotton counties of antebellum Mississippi, Alabama, Georgia, and South Carolina.

The counties—the Black Belt by both soil and population—also hosted the greatest concentrations in slaves along that ancient shoreline. Black majorities persist today, marking a swoop of 2012 Barack Obama victories across a swatch of Mitt Romney Red.

Walter Johnson suggests a number of other foundational holdovers in *River of Dark Dreams*, one of 2013's best books.[100]

By purchase and by violence the United States folded in hundreds of millions of acres upriver of New Orleans. Thomas Jefferson imagined his 1803 Louisiana Purchase—rolling over French conquest—two ways. At one and the same time it was a means to a republic of yeomen farmers free of capital's taint and a sink to which millions of potentially insurrectionist Upper South slaves, capital embodied, could be dispersed and defused:

> Between 1820 and 1860 as many as a million people were sold "down the river" through an internal slave trade, which, in addition to the downriver trade, included a coastal trade (Norfolk to New Orleans, for instance) and an overland trade (Fayetteville, North Carolina, to Florence, Alabama, for instance). Their relocation and reassignment to the cultivation of cotton—the leading sector of the emergent global economy of the first half of the nineteenth century—gave new life to slavery in the United States.[101]

The American ethos, once afraid of slave insurrection, now standing its ground one dead black teen at a time, incubated within whites' visceral terror of revolutionary Haiti.

Slavery's spatial fix along the Mississippi proved more than a projection of imperial might or an economic reorganization, however.[102]
It represented ecology's unprecedented transformation into manifest
economy:

> Most of the cotton picked by [Mississippi] Valley slaves was
> Petit Gulf (*Gossypium barbadense*), a hybrid strain developed in
> Rodney, Mississippi, patented in 1820, and prized for its "pick-
> ability." The hegemony of this single plant over the landscape of
> the Cotton Kingdom produced both a radical simplification of
> nature and a radical simplification of human being: the reduc-
> tion of landscape to cotton plantation and of human being to
> "hand." Cotton mono-cropping stripped the land of vegetation,
> leached out its fertility, and rendered one of the richest agricul-
> tural regions of the earth dependent on upriver trade for food.[103]

This strange cotton—resembling its natural ancestor as a Chihuahua
a wolf—emerged out of an idiosyncratic convergence of slavery, ecology, crop cycles, and global markets and trade:

> The "cotton market" . . . was in actual fact a network of mate-
> rial connections that stretched from Mississippi and Louisiana
> to Manhattan and Lowell to Manchester and Liverpool. The eco-
> nomic space of the cotton market was defined by a set of standard
> measures—hands, pounds, lashes, bales, grades—that translated
> aspects of the process of production and sale into one another.

The unsustainable agroecosystem repeatedly produced its own
material and conceptual crises, temporarily "solved" only by the expe-
dient crashes off which other classes of confidence men—in transport
or wildcat banking—profited:

> Overinvestment in slaves [but not in their most basic victuals],
> overproduction of cotton, and overreliance on credit made
> Valley planters vulnerable to precisely the sort of crisis they
> experienced during the Depression of 1837. Cotton planting was

extraordinarily capital intensive, and most of planters' money was tied up in land slaves. For the money they needed to get through the year—for liquidity—they relied on [New Orleans and Northern] credit. And to get credit they had to plant cotton. Their situation—the fact that they were "overaccumulated" in a single sector of the economy—was expressed in the antebellum commonplace [that planters] . . . "care for nothing but to buy Negroes to plant cotton & raise cotton to buy Negroes."

As capital gushed into cotton, the Southern economy's leading sop, its returns diminished. Nor were slaveholders able to liquidate for an easy exit. Even slaves treated like draft animals—with whole families sold off separately—proved too much of a structural drag.

So Jeffersonian expansionism represented the only way out. New land, new soil, and new slave sinks. First west and then south. The abolitionist movement, then, wasn't merely a metaphysical contretemps, but an existential threat. When the West was blocked off by the Kansas-Nebraska Act, Johnson argues, the slaveholder ideologues— think Charles Murray in sideburns—turned to linking the Mississippi River to the Amazon by way of Cuba and Central America.

Johnson portrays William Walker's Nicaraguan filibustering, Narcisco Lopez's Cuban (mis)adventures, and the failed efforts at reopening the Atlantic slave trade as slavery's efforts at its own foreign policy. Globalization or death! The Civil War would finish the job.

It wasn't that the South's mode of production wasn't profitable, but as Ann Markusen explains, its relative growth couldn't keep pace with Northeast-Midwest dynamism:

Cities like Baltimore and Louisville moved away from the southern fold as their manufacturing and commercial activities molded them increasingly in the image of northern cities. By the 1850s, it had become patently clear that if southern planters had not enjoyed disproportionate political power due to the three-fifths provision for each of their four million slaves, planter class national political power would have been broken.[104]

And yet slavery's agriculture didn't die at the Battle of Columbus, the Civil War's last. A hundred and fifty years before cosmetic arsenic and oestradiol-17, Johnson's economic ethnography intimates that many of agribusiness's key innovations, in both technology and organization, originated in slavery.[105]

HOW DID THE LARGEST MISSISSIPPI VALLEY slaveholders get their land in the first place? Early U.S. intervention—by treaty and by carbine—suddenly opened millions of acres straddling the Mississippi to even the poorest farmers of the East, turning, Johnson writes, "Indian land into white farms and conquest into cultivation: empire into equality."[106]

But the richest gamed even such grotesque ideals.

Surveyors hired by the General Land Office subdivided the rolling landscape into 160-acre rectangles still visible from space.[107] The expropriation was couched as an intellectual necessity. The white race must bring order to nature by pseudoscientific principles now long abandoned, but atop which all subsequent rounds of rationalized land grabbing, domestic and abroad, yesterday and today, were churned.

In an effort to actualize Jefferson's idealized yeoman, cultivators who "improved" the land in the gap between surveying and selling were permitted their plot at a minimal price (at the risk that if the land wasn't bought within a year the feds would foreclose on the now improved land).

As in post-Soviet Russia and now China, the danger produced a market in which the poorest farmers unable to make the year payment sold off their claims before the official auction.[108] In this way the richest farmers snatched up (and combined) the best lands along tributaries or outside towns.

The wealthiest were also the only ones with enough cheap labor— poor whites and black slaves—to best improve holdings for price subsidies, making "a mockery of the equivalence of land and labor upon which the law was based."

SO LATIFUNDIUM COTTON CAME A-CALLIN'.

As much as today's big-breast chickens, Petit Gulf's attributes were as much economic as biological.[109] While its long fibers were best for textiles, Johnson writes, the size and shape of the plant was selected for their "pickability," for slave picker productivity, gripping and pulling off 200+ pounds in boll a day.

Indeed, slaveholders, melding land and labor, calculated the cotton production line in terms of bales per hand. The slaves themselves were labeled "hands"—nursing mothers "half hands," children "quarter hands":

> Measuring crops and slaves "to the hand" was an ecological as well as an economic measure—an attempt to regulate the exchange between slaves and soil by prescribing benchmark measures for the process by which human capacity and earthly fertility were metabolized into capital.[110]

The quality of soil was transubstantiated into a narrow annual metric—yield per acre. The measures together produced a logistics matrix familiar to many an MBA candidate:

> Would their cotton bloom early and full enough to keep their hands busy through the picking season? Would there be hands enough to tend all the acres they had planted, or would their cotton end up choked in grass and blown away by the wind before it could be picked?

The answers were found in part in the innovations slaveholders developed in labor management, many held over to this day.

When overseers atop horseback or Mistress in the Big House spotted transgressions, discipline was scaled by kinds of "error." We're talking here the lash, of course, but the workplace panopticon, backed by gradated punishment and humiliation, assured labor was working in the right place and the right time, a critical convergence for exploitative productivity.

"Twenty-five [lashes]," former slave Solomon Northup, his life story now a movie, remembered, when a dry leaf or piece of boll is found in the cotton, or when a branch is broken in the field; fifty is the ordinary penalty following all the delinquencies of the next higher grade; one hundred is called severe: it is the punishment inflicted for the serious offense of standing idle in the field.[111]

As today, the work itself was its own discipline, the danger and damage their own message. When an immigrant meat packer loses her hand, the expectation that the line is restarted promptly is more than code for the replaceability of any of the other workers, but that each is as much a side of beef as the meat he or she is prepping. Johnson reports that slaveholders routinely made such an equivalence explicit.

Slavery's discipline originated as much off-plantation. Johnson quotes Northup that "a slave never approached the gin house with his basket of cotton but with fear." If the cotton quotas proved short, he or she would suffer the "appropriately" scaled lashing, what Johnson identifies as a metric of production:

The grading of cotton introduced the standards of exchange [from Lowell and Manchester] into the calculus of labor discipline in Louisiana, for quality depended on how quickly and carefully a crop was picked and processed.[112]

In the other direction, off the agricultural site, anyone caught helping a slave flee his master suffered severe punishment alongside the slave. Today "ag-gag" laws recently passed or pending in sixteen U.S. states against filming animal abuses on factory farms—but tellingly never workers' abuse—in effect extend factory rules to the general population.[113]

AS IOWA CAN ATTEST TODAY, despite all the fevered production and with some of the world's richest soil, the Lower Mississippi Valley couldn't feed itself.[114] The Valley produced a single crop for export. Johnson reports that wheat, corn, beef, and corn were imported from the Midwest.

Some "enlightened" slaveholders—Michael Pollan in a string tie—lamented an ecologically integrated slavery that would heal the metabolic rift between soil and economy.[115] Some of these "progressives" grew corn to feed plantation cattle and pigs, but as today, fierce competition for land, especially during economic crises, routinely put a premium on the moneymaker crop.

Slaves meanwhile bore the severest costs of efforts at controlling food imports. "One bushel of potatoes," Johnson quotes the *Cotton Planter's Manual*,

> or ten qts. corn meal, or eight qts. of rice, and four qts. of peas, with occasional fresh meat, and twenty barrels of salt fish and two barrels of molasses during the year. Number of people 170.[116]

The stores provided depended more on cost margins than on slave nutrition. Food, after all, also proved excellent discipline and many slaveholders kept close watch on the calories their slaves consumed, walking the fine lines between malnutrition, labor reproduction, and insurrection.

Indeed, Johnson writes, growing inedible cotton proved a part of the carceral infrastructure, although unbeknownst to the cruelest owners, forcing slaves to self-provision off-plantation permitted slaves looking for food in the nearby woods to discover, perhaps, a means of escape.

The more "liberal" slaveholders—think the Daryl and Melinda Gates Foundation—saw imported beef in terms of lost soil manure than food for slaves. Although those who attempted locally sourced cattle lost their shit, so to speak, when slaves stole cattle feed to supplement their own diets, as if stealing from slave masters who starve (and enslave) them were a crime.

Other slaveholders tried to vertically integrate their operations, feeding their slaves cottonseed oil, which, Johnson quotes fugitive slave John Brown, caused slaves to break out in running sores.

Progressive myopia proved pervasive. Johnson writes that M. W. Phillips—as if Dave Quammen with a bushier beard—argued against the ongoing ecological catastrophe of the cotton plantation, but solely within its perverse economy, tallying energy outflows and stock fertilities, including of his own slaves, as if their children were his own. Phillips, thinking of the sustainability of the system,

> was arguing that the slaveholding South needed to slow the rate at which it was converting human beings into cotton plants. He wanted to adjust the metabolism of social anthropophagy.[117]

Left to right, slavery became its own presupposition, turning its hideous compulsions into eschatological necessity. "The African," wrote the notorious Samuel Cartwright, around dispatches on drapetomania and spirometer readings, "will starve rather than engage in a regular system of agricultural labor, unless compelled by the stronger will of the white man."

No mere recapitulation of racist phylogenies dating back to Cuvier and Buffon. To Johnson, the metaphysics here, drawing repeatedly from farming and animal husbandry, is ecological in origin:

> The agricultural order of the landscape, the standing order of slavery, the natural order of the races, and the divine order of earthly dominion were not separable . . . they were fractal aspects of one another.[118]

Save for the small issue of the murders of millions of Africans in and after the Middle Passage, this would seem all P. G. Wodehouse if only for the fact that many important advances in cotton production and implementation, including seed selection, cotton grading, and perhaps even Eli Whitney's cotton gin, were invented by black slaves, whose ideas the slaveholders claimed for their own (an appropriation Paula Deen's antebellum party reminds us extends to the heart of the South's cuisine).[119]

Johnson relays Frederick Law Olmsted's observation that

> there is always on hand . . . some Negro who really manages his owner's plantation, his agricultural judgment being deferred to as superior to that of any overseer or planter in the country.[120]

As a result, Johnson writes, we're left with the slaveholder's contradiction,

> between not knowing and claiming knowledge expressed along the juncture of the unfathomable and the incomprehensible, the lived experience of slaves and the efforts of planters to explain what they themselves only half knew. And so the masters of the Cotton Kingdom left behind barely readable "explanations" of the very basis of their prosperity.

EXPERTISE—REAL OR PRETEND—CAN'T protect an ecological system built on growing money first.

Johnson describes how genetic homogenization and intensive production exposed antebellum cotton to the kinds of rusts, rots, and worms that continue to plague monocrops and GMOs.

The short time horizon imposed by debt payments meanwhile induced slaveholders to plant cotton along the east-west axis to maximize sun exposure, regardless of the pitch of the field, draining underlying water tables only ten to fifteen years after clearing. As today, the water that was used in so short an order helped slough topsoil into the river.

In carrying cotton, the mighty steamboats, on which Johnson's writing approaches the miraculous, ate away at their own success. Riparian forests were cleared for fuel, eroding banks, making the river meander more, and dumping larger keel-ripping obstacles in its flow. With so many boats on the water, competing for hauls in just about every tributary of any draft, companies installed high-pressure boilers to propel boats faster, over sandbars, and against the clock. Engines that were also more likely to explode.

Johnson's magical here at connecting such structural failures to exploitation's grand narrative. The death and destruction were chiseled into the cultural foundation:

> Steam power became, in these accounts, a sort of alibi for imperialism and dispossession: a *deus ex machina* that shifted the terrain

of conquest to a scale of action beyond politics and war—a literary conceit that acquired a terrible historical correlative when the steamboat *Monmouth*, packed with Creek Indians being forced out of their homeland, exploded about twenty miles north of Baton Rouge, killing hundreds of those aboard. The steamboat sublime took expropriation and extermination and renamed them "time" and "technology."

Perhaps the central clusterfuck, however, is the way global circuits of capital entrained slave agriculture. Johnson cuts through talk whether slavery was capitalist by switching directions: nineteenth-century capitalism could exist only by virtue of American slavery. Labor at so little cost, for one, undercut wages everywhere else, including strenuously abolitionist countries in Europe.

There were other mechanisms.

In leaning on loans from New Orleans and eventually New York, King Cotton abdicated control. To the South's chagrin, planters shipped to pay off debts first, making New York, and its banks, the leading port out to Liverpool and Manchester: "Distance was measured not in miles, but in dollars."

The debt cycle dictated agriculture for capital turnover rather than food or linens (much less sustainability). Virtual crops—annual debt payments, some packaged into derivatives—trumped actual crops on which they were based, often well in advance of a season's planting:

Capital entered the Mississippi Valley in the winter months, when cotton was sold. As the crop came to market in New Orleans, cotton merchants—who were often agents of merchant banks based in New York or Liverpool . . . provided advances against its eventual sale. In return for lending the factors (and thus the planters) money during the time the crops was traveling to market, these cotton merchants and their merchant-banker backers received the right to sell it on a consignment basis, thus earning the commission and perhaps, in the case of some of the larger firms, the right to ship it aboard their own ships.

Capital also flowed in as advances and futures, the investment in which provided planters liquidity to pay for supplies and services during the year. While smoothing out the spatiotemporal bumps in available cash, it also pushed risk toward the production end and separated finances from the source commodity backing it.

That made the entire financial apparatus increasingly rickety, prone to bubbles and panics.

INDEED, JOHNSON DESCRIBES, DROUGHT, pests, and the other risks natural to the planting cycle we discussed earlier, in actuality profoundly anthropogenic to this kind of agriculture, suddenly punted many an indebted farmer into bankruptcy. Even a good crop might not be good enough if it wasn't delivered on time to its creditors' satisfaction.

In other words, Johnson continues, cotton turned from crop to commodity, with responsibilities—marketability, money valuation, and fungibility—above and beyond its material qualifications as a fabric source. Its fluctuating price across seasons and circumstances turned it into an object of market speculation. Side bets on the killing floor.

The übermarket placed many local factors in direct opposition to the planters they ostensibly serviced. Shippers and creditors trafficked in large volumes across multiple crops that like today's bankers put them in the position of betting against (or flat-out fleecing) their own customers, who were absent at the point at which their cotton was actually sold:

> They would record sales at a lower rate in their books than they received in the market; or they would pay an extra quarter-cent on the pound on the first shipment of the season, only to deduct a half-cent on the rest once they had secured its promise. They might launder goods they owned themselves through third-party "sellers," thus adding a commission to their own price, or might pass on a higher price for suppliers to a planter while receiving a kickback from the grocer. They would add a commission for negotiating loans upon which they were already charging interest.[121]

Local moneybags were meanwhile under the gun themselves, short-selling one planter's bales to pay the debts of another, for instance. Or by virtue of their own dependence on particular higher-order creditors, they were forced to sell in that direction rather than at the highest market price. Summing to a series of takeaways cotton suffered all the way up to New York and Liverpool.

Beholden to debt schedules and unscrupulous commissions, slaveholders referred to themselves as "slaves" without a hint of irony. The low returns that resulted were meanwhile taken out on actual slaves, beaten for, well, obviously, failing to work hard enough to meet market demands. Or their very families were sold off separately to recoup slaveholders a bit of stopgap financing.

We see similar skeins across agricultural capital today.

Shuanghui International Holdings, China's largest meat company, is finalizing buying Smithfield Foods, the largest pork producer in the United States (and until recently a Paula Deen sponsor).[122]

The deal has NGOs atwitter. Food & Water Watch in coalition with a number of other groups issued a letter calling on the United States to reject Shuanghui's purchase on the basis of "significant risks of a Shuanghui takeover of Smithfield to food security, consumer food prices, food safety, farm and rural economies in the United States and national security."[123]

Vijay Prashad labeled such critiques Sinophobic, embodying both capital retraction and liberal impotence in the face of corporate dominance at home:

> Food & Water Watch acknowledges that Smithfield "is already the biggest, baddest bacon producer around, controlling about one third of the US pork supply, most of which is raised on factory farms." Yet Food & Water Watch believes that it needs to stand up to "protect" the consumer from the big, bad Yellow Peril. No sense that the Committee on Foreign Investment [still to review the deal] is an arm of US foreign policy, having targeted Venezuela, the Gulf Arabs (Dubai Ports) and the Chinese alone. US liberals have a serious problem confusing anti-capitalism with xenophobia.[124]

Helena Bottemiller's reporting initially suggests that the Smithfield purchase might even make pork safer: "China bans ractopamine, a controversial growth-promoting drug that is widely used by U.S. livestock producers."[125] Except that production for export won't fold in domestic meat:

> The U.S. pork industry, which sold more than a quarter of its products abroad last year, is now creating separate ractopamine-free supply chains to gain greater access to overseas markets and meet the demands of both Russia and China.

Tom Philpott also pushes back that China is offshoring meat production to alleviate a trifecta of environmental risk. The country is suffering water shortages, a pollution peak, and a land crunch:

> Reading these accounts—prime farmland abandoned and paved, aquifers sucked dry, water tables fouled—it makes perfect sense that a government-controlled company like Shuanghui would make a play for Smithfield, the globe's largest pork producer. Underlining these trends, the *Financial Times* reported in June that China's "shift towards a greater reliance on food imports could have profound implications for global food markets because China's total demand for grains is vast relative to the size of globally traded markets."[126]

All true, but production isn't solely the purview of nation-states or even their chartered companies. Institute for Agriculture and Trade Policy's Shefali Sharma splits the Gordian knot this way:

> The Smithfield acquisition acutely brings home one—albeit overlooked—fact: it's a globalized industry. Just look at Shuanghui's shareholders: CDH Investment, Goldman Sachs, New Horizon Capital, Kerry Group, Temasek and its own management and employees. As Peter Fuhrman from China First Capital puts it, "A Chinese company isn't buying Smithfield. A shell company based in the Cayman Islands is."[127]

It's a view shared by Chinese observers:

> For columnist Deng Yuwen, the deal is "not an overseas acqui-
> sition by a Chinese corporation, but a consolidation of industry
> control and profits by international finance."

THE STIRRINGS OF SUCH A Global Foods can be found in what
was slavery's economic space, which repeatedly strained at its national
borders.

As abolitionism of a variety of forms—including poor whites'
racist objections to increasingly skilled slaves—encroached on slavery's prerogative, slaveholders looked abroad for both new lands to
set up shop and markets to supply.

The project puts a premium on a separate foreign policy beyond or,
given recent U.S. diplomatic cables released by WikiLeaks, imposed upon
official Washington, D.C., that agribusiness pursues to this day.[128] Cargill
in Indonesia.[129] Smithfield in Mexico.[130] Monsanto in Africa.[131] And in
some cases, in this very day and age, supporting child labor and slavery
out in the open.[132] White supremacy with a Delaware corporate charter.

In some sense, the arrangements reconcile a long-standing dis-
agreement about the nature of profit between the likes of geographer
David Harvey, who emphasize accumulation by dispossession, and
traditional Marxists who focus on labor exploitation.[133] As Manifest
Destiny before it, imperialism signaled primitive accumulation by
sea—killing off natives or rival countries' slaveholders—what slavery's labor extraction would complete by land.

In the other direction, if liberal abolitionism balked at slavery's
expansion—to Central America and the Caribbean, for instance—
it wasn't necessarily on moral grounds. British objections, Johnson
echoes Eric Williams, appeared a mask for undercutting American
domination of the cotton market in favor of its nascent and British-
dominated rivals in Egypt and India.[134]

We see in U.S. slavery (and its descendants in agribusiness) a capacity for production, for gittin' 'er done, that emerges less in agricultural
technicalities than in turning political power into exclusive access to
what were previously other people's resources.

Despite pious psalms to the free market, agricultural powerhouses succeed only by virtue of massive state intervention, whether making slavery the law of the land or pushing free trade agreements that trash domestic protections. Whatever their technical provenance, genetically modified crops have little to do with food and are but a means by which pesticide companies turn independent farmers worldwide into sharecroppers locked into patented production spirals.

From James D. B. DeBow's K Street–ready African Labor Supply Associates to William Walker's Cornelius Vanderbilt–backed *Falanges*, and Bill Gates's Monsanto-linked Alliance for a Green Revolution in Africa, adventurers aim at externalizing internal contradictions dragging on their social reproduction.[135] All for the greater good, of course. Agribusiness penetrating markets abroad repeat the slaveholder's declensionist fallacy that the system will reverse alleged shortfalls in production it helped impose in the first place.

"Reopening the [Atlantic] slave trade," Johnson writes, paraphrasing the slaveholder position,

> would be the first cause in a chain of events that would transform untamed territory into productive land, redeem time with improvement, and thus trace out the natural course over space and time of the history of slavery (or, perhaps more accurately, history as slavery).[136]

He may as well be relaying the USAID's stance on GMOs in Kenya.[137]

WITH SLAVERY'S DEMISE AND THE collapse in land values that followed, the Civil War depressed Southern assets to less than half their prewar worth. "In reality," Ann Markusen writes, echoing Vladimir Lenin's American regionalism, "the major productive assets of the Southern economy remained in place—land and a huge black agricultural labor force."[138]

Reconstruction's efforts at radically altering the South's political economy stumbled into delivering blacks (and the poorest whites) to segregated sharecropping and tenancy. White supremacy ruled administratively by day, through terror by night.

Debt devolved to individual smallholders. Slaveholder capital rolled over to local confederations, some of which would regionalize into conglomerates, including, after a series of mergers, some of today's best known agricultural companies. The overdependence on cotton, and its ecological damage, continued. Advances in cultivation technology increased crop inequality. Smallholders abandoned farms in the thousands. The monocrop South, cultivating debt payments, remained unable to feed itself.

Monica Gisolfi traces the credit system backing King Cotton up through the mid-twentieth century when, with the Great Depression, the crop lien was reappropriated to pay cotton planters to raise chickens:

> Soon spring chickens or "fryers" that once ran about yards and were considered a seasonal crop were renamed "broilers" and were grown year-round in enclosed houses under tightly regulated conditions. What had been once the domain of women and children—who patched together makeshift chicken coops, read up on artificially heated incubators or "wooden hens," and became devotees of the country agent and home demonstration service—became the domain of hatchery-men, feed-dealers, poultry growers, poultry processing plants, poultry integrators, poultry scientists, and national corporations.[139]

John W. Tyson, the scion of what would become Tyson Foods, transported chickens to large Midwest markets from his Springdale, Arkansas, base before vertically integrating chicks and feed.[140]

The regime switch was as much based in relieving surplus capital in a strictly regulated period as in the ecology or the culinary:

> [Creditors] advanced chicks and feed to farmers. By the time the United States entered World War II, merchants had laid the foundation of contract farming. . . . By the 1950s poultry, once a sideline activity that buffered farmers against the whims of the cotton market, had become Georgia's most important farm product. Georgians came to depend on chicken in the way that they

and their ancestors had depended upon cotton, a dependence that
begot poverty and indebtedness.[141]

And the mode of production, despite New Deal intervention,
remained largely unchanged:

> By the late 1930s the demands of industrialized agriculture began
> to bear down on Upcountry farmers. They began to realize that
> they had traded one cash crop for another. In doing so, farmers
> had not escaped their creditors nor had they solved the problems
> associated with a one-crop system.

Once poultry replaced cotton as the dominant source of agricultural
income, Gisolfi continues, the problems of intensive monocropping
began to reappear. Rising integrators, increasingly contracting farmers to raise batches of chickens by a capital-led feed-conversion model,
tried to enjoin backyard poultry in an attempt to keep their commercial
flocks from being infected by circulating disease. It's an alleged epizoology to which smallholders are repeatedly imputed to this day.[142]

Solutions to problems became new problems. The manure poultry
farmers thought they would finally be able to reintroduce into cot-
ton-depleted soils polluted rivers and lakes, producing fishkills and
disease outbreaks.

We see, then, as Johnson's exquisite book suggests, that though
Northern modernization mechanized agriculture—which by reaper
and railroad fed Civil War troops in ways the South couldn't—slavery's legacy remains: labor extraction, state subsidies, breakneck
ecology, and foreign intrigue.

On the other hand, however confounding even to a nonagenarian's
experience, legacies aren't by definition cut in stone. Or perhaps they
are all too well. Carved by a receding glacier as far back as the eighth
century B.C.E., the Old Man of the Mountain, which we alluded to
along with agribusiness's near-geological inevitability, collapsed one
day in May 2003.

—*FARMING PATHOGENS*, 16 AUGUST 2013

UPDATE. Not long after I posted on Johnson's book, Steve McQueen's Oscar-winning adaptation of Solomon Northup's *12 Years a Slave* hit movie houses, depicting, along with slavery's hideous brutality, the calculus of the cotton field. Slave whippings are depicted scaled to the pounds deficit in bolls picked. Slave selves are quite literally commoditized even after their initial sale.

Meanwhile, Katie Johnston wrote a *Forbes* piece on Harvard Business School fellow Caitlin C. Rosenthal's ongoing book project.[143] In reviewing nineteenth-century accounting practices, Rosenthal discovered Southern plantation owners pioneered management techniques now widely used in business today. As Johnson describes, slaveholders, anticipating the railroad industry, experimented with units of production, including "bales per hand," demographically weighted by sex and age.[144]

Absentee slaveholders, for the first time separating ownership from management, "incentivized" work, if we can call anything under slavery that, depreciated laborers over time, migrated laborers across operations, and monitored their health and diets:

> This led owners to experiment with ways of increasing the pace of labor, Rosenthal explains, such as holding contests with small cash prizes for those who picked the most cotton, and then requiring the winners to pick that much cotton from there on out. Slave narratives describe how others used the data to calculate punishment, meting out whippings according to how many pounds each picker fell short.
>
> Similar incentive plans reappeared in early twentieth-century factories, with managers dangling the promise of cash rewards if their workers reached certain production levels.[145]

Incentives were also used to undercut the kinds of grim reaction such exploitation routinely inspired:

> Planters also used group incentives to encourage honesty, doling out a barrel of corn to each hand with the caveat that if anything was stolen from the farm and no one turned in the thief, double

the value of that corn would be deducted from each of their Christmas awards. Collective penalties would later be adopted by salesmen and companies like Singer Sewing Company to encourage workers to police one another.

"If you tried to do this with a northern laborer [at that time]," *Forbes* quotes Rosenthal, "they'd just quit."[146] And now it's business as usual.

Cave/Man

Newton often talked of the story of Belshazzar's impious feast and the secret writing that Daniel did decipher. Indeed the Book of Daniel was one of his most favourite in the Bible, being full of numerical prophecies. He wondered why those wise men of Belshazzar could not read the words: mene, mene, tekel, upharsin. *"Numbered, weighed and divided." Perhaps they feared to give bad news to the King, whereas Daniel feared only God.*

—PHILIP KERR (2002)

A NEW STUDY REPORTS THAT SEVERAL bacterial strains isolated from New Mexico's Lechuguilla Cave, shut away for over four million years, are resistant to up to fourteen different commercially available antibiotics.[147]

The implications are profound. At the risk of the overdramatic, they speak to the nature of our very existence, as well as, more practically, our relationship and responses to the pathogens that feed on us.

The horror of many a pathogen isn't just that they can "think" by an emergent cognition, or in how they outwit us by way of a near-ontological Hegelian dialectic, daily evolving resistance not only to every drug we've ever designed but to every one we will design.[148] It's that, if the cave bacteria are any indication, they outfox us in the course of solving some other problem entirely.

We are no vanquished competition. We are a speed bump on the road elsewhere. Our medical advances, a geochronological fleck, are routinely flicked aside with exaptations of a billion-year-old molecular Bauplan. However ingenious humanity may be, there isn't an R&D budget that can bust that problem.

There is, however, an ironic hope in there. The characterization puts the onus back on us. Without denying pathogens their agency or historicity, if many are only passing through a hyperdimensional ecological niche space, agnostic to our suffering, our worst outbreaks largely arise out of the world as we have made it.[149]

By pills and pushes alone we try wrangling what in fact has already wrangled us. Our microbiomes, our immune systems, our very cells and DNA, after all, are structured by parasitic artifacts. We'd do better in putting our socioecological houses in order, by multilevel interventions and ecological resilience, by a sociality that sees people before commodities, finessing from bug to bug an epidemiological detente.

And yet, incredibly, with the ancient and intrinsic failure of our present approaches scrawled in genetic code across the cave wall— Belshazzar's resistome—the study is instead spun as another bulk order for the pharmaceutical industry:

> While this may sound like bad news, the researchers explain that finding isolated, drug-resistant bacteria actually is a good thing. They say it suggests there are many types of previously unknown, naturally occurring antibiotics in the environment that can be developed for doctors to use against currently untreatable infections.[150]

—*Farming Pathogens*, 21 April 2012

PART SIX

[Medical doctor and public health activist Rudolf Virchow] was opposed to Bismarck's excessive military budget, which angered Bismarck sufficiently to challenge Virchow to a duel. Virchow, being entitled to choose the weapons, chose two pork sausages: a cooked sausage for himself and an uncooked one, loaded with Trichinella larvae, for Bismarck. Bismarck, the Iron Chancellor, declined the proposition as too risky.

—MYRON SCHULTZ (2008)

The Virus and the Virus

You cannot train yourself to successfully and sustainedly unsee and unhear. You do them all the time, but they also fail, repeatedly, and you cheat, repeatedly, in all sorts of small ways.

—CHINA MIÉVILLE (2009)

HENDRA, EBOLA, MALARIA, SARS, XDR-TB, Q fever, simian foamy virus, Nipah, and influenza. One of these bugs, or an as yet undiscovered cousin, will likely kill a few hundred million of us someday soon. It isn't *if*, as many of the scientists Dave Quammen interviews across his new book repeat, it's *when*, a when it so happens no one knows when.[1]

Spillover: Animal Infections and the Next Human Pandemic, surveying a variety of roads a wildlife pathogen might take to a deadly human infection, reads the gothic thriller, at 500+ pages epic in scope across levels of biocultural organization and locale. DNA to global geography. Quammen's Montana hometown to the deepest rainforest.

As he has in his other books, Quammen is here a generous narrator, patiently making complex ideas plain to an audience he repeatedly addresses across the proverbial canteen bar as fellow travelers. He roughs us through the places he describes, not only through the muck in the field, but in the lab and in and out of concepts. We're taken 0 to 60 on the differences between screening for antibodies and isolating a virus and through a history of mathematical modeling of susceptibles, infectious, and recovered.

Of course, people can go to a faraway place or outlandish idea and see not a damn thing. Indeed, while we come off churlish knocking good people for good work, Quammen's book is so well-written, so fleshed out, so comprehensive that, like Laurie Garrett's tomes, it gives the impression of an authority it doesn't quite possess. Think on the shitty conversationalist who refuses anyone else a word in edgewise.

The same can be said of the scientists Quammen covers, with whom he throws in unconditionally, querying them for guidance rather than cross-examining for answers.

Don't get me wrong, many of the scientists and medical staff Quammen tags along with are brave and bright beyond belief. *Spillover* channels George R.R. Martin, killing off its characters with aplomb. One researcher bites it in a bush-plane crash. Sixty hospital staff in Kikwit are eaten by Ebola. Doctors and nurses across Asia took the biggest blasts of secondary SARS infection. Malaria killed evolutionary biologist William Hamilton, at the time playing an epidemiological Livingstone looking for HIV's Congolese source.

But we would do well to add the more jaundiced view missing here. Leaving aside the field's Olympic plagiarism and backstabbing, disease scientists are actors within a broader political economy that pigeonholes many a researcher to an epistemological script. Not only within scientific metaphysics, but across naked economic interests. Several of the scientists Quammen interviews are flat-out mercenaries, taking Cargill money, for instance, to investigate outbreaks—vis-à-vis palm oil in Indonesia, for instance—of Cargill's own making.[2]

If these researchers profit from their sins of commission, Quammen, by taking these prevaricators at their word, even for what he genuinely believes to be a greater good, suffers (and inflicts) a bout of traumatic bonding.

What aim such noble sacrifice? The Big Idea Quammen flogs is that new diseases—viruses, bacteria, fungi, protists, prions, and worms spilling over from wildlife—arise out of human impacts on the population biology of host and pathogen alike:

> Make no mistake, they are connected, these disease outbreaks coming one after another. And they are not simply *happening* to us; they represent the unintended results of things we are *doing*. They reflect the convergence of two forms of crises on our planet.

The first crisis is ecological, the second is medical. As the two intersect, their joint consequences appear as a pattern of weird and terrible new diseases, emerging from unexpected sources.[3]

These sources? Previously marginalized pathogens turn ecological opportunity across suddenly juxtaposed landscapes into an evolutionary payoff. *Coxiella burnetti,* the bacterium behind Q fever, has infected

dairy cows in California, sheep in Greece, rodents in North Africa, and bandicoots back home in Queensland. It passed from one species to another in the form of minuscule airborne particles, often dispersed from the placenta or the dried milk of an infected female animal, inhaled and then activated through the lungs, or taken directly into the bloodstream from the bite of a tick.

In essence, causality—and any effective intervention—is found in the field, both quite literally and as a philosophical premise rather than in the object, say in the form of a bacterium or any single host population. The connections organisms make (and break) with one another embody the pathways over which pathogens evolve their distinctive adaptations.

Quammen places blame for the shifts in the landscape driving pathogen spillover squarely on humanity's shoulders, including population growth, global transport and travel, climate change, deforestation, and domesticated animals (which, for instance, it overtreats with prophylactic antibiotics and transports across great distances).

Explaining the ecosystemic dependencies out of which new pathogens arise isn't nearly enough, however. Quammen rarely touches the processes occurring farther upstream. Pathogens are embedded in circuits of capital in such a way as to reverse conclusions based on ecology alone.

Take highly pathogenic H5N1, the bird flu, which almost certainly emerged in the southeastern Chinese province of Guangdong in 1996 before spilling over into Hong Kong a year later.[4] When we include the economic relationship Hong Kong and Guangdong share, cause and effect shift direction.

By the 1990s the Pearl River Delta had returned to pre-revolution dynamics whereby the newly reintegrated Hong Kong turned back to acting the proverbial front of the store, providing capital and marketing to Guangdong—the back of the store—where industrial production of unnerving scale continues to this day.[5] Indeed, at the time of H5N1's emergence—and SARS's, which also arose in Guangdong—four-fifths of Hong Kong's foreign direct investment went to Guangdong, including backing the shifts in agriculture and land use implicated in the new infections there.

Contrary to the morality tale that repeatedly characterized Hong Kong as some innocent victim, Hong Kong proves as responsible as Guangdong for H5N1's emergence.

Or take Quammen's dispatch five klicks south of Yokadouma, Cameroon, at Mambele Junction,

> where Karl Ammann saw chimpanzee arms stashed under the hood of a log truck. It was also one of the locations featured in Bradon Keele's paper on the chimpanzee origins of HIV-1. Chimp fecal samples from hereabouts had shown high prevalence of the virus in its most fateful form. Somewhere very nearby was Ground Zero of the AIDS epidemic.[6]

Exactly the travel porn at which Quammen's advance reviewers hooted and hollered. But the characterization confuses mechanism for causality. It's true, the virus first emerged in Africa (although unlikely by the nigh racist caricature of a reluctant bushmeat hunter Quammen fantasizes at the heart of his HIV chapter). But the causes aren't African alone.

Mike Worobey's group dated the emergence of HIV's group M, the clade that seeded the pandemic, to 1908, give or take fifteen years. In this time frame French and German colonial administrations competed for land and labor, radically altering the region's landscape and social order.[7]

As Walter Rodney describes, African labor was redirected by force and economic compulsion to producing for European export.[8] The regime melded and juxtaposed pre-colonial and provincial social behaviors, including population fragmentation, cycle migration, sex and age biases urban and rural, with sex a commodity.[9]

Clear-cutting meanwhile broadened the wildlife-human interface. Animals, and their pathogens, until then more tightly integrated at the level of the local village and more marginalized at the regional scale, became more exposed to the new order. In short, as the forest's edge grew in extent, so did the epizoological traffic.

Deforestation concomitantly turned bushmeat from a subsistence food item into a commodity that supported logging camps in the thousands and, later, farming towns growing on the edges of the contracting forest.[10] Associated logging roads and rail integrated the deepest forest with regional cities.

In short, explanations of HIV's origins must be extended to an imperial epizoology, out of Africa and to Europe's capitals, a framework establishment researchers have started to assimilate, if by dint of overwhelming evidence.[11]

Even the methods scientists use to characterize diseases are freighted with such histories. As the geographer Peter Gould described, the susceptible-infectious-recovered modeling that Quammen takes the time to teach us is loaded with political assumptions, disappearing complex social epidemiologies inside billiard-ball simultaneous equations and cellular automata.[12]

Quammen, coming off as the folksy neoliberal, does address economic impacts on disease emergence, but in two ways that conveniently obfuscate responsibility for a particular economic order. First, he'll detail an impact without naming names: deforestation, agriculture, antibiotics, etc. Indeed, not a single corporation involved in said disturbances is named in the book.

Second, he'll riff on a Global South informal economy, local palate, or illegal trade cutting into forest and food web, but fail to address the regional neoliberalism and structural adjustment New York and London bankroll, turning subsistence consumption into an export economy. Quammen's cynicism is naively obstructionist.

There are exceptions. Quammen's description of the agroeconomics around Q fever in the Netherlands bears repeated reading:

Among the first things he mentioned, when I asked about the character of Herpen as a community, was the big change that had come in local farming practices within the past decade: the increase in goats.

This change had actually started back in 1984, when the European Community established quotas on cow milk that pushed Dutch farmers away from dairy cattle. Many continued as dairymen but started milking goats. The dairy-goat trend grew stronger after 1997 and 1998, when outbreaks of classical swine fever (caused by a virus, but not zoonotic) led to mass cullings of pigs, and many pig farmers, hard hit financially and scared about a recurrence, sought an alternative line of husbandry. . . . From a low of about 7,000 animals in 1983, the total Dutch goat population had increased to 374,000 by 2009. . . .

Another shot gave a clearer view of what he called a "deep litter shed," the standard arrangement for housing hundreds or thousands of dairy goats. The shed had a concrete floor, recessed below ground level so that it could contain weeks' or months' worth of bedding straw, goat shit, and urine, a savory mulch of organic waste that grew ever deeper and, warmed by decay, offered a lovely culture medium for microbes.[13]

But such glimmers aren't translated to the larger context. Indeed, Quammen and the One Health devotees he interviews prescribe scut work more tuned to cleaning up the next outbreak than preventing it:

The practical alternative to soothsaying, as Burke put it, is "improving the scientific basis to improve readiness." By "the scientific basis" he meant the understanding of which virus groups to watch, the field capabilities to detect spillovers in remote places before they become regional outbreaks, the organizational capacities to control outbreaks before they become pandemics, plus the laboratory tools and skills to recognize known viruses speedily, to characterize new viruses almost as fast, and to create vaccines and therapies without delay.

Emergency capacity is always critical. But that's what you're left with when you refuse to say the other "c-word."[14]

While Quammen and the researchers he champions see and hear viruses of a sort, others, a growing group, just as ensconced in representative sampling and statistics, see and hear viruses of another kind completely. These pathogens, our next generation in science is learning, transmit by surplus value and margin call, wearing molecular suits of the finest cut.

—*CounterPunch*, 14 June 2013

UPDATE. Less than a year later I called out Quammen on his characterization of the Ebola outbreak in West Africa.[15] Quammen spent five incensed tweets denouncing my post as "confused nonsense" from an "addled guy," who, it happens, has consulted for CDC and FAO. Quammen hoped my "loopy post" "doesn't mislead credulous people," including the Ecohealth Alliance, to whom I never referred, as the post is "all abt yr political agenda & my blinders." The sole hit he scored is that Ebola is of the *Filoviridae* family, not *Flaviviridae*, my original typo. But the spell-check and the *ad hominem* attack were the extent of his response. The internet is now a place where that's enough even for a *New York Times* bestselling author.

Coffee Filter

It's hard obviously to imagine a house which doesn't have a door. I saw one one day, several years ago, in Lansing, Michigan. It had been built by Frank Lloyd Wright. . . . There appeared something like an open-work roof that was practically indissociable from the vegetation that had invaded it. In actual fact, it was already too late to know whether you were indoors or out. . . . A dozen more or less similar houses were scattered through the surrounds of a private golf club. The course was entirely closed off. Guards . . . were on duty at the one entrance gate.

—GEORGES PEREC (1974)

DOSAGE AND TOLERANCE MARK the thin line between palliative and poison.

The caffeine that perks up one patron in the coffeehouses of snowbound Minnesota can rocket another into rare tachycardia and cardiovascular collapse.[16] It's a chance many are willing to take. Even the jitters tell us we're still alive in −40 wind chill. And look on the bright side, as one must here under the penalty of death, should a slurper keel over, a table in a popular joint is suddenly free for the rest of the day.

The devotional's exploding global appeal—and increasing consolidation—obfuscates its modest origins.[17] The genus *Coffea* grew naturally in the Horn of Africa, its purine alkaloids caffeine and theobromine herbivore irritants and insecticides.[18] Lure and lore parlayed the bean into a regional then an imperial prerogative and today a record 150 million-60-kg-bag and $100 billion-a-year global industry, second only to Big Oil, employing, across production, trade and retail, as many as 500 million people.[19]

Blue Mountain, Colombian, Ethiopian Harar, Hawaiian Kona, Java, SL28, and on and on, manifold varieties and hybrids are grown across seventy countries.[20] At $1,000 per kg, the priciest is an Indonesian bean swallowed and shat out by a caged luwak or Asian palm civet.[21] The kind of arbitrary appreciation slash commoditization that'll eventually slash slash slash the civet population to oblivion.

The differences in species, soils, sunlight, and cultivation help produce beans of a variety of balance, bouquet, and body. According to an extraordinary line of research by University of Michigan's Ivette Perfecto, John Vandermeer, and their colleagues, coffee ecosystems also differ in their capacity to naturally control pest insects and plant diseases that can devastate a *Coffea* crop.

Control in *Coffea* canephora, the major Latin American variety, emerges from more than the plant's biochemistry and bred-in disease resistance. The thatch of ecological relationships—predation, mutualism, competition, and the like—up and down the food web in which the plant finds itself can box out pest damage. Resistance and resilience are found in the field rather than the object, emerging out of these interconnections and their redundancy. Should one control cascade fail, another steps up or steps in.

For ten years plus, on a 300-hectacre organic coffee farm in operation for nearly a hundred years in the Soconusco region of Chiapas, Mexico, Perfecto and Vandermeer's team have worked to tease out the multiple spatioecological layers that buffer shade coffee from the worst of pest outbreaks.[22]

Coffee rust disease fungus *Hemileia vastatrix*, the coffee berry borer *Hypothenemus hampei*, the green coffee scale *Coccus viridis*, and the leaf-mining moth *Leucoptera coffeella* are four of potentially 200 now-endemic pests, each alone capable of destroying a coffee crop, and yet, here, have not. The PVC team identified a web of dynamic and contingent relationships across, if you're keeping score at your café, thirteen kinds of organisms and six ecological processes, keeping the four pests largely in check.

THE SWARMING *AZTECA INSTABILIS* ANT, of no common name, serves as the keystone species for the control network. Queens of the polygynous ant "bud" off and with some of their brood colonize new nests on coffee plants nearby. Colony diffusion is constrained in part by a *Pseudacteon* phorid fly, which lays brain-eating offspring inside the worker ants. Phorid attacks are nest-density-dependent. The more *Azteca* nests in the vicinity, the more attacks in the area, producing a power law distribution of nests across the farm.

That distribution, in turn, helps a lady beetle species *Azya orbigera* control the green coffee scale, our first pest. How? It gets all Robert Altman, so pay attention.

The ants and green scales are—perhaps a surprise—mutualists. *Azteca* offer the scale protection, including against the adult beetle, in return for honeydew the scales secrete. Protection *Azteca* cannot provide, however, against the beetle larvae. The larvae's waxy protuberances gum up *Azteca* mandibles and the young'uns chaw on the scale to their heart's content. The larvae score a daily double as *Azteca* also scares away parasitic wasps that feed on—and would control—the larvae in the ant's favor.

Without *Azteca*'s indirect protection, the beetle larvae wouldn't be able to survive its own parasitic tormenters in order to control the green scale. In short, as Perfecto and colleagues describe, the beetle helps produce the very spatial distribution it needs to survive. Dialectical biology in action.

There is a second, if indirect, means by which the distribution of *Azteca* is circumscribed to 3 to 5 percent of the farm. The white halo fungus *Lecanicillium lecanii* attacks the scale on which *Azteca* depends when the scale is locally abundant (which occurs largely under *Azteca* protection).[23]

White halo also attacks the coffee rust, our second pest, but, as we see, does so only because *Azteca* protects scales to densities white halo attacks. In other words, the scale and rust are by indirect means mutually constraining.

SOMETHING PUZZLED THE PVC TEAM. How do adult beetles— viciously attacked by *Azteca*—oviposit their similarly vulnerable eggs on a plant on which only their larvae survive?

Remember the phorid fly whose larvae feed on *Azteca*? What do we want? Brains! When do we want it? Brains! The fly offspring locate the ant colony by detecting its alarm pheromone and any one individual host by its movement. The ants respond by retreating to the nest or standing stock still in such a way as to avoid the fly's motion detection and, when able, attack its phorid tormenter.

The ants produce a second "phorid" pheromone alerting other ants to enter their defensive catatonia. The female beetles looking to oviposit their eggs unmolested can detect this second pheromone, finding areas of the plant in which *Azteca* have entered their collective freeze frame.

It appears, then, that *Azteca* distribution, natural pest control, and likely other such distributions in the forest and farm, arise from no single cause but a nonlinear complex of interactions distributed across the ecological network, an important lesson for those of us in the fields of livestock disease and public health.

The complications pile on, however.

If the coffee scale needs *Azteca*'s protection, how does a new ant colony find scale elsewhere? PVC discovered that although not nearly as effective as *Azteca*, at least five other ant species that forage in the area tend scales. In essence, the various species, occupying different parts of the farm canopy act as indirect mutualists maintaining scale densities across the farm, including the local outcrops a new *Azteca* colony needs.

One ground ant, *Pheidole* ctp, which while feeding on scales (and like *Azteca* on leaf miners and berry borers, our final two pests), offers *Azteca* additional help by outcompeting a third ant, an *Azteca* competitor, *Pseudomyrmex simplex*.

Other ant species meanwhile act as *Azteca* antagonists, if only because they do not co-tend scales. *Pheidole protensa*, for one, which also feeds on berry borers in old fallen seeds that offer borers off-season refuge, outcompete *Azteca* ally *Pheidole* ctp on the ground.

We are speaking here of an ecological guild of more than eighty ant species that engage in complex interactions of various—and at times simultaneous—mutualisms and competition across canopy niches.

WE—OR RATHER NATURE—CAN ADD yet another layer.

To test the effects birds have on pest numbers, the Perfecto-Vandermeer team conducted an exclosure experiment across shade and intensive farms in Soconusco.[24] With 5-cm mesh fishing nets, the researchers excluded birds from 10 x 5 x 3-meter plots of at least ten coffee plants. They selected control plants open to the elements from parallel rows nearby.

The team placed third- and fourth-instar larvae of the salt marsh moth and fall armyworm ten per plant in the experimental and control plots, modeling a sudden pest surge from a 2.1 average larvae density.

For each of four days the team placed larvae on the plants before sunrise and counted every three hours until 2 p.m. The researchers also identified the birds feeding at the coffee layer.

The censuses showed significant differences in the number and density of birds feeding on coffee plants between the shade and intensive plants, with a significant synergistic effect for treatment and site. Many more birds and bird species fed on the shade site, with a significant difference between exclosure and control plots not found on the intensive farm.

In other words, larvae were being removed from the shade controls in a way they were not from those on the intensive farm.

Behavioral observation qualified the results. Contrary to expectations, bird diversity did not appear the direct mechanism by which shade coffee was better protected. Instead, it appeared that particularly effective insectivores—including the rufous-capped warbler—foraged repeatedly in shade coffee.

That is, there may be a third effect. Despite the traditional troubles in segregating the effects of bird diversity and density out in the field, it appears the more birds feeding here, the more likely one or a few will be particularly effective, if by chance alone. A sampling effect.

COFFEE PLANTS MAY KEEP THE North Country—and the birds south—awake during the day. But there's no rest for pests at night. While the rufous-capped warbler and other birds coop, bats—many seed dispersers and pollinators—take to the air, some to eat pest insects. To weigh the predatory effects of bats and birds, Perfecto and Kim Williams-Guillen's team set up a series of exclosure treatments in Soconusco: birds-only during the day, bats-only during the night, both sets day and night, and a control of no netting.[25] The group censused non-colonial arthropods—insects, spiders, harvestmen, and mites—every two weeks over a seven-week period during the dry season and over eight weeks during the wet season.

The dual exclusion left the greatest density of arthropods on individual coffee plants, 46 percent greater than on the controls. Bats had a significant effect in the wet season, their exclusion leaving 89 percent greater arthropod density than controls, but less so in the dry. Finally, there appeared no significant interaction between birds and bats, indicating their predation is additive and each predates on different types of pests.

The seasonal difference may arise in part from the influx of overwintering songbirds during the dry season and an increase in bat abundance during the wet season when mothers, doubling their typical food intake, must nurse their offspring.

Which bats are gleaning what? By netting bats over forty-four nights and acoustically monitoring echolocation calls sensitive enough to detect a caterpillar chewing a leaf, the team identified twenty-four insectivores across a continuum of shade and intensive coffee plantations.[26]

Few species were captured on a single type of farm, but they did differ in their preferences. Indeed, while species richness differed little across the farm gradient, open-space bats, such as the greater sac-winged bat, appeared most frequent in the more intensive farms whereas forest bats, including the Argentinean brown bat, appeared more shade-prone.

A follow-up PCR study identified DNA of the berry borer and cicada *Idiarthron subquadratum* in bat fecal samples.[27] So, yes, the bats are indeed consuming the insects.

While forest bats fed less the more intensive the farming, as measured by their feeding buzzes, open-space bats did not feed more along the gradient, indicating that intensive coffee, some plantations with higher abundances of pests, scored little protection across the bat ensemble.

What's the take-home? The team concluded that even areas dominated by intensive agriculture would benefit from forest fragments, which offer roosts for all bat insectivores, including open-air species. However, they report, fine-grain, spatially contiguous agricultural matrices, including shade cultivation, would offer forest bats and other insectivores the kinds of wildlife-friendly refugia in which they could better survive.

Indeed, Williams-Guillen and Perfecto write, with the pressures of poverty and food insecurity also in the mix, blocking off agroecological landscapes into patches of forest and intensive farming, at the heart of much conservation modeling, can cause *declines* in local biodiversity.[28] When boxed out of all available land, the poorest farmers clear-cut the forest, and the largest operations, Perec's guard at the entrance, surf their own destructive production along an ever-expanding forest edge.[29]

A SELF-ORGANIZED PEST CONTROL emerges here out of ecological interactions.

Such systems are neither preplanned nor static projects. They're historically contingent. As PVC describe, coffee plants, and their rusts and berry borers, were imported from Africa. White halo fungus are common to the tropics, the leaf-mining moth to tropics of the Western Hemisphere, and the ants native to southern Mexico. By dint of conscious cultivation and chance biogeography, this particular combination of organisms happened to converge upon this specific and in all likelihood—at the geological time scale—passing control program.

While nature bears a connotation of ancient origins, over geologically short, if anthropologically long, intervals, functional ecologies are time and again disassembled and reconstituted.

To scale us back into humanity's present and pressing needs, in the short term, say the next few hundred years, if ecosystems were to be conserved and agriculture integrated into local forest matrices, farmers could enjoy such autonomous ecosystem services largely free of charge.

How exactly such services—soil enrichment, water conservation, pest control, etc.—emerge from place to place and how farmers might harness them, for lack of a better term, will require much more of the kind of research the Perfecto and Vandermeer team has pursued. Forget genetic engineering—that's all cave man brushing his teeth with a smartphone. This, on the other hand, is the cutting-edge research of the twenty-first century.

Think on what modern agriculture does in contrast. It strips out the forest and destroys the kind of self-integrated services nature often offers, or, better said, embodies. Agribusiness acts as one big exclosure keeping larger fauna out while soil degrades and bugs continue to munch on. Farmers are left to reproduce these services by firebombing their crops and soils with destructive petrochemicals.

Along with the model's unsustainability, which serves as a tautological rationale for cutting deeper into the forest that remains, intensive agriculture assigns farmers the absurdist task of nailing—like little Maxwell's demons—every minuscule pest that comes along.[30] What a waste of time and effort, especially as pests evolve resistance to pesticides as a matter of course. Instead farmers could have a whole ecosystem moving that bit of bother off their margins.

Farmer convenience, however, was never really the point of corporate agriculture. On the contrary. "Cargill is engaged in the commercialization of photosynthesis," CEO Gregory Page said in 2008.[31] "That is at the root of what we do." By dispossession, monetizing the sun and soil and air out from underneath the farmer and the forest.

—*Farming Pathogens*, 4 February 2013

Homeland

A NEW REPORT SHOWS AN INCREASING global population exposed to the risk of accidents from biosafety laboratories (BSL) studying some of the world's most dangerous diseases.[32]

Princeton University post-doc Thomas Van Boeckel and colleagues show the population living within the commuting field of BSL-4 labs increased by a factor of four from 1990 to 2012. The fields encapsulate nearly 2 percent of the world's population, but by virtue of infectivity any one escaped pathogen may turn epidemic.

The team mapped friction surfaces of the commuting time over which a potentially infected lab worker would carry an infection home. The resulting isochronal belts were used to determine the population within the direct vicinity of each lab.

The increase in the population at risk appears largely driven by a surge in global BSL-4 labs, from twelve in 1990 to fifty-two in 2012. Though an estimate of nearly 250 million people appear within a sixty-minute commute of these labs, smaller commuting fields, embodying urban cores, contained much greater proportions of the population than expected by geometry alone.

The effect was particularly pronounced for many newly built BSL-4 in Asia, writes Van Boeckel's team, but apparent elsewhere:

> By 2010, new facilities had been constructed in densely-populated areas in Europe (London, Milan, Hamburg) and in Asia (Taiwan, Singapore). According to the predictions for the post-2010 era,

India will make a noticeable entry in this ranked list, with the country's first two BSL-4 facilities being built in Pune (5.5 million inhabitants) and Bhopal (1.8 million inhabitants).

Since 9/11 thousands of BSL-3 and -4 labs have been built across the world for studying pathogens, among others, that terrorists might use.[33] Accidents have been occurring in these labs with "alarming regularity," Laurie Garrett reported in 2011.[34]

The accidents suggest the possibility, if not the probability, that the release of a bioengineered agent will be inflicted by the government-industrial complex dedicated to blocking such attacks.

The growing sample size of labs turns accidental unlikelihoods toward graver possibilities. "A chance event with low probability," biologists Richard Levins and Richard Lewontin wrote of scale effects of randomness, "becomes a determinate certainty when there are a large number of opportunities."[35]

Unfortunately, the development, a postmodern appointment in Samarra, operationalizes terrorist strategy by which industrial powers are goaded into overreacting.[36] Blowback now extends beyond the battlefield and into civilian infrastructure.

Van Boeckel and colleagues call for global regulation of bio-safety labs, the proliferation of which, in my view, appears driven by ideological compulsion, scientific competition, and bastardized Keynesianism.[37] Under the present political order, any such moratorium largely involves appealing to the very authorities building the labs.

—*FARMING PATHOGENS*, 16 DECEMBER 2013

Disease's Circuits of Capital

I co-wrote the following critique of One Health with colleagues Luke Bergmann, Richard Kock, Marius Gilbert, Lenny Hogerwerf, Rodrick Wallace, and Mollie Holmberg. It was published in Social Science & Medicine as part of the journal's special issue on One Health.[38]

THE NEW "ONE WORLD–ONE HEALTH" approach integrates investigations of wildlife, livestock, crop and human health in an ecosystemic context.[39] The approach convenes medical doctors, veterinarians, and ecological biologists under the rubric that many species share infectious, chronic, and environmental illnesses.[40] The approach is not without precedence. Calvin Schwabe's "One Medicine," the "Disease in Evolution" conference at Woods Hole, and investigators as far back as social medicine founder Rudolf Virchow and eighteenth-century veterinarian Félix Vicq-d'Azyr connected human and animal health within varying degrees of social and ecological contextualization.[41] The renewed interest appears driven as much by practical matters as by theoretical development in related fields such as ecohealth and complexity science.[42] The complications associated with the surprising spillover of highly pathogenic influenza A (H5N1) (bird flu) from poultry to humans at century's end galvanized international health agencies to gather scientists across disciplines to address influenza and other emergent diseases.[43]

The new One Health has been presented as a crucible in which to test combinations of specialist approaches in population health.[44] The animal and human diseases that are now most difficult to intervene

in arise from and are spread by a multitude of causes interacting at multiple scales and across biocultural domains. A variety of
epistemologies are required to address such infections. Indeed, retrospectively many of today's most common human infections first arose
in ancient civilizations by way of such synergies.[45] Domesticated stock
served as sources for human diphtheria, influenza, measles, mumps,
plague, pertussis, rotavirus A, tuberculosis, sleeping sickness, and
visceral leishmaniasis.[46] Ecological changes brought upon landscapes
by human intervention selected for spillovers of cholera from algae,
malaria from birds, and HIV/AIDS, dengue fever, malaria, and yellow
fever from wild primates.

The new pathogens stimulated innovations in medicine and public
health, including individual treatment and prophylaxes, land and
marine quarantines, compulsory burial, isolation wards, water treatment, and subsidies for the sick and the unemployed.[47] Each of the
series of agricultural and industrial inventions to follow accelerated
demographic shifts and new settlement and rejuxtaposed potential
host populations, prompting additional rounds of novel spillover.[48]
Environmental impacts, climate change among them, have since
scaled geological.[49] While producing an unprecedented array of
commodities, attendant increases in resource extraction, producing
material and conceptual rifts between economy and ecology, have
degraded habitats, biodiversity, ecosystem function, resource bases,
waterways, soil nutrients, and oceanic stock.[50] The impacts have
together promoted disease emergence across multiple host taxa.[51]

In particular, the "Livestock Revolution," in which the breeding,
processing and distribution of fast-growth livestock are vertically
integrated under a few large agribusinesses, makes repeated appearances across these latest impacts.[52] Industrial stockbreeding drives
as much as services a new demand in meat protein, particularly in
so-called developing countries, where, like its Neolithic predeces-
sors, it promotes pathogen spillover.[53] Livestock effects are indirect
as well. While the sector's growth presents economic opportunities,
competition from integrated producers marginalizes smallholders
out of markets.[54] In turn, the resulting food insecurity, environmental destruction, and perceptions thereof serve as rationales for a

particular capital-securitized science tied into spreading the very agri-food model precipitating cycles of economy and disease.[55]

Social scientists have begun to help catalog the mechanisms by which such disease spillover is socially mediated. Anthropologists Goldberg et al. describe the Kibale EcoHealth Project in Kibale National Park in western Uganda, testing for area-specific connections among human health, animal health, and the surrounding landscape, including population growth, forest fragmentation, rural poverty, cultural beliefs, and shifts in agriculture.[56] Multispecies infection dynamics, including for *E. coli,* appear as connected to higher-level agroecological changes as to behavioral practices directly related to transmission. For instance, humans tending livestock there proved at elevated risk of carrying *E. coli* strains specific to local wild primates that have been increasingly marginalized to dwindling forests. Red-tailed guenons raiding crops out of said forests tended to carry *E. coli* characteristic of humans and livestock.

Other studies have investigated disease pathways appropriate to more industrialized contexts. For example, Paul et al. apply a value-chain analysis to traditional poultry production in Phitsanoulok, Thailand.[57] The team found across twenty-eight poultry collectors, slaughterhouses, and market retailers that collectors—intermediaries between farmers and slaughterhouses—played an unrecognized role in spreading HPAI H5N1 in Phitsanoulok. The rapid destocking of poultry upon an outbreak facilitated H5N1 spread and appeared influenced by risk perception, economic margins, and compensation for the players along the commodity chain.

Other social science has positioned One Health within local and global political economies. Giles-Vernick et al., for instance, review the historical roots of a number of pandemics with the expectation that comparative studies should help divulge unexpected differences and similarities across outbreaks.[58] Such work aims to draw out the complexities inherent to societal responses that single-site studies routinely miss, including "the unequal burdens of suffering . . . subsumed under the rubric of globalization." Sparke and Anguelov situate the politics of epidemiological knowledge within such a socioeconomic divide between the Global North and South, specifically within risk management, access to medicines, media portrayals of risk, and the emergence of new diseases in the first place.[59] Forster and Charnoz find these inequalities also arise out of a coercive "global health diplomacy"—both governmental and philanthropic—ostensibly undertaken to bridge the divide.[60] Keck describes such power dynamics as an extension of colonial medicine.[61] The contests are part and parcel of higher-order struggles over the political course of economically developing "sentinel borderlands" where new epizootics arise and at the epistemological junctures where disciplines meet.

Research gaps remain, however. Here we first critically review One Health as conceived to this point, suggesting additional points of departure for social scientists of a variety of stripes, including in medical anthropology, ecosocial epidemiology, biopolitics, and the political ecology of health, all of which have addressed various aspects of the relationships between social science and epidemiology.[62] As integral as these approaches are to understanding the social context of population health, none to date have pursued statistical tests of what Krieger and others have hypothesized are the likely connections between global capital accumulation and determinants of ecosystemic health.[63]

To that aim we also introduce here an approach that seeks to model the mechanisms by which the broader socioeconomic context, largely missing from One Health, helps select for xenospecific spillover. Specifically, for the first time in any field we introduce ongoing research *quantifying* the relationship between the circuits of capital out of which many new diseases emerge and their subsequent dynamics, including, from the vantage point of pathogens, their genetic evolution and sociospatial spread. That is, we propose a Structural One Health that empirically formalizes the connections among capital-led changes in the landscape and shifts in wildlife, agricultural, and human health. Should such efforts eventually succeed, researchers will be able to identify the statistically supported combinations of local agroecological circumstances and economic relations that—extending out beyond specific epicenters—drive disease spillover across species.

THE SCIENCE AND POLITICAL ECONOMY OF ONE HEALTH

Integrating health studies across species appears a step forward for disease prediction and control. A literature search by Rabinowitz et al. showed a series of studies offering evidence for the feasibility of intersectoral cooperation, including the xenospecific benefits of animal vaccination.[64] Rabinowitz et al. review other studies showing improvement in predicting site-specific disease dynamics and in implementing successful intervention. As presented so far, however, the One Health approach also repeatedly misses key sources of causality, an omission that for some of its analyses may reverse initial conclusions. For instance, descriptions of effort in disease control can conflate proximate risk factors—and the contact tracing, vaccination, culling, and biosecurity deployed in response—with the underlying *causes* of an outbreak.[65] A disease is synonymous neither with its pathogen, nor a map of its infecteds, whether or not either is placed within a One Health context that acknowledges the functional ecologies humans, livestock, and wildlife share.

Among many such investigations, there is Preston et al.'s description of the effects of Peruvian land use on disease emergence.[66] Although the specifics as to deforestation's effects on Amazonian malaria are rigorously documented, the study is emblematic of a model of health that confounds where a pathogen emerges with the geography of causality.[67] Such absolute geographies often miss the sociospatial relations across global economic actors, the effects of which can reach into the very mechanics of modeling.[68] In presenting updated maps of global livestock, Robinson et al. report that as agricultual production intensifies

it becomes increasingly detached from the land resource base (for example as feeds are brought in that are grown in completely different places) and thus more difficult to predict based on spatial, agroecological variables. The effect is particularly marked for chickens and pigs, where the locations of intensive farming units often have more to do with accessibility to markets or to inputs of one sort or another, than to the agro-ecological characteristics of the land that can be quantified through remotely sensed variables.[69]

The consequences for epidemiology extend beyond the technical. Harking back to the core assumptions underlying colonial medicine, which Tilley notes included at its peak its own "ecology of complexity," an absolute One Health can steer scientists of what Connell identified as a modern-day North American and European metropole into lecturing the Global South about deforestation and disease risk.[70] For instance, Robbins quotes one EcoHealth scientist:

> By mapping encroachment into the forest you can predict where the next disease could emerge. . . . So we're going to the edge of villages, we're going to places where mines have just opened up, areas where new roads are being built. We are going to talk to people who live within these zones and saying, "What you are doing is potentially a risk."

Though the impulse is understandable, such environmental crises are in actuality confined to no one outbreak zone, and are presently driven largely by structural adjustment of a variety of permutations and a doctrine of export economics originating at capital's core.[71] The capital backing the kinds of development and production driving disease emergence in the underdeveloped parts of the globe potentially reverses causality, turning New York, London, and Hong Kong, key centers of global capital, into three of the world's worst "hotspots" instead.[72] Alongside sovereign wealth funds, state-owned enterprises, and governments, private equity in the form of agribusiness and agrifood companies, biofuels developers, and private institutional investors—mutual funds, banks, pension funds, hedge funds, university endowments, and private equity funds—are accelerating purchases of farmland in the Global South, consolidating domestic food production there, speculating on land prices, and exporting output to the global market at grave costs to smallholders and the environment alike.[73] The Land Matrix Observatory lists 959 transnational land deals concluded worldwide as of June 2014, covering nearly 36 million hectares.[74] The Oakland Institute estimated $500 million invested in African farmland alone, with expectations of 25 percent returns from production and land appreciation on leases running for as long as ninety-nine years and, depending on the deal, unlimited water rights, profit and equity repatriation, and exemptions or reductions in custom duties, VAT taxes, and profit taxes.[75]

In this way One Health *as a science* can obfuscate context, even in the course of describing multiple sources of epidemiological cause and effect. Kahn et al., among a variety of examples, describe the process by which Nipah virus emerged in 1998 Malaysia when deforestation destroyed fruit bat habitat.[76] The bats migrated to trees nearby live-stock pens where they spread Nipah to pigs, from which humans were subsequently infected. As in other studies, Kahn et al.'s description leaves the companies and land deals backing the hog intensification associated with the spillover unnamed, as are the broader economic shifts in regional stockbreeding undergirding local dynamics.[77]

One Health practitioners are certainly cognizant of the notion of a larger context. Considerable attention is paid to the epistemological boundaries of the perspective. In writing cogently on the economic and social inputs on disease emergence for one of a series of *Ecohealth* editorials, Zinsstag et al. propose that

> intercultural work on the human–animal relationship requires a clarification of one's own perspective in a self-reflective way. "What is my personal cultural/and ethical background that determines my relationship with animals and my concept of one health?" Answers critically determine the emotional or financial value assigned to animals. Could this lead to a new subjectivism in Science? One Health, for example, can be influenced by philosophical ramifications, that determine the method of economic analyses of the cost of infections that are transmissible between humans and animals.[78]

The research out of such a formulation is cast in the mildest of cross-cultural terms: pursue One Health from other vantage points. Such a modest expectation may limit the One Health produced. Little effort appears to have been made to identify specific owners and producers. Disease actors are classed in abstractions—susceptibles, infectious, and recovered—coded for simultaneous equations that can disappear socialized epidemiologies.[79] Even the "socioeconomic" work under such a rubric has until now tended toward tracing out the broadest of logistics underlying the geography of disease. Hosseini et al., for instance, combine direct and indirect airline flights, total poultry and swine trade, and health care spending as a marker of a country's ability to detect new cases to retrospectively project early spread of swine flu H1N1 in 2009 (and ostensibly other pandemic influenzas to follow).[80]

Such studies are useful. There is great value in discovering how to block a novel pathogen from spreading through animals and humans alike, whatever the system in which we find ourselves historically. At the same time, there are profound costs associated with reifying a status quo that brought about the threat in the first place. Such work can advance a technicism that acts as an ideology in absentia, implicitly delegitimizing alternatives by way of a narrow approach to an unexamined grand project already underway.[81] Indeed, if the vantage points proposed are limited enough, disease research presumes state and market neoliberalism as a part of the natural order even should other studies show the system's mechanisms are central to the problem of disease.[82]

Such a political economy raises the issue of whether the current epidemiological infrastructure can address the totality of inputs impinging upon the problems it addresses.[83] How, for one, does the World Bank or the World Health Organization approach outbreaks that originate with the very institutions on which the organizations depend for funding and legitimization? One recent World Bank report offers a well-documented economic case for One Health. Smith et al. aim at convincing the world's richest countries to invest in ecohealth and conservation by appealing to the underlying costs of a failure to act: at least $80 billion in losses from Nipah, West Nile Fever, SARS, HPAI, BSE, and Rift Valley Fever in 1997–2009.[84] The authors propose that paying a little now—$1.9 billion to $3.4 billion annually across 139 countries—can prevent considerable epidemiological damage, even with a low year-to-year probability a deadly pandemic will strike. The gains should compound, advancing campaigns in poverty reduction, food security, and food safety. The report also positions One Health, sharing lab and vaccination costs across animal and human projects, as a way of institutionalizing the kinds of service consolidations routinely proposed under the doctrine of budgetary austerity.[85] The NGO literature is filled with such promethean appeals. The reports also regularly omit addressing capital's structural momenta that growing evidence indicates help select for deadly pathogens.[86] Together the latter citations describe a system at best insensitive to the platforms it creates for pathogen emergence. Its production cycles degrade ecosystemic resilience to disease as natural resources are transformed into commodities, complicate epidemiological interventions by treating humans and animals as markets and commodities first, and globalize the transport of goods, people, livestock, and pathogens. Indeed, following geographer Jason Moore, capitalist production does not *have* an epidemiology so much as it *is* an epidemiology.[87]

The failure to address such a fundamental context may itself serve a purpose, however unintended. Within the current global recession, epidemiological interventions increasingly represent declensionist rationales for the neoliberal land grabs, wholesale deforestation, and agricultural intensification that underpin many of the epizootic outbreaks in the first place.[88] The outbreaks of the Global South are presented as due cause for clearing the field of all agricultures and alternate economies save the most highly capitalized and "biosecure," which in actuality, suffering diseconomies of scale, have been implicated in recent outbreaks and new strains: among them, LPAI, HPAI, Q-fever, foot-and-mouth disease, porcine reproductive and respiratory syndrome virus, the salmon louse *Lepeophteirus salmonis*, and West African Ebola.[89] Specifically, genetic monocultures of host livestock, high population densities, rapid throughput, and increased exports appear to promote greater pathogen spread and evolution.

On the other hand, other One Health work appears immediately amenable to expanding its purview. Engering et al. place infectious disease events into four categories.[90] While each category has its own set of typical drivers as the authors describe them, each also has its own apparent link to production and capital flows. For example, endemic diseases, the first of Engering et al.'s categories, are important mainly in underdeveloped countries and are often associated with poverty.[91] The emergence of pathogens in novel hosts is related to the economic models underlying the destruction of wildlife habitat, from which wildlife diseases spill over into humans, as well as those backing poultry and livestock production.[92] Pathogen introgressions are oft-related to trade or more gradual expansions brought about by climate change and shifts in land use.[93] Finally, the emergence of pathogens with novel traits by virulence jump or antimicrobial resistance has been connected repeatedly to intensified husbandry and preventive antibiotic use in livestock.[94]

THREE POSTULATES OF A STRUCTURAL ONE HEALTH

What would an alternate science look like? At its most comprehensive, a Structural One Health might include all the foundational processes underlying health ecologies, including, but not limited to, the ownership and production, deep-time historical holdovers, and cultural infrastructure behind the landscape changes driving health threats. Wallace et al., for instance, explain influenza in southern China in terms of a "historical present" within which multiple virulent recombinants arise out of a mélange of agroecologies originating at different times by both path dependence and contingency: in this case, ancient (rice), early modern (semi-domesticated ducks), and present-day (poultry intensification).[95]

Such a One Health would act as a base upon, or offer limits within, which other approaches must respond to their own problematics. The closer the approach is to the base of the schematic pyramid relating health approaches shown in Figure 1, the broader the set of disciplines that are essential for researching a disease, as well as for the balance of positive and negative impacts of potential interventions. Mechanisms promoting disease at the base of the pyramid may be located elsewhere in time and space than the actual disease, including circuits of capital and historical practices. Mechanisms at

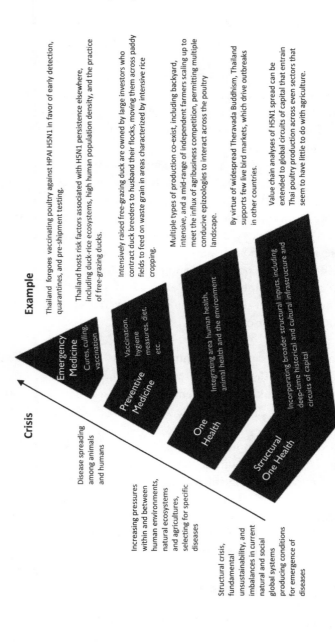

Figure 1. Schematic pyramid of health approaches and interventions. Structural One Health investigates the broader context of a disease, including out beyond the local, more proximate mechanisms of emergence on which more episodic One Health focuses. Preventive and emergency medicine are deployed in response to threats on the health of specific populations and individuals. For all mechanisms that promote disease—under "crisis"—the proximity in space, time and causal origin to any given outbreak increases up the pyramid. The relative importance of each point along the scale is dependent on the collective interplay between all parts of the pyramid. An array of inputs and outcomes for highly pathogenic avian influenza H5N1 in Thailand is shown across the schematic.

the top of the pyramid are directly connected to disease dynamics (such as pathogen transmission, dietary habits of individuals, etc.). The schematic is clearly an oversimplification, omitting complex interactions across conceptual scales, but, as its Thai example hints, may offer a start for conceptualizing how disease vulnerabilities emerge out of structural processes that, though impacting ground zeros both directly and indirectly, may also originate distally in time, space, and causality.[96]

The geographically explicit program could be supplemented with a "life history" perspective that tracks the means by which market demands upon livestock production at the levels of the lab, barn and/ or commodity chain shape disease dynamics.[97] Alternately, traditional mathematical epidemiology has already begun to merge economic and disease modeling.[98] Such agricultural microeconomics could be expanded to broader political economies of disease spillover. As we will explore below, other additions are feasible. In this section we introduce three base postulates around which such a wide array of research efforts could be organized.

Differentiate domains of crisis. Figure 1 suggests that some of the crises and opportunities to which various agroecological actors, human and animal alike, respond emerge across a broad scope of causes, wider even than nascent One Health has proposed to this point.

As the previous section intimated, the distinction between types of crisis is definitional, framing the very nature of the diseases described. Philosopher István Mészáros differentiates between episodic or periodic crises resolved within the established framework and foundational crises that affect the framework itself.[99] In the latter structural crises, unfolding in an epochal fashion through the very limits of a given order, the systemic contradictions start to run up against one another. As the World Bank example exemplified, palliative efforts in the name of the system that brought about the calamities may deepen the very crisis such efforts were ostensibly undertaken to alleviate. It follows that unpacking the broader economies—financial, political, and epistemological—upon which institutions and dominant paradigms depend is a critical part of a systemic characterization of health crises.

Such contextualization can be extended beyond descriptive caveats and empirically operationalized. For instance, the episodic changes much One Health addresses can be tracked as the overflow of capital-structured regime shifts from one ecosocial equilibrium to another as measured by Ives models of stochastic resilience.[100]

Let the scope of the crisis define the questions addressed. The variables One Health scientists include in their models are a social decision.[101] What researchers choose to make internal or external to a model, including which data to concatenate or exclude, can have a significant impact on its outcome—not only in the magnitude of effect, or even in direction, but in the very nature of causality.

An analysis conducted under an open sociality, one that simultaneously articulates the social processes under which the science is practiced, can modify the very premises under which the project is initiated. Indeed, such an exploratory approach may circumvent the distinction between structural and episodic. The nature of the health problems studied may suggest more aleatory and anti-foundational resolutions.[102]

For instance, anthropologist Lyle Fearnley tracked the mechanism by which the science of one group of One Health practitioners was forced into matching the conceptual flexibility of the problem they addressed.[103] The team aimed to study how zoonotic influenzas emerged in and around Poyang Lake, China, thought to be a source of multiple recombinants.[104] The researchers discovered the distinction between domestic poultry and wild waterfowl, a key premise of their study (and of the larger literature), to be effectively nonsensical (see Figure 2, page311):

> When [FAO ecologist Scott Newman] visited Wang's farm, the Wang family graciously invited him for lunch, refusing to be dissuaded from their misrecognition of Newman as an American investor. Showing him the flock of swan geese hundreds strong, as well as mallard ducks, Wang proudly told Newman that bird

production could easily be increased, and birds could be exported overseas. Wang also emphasized that the wildness (*yexing*) of his geese made them particularly valuable.

Here, the relationship between farming and the epizootic research around it becomes dynamically codetermined, if on terrain far different than the agribusiness-university complex. As Fearnley describes, Poyang farmers repeatedly manipulate the distinction between wild and domestic as an economic signifier, producing new meanings and values, including in response to the very epidemiological alerts issued in kind. In turn, the One Health team, intent on learning how recombinant influenzas actually emerge, chose against their field's practice to let the crisis define the study question, integrating economy and ecology.

Integrate sources of causality. Integration extends beyond introducing different disciplines, however. Anthropologist Steve Hoffman contends that institutionalized interdisciplinarity in more capitalized economies can cater to the new labor demands of profit-based state and private universities and the "problem-driven" research championed by private foundations and corporate R&D.[105] Biologists Richard Levins and Richard Lewontin include in the resulting epidemiological fallout a series of ontological dichotomies that scientists, epidemiologists included, traffic into their own work: between chance and necessity, randomness and determinism, organism and environment, and nature and society.[106]

A Structural One Health might better match the pathogens it studies by integrating across these divisions. For instance, in a vital contribution Leibler et al. pursue an ecohealth of industrial animal production, describing disease vulnerabilities at selected links in the value chain.[107] Some nodes in poultry production, for instance, are more vulnerable to producing influenza outbreaks than others. Their analysis, as sophisticated as any in One Health to date, also reproduces one of the field's faulty presuppositions. Although as the team describes, biology and economy—bird ontogeny and commodity production—operate in parallel, even interacting with each

Figure 2. Semi-domesticated ducks returning to their host farm of their own volition after a day out on Poyang Lake, Jiangxi Province, China, October 2007. Photo by Marius Gilbert.

other, another pathway goes unaddressed. Biology and economy also repeatedly meld into composite objects, often with complex webs of human, livestock, and pathogen agency.[111] Wallace, for instance, hypothesizes that avian influenza has converged upon agribusiness's production schedule, with the virus "husbanding" cohorts of infected birds not for market but for the next available barn of susceptibles.[108]

OPERATIONALIZING STRUCTURAL ONE HEALTH

Geographer Luke Bergmann's group extends the convergence of biology and economy beyond a single commodity chain and up into the fabric of the global economy, putting us at the precipice of operationalizing one possible Structural One Health. In recent research, Bergmann et al. have been examining the ways processes of globalization contribute to the emergence and persistence of diseases. In searching for the covariates to be inputted into a niche analysis of disease presence, Bergmann et al. are considering the potential role for local ecological variables such as land cover, host species distributions, and climate, but in addition social variables and human-ecological interaction terms. Beyond those potentially causal variables that are easily available in both practical and conceptual terms, such as population density rasters, the team is exploring the roles played by global interconnections. Such a relational approach is ubiquitous within the contemporary social sciences, but still as yet underexamined within One Health.

Bergmann et al. are including candidate covariates that for the first time quantify the extent to which local agroecological landscapes such as fields and forests—and the natural and cultural processes that crisscross them—have been globalized. Landscapes are entrained by transnational commodity chains and circuits of capital, including financial and productive circuits, with critical local effects. Geographer David Harvey argued that even globalized markets introduce anisotropic distributions to labor, exchange, and production.[109] Indeed, as economic geographers since Karl Marx have noted, such polarities, dynamic in time and space, drive innovations in capital's geographic deployment, serving as sources of new profit in inherently stagnating markets.[110] By shifts in technology, transport, fixed capital, land price, effective demand, locational competition, credit availability, management, labor discipline, and state investment, a locale may suddenly become transiently conducive to cheap livestock production and advantageous exchange.[111] The new geography of production and the "spatial fixes" companies undertake link intensive transformations of human-environmental relations to extensive global trade, with, Bergmann's group hypothesizes, statistically significant impacts upon pathogen evolution and spread. As in the historical precedents we explored in the first section, changing husbandry's economic geography should reset the mix of ecological opportunities and evolutionary selection pressures acting on infections.

By reconstructing Global Trade Analysis Project 7 data commonly used to model all the connections of the global economy for the purposes of trade negotiations,[112] Bergmann and Holmberg have estimated capital's agroecological footprints (see Figure 3).[113] Products from globalized croplands, forests, or pastures eventually contribute to consumption or capital accumulation in other countries. Other landscapes are enmeshed primarily within local circuits

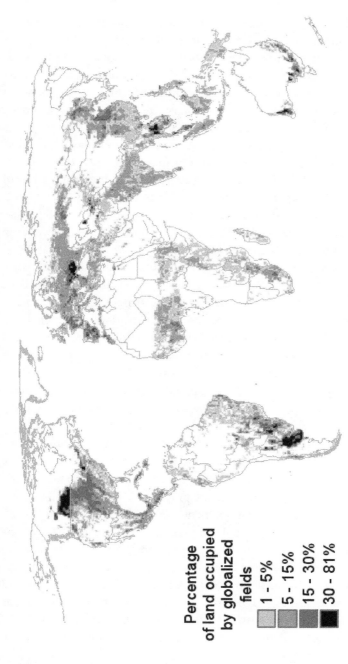

Figure 3. Globalization of croplands, 2004. Percentage of landscape area occupied by croplands whose products are incorporated as part of commodity chains (agricultural or otherwise) whose first consumers are located internationally (calculations by Bergmann and Holmberg).

of production and exchange.[114] Bergmann extends beyond characterizing landscapes that directly produce traditional agricultural exports to identifying the forests and fields that are part of commodity webs supporting export-oriented development producing goods or services for overseas benefit.[115] Bergmann further differentiates between foreign consumption/accumulation of "direct" agricultural goods (for example, fruit or grain); refined or processed agricultural goods (cloth, peanut butter, meat products); manufactured goods (electronics and vehicles); and services (air transport, insurance, education).

How are half-degree rasters of such moments in global circuits of capital to be connected to emergent disease? Are any of these landscapes better related to particular geo-coded outbreaks, as captured, for instance, by FAO's EMPRES Global Animal Disease Information System (EMPRES-i), than simple maps of global land use that fail to differentiate by positionality with respect to circuits of capital? One may wish to control for a variety of other variables, but regardless, this particular Structural One Health seeks more than mere spatial correlations between land uses and particular diseases, which as we previously noted Robinson et al. have called into question.[116] It should be able to differentiate, on the one hand, between the proximity of outbreaks to transnational capital as opposed to transnational consumers/laborers and to local livelihoods or local capital. On the other hand, such an approach should be able to help researchers develop a sense for whether diseases that emerge in economic/agroecological landscapes are connected to export-oriented agriculture, manufacturing, or even services. With the synergistic nature of disease emergence, more-than-local and nonlinear approaches to the empirical study of human-environment processes within One Health are increasingly feasible and fundamental to the future of the field.

For instance, Wallace et al. (in preparation) are using Bergmann's circuits of capital in a statistical phylogeography of Asian H7 and N9 isolates dating back to the 1980s to identify the sociospatial pathways by which the new avian influenza A (H7N9), first detected around Shanghai in 2013, emerged. The team is developing a niche analysis on the MaxEnt and Boosted Regression Trees models to test which of a series of geo-coded social and environmental covariates, including connections to said circuits of capital, characterizes the isolate locales and the localities visited by the virus as inferred by the phylogeographies.[117] The scale and mechanisms of H7N9's emergence are to be arrived at by an automated (if confidence-bounded) exploration of the multidimensional data space over which viral genetics, locales, and the socioecological matrix are related, rather than out of a strict set of *a priori* (and ultimately arbitrary) categories.

Caveats around such work abound—especially around data resolution and availability—but in effect researchers should be able to assign a matrix of indices of export to each disease or strain included in such analysis. Some pathogens, such as some of the avian influenzas, may emerge by local or cross-sectoral agricultural practices (i.e., in a mosaic landscape of backyard and intensive husbandry).[118] Others, such as porcine reproductive and respiratory syndrome and porcine epidemic diarrhea virus, may be more or even exclusively globalized in their agroecologies, perhaps by some combination directly related to agriculture and indirectly to manufactured goods and services as far afield as, for instance, computers and insurance. Still others may take on multiple identities across time and space. In other words, for the first time epidemiologists may be able to statistically test for, numerically weigh, and qualify the world's "agribusiness diseases," which until now have been characterized largely descriptively. More generally, the new approach should offer a novel, intuitive, and rigorous means of coding the economic character of emergent diseases.

The One Health perspective reintroduced scientific investigation to the questions its constituent disciplines have long avoided as a matter of epistemological course. On the other hand, the approach's present episodic abstraction appears overdetermined in time and place while maneuvering causality away from systemic sources. The Structural One Health we introduce here aims to place all sources of cause and effect atop the metaphorical table, including episodic circumstances, foundational and historical contexts, and scientific practice itself. Other structural approaches to multispecies health are also open to exploration.

Flu the Farmer

Leopards break into the temple and drink to the dregs what is in the sacrificial pitchers; this is repeated over and over again; finally it can be calculated in advance, and it becomes a part of the ceremony.

—Franz Kafka (1935)

I DESCRIBED ELSEWHERE THE POSSIBILITY that reducing finishing time may select for greater virulence in influenzas.[119] That is, reducing the age at which poultry are sacrificed may select for increasing the damage influenza incurs.

There may be immunological fallout as well:

By increasing the throughput speed, and reducing the age of food animals at slaughter, the livestock industry may also be selecting for strains able to transmit in the face of younger, more robust immune systems, including, should spillover occur, in humans.

A friend and colleague points out that younger immune systems in poultry may *not* be the more robust. Indeed, it takes up to six weeks for a bird's full immunity to come online. As J. J. Dibner and colleagues describe it:

The seeding of the bursa by lymphocytes occurs between embryonic Days 10 and 15. These cells are committed B cells but are capable of only IgM expression at hatch. The secondary immune organs, such as the spleen, cecal tonsils, Meckel's diverticulum,

Harderian gland, and the diffuse lymphoid tissue of the gut and respiratory systems are incomplete at hatch. There are B cells in the cecal tonsils, but these only express IgM. Similarly, there are T cells in the lamina propria and epithelium of the gut and in other secondary immune organs, but these do not develop helper or cytotoxic capability until some period after hatch. The ability to mount a secondary response, as indicated by the presence of germinal centers or circulating IgG and IgA, begins to appear between 1 and 4 wk of post-hatch life in the broiler chick.[120]

Dibner's team recommend reversing what was at publication the industrial practice of waiting to feed and water hatchlings. The earlier new poults are fed and watered—and, interestingly, by feeding, the earlier they are *exposed to antigens*—the faster the immune system develops.

The notion of immune development—and the health costs of too much biosecurity—introduces an interesting convergence here.

The industry makes an economic distinction between food animals of different ages.[121] If neonatals get sick and die, no problem. Little investment—feed per unit gain—is lost. But if poultry or livestock approaching sacrifice get sick, that's bad business. The company has invested considerable feed by this point. There is, then, a premium placed on a well-oiled immune response in poultry approaching sacrifice.

Some preliminary modeling I'm a part of suggests *influenza* may be on a similar schedule.

We found the individual host's recovery time post-infection and the expected fitness of a flu strain are apparently independent of the duration of a poultry cohort, even under industrial conditions. Influenza's infectious period (no more than a week for any individual host) will likely never approach the finishing time, even under the most rapid throughput speed (presently forty days).

However, selection occurring at another *level of organization*—namely across the cohort—may better bear down on the relationship between finishing time and virulence:

Even as individual hosts die off, the outbreak chain continues to propagate on the farm over several viral generations until a strain can infect enough birds to threaten violating biocontainment and spreading to the next barn or farm. If so, the time it takes to successfully propagate to such a threshold of infected birds may approach the finishing time. From this perspective, it's the *final number of birds* infected that is the controlling variable, not the individual infectious period.

If so, and we're still modeling this, mind you, reducing finishing time could indeed affect the evolution of virulence. A shortened finishing time may select for strains able to reach the propagation threshold faster (before the cohort is slaughtered).

By that backdoor—by which both flu and farmer put a premium on a near-slaughter bird—evolving virulence in the face of an increasingly active, if not robust, immune system may indeed be selected for.

Incredibly, it would also mean flu's now a farmer too, husbanding cohorts of infecteds not for market but the next available barn of fresh susceptibles.

—*Farming Pathogens*, 17 April 2013

Protecting H3N2v's Privacy

THE *GUARDIAN* PUBLISHED A SERIES of stunning articles on the extent of surveillance the National Security Agency has been conducting on U.S. citizens and millions of others worldwide.[122] Proponents of such programs, including President Obama, have contended that secretly collecting our internet and phone metadata—when, where, and with whom we connect—is about our protection.[123] I must say that as an evolutionary epidemiologist I find it a fascinating defense, if only because there have been several failed efforts at producing geographies of deadly influenzas because governments across the globe, including the United States, refuse to provide the locales and dates of livestock outbreaks.[124]

It's as if the privacy rights of these viruses—and really the farms over which they spread—are better protected than those of the populations epidemiologists are ostensibly trying to protect.

As Helen Branswell describes it, the strain typing and pathogen genetic sequencing conducted by the National Animal Health Laboratory Network here in the United States, including at several federally funded public universities, remains strictly confidential and for the livestock industry's eyes only.[125]

Paul Sundberg, vice president for science and technology for the National Pork Board, explains:

> The pigs are owned by the farmer. And what happens to their pigs is the farmer's business, not the government's business, as long as the infection that is going on in those pigs is not what's termed a program disease that is considered to be a risk to the national herd.[126]

As if a new pandemic would emerge only when the whole of the national herd was infected first.

By the time swine flu H1N1 (2009) rolled around, clearly arising from industrial pigs, hog producers, worried about the bad publicity's impact on the bottom line, stopped sending samples.[127] To solicit some kind of cooperation from the industry, the CDC and USDA built in anonymity.

Any viruses found, including data describing on which farm or even in which county an outbreak has occurred, would be made available to a larger network of scientists only with the affected producer's permission. But as a rule researchers are allowed only what state the virus is found, trivial data as we can see from the incomplete if heroic work of Eddie Holmes and Matthew Scotch's phylogeography groups.[128]

In other words, a federal government of a major industrial country won't allow itself—much less anyone else—the geocoded data needed to determine where an outbreak of deadly pandemic influenza might emerge within its own borders, a possibility experts have long argued could kill hundreds of millions of people worldwide.[129] Indeed, even if a person is subsequently infected by pigs, the U.S. government still needs approval from the owner before the source pigs can be tested.

In contrast, we now learn NSA programs such as Boundless Informant and PRISM have mapped trillions of private calls and emails down to even the IP address, including under some protocols the content of the communication.[130]

The revelations follow reports that the Department of Homeland Security has been monitoring social media sites for keywords indicative of terrorist threats.[131] DHS search terms include "Outbreak," "Contamination," "H1N1," "H5N1," "Avian Flu," "Influenza," "Tamiflu," "Human to Human," "CDC," "FDA," "WHO," "Swine," "Pork," "Agriculture," "Resistant," "Infection," "Pandemic," and "Wave," a veritable tag cloud for many a research blog, including this one.

Does the difference between the privacy offered pathogens and people speak to the nature of our democracy? It is as if *talking* about an outbreak is thought more of a danger than the outbreak itself.

—*Farming Pathogens*, 10 June 2013

UPDATE. In July 2013 the National Pork Producers Council and the American Farm Bureau Federation demanded that a federal judge reverse successful efforts by environmental groups to get the U.S. Environmental Protection Agency to release the contact and locale information for farmers across thirty-five states: names, addresses, emails, and global positioning coordinates of thousands of poultry and livestock farmers and ranchers.[132] The environmental groups had sought the data to help discover the sources of wastewater pollution.

The industry groups are concerned that the data would be used to "harass" the farmers, including suing individual producers for violations of the Clean Water Act.

The EPA had at this point already sent out discs with the contact information of farmers across twenty-nine states to Earthjustice, Sierra Club, and the Pew Charitable Trusts. When pork producers complained, the EPA collected the discs back and reissued them with some of the data redacted.

In a letter to the EPA, Pew wrote that it believes strongly that gathering basic information regarding the location, nature and extent of pollution sources associated with . . . Concentrated Animal Feeding Operations . . . is a fundamental first step to carrying out the objectives of the Clean Water Act. . . . We were disappointed when the agency withdrew its proposed reporting rule.

Distress of Columbia

So far as Slavery is concerned, we of the South must throw
ourselves on the constitution & defend our rights under [it] to the
last, & when arguments will no longer suffice, we will appeal to
the sword, if necessary to do so. I will be the last to yield one inch.

—Zachary Taylor (1847)

THERE'S SOME ROUGH JUSTICE in three antebellum-era presidents getting killed drinking the water at the slave-built White House.[133]

For decades the water was drawn just seven blocks downstream from where the White House dumped its shit.

James Polk and Zachary Taylor, both of whom owned slaves during their presidencies, suffered severe gastroenteritis, Taylor dying in office and Polk three months following his term.[134]

According to Jane McHugh and Philip Mackowiak, the ill-advised enemas William Henry Harrison's doctor prescribed—now there's a vision—likely burst intestinal ulcers produced by typhus and paratyphus, leaching bacteria into the bloodstream for a painful death by septic shock.[135]

No grindhouse moral, nor art house redemption, but perhaps still an epiphenomenon of empire. On what was a glorified plantation, growing not crops but imperial designs alienated from people and place alike, enslaved men and women were obligated to kill their masters bucket by bucket.

—*Farming Pathogens*, 8 April 2014

PART SEVEN

If we listen closely to twentieth-century writers and thinkers about modernity and compare them to those of a century ago, we will find a radical flattening of perspective and shrinkage of imaginative range. Our nineteenth-century thinkers were simultaneously enthusiasts and enemies of modern life, wrestling inexhaustibly with its ambiguities and contradictions; their self-ironies and inner tensions were a primary source of their creative power. Their twentieth-century successors have lurched far more toward rigid polarities and flat totalizations. Modernity is either embraced with a blind and uncritical enthusiasm, or else condemned with a neo-Olympian remoteness and contempt; in either case, it is conceived as a closed monolith, incapable of being shaped or changed by modern men.

—MARSHALL BERMAN (1982)

We were dreamers but not easily impressed. This is an engaging combination. It insists on its own accounting system, and the columns never align.

—MEGAN HUSTAD (2014)

Did Neoliberalizing West African Forests Produce a New Niche for Ebola?

I co-authored the following commentary with Richard Kock, Luke Bergmann, Marius Gilbert, Lenny Hogerwerf, Claudia Pittiglio, Raffaele Mattioli, and Rodrick Wallace for the International Journal of Health Services.[1] *For clarity's sake, I've edited out the few equations we originally included.*

PRELIMINARY RESULTS INDICATE RESEARCHERS have developed a successful vaccine against Ebola Makona, the *Zaire ebolavirus* variant underlying the regional outbreak in West Africa.[2] A cluster-randomized vaccination trial of nearly 8,000 people across Guinean location and ring size found that all contacts around a confirmed infection (and contacts of contacts) vaccinated immediately went uninfected. In contrast, sixteen cases emerged in those rings vaccinated twenty-one days after an index case.

Good news indeed, even should the vaccine prove less efficacious in subsequent clinical testing. Vaccines are a fundamental public health intervention when not ensnared in market failures, which are as effective a barrier to the availability of health technologies as any anti-vaxx campaign.[3] A series of mergers and acquisitions have left only four pharmaceutical companies—GlaxoSmithKline, Sanofi-Pasteur, Merck, and Pfizer—producing vaccines for diseases other than influenza, primarily for developed markets.[4] With little competition, many such vaccines are overpriced and effectively unavailable in the poorest countries.[5] The Ebola vaccine trial in West Africa was funded as a non-commercial effort by WHO, Wellcome Trust, Médecins Sans Frontières, and the Norwegian and Canadian governments. There is an adjunct danger in the latter success. Vaccination is based on a molecular model of disease etiology. Such thinking is necessary, of course. Viruses and immunity interact at the molecular level, even as they also do so pleiotropically, cognitively, and across multiple physiological systems.[6] For a broad constituency, however, a successful vaccine implies the approach is also sufficient.[7] An ebullient *Nature* editorial, for instance, charges:

> Roll-out of the vaccine to more people will provide data to confirm its effectiveness. But by vaccinating the families, friends, healthcare workers and others who come into contact with infected people, Ebola outbreaks could be stopped in their tracks—the same strategy that was used to eradicate smallpox in the 1970s. This means that this vaccine can, in principle, be deployed immediately to help to end the Ebola epidemic in West Africa. As aptly conveyed by the trial's French name, *"Ebola, ça suffit!"* (Ebola, that's enough!), it is time to finish the job.[8]

If only diseases responded to such heroic appeals to consequences alone. Many intractable pathogens, among them HIV, malaria, and tuberculosis, act decidedly unlike smallpox and other diseases that respond to the reductionist model of intervention.[9] In a world in which viruses and bacteria evolve in response to humanity's multifaceted infrastructure—agricultural, transportation, pharmaceutical, public health, scientific, political—our epistemological and epidemiological intractabilities may be in fundamental ways one and the same.

The more socioecologically complex pathogens can evolve into population states that even the most well-intentioned researchers fail to parse, if by dint of the demands of research and development alone.[10] Models of biology and the economic doctrine under which they are produced are often tightly intertwined, down to their mathematical formalisms.[11] Many pathogens meanwhile plot their own paths, deriving solutions to interventions at one level of biocultural organization with adaptations at another.[12] As a result, pathogen evolution routinely fails to cooperate with market expectations and scientific hypotheses alike.

NEOLIBERAL EBOLA

Ebola offers an archetypical example of such a disjunction between method and medical phenomenon.

The Makona variant appears conventional in its phenotype, if one could say so of such a dangerous pathogen, with a typical case fatality rate, incubation period, and serial interval, the latter the time between successive cases.[13] The virus had been spilling over in the region for years. Schoepp et al. found antibodies to multiple species of Ebola in patients in Sierra Leone as far back as five years ago, including to the Zaire species from which the outbreak variant evolved.[14] Phylogenetic analyses meanwhile show the species circulating in West Africa as far back as a decade.[15] Hoenen et al. showed the outbreak variant as initially possessing no molecular anomaly, with nucleotide substitution rates typical of Ebola outbreaks across Africa, even as Makona would phylogeographically diversify and adapt, largely by antigenic drift.[16]

As we raised last year, these results beg an explanation for Ebola's ecotypic shift from intermittent forest killer taking out a village here and there, to a protopandemic infection infecting 28,000 and killing 11,000 across the region, leaving bodies in the streets of capital cities Monrovia and Conakry.[17] Even with contagion presently below replacement, the outbreak continues. Many of the thousands who survived infection suffer long-term symptomatic sequelae, including eye disease, hearing loss, arthralgia, anorexia, difficulty sleeping, and PTSD, and, as documented in one recent patient, can pass on the virus by sexual transmission.[18]

Some commentary has noted that the structural adjustment to which West Africa has been subjected the past decade included the kinds of divestment from public health infrastructure that permitted Ebola to incubate at the population level once it spilled over.[19] The effects, however, extend further back in the causal chain. The shifts in land use in the Guinea Forest Region from where the Ebola epidemic first emerged were also connected to neoliberal efforts at opening the forest to global circuits of capital. Apparently Ebola did not fundamentally change, but West Africa had.[20]

Daniel Bausch and Lara Schwarz characterize the Forest Region as a mosaic of isolated populations of a variety of ethnic groups that hold little political power and receive little social investment.[21] The forest's economy and ecology are also strained by thousands of refugees from civil wars in neighboring countries. The region is subjected to the tandem trajectories of accelerating deterioration in public infrastructure and concerted efforts at private development dispossessing smallholdings and traditional foraging grounds for mining, clear-cut logging, and increasingly intensified agriculture.

The Ebola epicenter is located in the larger Guinea Savannah Zone that the World Bank describes as "one of the largest underused agricultural land reserves in the world."[22] Continental Africa hosts 60 percent of the world's last farmland frontier. The Bank sees the Savannah as an opportunity best developed by market commercialization, if not solely on the agribusiness model. As the Land Matrix Observatory documents, such prospects are in the process of actualization.[23] The Observatory lists ninety deals by which U.S.-backed multinationals have procured hundreds of thousands of hectares for export crops, biofuels, and mining around the world, including multiple deals in Sub-Saharan Africa. The Observatory's online database shows similar land deals contracted by other world powers, including the United Kingdom, France, and China.

Under the newly democratized Guinean government, the Nevada-based and British-backed Farm Land of Guinea Limited secured ninety-nine-year leases for two parcels totaling nearly 9,000 hectares outside the villages of N'Dema and Konindou in Dabola Prefecture, where a secondary Ebola epicenter developed, and 98,000 hectares outside the village of Saraya in Kouroussa Prefecture.[24] The Ministry of Agriculture has now tasked Farm Land to survey and map an additional 1.5 million hectares for third-party development. While these as of yet undeveloped acquisitions are not directly tied to Ebola, they are markers of a complex, policy-driven phase change in agroecology our group has hypothesized undergirds Ebola Makona's emergence.[25]

In an effort to connect this broader context to data accumulating about the epizoology of Ebola and the ecology of its hosts, we centered our thesis on palm oil.

Natural and semi-wild groves of different oil palm types have long served as a source of red palm oil in the Guinea Forest Region.[26] Forest farmers have been raising palm oil in one or another form for hundreds of years. Fallow periods allowing soils to recover, however, were reduced over the twentieth century from twenty years in the 1930s to ten by the 1970s, and still further by the 2000s, with the added effect of increasing grove density even should no new plots break ground. Concomitantly, semi-wild production has been increasingly replaced with intensive hybrids, and red oil replaced by, or mixed with, industrial and kernel oils.

Other crops are grown in the forest.[27] Regional shade agriculture includes coffee, cocoa, and kola. Slash-and-burn rice, maize, hibiscus, and corms of the first year, followed by peanut and cassava of the second and a fallow period, are rotated through the area. Lowland flooding supports rice. In essence, the region has long been characterized by a move toward increased intensification without private capital in the technical sense while still remaining classifiably agroforest.

Even this passing juxtaposition has since been transformed. The Guinean Oil Palm and Rubber Company (with the French acronym SOGUIPAH) began in 1987 as a parastatal cooperative in the forest but since has matured into a state company.[28] SOGUIPAH is leading efforts that began in 2006 to develop plantations of intensive hybrid palm for commodity export. The company economized palm production for the market by forcibly expropriating farmland, which to this day continues to set off violent protest. During the outbreak itself, a medical team dispatched by SOGUIPAH to educate locals about Ebola and distribute chlorine was met with stones and briefly taken hostage in Bignamou, Yomou, on the Liberian border.[29] Trust and its collapse are eminently epidemiological variables.[30]

International aid accelerated forest industrialization. SOGUIPAH's new mill, with four times the capacity of one it previously used, was financed by the European Investment Bank.[31] The mill's capacity ended the artisanal extraction that as late as 2010 provided local populations full employment. The subsequent increase in production has at one and the same time led to harvesting above the mill's capacity and operation below capacity off-season, leading to a conflict between the company and some of its 2,000 now partially proletarianized pickers, some of whom insist on processing a portion of their own yield to cover the resulting gaps in cash flow. Pickers who insist on processing their own oil during the rainy season now risk arrest.

The new economic geography instantiates a classic case of land expropriation and enclosure, turning a tradition of shared forest commons toward expectations that informal pickers working fallow land outside their family lineage obtain an owner's permission before picking palm.[32]

Out of the new agricultural regime an archipelago of oil palm plots has emerged in and around the Guéckédou area, the outbreak's apparent ground zero.[33] The characteristic landscape is a mosaic of villages surrounded by dense vegetation and interspersed by crop fields of oil palm and patches of open forest and regenerated young forest. The general pattern can be discerned at a finer scale as well, west of the town of Meliandou, where the index cases of the new Ebola appeared.

The landscape may embody a growing interface between humans and frugivore bats, a key reservoir for Ebola, including hammer-headed bats, little collared fruit bats, and Franquet's epauletted fruit bats.[34] Shafie et al. document a variety of disturbance-associated fruit bats *attracted* to oil palm plantations.[35] Bats migrate to oil palm for food and shelter from the heat while the plantations' wide trails permit easy movement between roosting and foraging sites. As the forest disappears, multiple species of bat shift their foraging behavior to the food and shelter that are left.

Bushmeat hunting and butchery are one means by which subsequent spillover may take place, but agricultural cultivation may be enough of a mechanism. Anti et al. report more than a third of survey respondents in Ghana were bitten by bats, scratched, or exposed to bat urine.[36] Plowright et al. characterize bat roosting structures as conducive to indirect transmission of viruses by droplets or aerosols and warn that continual exposure "may lead to a high probability of infection."[37] Fruit bats in Bangladesh transmitted Nipah virus to human hosts by urinating on the date fruit humans cultivated.[38] Even transmission by hunting may be dependent upon agriculture if by second-order effects. Leroy et al. report that not long before a village outbreak, large-scale hunting of Ebola-prone bats along the Lulua River in the Congo took place among the palm trees of a massive abandoned plantation that bats had been visiting for half a century.[39]

Saéz et al. have since proposed that the initial Ebola spillover in Guinea occurred outside Meliandou when children, including the putative index case, caught and played with Angolan free-tailed bats in a local tree.[40] The bats are an insectivore species also previously documented as an Ebola virus carrier. As we describe elsewhere, whatever the specific reservoir source, shifts in agroeconomic context still appear a primary cause.[41] Previous studies show the free-tailed bats also attracted to expanding cash crop production in West Africa, including sugarcane, cotton, and macadamia.[42]

Indeed, nearly every Ebola outbreak to date appears connected to capital-driven shifts in land use, including logging, mining, and agriculture, back to the first outbreak in Nzara, Sudan, in 1976, where a British-financed factory spun and wove local cotton.[43] When Sudan's civil war ended in 1972, the area rapidly repopulated and much of Nzara's local rainforest—and bat ecology—was reclaimed for subsistence farming, with cotton returning as the area's dominant cash crop.[44] As if to punctuate the point, hundreds of bats were discovered roosting in the factory itself where several workers were infected.

STRUCTURAL ONE HEALTH

Clearly such outbreaks are embedded beyond shifts in local ecologies brought about by the actions of specific companies in specific countries. Causality extends in space and scope. By a Structural One Health we can determine whether the world's circuits of capital as they relate to husbandry and land use, producing pronounced interconnections across the globe, are related to disease emergence.[45]

Some landscapes are enmeshed primarily within local circuits of production and exchange. Other landscapes produce traditional agricultural exports. But maps by Bergmann and Holmberg show calculations of the percentages of land (croplands, pasturelands, and forests) whose harvests are effectively consumed abroad, not only directly as agricultural goods, but also indirectly as manufactured goods and services.[46] Further, they show how West African forests and fields are much more globalized when viewed from the perspective of the largely foreign capital investment and accumulation they directly and indirectly support, even when compared to the many overseas consumers to whose lives they contribute.

In presenting updated maps of global livestock, Robinson et al. report:

> As [agricultural] production intensifies it becomes increasingly detached from the land resource base (for example as feeds are brought in that are grown in completely different places) and thus more difficult to predict based on spatial, agro-ecological variables. The effect is particularly marked for chickens and pigs, where the locations of intensive farming units often have more to do with accessibility to markets or to inputs of one sort or another, than to the agro-ecological characteristics of the land that can be quantified through remotely sensed variables.[47]

If landscapes, and by extension their associated pathogens, are globalized by circuits of capital, the source of a disease may be more than merely the country in which the pathogen first appeared. As a matter of methodological completeness, we need identify which sovereign wealth funds, state-owned enterprises, governments, and private equity—companies, developers, mutual funds, banks, pension funds, hedge funds, university endowments, and equity funds—finance the development and deforestation leading to disease emergence in the first place.[48]

The implications are more than technical in nature, however. Such an epidemiology begs whether we might more accurately characterize such locales as New York, London, and Hong Kong, key sources of capital, as disease "hotspots" in their own right. Diseases are relational in their geographies, which are never confined to within the borders of a "hot zone."[49]

The new approach speaks to the nature of public health campaigns. The current Ebola response appears largely organized around segregating emergency operations and broader structural interventions.[50] Emergency responses are critical, of course, but such logistics are an indirect, if perhaps in most cases unintended, means by which to avoid addressing the greater foundational contexts driving the emergence of diseases. That is, however critically unaware its practitioners, the omission serves as an ideological design feature partial to the present political and economic orders.

The philosopher István Mészáros differentiates between episodic or periodic crises resolved within the established global framework and foundational crises that affect the framework itself.[51] In the latter structural crises, unfolding in an epochal fashion through the very limits of a given order, the systemic contradictions start to accumulate in such a fashion that none can be adequately addressed. Beyond ill-defined references to "upstream" causes,[52] we need instead to explicitly acknowledge that many of our emergencies, pathogens among them, arise from the very structural apparatus called upon to respond.

FOREST BACKGROUND FRONT AND CENTER

A second false dichotomy divides pathogen and outbreak from their contextual fields. In Ebola's case, the deterministic effects of the pathogen and its evolution are treated as if divorced from the forest's ecosystemic noise—the sum of chance encounters among the various agroecological actors in the region. The reality is much more complicated, with networks of causes highly interlinked and conditional in time, space, and direction. The ostensible "background" of the forest on which Ebola and other pathogens emerge may in fact be a front-and-center explanation for the outbreak.

Our group developed a simple stochastic differential model of exponential growth in a pathogen population that includes the "noise" of stochastic ecological interactions across and within species imposed by the complexity of the forest.[53] When below a threshold, the noise exponent is small enough to let a pathogen population explode in size. When above the threshold, the noise is large enough to control an outbreak, frustrating efforts on the part of the pathogen to string together a series of susceptibles to infect above replacement.

The formalism implies that under certain conditions the forest acts as its own epidemiological protection and we risk the next deadly pandemic when we destroy that capacity. When the forest's functional noise is stripped out, the epidemiological consequences are explosive.

Control efforts are similarly impacted. Much of public health intervention, by vaccine or sanitary practices, aims at lowering an outbreak below an infection's Allee threshold, under which a population can't reproduce enough to replace its dead.[54] A pathogen, unable to find enough susceptibles to sustain itself, can be maneuvered into burning out on its own. But in this case, commoditizing the forest may have lowered the region's ecosystemic threshold to such a point that no emergency intervention can drive the Ebola outbreak low enough to burn out. Novel spillovers suddenly express larger forces of infection. On the other end of the epicurve, a mature outbreak continues to circulate, with the potential to intermittently rebound.[55]

In short, neoliberalism's structural shifts are no mere background on which the emergency of Ebola takes place. The shifts *are* the emergency as much as the virus itself. Changes in land use brought about by policy-driven transitions in ownership and production appear to be fundamental contributions to explaining Ebola's area-specific emergence. Deforestation and intensive agriculture may strip out traditional agroforestry's stochastic friction, which typically keeps the virus from lining up enough transmission.

We can formalize the connections between economy and epizoology more explicitly. Members of our group inductively modeled the effects of environmental stochastic noise on the resulting financial costs of an outbreak for industrial livestock on the one hand and agroecological production on the other.[56] We adapted the Black-Scholes approach to option pricing in finance to modeling the cost in resources needed to control epizootic outbreaks under the two models of production.[57]

Our model shows that the costs are dependent on a constant of proportionality dampening the environmental noise. If the constant is effectively zero, as occurs under agroforestry, then the cost of epidemic control grows only as the log of the policy-driven stochasticity. If the constant exceeds zero, as occurs under most industrial production, then the cost will be dominated by linear growth in the stochasticity. In short, the overall financial costs of an outbreak—including direct and opportunity costs—are dependent upon the impacts of agroeconomic policy on environmental stochasticity. The inherently explosive epizoologies of commodity agricultures—however biocontained—appear exorbitantly expensive as a first principle.

Although the contention requires field testing, the Ebola outbreak in West Africa is suggestive. Bartsch et al. estimate the direct societal costs of all cases in Guinea, Liberia, and Sierra Leone through mid-December 2014 ranging from $82 million to $356 million.[58]

The Political Will for a Research Way

To test these various hypotheses, we could combine remote sensing, demographic data, and trade data to spatially project the risk of another outbreak across Africa's Guinea Savannah Zone. By a number of spatial approaches, including potential surface analyses, we could project Ebola zoonotic risk across the Zone based on a number of socioecological factors, including host reservoirs, health infrastructure, human population density and mobility, shifts in land use, and globalized capital accumulation and consumption across local croplands, pasturelands, and forests, with a particular emphasis on how those factors may have evolved over time.

We could develop historical political-economic studies for the areas identified by the projection models to be at risk for novel Ebola outbreaks. Each risk area is characterized by its own place-specific social and agroeconomic trajectories. Working through local communities and supporting agencies, we could make site visits to locales already affected by outbreaks and, once the risk maps have been produced, visit areas projected to be of the gravest risk. Though such site visits have been previously made for Ebola, none to date has done so incorporating the broader global agroeconomics at the heart of the changes in land use behind disease spillover. Nor have such visits been made to areas of projected risk.

The question remains, however, whether in the face of current research imperatives there exists the political will to fund a project undergirded by such a set of premises. Concepts of pathogen biology can act as both a spur to and a brake upon new interventions in public health. Unwittingly or not, the new Ebola vaccine is presently applied as much as a proverbial inoculation against discussing the problems of neoliberalism's impacts upon deadly pathogens as it is a welcome addition to public health's arsenal.[59] At bottom, the two conditions are a false equivalence in practice and proposition. Blocking Ebola with a vaccine does not make the social context driving Ebola's circulation disappear. Indeed, ignoring the latter condition increases the likelihood that the vaccine will fail at any number of levels, from the molecular to the socioeconomic.[60]

As Ebola and other pathogens evolve from underneath our passing technicist responses, the agroeconomic matrix, a global specter, looms as the critical cause the health sciences are leaving largely unaddressed. That needn't be the case.

—*International Journal of Health Services,*
January 2016

Collateralized Farmers

IN THE COURSE OF HIS SENSATIONAL exposé of Big Meat, Christopher Leonard falls upon both a solution to a mystery central to influenza epizoology and a foundational admission on the part of the poultry industry.[61]

It's common knowledge that agribusinesses are vertically integrated.[62] All nodes of poultry or pig production are placed here in the States under each of the Big Five's roofs. Cargill, Smithfield, JBS Swift, Pilgrim's Pride, and Tyson raise their birds and hogs and beef from fertilization to freezer.

But that isn't quite correct. "There is one link in the chain that Tyson [much as the other companies] has decided not to own," Leonard writes,

> one part of the rural economy that the company has pushed far outside the limits of its property. While most businesses are drawn steadily into the integrator's body, the force of gravity has been reversed when it comes to the farms. The farms [on which poultry spend much of their albeit short lives] are exiled, shoved away, and dumped from the balance sheets.[63]

Plumping up birds for sacrifice is contracted out to local freelancers as modern-day sharecroppers:

> During the 1960s, Tyson Foods realized that chicken farming was a losing game. When Tyson executives examined operations at the company, they saw that farming was the least profitable, and most

risky, side of the business. . . . "You need to allocate whatever capital you have where it produces the most return on your investment."

While cutting-edge machinery, as it were, for slaughtering and processing poultry saves thousands of hours of labor, owning the land and raising birds under difficult circumstances add limited value.

"You can't crowd the chickens in [a 400-by-40-foot chicken house]," Leonard quotes former Tyson attorney Jim Blair. When "there's too much chickens you create disease and you lose efficiency. You can't keep a curve on the growth of production in the chicken house."

Ventilation, vaccines, and automated feed distribution only incrementally boost profits.

In effect, the companies are implicitly admitting that squeezing thousands of animals together produces repeated and devastating outbreaks that undercut margins. As Tommy Brown, a former Tyson field technician Leonard interviewed, describes it:

> The chickens seemed as delicate as a crop of indoor snow being grown in the Ozark summer. With just the slightest glitch, a broken fan or feed line or dirty water tank, the birds would expire fast as melting ice. More than anything, [Brown thought,] it took vigilance to raise chickens. This is what he preached to farmers. This was his solution when he entered a barn and saw that the feeder was broken and the birds were pecking each other to death.

The admission is spelled out in something more damning than a leaked document or by candid informers however helpful these may be. It's found in the structure of the sector.

Raising animals this way is so unsustainable that the companies ostensibly rearing them, control freaks extraordinaire, refuse to fold it into their incorporated operations. Instead, by a complex bureaucratization the companies maneuver contract farmers into taking on all the risk but without any of the authority:

> Tyson has offlanded ownership to the farms, but it maintains control. The company always owns the chickens, even after it drops

them off at the farm. . . . So the farmer never owns his business's most important asset. Tyson also owns the feed the birds eat, which is mixed at the Tyson plant according to the company's recipe and then delivered to the farm on Tyson's trucks according to a schedule that Tyson dictates. . . . Tyson dictates which medicine the birds receive to stave off disease and gain weight.

As if this wasn't command enough, Tyson plays the farmers off each other:

> Tyson also sets the prices for its birds . . . subtract[ing] the value of the feed it delivered to grow the birds. . . . But the farmer isn't paid this flat fee. Instead, final payment is based on a ranking system, which farmers call the "tournament." Tyson compares how well each farmer was able to fatten the chickens, compared to his neighbors who also delivered chickens that week.

That is, the diligence and vigilance Brown counseled farmers are never enough:

> [Brown] also knew what the farmers didn't: that no matter what they did, no matter how many hours they worked or what new equipment they bought or innovations they tried, it wouldn't affect their profitability at the end of the day. That profitability was determined before the loads of baby chicks were placed on the bed of fresh litter. It depended on how healthy the birds were at birth, and whether Tyson delivered good feed or the dregs from the bottom of the feed mill silos. . . . Older hens produced weaker chicks, while younger hens laid more vigorous broods.

Indeed, access to the best birds, feed, and ranking appears a means by which to discipline farmers. "Fear of economic punishment for upsetting the company," Andrew Jenner writes,

> is pervasive among growers. Even worse is the prospect of being "cut off," or dropped altogether by a company, which generally

can terminate a grower's contract at will with 90 days' notice—
potentially devastating to a grower with mortgage payments to
make on his poultry houses.

As a result, very few growers are as willing to be as outspoken
as [Pilgrim's contract farmer and labor organizer Mike] Weaver
about difficult circumstances they may be facing. . . . As a case in
point, Weaver says he used to regularly earn production bonuses
by topping the weekly pool of growers. He says it hasn't happened
once in the past three years.[64]

One Tyson office worker Leonard interviewed discovered that
some farmers repeatedly received the cream of the day-old chicks,
from younger hens, while another batch routinely were sent the
worst, from older hens. "Complainers," among them those attempting to organize fellow poultry growers, were shipped the bad eggs:

It was understood within the office that those who complained
would be marked. And it was as obvious as a list of names on a
bulletin board who was who. Some farmers went with the program and ensured the system ran smoothly. And others . . . posed
a threat by complaining, calling the office, or demanding more
money.[65]

Prices, feed, and birds aren't the only inputs fixed. Even the financial risk of running a farm, superficially a matter between a farmer
and his or her bank, is tightly controlled. "Farmers take out bank
loans to finance the operations," Leonard explains,

and rural banks have become proficient at helping the farmers become indebted. The banks have learned to break down a
farmer's debt payments into a schedule that perfectly coincides
with the life cycle of a flock of chickens. The farmer pays the bank
every six weeks or so, just when his paycheck arrives from Tyson.
In many cases Tyson cooperates with the bank and draws the
loan payment from the farmer's pay, directly depositing it into the
bank. So with every flock, the farmer is racing against his debt,

hoping the birds Tyson delivers will gain enough weight to earn
a payment that will cover the mortgage and bills from electricity,
heating fuel, and water [for the birds].

While a farmer's debt is measured in decades, the contracts run a
matter of weeks and are reissued flock-by-flock, to be terminated at
the company's whim.

The epizootic thunderbolt is that pathogens likely evolve in
response to the company town.

Mathematical modeling that I'm involved in previously hypothesizes that influenza strains have evolved virulence schedules
convergent with agribusiness production.[66] Flus may "grow" cohorts
of infected chickens not for market but the next barn of susceptibles
in the value-added chain.

We can now add another perversity. Agribusiness grows farmers as
trap crops, sopping up structural diseases with externalized debt. The
market protects influenzas and other pathogens inherent in raising so
many birds so fast and so close together by dumping the costs of the
outbreaks on contingent labor.

The damages smallholders shoulder extend beyond financial ruin.
Stressed U.S. farmers, like their counterparts in India, are killing
themselves at a prodigious rate.[67]

"[The 1980s] economic undertow sucked down farms and the
people who put their lives into them. Male farmers became four times
more likely to kill themselves than male non-farmers," *Newsweek*
recently reported, "Since that crisis, the suicide rate for male farmers has remained high: just under two times that of the general
population."[68]

—*Farming Pathogens*, 8 May 2014

Mickey the Measles

I only hope that we never lose sight of one thing—that it all started with a mouse.

—WALT DISNEY (1954)

AN OUTBREAK OF HIGHLY INFECTIOUS measles starting at Disneyland in Anaheim, California, has spread to eight U.S. states and Mexico.[69] Arizona, one state hit, is presently monitoring 1,000 people linked to Disneyland visitors and subsequent exposures.[70]

With good reason, much attention has been placed on the role the anti-vaxx movement has played in both the initial outbreak and its subsequent spread.[71] In 2014, before the outbreak, U.S. measles clocked in at three times the cases (644) than any of the ten years previous.[72]

The outbreak may represent a second scandal.

Five years ago Disney objected to suggestions that the theme park and resort, drawing 15 million visitors a year from around the world, was a potential amplifier for infectious diseases.

In late 2009, with swine flu H1N1 still circulating, a colleague and I produced a report on the occupational epidemiology of influenza for UNITE HERE Local 11, a union representing Disneyland employees.[73]

We placed Disneyland within the geography of global disease:

Disney's park draw may have epidemiological implications. Each year millions of visitors from around the world visit Disney parks, some for as long as a week. Given such traffic, a reasonable inference is that at least some of the pathogens that annually emerge elsewhere in the world, influenza included, find their way into Disney venues. . . .

As a major destination site the resort has the potential to amplify the geographic spread of the virus. Any Disney pandemic plan should account for the possibility the company's parks may contribute to the spread of influenza both locally and abroad. . . .

The draw may produce a funnel-like effect, in which sick individuals from numerous geographically diffuse locations are brought to a specific location, in this case a resort at which thousands of employees work.

There were already apparent precedents:

Long-distance travel also offers a primary mechanism by which newly evolved variants of a pandemic strain, characterized by shifts in inherent virulence, can geographically spread. Maria Koliou and her colleagues reported some of the first H1N1 cases in Cyprus were in younger people who had visited tourist resorts. Similarly many of the first cases in the United States were reported among young adults returning from their spring break vacations in Mexico.

Indeed, there is anecdotal evidence from media reports that Disney parks and hotels, including at Disneyland, have already served as hubs through which swine flu H1N1 (2009) has been both brought in from abroad and transmitted locally. In mid-May three Melbourne siblings tested positive for swine flu on their return from a family holiday to Disneyland. Victorian health authorities subsequently quarantined and administered anti-viral medication to their classmates. In mid-July a group of Mississippi tourists who had stayed at Disney's Pop Century Hotel were treated at a Celebration, Florida, hospital for flulike symptoms thought to be caused by H1N1.

Of the mechanisms by which a pathogen can be amplified once on Disney properties, we wrote:

If one person, whether a customer or employee, becomes infected, there is a real potential that he or she could spread it to others, given the large number of people with whom he or she might come in contact. . . .

Customer behavior may augment risk. Guests may not realize that they are ill until they have already traveled a long distance to visit Disneyland. Many may be unwilling to stay out of public after they have already paid for their vacations. This places employees at such sites in a position where they may be exposed to visitors who are ill with influenza, even as the level of influenza infection in the surrounding community may be comparatively low . . .

In effect, hotel workers are being asked to act as public health workers, commensurate with medium-risk exposure. Should the pandemic turn severe they could be asked to expose themselves still further. If public health authorities were to quarantine a hotel with severely sick guests, a scenario for which the [American Hospitality and Lodging Association] asks its members to prepare, the hotel's employees, preparing and attending an isolation ward for guests and coworkers, could be shifted into high-risk exposure commensurate with hospital professionals.

We projected beyond influenza to other pathogens:

In preparing for a pandemic today, public and private organizations—employees and management—can better organize their operations to withstand outbreaks and other public health emergencies that may emerge in the near and extended future.

We capped our review with a list of detailed recommendations. These included employee-employer collaborative pandemic planning, an off-site employee response team, and, as employees' lives extend beyond the park gates, regional planning.

We concluded by alluding to the responsibility Disneyland bears to its employees and customers both:

In bringing over 15 million people through its park gates and thousands into its hotels each year, the Disneyland Resort takes on enormous responsibilities. These obligations, however, extend beyond the health and safety of its employees and customers day-to-day and on to acting responsibly under even the worst of community and public health threats. The company is not indemnified by the severity of an emergency. As one of Southern California's largest employers, Disneyland can and should act to assure its employees and their families are protected to the fullest extent possible. By doing so, the company will also help protect its customers from near and far, as well as the surrounding community.

Catching wind of the draft report, Disney trotted out CDC's Phyllis Kozarsky to preempt calls for long-term pandemic preparations. Kozarsky, of the CDC's Travelers' Health Branch, emailed the *New York Times*:

> To single out Disneyland and Disney World is not appropriate with regard to transmission of H1N1. There are too numerous to count opportunities for people to be in close spaces together, whether in movie theaters, in crowded shopping malls, on public transportation as well as during most individuals' daily activities.[74]

In other words, Disneyland is like anywhere else, so, against OSHA, Homeland Security, and yes, CDC recommendations, don't bother with special preparations.

And yet, at the same time, CDC researchers offered very different conclusions for another global attraction.

Shahul Ebrahim and colleagues reviewed the epidemiological implications of the annual Hajj, when two and a half million Muslim pilgrims converge on Mecca, Saudi Arabia, from around the world.[75] According to Ebrahim's team:

> Hajj-related exportation of H1N1 virus by returning pilgrims could potentially initiate waves of outbreaks worldwide. . . .

Pilgrims originating from North America (more than 15,000) and Europe (more than 45,000) pass through major airline hubs of the world on their journey, which increases the risk of international spread of the virus.

The authors offered control recommendations for the Hajj under the principle that those administrating mass gatherings, including, for instance, Disneyland, should act in as cautious a way as possible in case such places or the events they host are in fact instrumental in the virus's spread. In short, it is better to be safe than sorry.

The difference here is that unlike the travel industry, Hajj organizers do not deploy the kinds of ruffian lobbyists and envelopes of PAC money we see from Mickey the Measles.[76]

Five years later and this outbreak wave is followed by a wake of post-hoc rationalization.

The California Department of Public Health reports:

> Measles has been eliminated in the United States since 2000. However, large measles outbreaks have occurred in many countries, particularly in Western Europe, Pakistan, Vietnam and the Philippines in recent years. Travelers to areas where measles circulates can bring measles back to the U.S., resulting in limited domestic transmission of measles. California has many international attractions and visitors come from many parts of the world.[77]

For an outbreak, "this is the ideal scenario," pediatric infectious diseases expert James Cherry told the *Los Angeles Times*.[78] "People go to Disneyland from all different countries and all different states."

We always knew what we refused to acknowledge.

—*FARMING PATHOGENS*, 29 JANUARY 2015

UPDATE. Five Disneyland employees were confirmed infected with measles.[79] Other employees who may have been in contact with them were sent home on paid leave while awaiting test results. Disneyland employees meanwhile observed an apparent decline in attendance to the park.[80] Disney Chair and CEO Bob Iger claimed attendance and bookings were up.

Turns out this wasn't the first time that a measles outbreak started at Disneyland. In 1982, an outbreak of fourteen cases began there, as did another of five cases in 2001. The *San Francisco Chronicle* reports that both also started when someone infected from abroad visited the theme park while contagious.[81]

Made in Minnesota

From the outside, the headquarters of the Cankor Health Group resembles a garage. The interior is modeled after an industrial poultry factory. The lobby is a dank, low-ceilinged concrete chamber. Upon entering, employees and visitors are asked to ingest a small capsule. . . . The fast-acting drug produces a series of vivid hallucinations.

—BEN KATCHOR (2013)

INDUSTRIAL TURKEY AND CHICKEN in Minnesota, and other states Midwest and South, have been hit by a highly pathogenic strain of avian influenza A (H5N2). Millions of birds have been killed by the virus or culled in an effort to control the outbreak.

The epizootic began with a soft opening, hitting a handful of backyard farms and wild birds in December in Washington and Oregon before spreading east.[82] Suddenly in early March, H5N2 wiped out 15,000 turkeys on an industrial farm in Pope County, Minnesota, the first of what would be nearly 9 million birds and counting killed or culled across 108 farms over 23 counties.[83]

The virus would spill over into turkeys in North and South Dakota, the chicken egg belt along northern Iowa, industrial turkeys and chickens in Wisconsin, and down the Mississippi to the concentrations of Cargill poultry in Missouri and northwestern Arkansas.[84]

Twenty-one thousand turkeys in Otter Tail County. Forty-five thousand in Meeker County. Fifty-thousand in Kandiyohi. Fifty-six thousand in Redwood. Sixty-seven thousand in Stearns. Another 76,000 in Stearns. One hundred and twenty-seven thousand on a Hormel farm in western Wisconsin.

Another 152,000 in Kandiyohi, whose outbreak has since expanded to forty separate farms. One million plus hens in Nicollet County owned by Michael Foods, a division of Post Holdings.[85] Nearly four million hens in Osceda County in Iowa, just south of Worthington, Minnesota. Five-and-a-half million birds at Rembrandt Enterprises in Buena Vista County, Iowa, owned by *Star Tribune* owner Glen Taylor (which may account for the newspaper's coverage of the outbreak for better and for worse).[86] And on and on.

H5N2 has proved extremely deadly. Farmers report an eerie quiet.[87] The birds cough. Their eyes run. They lose their appetite. Diarrhea ensues. The virus takes two to four days to wipe out a barn. Infected layers meanwhile stop laying eggs or lay eggs with weak and misshapen shells.

The virus alone wiped out 99 percent of the birds on that first Pope County turkey farm. On a second farm, the virus killed all 22,000 turkeys in one of three barns.

MINNESOTA IS THE COUNTRY'S LARGEST turkey producer. According to the Minnesota Department of Agriculture and the USDA, as of 2012 the state produced 47 million turkeys, 42 million chicken broilers, and 13 million layers, laying 3 billion chicken eggs.[88] Its poultry sector accounts for $2 billion a year in sales.

Upon announcement of the first outbreaks in Minnesota, 40 countries banned Minnesota turkey imports.[89]

There appears, then, a strong economic compulsion to protect the sector at all costs, including blaming everything other than the industrial model for the outbreak: wild birds, smallholders, farm workers, the weather, the wind, flies, and rodents.[90] The Yellow Peril of Asia, where we began this book, is repeatedly blamed as if influenza reassortment doesn't accrue across much of the world by both overlapping flyways and intercontinental live animal trade.[91]

Surely the outbreak needs to be stopped if it doesn't burn out on its own, a dubious hope. But the bipartisan nature of the government's response also speaks to the state's prime directives.[92] The fate, and certainly fortune, of the poultry sector reverberates down the hierarchy of state agencies and university research units responsible for responding to the outbreak.

Indeed, the ideological engine protecting Big Poultry, pumping on six cylinders, lurched into action right off the first outbreak. The first doctrine is one of dismissal and denial. According to turkey farmer John Zimmerman, "We never expected [bird flu] to jump to the Western Hemisphere."[93] Once H5N2 hit the Northwest, "we thought it wouldn't cross the Rocky Mountains."

"We think the lid is on, but we are concerned about the possibility of spread," said Steve Olson, executive director of the Minnesota Turkey Growers Association.[94]

Carol Cardona, a veterinary professor at the University of Minnesota, noted the loss of only one of three barns on the second Minnesota farm hit as a good sign: "I don't think it will spread between turkey flocks."

Only weeks later, with H5N2 splattered across the state, Cardona would revise her expert opinion for the Minnesota House Committee on Agriculture that once the virus emerges in waterfowl population—note it's the wild birds' fault—it can persist three to five years.[95]

By late April Cardona had walked her views further back: "We are really in research mode. There's a bunch of stuff we don't know."[96]

Conflating frequency and impact, Alicia Fry of the National Center for Immunization and Respiratory Diseases claimed person-to-person infection of any H5 strain extremely rare.[97] One of the dangers of influenza, however, is that it evolves. Given enough opportunities—millions of birds already—a rare possibility, repeated over multiple reassortants, bends toward inevitability, whether that be H5N2 or another of the many circulating strains.

"This virus gives no indications that it would do that," Fry adds, as if she can predict the virus's course.

Simon Shane, a poultry industry consultant and adjunct professor of poultry science and veterinary medicine at North Carolina State University, a conflict of titles, proclaimed the year's failure a grand success.[98]

Shane claimed the salmonella protections instituted in 2011 "caused the industry to upgrade biosecurity, and I believe inadvertently their salmonella rule has helped with protection of the egg industry against viral diseases like avian influenza." And yet a nationwide outbreak that sickened thousands of Americans in 2010 following two decades over which agribusiness blocked federal implementation of egg safety rules appears in actuality to have done little to prevent the deaths of 38 million chickens this round, 29 million in Iowa alone.[99]

"I do not believe we will have a wholesale mass uncontrollable outbreak of influenza," Shane would say of a wholesale mass uncontrollable outbreak of influenza.[100]

SECOND, CONFLATING FARM SIZE AND SECURITY, industry spokesmen and their colleagues in the state's veterinary services repeatedly essentialize the protection intensive production embodies. Big farms are by definition safe farms:

> "Jennie-O Turkey Store raises its turkeys in barns to protect them from inclement weather, predators, and migratory birds, which are a common source of influenza viruses," Hormel reported. "While turkey raised in barns aren't resistant to influenza infection, they are at a reduced risk of becoming exposed to the virus."[101]

And yet, in contrast to the hundreds of intensive operations hit nationally, only twelve cases of backyard birds infected were reported, five of which struck in Washington State back in January and February. In one of the few pieces to clear an apparent media blockade, Ortonville farmer Rebecca White notes that thirteen backyard flocks in Lac qui Parle County here in Minnesota tested negative as did thirty backyard flocks in Pope.[102]

She follows through with the obvious implications:

> Instead of racing to plug gaps in the existing system, maybe it's time to question the system itself. Raising thousands of birds (or cows, or hogs) in the confined space may be considered "efficient," but it results in a high-stress environment that sets out the welcome mat for disease, as well as concentrating waste in a way that pollutes rather than enriches. . . . What if, instead of being the state that produces the most turkeys, we became the state that produced the best turkeys.

For obvious reasons, researchers whose programs are paid for by the industry didn't like that suggestion. And there may be something in their objection, if only in the specifics of the ongoing outbreak.[103] The backyard season is only beginning and free-range turkeys may still be vulnerable, regardless of their diet and cross-immunity to multiple pathogens.

On the other hand, should backyard birds die en masse, industrial poultry would score no free pass. In many other bird flu outbreaks globally, the virulence to poultry, and indeed even blown back to waterfowl, developed only after the virus passed through industrial farms.[104]

Industry scientists at the University of Minnesota have since pivoted off that argument to one in which the size and economic organization of farms hit shouldn't matter, erasing all causality save, ironically, the sector's financial margins.

Montserrat Torremorell, a professor of veterinary medicine, told the *Star Tribune* the state's response should only be about plugging gaps:

> "To me, it's a discussion of how do we manage the food supply to decrease the risk," not just for disease, but for the industry's bottom line and the stability of the food system as well, said Torremorell.
>
> The critical question, she said, is not how animals are raised, but how they are protected from disease–whether they are free-range, organic or from larger operations. All domestic poultry is vulnerable to these diseases, she said.[105]

A THIRD MANIFESTATION OF THE IDEOLOGICAL infrastructure protecting Big Poultry, the identities of the initial Pope farm and all farms subsequently hit in Minnesota are never revealed.

A 2005 state law, addressing agribusiness concerns about "privacy" and the threat of animal rights activists, exempts "animal premises data" from the open records law. The law is modeled after federal efforts, providing viruses, in this age of an NSA off the leash, more privacy than the humans the government ostensibly represents.[106]

There is a loophole, however. "The law does allow the Board of Animal Health to release the farm data to the public," columnist James Shiffer writes,

> "if the board determines that the access will aid in the law enforcement process or the protection of public or animal health or safety." The board has shared the information with other agencies and adjoining property owners, but "an argument has not been made that we need to disclose it to the public," said Beth Thompson, the Minnesota Board of Animal Health's assistant director.[107]

A curious turn of phrase on Thompson's part, citing a statement that hasn't been made—or rather, given Shiffer's column, heard—as due cause against releasing the data. But clearly there is a discretion built into the albeit terrible law health officials repeatedly spurn in favor of the argument that their hands are conveniently tied.

Thompson, modeling an apparent talking point that has spread across state and industry functionaries, including among others Randy Olson and Ed Ehlinger,[108] goes on that "we haven't seen any humans coming down with the virus. . . . We've also not seen it spreading barn to barn."

Shiffer responds to Thompson that

> at a time when agencies are mobilizing and hundreds of thousands of birds are being slaughtered, it's hard to see how the public is served by this secrecy. If this isn't a situation where the board should disclose what farms are affected, I don't know what is.[109]

The public may not be served, but agribusiness sure is. Indeed, in the face of the talking point and Thompson's sangfroid, 101 farm workers were placed under observation as of mid-April and the state recommended 93 take preventative Tamiflu.[110] Seventy-three did. Clearly the state is concerned about a human-to-human infection emerging. In ways industry-funded scientists have not, more practically minded industry officials have meanwhile moved past the notion that it's all wild birds. As reported by CIDRAP:

John Brunquell, president of Egg Innovations, Port Washington, Wis., which owns 60 farms, said, "We believe all these infections you're hearing about now are from facility to facility" and that migratory waterfowl are no longer the main vehicle for the virus.[111]

In an age when influenza samples are increasingly labeled by GPS coordinates, national policy, followed by additional protocols at the state level, is organized around reducing geographic resolution for independent scientists and the public alike.[112]

The official blanket extends to photographs of the present outbreak. I have found several shots of piles of dead birds onsite in Iowa, but not a single photo here in Minnesota.[113]

At best, it took the *Star Tribune* to photograph the perimeter of a barn on its own—a farm it still refused to name—just up the Sauk River near Melrose, with a sign, "KEEP OUT. Disease control."[114]

In my decade studying bird flu, I have never seen such control exercised on coverage of an outbreak, including in China, whose post-SARS media regularly print photos of infected birds and their disposal. Think about that—China.

FOURTH, THE INDUSTRY HAS CIRCLED the barns to blame anyone and everyone else for the outbreak regardless of its epidemiology.

While migratory waterfowl are a reservoir for multiple reassortants, the repeated focus begs the question: Does it matter that waterfowl are the ultimate source? It certainly doesn't wash out the poultry sector's responsibility for the virus's case fatality rates on industrial farms.[115]

Perhaps the suggestion that causality need extend into what drives virulence explains officials' tautological treatment of waterfowl input. T. J. Myers, associate deputy administrator in veterinary services for the USDA, made this cogent observation: "When you look at a map, you see a lot of turkey farms in Minnesota. When you look at a map of Minnesota, you also see a lot of lakes."[116]

There may be something in this gem other than what Myers intended, however.

Wetlands, under enormous pressure worldwide, have traditionally served as *Anatidae* migration stops. As we've described elsewhere, a growing literature shows many migratory birds have responded to the destruction of their natural habitat.[117] Geese, for example, display an alarming behavioral plasticity, adopting entirely new migratory patterns and nesting in new types of wintering grounds, moving from deteriorating wetlands to food-filled farms. Wintering lesser snow geese, for instance, switched from wetlands along the Gulf Coast developed out of existence to foraging on the great expanse of Midwest agriculture as far north as Minnesota.[118]

In 2013 the Environmental Working Group issued a report, echoing other analyses, showing precipitous declines in available wetlands across the Prairie Pothole Region as these are drained and plowed for new agricultural land.[119]

The EWG map overlaps with many of the initial counties hit by H5N2 across Minnesota and North Dakota.[120] We needn't repeat Myers's stumble over correlation and causality, but the overlay suggests a mechanism by which the interface between wild waterfowl and poultry has increased in the region, a shift for which agribusiness appears responsible on both ends.

In a fascinating development, the attempt to blame migratory waterfowl has been subjected to a subtle but not indirect pushback, including from colleagues who share the same departmental affiliations as researchers pushing the story for their industrial sponsors.

As of late April, 2,200 Minnesota samples across wild birds tested negative.[121] The USDA reported no environmental fecal samples from waterfowl positive for HPAI H5N2 across the country. Nationally, fifty waterfowl have tested positive, mostly mallards, but also geese.

One Cooper's hawk was found H5N2-positive in Minnesota, a result somehow presented as explanation enough, but as Pat Redig of the University of Minnesota's Raptor Center clarified, the hawk was killed hitting a window and not by the virus.[122] The Raptor Center has since tested live eagles, owls, hawks, and falcons and found no flu.

Lou Cornicelli, wildlife research manager for the Department of Natural Resources, bent the results toward a broader implication,

telling the *Star Tribune* that the virus spreads quic'
flocks, but wild bird populations such as raptors ?
aren't as vulnerable because they are dispersed, a rounda
turning the focus back on industrial poultry.[123]

Cornicelli would continue in Minnesota Nice noting the discovery of the Cooper's hawk doesn't indicate the virus in wild birds is the direct cause of the bird flu. Ostensibly he's referring to where the virus has been found. Yellow Medicine County, where the hawk was discovered, hasn't hosted a single poultry outbreak.

FIFTH, CALLS FOR INCREASING BIOSECURITY were broadcast right from the first outbreak. We're talking changing clothes and boots, disinfecting equipment and vehicles, different farm workers for different barns, and refraining from storing feed outdoors as spilled feed could attract wild birds.

The latter intervention cops to the increasing interface between waterfowl and poultry.

And yet despite the forewarning months in advance, the outbreak has burned through the Midwest and beyond. That tells us that H5N2 has cracked the code of industrial poultry here in Minnesota and continues to spread even as the industry was fully apprised and its response operationalized.

It tells us no level of biosecurity is apparently secure enough, as has long been raised in the literature, however much it may have helped individual farmers.[124] Proposals to protect against fomites carrying flu would require barn filters at a cost beyond the margins the sector is willing to dedicate to biosecurity.

It tells us, contrary to Torremorell's wishful thinking, that the model of production is the heart of the problem. And the industry, if not its scientists, knows this.

We need only look at how the industry is structured. Contrary to the prevalent notion, industrial poultry is not totally vertically integrated. All nodes are integrated, except, largely growing out the birds. That's offloaded onto contract farmers who, as employees, must take out millions in loans to buy the land, barns, equipment, and other inputs to raise the birds to company specifications.

Why? Because decades ago agribusinesses calculated actual farming to be a losing proposition. It represents a severe diseconomy of scale. Raising birds in huge monocultures of 50,000 turkeys or 250,000 chickens per barn is entirely too precarious. The birds too often get sick and die, from infectious disease and stress morbidities. So the companies are using the contract farmers and their debts as veritable trap crops by which to sop up the costs of such dysfunctional production.[125] With the help of the banking sector, the costs are moved off the industry's balance sheets and onto contractors.

Indeed, we see here, while the USDA is covering the costs of culling birds—another externalized cost taxpayers must bear—farmers, with no insurance available, are stuck with the direct costs of birds killed by H5N2. There are too the indirect costs farmers must bear with their barns out of commission for the 28 days of composting to which dead birds must be subjected (and subsequently sold as crop fertilizer). Barns must lay empty for an additional 21 days before they can be repopulated and brought back into production.

With their loan payments still on the clock—outbreak or no—farmers are so desperate they've requested the second half of composting be allowed outside to free up their barns earlier.[126] Economics before epidemiology.

The virus, however, cares little about the econometric measures, our sixth doctrine, companies have spun out of thin air, tethering poultry and people alike. Gate prices, throughput, sales value, profits per bird, and on and on, are a semantics by which our economy is separated from the ecology in which it is in actuality embedded. With real world consequences supply and demand can't address.

CONSUMERS ARE MEANWHILE STUCK WITH increasing egg prices.[127] Rembrandt and Hormel have hit their processing lines with layoffs.[128] Everyone else is to blame and bear the brunt.

The one constituency to which regional agribusiness appears responsive is that of market analysts, whose pronouncements can send stocks tumbling.

During a May conference call with a group of the new priesthood, Hormel CEO Jeffrey Ettinger appeared nigh on solicitous.[129]

He responded with a level of detail if not candor that neither media nor public elicits. After 310,000 turkeys were killed at a Hormel farm in Meeker County, the company refused to make a single executive available for media comment.[130]

When one analyst asked if the company is considering geographically diversifying turkey production, Ettinger responded:

> Given this unprecedented and rare incident, it's kind of exposed a little bit of an Achilles' heel to the strategy of being centralized. We are still in the triage mode right now, and I guess that [geographic diversification] is something on a strategic long-term basis I will be talking with the team about…. But it is a valid question.[131]

If the outbreak is "unprecedented and rare" that begs why Hormel need consider moving turkey out of Minnesota. But setting that dissonance aside, Ettinger's reply certainly puts to question the solidarity between state and capital at the heart of the epidemiological response. To protect a $265.6-billion-a-year industry, the poultry sector and regulators across the United States have laid blame upon poultry workers and wild waterfowl. H5N2, however, demonstrates, that the sector is defined by inherent diseconomies of scale that it survives solely by externalizing costs to consumers, workers, governments and the environment.[132] In a market economy, such costs, moved back onto company margins, would end the industry as we know it.

But apparently what's best for Hormel isn't necessarily about what's best for the state, whatever the lengths to which the latter goes for the former. At this point, no worker-environmentalist alliance building a better food landscape is driving business out. The companies *themselves* see the virus made in Minnesota and moving out an economic necessity.

—*Farming Pathogens*, 10 June 2015

UPDATE. In January 2016, the *Star Tribune*, owned by agribusiness investor Glen Taylor, reported on a University of Minnesota study funded by Hormel's Jennie-O—a funding source the newspaper failed to mention—that showed Upper Midwest farmers tilling fields near poultry barns, producing clouds of fomites, that likely helped spread the H5N2 virus early in the outbreak.[133] The study also statistically indicted the spatially proximity of infected farms, the rendering of infected birds near barns, and truck-washing stations, which, deployed to stop the outbreak, may have spread it.

In short, it's the farmers' fault (as well as that of the state's botched cleanup). The problems are found in specific practices on-site and not in the industrial model that selected for a strain that hit only the region's largest operations. The conclusions, if not the specifics, are hardly a surprise as the study's answers were locked in by its questions:

> To identify possible risk factors, the research team developed a detailed survey that asked turkey farmers questions about the farm and surrounding environment, presence of wild birds, and farm management practices.[134]

The study is honest as far as one must start somewhere, and why not with such a survey? Setting aside the limits of case-control studies, including this one's small sample size restricted to Jennie-O farms, the analysis is righteous in its albeit simplistic risk modeling.

And yet the study is corrupt to its metaphysical heart.

If spatial proximity represents nearly five times the odds risk than the next factor, why the focus on individual farm practices? What about the size, density, and interconnectedness of monoculture poultry operations arrayed across whole counties? What alternate food models are left out when only Jennie-O farms make up the universe of samples?

What of the political power agribusiness exercises on local counties, including staffing their regulatory agencies? What does it mean to fail to investigate the conceptual premises of your own funding source? What gets lost along the way when land grant universities are turned into agribusiness R&D?

Missed Anthropy

A brilliant blue jay is springing up and down, up and down, / On a branch. / I laugh, as I see him abandon himself / To entire delight, for he knows as well as I do / That the branch will not break.

—JAMES WRIGHT (1963)

A TRAILER FOR DAVID QUAMMEN'S NEW book, *Spillover*, detailing the pathogen blowback our environmental destruction has set off,[135] elicited a number of like-minded comments online on *CounterPunch* editor Jeffrey St Clair's Facebook page:

Earth, healing itself.

and

The Tibetans say that Mother Earth will shake us off the way a dog shakes off his fleas.

I could say Earth isn't a person (or a dog), but even a well-deserved allegorical warning needn't be served with such resplendent misanthropy. We'd hope all parties—even pro-sustainability—would recognize we are—the planet—an integrated ecosystem. Indeed, even if our entire race of "fleas" were wiped out tomorrow, by our impact Earth's biospheric trajectory would still be altered forever.

If you're not a misanthrope you're delusional.

As a daily meditation, I get it. As a political program, meh. Perhaps it smells a whiff of the population-control wing of the ecological movement.[136] One can despise capitalists, and their role in promoting outbreaks,[137] without wishing Armageddon as just desserts.

That's too much of a price came the reply:

> There's no political program which will deter climate change, species extinctions, rainforest liquidation or the global ecological consequences that are the foreseeable result. None of these issues are even on the table. So we're left only with our rage and our empathy for the victims, human and non. Are you asking us to surrender that as well?
>
> I take part of that back. The issues are on the table—but only how fast to accelerate them.
>
> And I think we should note for the record that Misanthropy is not the same as Malthusianism, since Malthusianism by definition favors one class over all others. Misanthropy is a kind of multi-species chorus of the oppressed, the abused, the targeted.

Behind Malthusianism and the ecological misanthropy expressed across the comments is the precept that humanity has overreached its carrying capacity (and by a moral justice embodies its own worst revenge). Not an identity, but an intersection nonetheless.

I can't say things are looking good for our heroes at this point, but communal projects in conservation agriculture the world over, some feeding millions, are living refutations of the present production paradigm.[138]

Mind you, I'm a cynic through and through—it's an occupational hazard—but I've decided I will no longer be my own defeat. There is a world to win, even if at best "these days we're shy imaginers of Utopias on hold," as the recently deceased Alexander Cockburn put it:

> We know we live in the age of iron, lamented by Hesiod and Ovid. All the more reason not to lose heart. There is abundance, if we arrange things differently. The world can be turned upside down; that is, the right way up. The Golden Age is in us, if we know where to look, and what to think.[139]

—*Farming Pathogens* blog, 9 October 2012

Notes

Introduction

1. Quinn JT (2004) Memorandum for the Record: Boston, Massachusetts Summary. Available online at https://catalog.archives.gov/id/2609657.
2. Hulse C (2015). "Claims against Saudis case new light on secret pages of 9/11 report." *New York Times.* 5 February. Available online at http://www. nytimes.com/2015/02/05/us/claims-against-saudis-cast-new-light-on-secret-pages-of-9-11-report.html.
3. Chung J (2014). "This 9/11 Cheese Plate May Be The 9/11 Museum's Most Tasteless Souvenir." *The Gothamist.* 22 May 22. Available online at http://gothamist.com/2014/05/22/photo_finally_you_can_buy_a_911_che.php#photo-1.
4. Wallace RG, HM HoDac, R Lathrop, and WM Fitch (2007). "A statistical phylogeography of influenza A H5N1." *Proceedings of the National Academy of Sciences* 104: 4473-8.
5. Wallace R, D Wallace, and RG Wallace (2009). *Farming Human Pathogens: Ecological Resilience and Evolutionary Process* Springer, Dordrecht.
6. Wallace RG (2009). Farming Pathogens: Disease in a World of Our Making. Available online at www.farmingpathogens.wordpress.com.
7. Wallace RG (2004). "Projecting the impact of HAART on the evolution of HIV's life history." Ecological Modelling 176: 227-53.
8. Davis M (2005). *The Monster at Our Door: The Global Threat of Avian Flu.* New Press, New York.
9. McKelvey T (2013). "Drones kill rescuers in 'double tap', say activists." BBC News. 22 October. Available online at http://www.bbc.com/news/world-us-canada-24557333; Chandrasekaran R (2012). *Little America: The War within the War for Afghanistan.* Alfred A. Knopf, New York; Physicians for Social Responsibility, Physicians for Global Survival, and the International Physicians for the Prevention of Nuclear War (2015). Body Count: Casualty Figures after 10 Years of the "War on Terror". First international edition. Washington DC. Available online at http://www.psr.org/assets/pdfs/body-count.pdf.

PART ONE
The Great Bird Flu Blame Game

10.   WHO, *Towards a Unified Nomenclature System for the Highly Pathogenic H5N1 Avian Influenza Viruses*. Available online at http://www.who.int/csr/disease/avian_influenza/guidelines/nomenclature/en/index.html.

11.   Salzberg SL, C Kingsford, G Cattoli, DJ Spiro, DA Janies et al. (2007). "Genome analysis linking recent European and African influenza (H5N1) viruses." *Emerg Infect Dis*. 13: 713.

12.   Chen H, GJD Smith, JS Li, J Wang, XH Fan et al. (2006). "Establishment of multiple sublineages of H5N1 influenza virus in Asia: implications for pandemic control." *Proc Natl Acad Sci U S A* 103: 2845.

13.   Patterson KD (1986). *Pandemic Influenza, 1700-1900: A Study in Historical Epidemiology*, Rowman & Littlefield Publishers, Totowa, NJ.

14.   Smith GJD, XH Fan, J Wang, KS Li, K Qin, JX Zhang et al. (2006). "Emergence and pre-dominance of an H5N1 influenza variant in China." *Proc Natl Acad Sci SA* 103: 16936.

15.   Reuters (2006). "China shares bird flu samples, denies new strain report." 10 November. Available online at http://www.alertnet.org/thenews/ newsdesk/PEK2663.htm.

16.   Greenfeld KT (2007). *China Syndrome: The True Story of the 21st Century's First Great Epidemic*. Harper Perennial. In 2003 the Chinese government took months to inform the world of SARS, a deadly respiratory coronavirus that originated in the southeastern province of Guangdong before infecting 8000 people across several countries worldwide.

17.   Anonymous (2006). "Ministries refute bird flu virus rumour in China." *China Daily*. 3 November. Available online at http://english.peopledaily.com.cn/ 200611/03/eng20061103_317874.html.

18.   Wallace RG, H HoDac, RH Lathrop and WM Fitch (2007) "A statistical phylogeography of influenza A H5N1." *Proc Natl Acad Sci USA* 104: 4473.

19.   Wan X-F, T Ren, K-J Luo, M Liao, G-H Zhang et al. (2005). "Genetic characterization of H5N1 avian influenza viruses isolated in southern China during the 2003–04 avian influenza outbreaks." *Archives of Virology* 150: 1257.

20.   Huang K and MA Benetiz (2007). "Guangdong ridicules H5N1 claims." *South China Morning Post*. 7 March.

21.   CIDRAP News (2007) "H5N1 death in Laos confirmed; Chinese reject research report." 8 March. Available online at http://www.cidrap.umn.edu/cidrap/cotent/influenza/avianflu/news/mar0807avian.html.

22.   Tang X, G Tian, J Zhao and KY Zhou (1998) "Isolation and characterization of prevalent strains of avian influenza viruses in China." *Chin. J.*

Anim. Poult. Infect. Dis. 20: 1 (in Chinese); Mukhtar MM, ST Rasool, D Song, C Zhu, Q Hao et al. (2007). "Origins of highly pathogenic H5N1 avian influenza virus in China and genetic characterization of donor and recipient viruses." *Journal of General Virology* 88: 3094. In 1999, the 1996 genotype was again isolated in Hong Kong in a shipment of geese from Guangdong. Mainland scientists recently hypothesized the 1996 Guangdong genotype arose from a recombination of H3 and H7 strains isolated in nearby Nanchang and a Japanese H5 virus. Low-pathogenic H5 strains circulate worldwide, including a recent outbreak in Pennsylvania.

23. Kang-Chung N (1997). "Chicken imports slashed by third." *South China Morning Post.* 15 December.

24. Yang Y, ME Halloran, JD Sugimoto and IM. Longini, Jr. (2007). "Detecting human-to-human transmission of avian influenza A (H5N1)." *Emerg Infect Dis.* 13: 1348.

25. Reuters (2007). "Indonesia dismisses human-to-human bird flu report." 3 September. Available online at http://www.reuters.com/article/ healthNews/idUSPAR36484220070903.

26. Horton R (2006). "WHO: strengthening the road to renewal." *Lancet* 367: 1793.

27. Enerink M and D Normille (2007). "More bumps on the road to global sharing of H5N1 samples." *Science* 318: 1229.

28. Shulman S (2006). *Undermining Science: Suppression and Distortion in the Bush Administration.* University of California Press. Berkeley, CA.; Mooney C (2005). *The Republican War on Science.* Basic Books, New York; Reuters (2007). "Former Bush surgeon general says he was muzzled. 10 July. Available online at http://www.reuters.com/article/ politicsNews/ idUSN1034212120070710; Hebert HJ (2007). "White House edited CDC climate testimony." Associated Press. 24 October. Available online at http://news.yahoo.com/s/ap/20071024/ap_on_go_ ca_st_pe/global_warming_health_21. There is also the litany of lies and subterfuge surrounding scientific issues related to the occupation of Iraq and the war on terror. Yellow cake from Niger. White phosphorous biowarfare in Fallujah. Psychologists in Guantánamo. Anthrax from Fort Detrick. Estimates of Iraqi dead. The billions of dollars and political capital spent in visiting death and destruction on Iraq could have been used against bird flu, a substantiated threat to U.S. interests and global stability. The war also renders Iraq vulnerable to bird flu. As Iraq's recent cholera outbreaks show, war destroys public health infrastructure with devastating consequences.

29. Barry JM (2004). *The Great Influenza: The Epic Story of the Deadliest Plague in History.* Viking Penguin, New York.

30. Fidler DP (2008). "Influenza virus samples, international law, and global health diplomacy." *Emerg Infect Dis.* 14: 88.
31. Revere (2007). "Flu virus sharing summit: wrap up." *Effect Measure* blog. 24 November. Available online at http://scienceblogs.com/effect-measure/2007/11/flu_virus_sharing_summit_wrap_1.php. Hammond reports the conference was crawling with pharmaceutical representatives that WHO invited.
32. Chang WK (1969). "National influenza experience in Hong Kong." *Bull World Health Organ.* 41: 349; Shortridge KF and CH Stuart-Harris (1982). "An influenza epicenter?" *Lancet* 2: 812; Xu KM , GJ Smith, J Bahl, L Duan, H Tai et al. (2007). "The genesis and evolution of H9N2 influenza viruses in poultry from southern China, 2000 to 2005." *J Virol.* 81: 10389; Cheung CL, D Vijaykrishna, GJ Smith, XH Fan, JX Zhang et al. (2007). "Establishment of influenza A virus (H6N1) in minor poultry in southern China." *J Virol.* 81: 10402.
33. Shortridge KF (1982). "Avian influenza A viruses of southern China and Hong Kong: ecological aspects and implications for man." *Bull World Health Organ.* 60: 129.
34. Fan CC (2005). "Interprovincial migration, population redistribution, and regional development in China: 1990 and 2000 census comparisons." *The Professional Geographer* 57: 295.
35. Sun AD, ZD Shi, YM Huang and SD Liang (2007). "Development of out-of-season laying in geese and its impact on the goose industry in Guangdong Province, China." *World's Poultry Science Journal* 63: 481; Luo X, Y Ou and X Zhou (2003). *Livestock and Poultry Production in China.* Paper presented at Bioproduction in East Asia: Technology Development & Globalization Impact, a pre-conference forum in conjunction with the 2003 ASAE Annual International Meeting, 27 July 2003, Las Vegas, Nevada. ASAE Publication Number 03BEA-06, ed. Chi Thai. Available online at http://asae.frymulti.com/request.asp?JID=5& AID=15056&CID=bea2003&T=2; Burch D (2005). "Production, consumption and trade in poultry: Corporate linkages and North-South supply chains." In N Fold and W Prichard (eds). *Cross-continental Food Chains.* Routledge, London.
36. Shortridge KF (1995). "The next pandemic influenza virus?" *Lancet* 346: 1210.
37. Shortridge KF and CH Stuart-Harris (1982). "An influenza epicenter?"
38. Greenfeld KT (2007). *China Syndrome: The True Story of the 21st Century's First Great Epidemic.*
39. York G (2005). "China hiding bird-flu cases: expert." *Globe and Mail.* 9 December.

40. Zamiska N (2006). "How academic flap hurt effort on Chinese bird flu." *Wall Street Journal.* 24 February.
41. Greenfeld KT (2007). *China Syndrome: The True Story of the 21st Century's First Great Epidemic.*
42. Wan X-F, T Ren, K-J Luo, M Liao, G-H Zhang et al. (2005). "Genetic characterization of H5N1 avian influenza viruses isolated in southern China during the 2003–04 avian influenza outbreaks."
43. AFX News Limited (2007). "Parts of China not fully ready against bird flu—official." 19 September.
44. Patterson KD (1986). *Pandemic Influenza, 1700–1900: A Study in Historical Epidemiology;* Pyle GF (1986). *The Diffusion of Influenza.* Rowman & Littlefield, Totowa, NJ.
45. Wallace RG, H HoDac, RH Lathrop and WM Fitch (2007). "A statistical phylogeography of influenza A H5N1."; Kidd DM and MG Ritchie (2006)."Phylogeographic information systems: putting the geography into phylogeography." *Journal of Biogeography* 33: 1851. ℛ?
46. Boyd W and M Watts (1997). "Agro-industrial just in time: the chicken industry and postwar American capitalism." In D Goodman, MJ Watts (eds). *Globalising Food: Agrarian Questions and Global Restructuring.* Routledge, London.
47. Kilpatrick AM, AA Chmura, DW Gibbons, RC Fleischer, PP Marra and P Daszak (2006). "Predicting the global spread of H5N1 avian influenza." *Proc Natl Acad Sci USA.* 103: 19368; Wallace RG and WM Fitch (2008). "Influenza A H5N1 migration is filtered out at some international borders." *PLoS ONE.* 3(2): e1697.
48. Cristalli A and I Capua (2007). "Practical problems in controlling H5N1 high pathogenicity avian influenza at village level in Vietnam and introduction of biosecurity measures." *Avian Disease* 51(1 Suppl): 461; Ferguson N (2006). "Poverty, death, and a future influenza pandemic." *Lancet* 368: 2187. In an act of international goodwill, China recently donated over $500,000 to Nigeria's effort to fight bird flu. Of course, Nigeria would never have needed the aid if China hadn't infected it with bird flu in the first place. The Qinghai-like strain that Nigeria now hosts originated in southern China.
49. Rweyemamu M, R Paskin, A Benkirane, V Martin, P Roeder et al. (2000). "Emerging diseases of Africa and the Middle East." *Annals of New York Academy of Sciences* 916: 61.
50. Greger M (2006). *Bird Flu: A Virus of Our Own Hatching.* Lantern Books.
51. Gilbert M, X Xiao, W Wint and J Slingenbergh (2014). "Poultry production dynamics, bird migration cycles, and the emergence of highly

pathogenic avian influenza in East and Southeast Asia." In R Sauerborn, LR Valérie (eds). *Global Environmental Change and Infectious Diseases: Impacts and Adaptations*. Springer Verlag, Berlin; Rapport D, J Howard, L Maffi and B Mithell (2006). *Avian Influenza and the Environment: An Ecohealth Perspective*. UNEP, New York. Available online at http://www.unep.org/dewa/products/publications/2006/DRapport_AI_Final_180506_Edit3.doc.pdf.

52. Garrett L (2001). *Betrayal of Trust: The Collapse of Global Public Health*. Hyperion, New York.

53. Kim JY, JV Millen, A Irwin and J Gershman (eds) (2000). *Dying for Growth: Global Inequality and the Health of the Poor*. Common Courage Press, Boston.

54. Davis M (2005). *The Monster at Our Door: The Global Threat of Avian Flu*. New Press, New York.

55. Greenfeld KT (2007). *China Syndrome: The True Story of the 21st Century's First Great Epidemic*.

56. At the time China's government warned local press to print nothing more about new outbreaks than official statements, including on a Guangzhou outbreak that erupted in November 2007. No news is good news, especially with the 2008 Beijing Olympics approaching.

The NAFTA Flu

57. Pyle GF (1986). *The Diffusion of Influenza*. Rowman & Littlefield Publishers, Totowa, NJ.

58. Wallace RG (2009). "The agro-industrial roots of swine flu H1N1." Available online at https://farmingpathogens.wordpress.com/2009/04/26/the-agro-industrial-roots-of-swine-flu-h1n1/.

59. Vijaykrishna D, Bahl J, Riley S, Duan L, Zhang JX et al. (2008). "Evolutionary dynamics and emergence of panzootic H5N1 influenza viruses." *PLoS Pathog* 4(9): e1000161. doi:10.1371/journal.ppat.1000161.

60. Burch D (2005). "Production, consumption and trade in poultry: corporate linkages and North–South supply chains." In N Fold and W Pritchard (eds). *Cross-Continental Food Chains*, 166–78. Routledge, London.

61. Tuckman J (2009). "Four-year-old could hold key in search for source of swine flu outbreak." *The Guardian*. 29 April. Available online at http://www.theguardian.com/world/2009/apr/27/swine-flu-search-outbreak-source.

62. Batres-Marquez SP, R Clemens, and HH Jensen (2006). *The Changing Structure of Pork Trade, Production, and Processing in Mexico*. MATRIC Briefing Paper 06-MBP 10. Midwest Agribusiness Trade Research and

Information Center, Iowa State University. Available online at http:// www.card.iastate.edu/publications/DBS/PDFFiles/06mbp10.pdf.

63. Davis M (2009). "Capitalism and the flu." *Socialist Worker.* 27 April. Available online at http://socialistworker.org/2009/04/27/ capitalism-and-the-flu.

64. Associated Press (2009). "Where did swine flu start? Official says it's not necessarily Mexico, could be Texas, Calif." 28 April. Available online at http://www.nydailynews.com/news/world/swine-flu-start-official-not-necessarily-mexico-texas-calif-article-1.359793.

The Hog Industry Strikes Back

65. World Health Organization (2009). "Global Alert and Response: Influenza A(H1N1) – update 41. 29 May 2009." Available online at http://www.who.int/csr/don/2009_05_29/en/.

66. Barry JM (2004). *The Great Influenza: The Epic Story of the Deadliest Plague in History.* Viking Penguin, New York.

67. Wallace RG (2009). "Breeding influenza: the political virology of off-shore farming." *Antipode.* 41: 916–951.

68. Wallace RG (2009). "The agro-industrial roots of swine flu H1N1." *Farming Pathogens.* 26 April. Available online at https://farmingpathogens.wordpress.com/2009/04/26/the-agro-industrial-roots-of-swine-flu-h1n1/.

69. Wallace RG (2007). "The great bird flu name game." *H5N1* blog. 27 December. Available online at http://crofsblogs.typepad.com/h5n1/files/rg_wallace_the_great_bird_flu_name_game.pdf.

70. Ginsburg M et al. (2009) "Swine Influenza A (H1N1) infection in two children—Southern California, March–April 2009." *MMWR* 58(15): 400-402.

71. Garten R et al. (2009). "Antigenic and genetic characteristics of Swine-Origin 2009 A(H1N1) Influenza viruses circulating in humans." *Science* 325: 197-201.

72. Kahn M (2009). "Swine flu source spawns wild theories." Reuters, 30 April. Available online at http://www.reuters.com/article/2009/04/30/us-flu-theories-idUSTRE53T3ZK20090430.

73. Wallace RG (2009). "NAFTA flu." *Farming Pathogens.* 28 April. Available online at https://farmingpathogens.wordpress.com/2009/04/28/the-nafta-flu/.

74. Pope L (2009). "Smithfield Swine Herd in Veracruz, Mexico Tests Negative for Human A(H1N1) Influenza." Available online at http://www.prnewswire.com/news-releases/smithfield-swine-herd-in-veracruz-mexico-tests-negative-for-human-ah1n1-influenza-61875212.html.

75. Randewich N and M Rosenberg (2008). "UPDATE 2-Mexico clears

more US meat plants, beefs up controls." Reuters, 30 December. Available online at http://www.reuters.com/article/2008/12/30/mexico -meat-ban-idUSN3035118520081230.

76. Cohen J (2009). "Out of Mexico? Scientists ponder swine flu's origins." *Science* 324: 700-702. Available online at http://www.sciencemag.org/ content/324/5928/700.full.

77. Lopez JH (2009). "Astillero." *La Jornada.* 29 April. Available online at http://www.jornada.unam.mx/2009/04/29/index.php?section=politica &article=004o1pol.

78. Carvajal D and S Castle (2009). "A U.S. hog giant transforms Eastern Europe." *New York Times.* 5 May. Available online at http://www.jornada.unam.mx/2009/04/29/index.php?section=politica&article=004o 1pol.

79. Blackwell JR (2009). "Smithfield seeks to ease flu concerns." *Richmond Times-Dispatch.* 6 May. Available online at http://www.richmond.com/ business/article_3477015d-0e1e-5e9a-bb1c-fae06f1bee80.html.

80. Philpott T (2009). "Smithfield: Don't worry, we're testing our Mexican hogs for swine flu." *Grist.* 7 May. Available online at http://grist.org/ article/2009-05-06-smithfield-self-regulate/.

81. Anonymous (2009). "Swine Influenza A (H1N1) infection in two children—Southern California, March–April 2009." *MMWR* 58 (Dispatch): 1-3. Available online at http://www.cdc.gov/mmwr/pre-view/mmwrhtml/mm58d0421a1.htm.

82. Gillan C (2009). "Farmers fear pigs may get 'swine' flu from people." Reuters, 1 May. Available online at http://www.reuters.com/ article/2009/05/02/us-flu-hogs-idUSTRE5401DJ20090502.

83. Branswell H (2009). "Circumstantial evidence the only proof of person-to-pig H1N1 infection: CFIA." *The Canadian Press.* 9 May. Available online at http://www.winnipegfreepress.com/special/flu/ Circumstantial-evidence-the-only-proof-of-person-to-pig-H1N1-infection-CFIA.html.

84. Carvajal D and S Castle (2009). "A U.S. hog giant transforms Eastern Europe."

85. Singer P (2005). "Who pays for bird flu?" Commentary available at http://www.projectsyndicate. org/commentary/singer5.

86. Gibbon E (1788). *The History of the Decline and Fall of the Roman Empire.* Vol. 6. Strahan and Cadell, London.

87. Kelly H, Peck HA, Laurie KL, Wu P, Nishiura H et al. (2011). "The age-specific cumulative incidence of infection with pandemic Influenza H1N1 2009 was similar in various countries prior to vaccination." *PLoS ONE* 6(8): e21828. doi:10.1371/journal.pone.0021828.

88. Belongia EA, SA Irving, SC Waring, LA Coleman, JK Meece, M

Vandermause, S Lindstrom, D Kempf, DK Shay (2010). "Clinical characteristics and 30-day outcomes for Influenza A 2009 (H1N1), 2008-2009 (H1N1), and 2007-2008 (H3N2) infections." *JAMA.* 304(10): 1091–98. doi:10.1001/jama.2010.1277

89. Dawood FS et al. (2012). "Estimated global mortality associated with the first 12 months of 2009 pandemic influenza A H1N1 virus circulation: a modelling study." *Lancet Infect Dis.* 12(9): 687-95. doi: 10.1016/S1473-3099(12)70121-4. Epub 2012 Jun 26.

90. Nelson MI, J Stratton, ML Killian, A Janas-Martindale, and AL Vincent (2015). "Continual re-introduction of human pandemic H1N1 influenza A viruses into US swine, 2009-2014." *J Virol.* April 1. pii: JVI.00459-15; Stincarelli M et al. (2013). "Reassortment ability of the 2009 pandemic H1N1 influenza virus with circulating human and avian influenza viruses: public health risk implications." *Virus Res.* 175(2): 151–54.

The Political Virology of Offshore Farming

91. Yuen KY and SS Wong (2005). "Human infection by avian influenza A H5N1." *Hong Kong Medical Journal* 11: 189–99.

92. Buxton Bridges C et al. (2000). "Risk of influenza A (H5N1) infection among health care workers exposed to patients with influenza A (H5N1), Hong Kong." *Journal of Infectious Diseases* 181: 344–48; de Jong MD et al. (2006). "Fatal outcome of human influenza A (H5N1) is associated with high viral load and hypercytokinemia." *Nature Medicine* 12: 1203–7.

93. de Jong MD et al. (2006). "Fatal outcome of human influenza A (H5N1) is associated with high viral load and hypercytokinemia."

94. Li KS et al. (2004). "Genesis of a highly pathogenic and potentially pandemic H5N1 influenza virus in eastern Asia." *Nature* 430: 209–13; Webster RG, M Peiris, H Chen and Y Guan (2006). "H5N1 outbreaks and enzootic influenza." *Emerging Infectious Diseases* 12: 3–8.

95. Salzberg SL et al. (2007). "Genome analysis linking recent European and African influenza (H5N1) viruses." *Emerging Infectious Diseases* 13: 713–18.

96. Smith GJD et al. (2006). "Emergence and predominance of an H5N1 influenza variant in China." *Proceedings of the National Academy of Sciences USA* 103: 16936–41.

97. Kandun IN et al. (2006). "Three Indonesian clusters of H5N1 virus infection in 2005." *New England Journal of Medicine* 355: 2186–94; Yang Y, ME Halloran, J Sugimoto and IM Longini (2007). "Detecting human-to-human transmission of avian influenza A (H5N1)." *Emerging Infectious Diseases* 13: 1348–53.

98. Rweyemamu M, R Paskin, A Benkirane, V Martin, P Roeder, and K
     Wojciechowski (2000). "Emerging diseases of Africa and the Middle
     East." *Annals of New York Academy of Sciences* 916: 61–70.
99. Cristalli A and I Capua (2007). "Practical problems in controlling
     H5N1 high pathogenicity avian influenza at village level in Vietnam
     and introduction of biosecurity measures." *Avian Disease* 51(Suppl):
     461–62; Gilbert M, X Xiao, W Wint and J Slingenbergh (2012).
     "Livestock production dynamics, bird migration cycles, and the emer-
     gence of highly pathogenic avian influenza in East and Southeast Asia."
     In R Sauerborn and LR Valerie (eds), *Global Environmental Change
     and Infectious Diseases: Impacts and Adaptation Strategies*. Springer,
     Berlin.
100. Fasina FO, SP Bisschop and RG Webster (2007). "Avian influenza H5N1
     in Africa: An epidemiological twist." *Lancet Infectious Diseases* 7: 696–
     97; Guldin GE (1993). "Urbanizing the countryside: Guangzhou, Hong
     Kong and the Pearl River Delta." In GE Guldin (ed), *Urbanizing China*,
     157–84. Greenwood Press, Westport, CT.
101. Wallace RG and R Wallace (2003). "The geographic search engine: One
     way urban epidemics find susceptible populations and evade public
     health intervention." *Journal of Urban Health* 80(S2): ii15.
102. Braun B (2007). "Biopolitics and the molecularization of life." *Cultural
     Geographies* 14: 6–28.
103. Castree N (2008). "Neoliberalising nature: The logics of deregulation
     and reregulation." *Environment and Planning A* 40: 131–52; Castree
     N (2008). "Neoliberalising nature: Processes, effects, and evaluations."
     Environment and Planning A 40: 153–73.
104. Benton T (1989). "Marxism and natural limits." *New Left Review* 178:
     51–81.
105. Davis M (2005). *The Monster at Our Door: The Global Threat of Avian
     Flu*. New Press, New York.
106. Cliff AD, P Haggett, and JK Ord (1986). *Spatial Aspects of Influenza
     Epidemics*. Pion, London.
107. Dieckmann U, JAJ Metz, MW Sabelis, and K Sigmund (eds) (2002).
     *Adaptive Dynamics of Infectious Diseases: In Pursuit of Virulence
     Management*. Cambridge University Press, Cambridge, UK; Ebert D
     and JJ Bull (2008). "The evolution and expression of virulence." In SC
     Stearns and JC Koella (eds), *Evolution in Health and Disease*, 153–67.
     Oxford University Press, Oxford.
108. Lipsitch M and M Nowak (1995). "The evolution of virulence in sexu-
     ally transmitted HIV/AIDS." *Journal of Theoretical Biology* 174: 427–40.
109. Food and Agriculture Organization of the United Nations (2004).
     Questions and Answers on Avian Influenza: Briefing Paper Prepared by

AI Task Force. Internal FAO document, 30 January. http://www.animal-health-online.de/drms/faoinfluenza.pdf; Graham JP, JH Leibler, LB Price, JM Otte, DU Pfeiffer, T Tiensin, and EK Silbergeld (2008). "The animal–human interface and infectious disease in industrial food animal production: Rethinking biosecurity and biocontainment." *Public Health Reports* 123: 282–99; Greger M (2006). *Bird Flu: A Virus of Our Own Hatching.* Lantern Books, New York; Shortridge KF (2003). 'Avian influenza viruses in Hong Kong: Zoonotic considerations." In R S Schrijver and G Koch (eds), *Proceedings of the Frontis Workshop on Avian Influenza: Prevention and Control,* 9–18. Wageningen University and Research Centre, Wageningen; US Council for Agricultural Science and Technology (2005). "Global risks of infectious animal diseases." Issue Paper 28. Available online at http://www.cast-science.org/publications/?global_risks_of_infectious_animal_diseases&show=product&productID=2900.

110. Capua I and DJ Alexander (2004). "Avian influenza: Recent developments." *Avian Pathology* 33: 393–404.

111. Graham JP, JH Leibler, LB Price, JM Otte, DU Pfeiffer, T Tiensin, and EK Silbergeld (2008). "The animal–human interface and infectious disease in industrial food animal production: Rethinking biosecurity and biocontainment."

112. Otte J, D Roland-Holst, D Pfeiffer, R Soares-Magalhaes, J Rushton, J Graham, and E Silbergeld (2007). *Industrial Livestock Production and Global Health Risks.* Food and Agriculture Organization Pro-Poor Livestock Policy Initiative research report. Available online at http://www.fao.org/ag/againfo/programmes/en/pplpi/docarc/rephpai_industrialisationrisks.pdf.

113. Garrett KA and CM Cox (2008). "Applied biodiversity science: Managing emerging diseases in agriculture and linked natural systems using ecological principles." In RS Ostfeld, F Keesing and VT Eviner (eds), *Infectious Disease Ecology: Effects of Ecosystems on Disease and of Disease on Ecosystems,* 368–86. Princeton University Press, Princeton.

114. Striffler S (2005). *Chicken: The Dangerous Transformation of America's Favorite Food.* Yale University Press, New Haven.

115. Shim E and AP Galvani (2009). "Evolutionary repercussions of avian culling on host resistance and influenza virulence." *PLoS ONE* 4(5): e5503.

116. Duan L et al. (2007). "Characterization of low-pathogenic H5 subtype influenza viruses from Eurasia: Implications for the origin of highly pathogenic H5N1 viruses." *Journal of Virology* 81: 7529–39.

117. Vijaykrishna D, J Bahl, S Riley, L Duan, JX Zhang, H Chen, JS Peiris, GJ Smith and Y Guan (2008). "Evolutionary dynamics and emergence of panzootic N5N1 influenza viruses." *PLoS Pathogens* 4(9): e1000161.

118. Cecchi G, A Ilemobade, Y Le Brun, L Hogerwerf and J Slingenbergh (2008). "Agroecological features of the introduction and spread of the highly pathogenic avian influenza (HPAI) H5N1 in northern Nigeria." *Geospatial Health* 3: 7–16.

119. Lu CY, JH Lu, WG Chen, LF Jiang, BY Tan, WH Ling, BJ Zheng and HY Sui (2008). "Potential infections of H5N1 and H9N2 avian influenza do exist in Guangdong population of China." *Chinese Medical Journal* 121: 2050–53.

120. Wang M, C-X Fu, and B-J Zheng (2009). "Antibodies against H5 and H9 avian influenza among poultry workers in China." *New England Journal of Medicine* 360: 2583–84.

121. Zhang P, Y Tang, X Liu, D Peng, W Liu, H Liu, S , and X Lin (2008). "Characterization of H9N2 influenza viruses isolated from vaccinated flocks in an integrated broiler chicken operation in eastern China during a 5-year period (1998–2002)." *Journal of General Virology* 89: 3102–12.

122. Meyers KP, SF Setterquist, AW Capuano, and GC Gray (2007). "Infection due to 3 avian influenza subtypes in United States veterinarians." *Clinical Infectious Diseases* 45: 4-9; Ogata T et al. (2008). "Human H5N2 avian influenza infection in Japan and the factors associated with high H5N2-neutralizing antibody titer." *Journal of Epidemiology* 18: 160–166; Puzelli S et al. (2005). "Serological analysis of serum samples from humans exposed to avian H7 influenza viruses in Italy between 1999 and 2003." *Journal of Infectious Diseases* 192: 1318–1322; WHO (World Health Organization) (2005). *Avian Influenza: Assessing the Pandemic Threat.* Available online at http://www.who.int/csr/disease/influenza/H5N1-9reduit.pdf.

123. Smith GJD et al. (2006). "Emergence and predominance of an H5N1 influenza variant in China."

124. Escorcia M, L Vazquez, ST Mendez, A Rodrıguez-Ropon, E Lucio, and GM Nava (2008). "Avian influenza: Genetic evolution under vaccination pressure." *Virology* 5(1). Available online at http://www.virologyj.com/content/5/1/15; Suarez DL, CW Lee, and DE Swayne (2006). "Avian influenza vaccination in North America: Strategies and difficulties." *Developmental Biology* 124: 117–24.

125. O'Connor J (1998). *Natural Causes.* Guilford Press, New York.

126. Yaron Y, Y Hadad, and A Cahaner (2004). "Heat tolerance in featherless broilers." Proceedings of the 22nd World Poultry Congress, Istanbul, Turkey, 8–12 June.

127. Luo X, Y Ou, and X Zhou (2003). "Livestock and poultry production in China." Paper presented at Bioproduction in East Asia: Technology Development & Globalization Impact, a pre-conference forum in

conjunction with the 2003 ASAE Annual International Meeting, Las Vegas, Nevada, 27 July. ASAE Publication Number 03BEA-06. Available online at http://asae.frymulti.com/azdez.asp?search=1&JID =5&AID=15056&CID=bea2003&v=&i=&T=1.

128. Sun AD, ZD Shi, YM Huang, and SD Liang (2007). "Development of out-of-season laying in geese and its impact on the goose industry in Guangdong Province, China." *World's Poultry Science Journal* 63: 481–90.

129. Marx K (1867;1990). *Capital: A Critique of Political Economy.* Vol 1. Penguin, London.

130. Castree N (2008). "Neoliberalising nature: The logics of deregulation and reregulation." *Environment and Planning A* 40: 131–52; Foster JB (2000). *Marx's Ecology: Materialism and Nature.* Monthly Review Press, New York; Heynen N, J McCarthy, S Prudham, and P Robbins (eds) (2007). *Neoliberal Environments: False Promises and Unnatural Consequences.* Routledge, London; Kovel J (2002). *The Enemy of Nature: The End of Capitalism or the End of the World?* Zed Books, London.

131. Boyd W and M Watts (1997). "Agro-industrial just in time: The chicken industry and postwar American capitalism." In D Goodman and MJ Watts (eds), *Globalising Food: Agrarian Questions and Global Restructuring.* 139–65. Routledge, London.

132. Striffler S (2005). *Chicken: The Dangerous Transformation of America's Favorite Food*; Manning L and RN Baines (2004). "Globalisation: A study of the poultry-meat supply chain." *British Food Journal* 106: 819–36.

133. Graham JP, JH Leibler, LB Price, JM Otte, DU Pfeiffer, T Tiensin, and EK Silbergeld (2008). "The animal–human interface and infectious disease in industrial food animal production: Rethinking biosecurity and biocontainment."

134. Food and Agriculture Organization of the United Nations (2003). *World Agriculture: Towards 2015/2030: An FAO Perspective.* Earthscan, London.

135. Gilbert M, X Xiao, W Wint and J Slingenbergh (2012). "Livestock production dynamics, bird migration cycles, and the emergence of highly pathogenic avian influenza in East and Southeast Asia."

136. Burch D (2005). "Production, consumption and trade in poultry: Corporate linkages and North–South supply chains." In N Fold and W Pritchard (eds). *Cross-Continental Food Chains,* 166–78. Routledge, London.

137. Manning L and RN Baines (2004). "Globalisation: A study of the poultry-meat supply chain."; McMichael P (2006). "Feeding the world: Agriculture, development and ecology." In L Panitch and C Leys (eds),

Socialist Register 2007: Coming to Terms With Nature, 170–194. Merlin Press, London.

138. Harvey D (1982/2006). *The Limits to Capital.* Verso, New York.
139. Burch D (2005). "Production, consumption and trade in poultry: Corporate linkages and North–South supply chains."
140. Manning L, RN Baines, and SA Chadd (2007). "Trends in global poultry meat supply chain." *British Food Journal* 109: 332–42; Sanders TAB (1999). "Food production and food safety." *British Medical Journal* 318: 1689–93.
141. Phongpaichit P and C Baker (2004). *Thaksin: The Business of Politics in Thailand.* Silkworm Books, Suthep, Thailand.
142. Davis M (2005). *The Monster at Our Door: The Global Threat of Avian Flu.*
143. Delforge I (2007). *Contract Farming in Thailand: A View from the Farm. Occasional.* Paper 2, Focus on the Global South, CUSRI. Bangkok, Thailand: Chulaongjorn University. Available online at http://www.focusweb.org/pdf/occasional-papers2-contract-farming.pdf.
144. Singer P (2005). "Who pays for bird flu?" Available online at http://www.projectsyndicate. org/commentary/singer5.
145. Chang WK (1969). "National influenza experience in Hong Kong." *Bulletin of the World Health Organization* 41: 349–51; Cheung CL et al. (2007). "Establishment of influenza A virus (H6N1) in minor poultry in southern China." *Journal of Virology* 81: 10402–412; Shortridge KF and CH Stuart-Harris (1982). 'An influenza epicentre?" *Lancet* 2: 812–13; Xu KM et al. (2007). "The genesis and evolution of H9N2 influenza viruses in poultry from southern China, 2000 to 2005." *Journal of Virology* 81: 10389–401.
146. Shortridge KF (1982). "Avian influenza A viruses of southern China and Hong Kong: Ecological aspects and implications for man." *Bulletin of the World Health Organization* 60: 129–35.
147. Shortridge KF (2003). "Severe acute respiratory syndrome and influenza: Virus incursions from Southern China." *American Journal of Respiratory and Critical Care Medicine* 168: 1416–20.
148. Fan CC (2005). "Interprovincial migration, population redistribution, and regional development in China: 1990 and 2000 census comparisons." *The Professional Geographer* 57: 295–311.
149. Luo X, Y Ou, and X Zhou (2003). "Livestock and poultry production in China."; Sun AD, ZD Shi, YM Huang, and SD Liang (2007). "Development of out-of-season laying in geese and its impact on the goose industry in Guangdong Province, China"; Burch D (2005). "Production, consumption and trade in poultry: Corporate linkages and North–South supply chains."

150. Davis M (2005). *The Monster at Our Door: The Global Threat of Avian Flu.*
151. Tang X, G Tian, J Zhao, and KY Zhou (1998). "Isolation and characterization of prevalent strains of avian influenza viruses in China." *Chinese Journal of Animal Poultry Infectious Diseases* 20: 1–5 (in Chinese).
152. Kang-Chung N (1997). "Chicken imports slashed by third." *South China Morning Post,* 15 December.
153. Wallace RG, H Hodac, RH Lathrop, and WM Fitch (2007). "A statistical phylogeography of influenza A H5N1." *Proceedings of the National Academy of Sciences USA* 104: 4473–78.
154. Wan XF et al. (2005). "Genetic characterization of H5N1 avian influenza viruses isolated in southern China during the 2003–04 avian influenza outbreaks." *Archives of Virology* 150: 1257–66.
155. Wang J et al. (2008). "Identification of the progenitors of Indonesian and Vietnamese avian influenza A (H5N1) viruses from southern China." *Journal of Virology* 82: 3405–14.
156. Mukhtar MM et al. (2007). "Origins of highly pathogenic H5N1 avian influenza virus in China and genetic characterization of donor and recipient viruses." *Journal of General Virology* 88: 3094–99.
157. Guan Y, KF Shortridge, S Krauss, and RG Webster (1999). "Molecular characterization of H9N2 influenza viruses: Were they the donors of the 'internal' genes of H5N1 viruses in Hong Kong?" *Proceedings of the National Academy of Sciences USA* 96: 9363–67; Hoffmann E et al. (2000). "Characterization of the influenza A virus gene pool in avian species in southern China: Was H6N1 a derivative or a precursor of H5N1?" *Journal of Virology* 74: 6309–15.
158. Li KS et al. (2004). "Genesis of a highly pathogenic and potentially pandemic H5N1 influenza virus in eastern Asia." *Nature* 430: 209–13.
159. Cheung CL et al. (2007). "Establishment of influenza A virus (H6N1) in minor poultry in southern China." Liu JH, K Okazaki, WM Shi, QM Wu, AS Mweene, and H Kida (2003). "Phylogenetic analysis of neuraminidase gene of H9N2 influenza viruses prevalent in chickens in China during 1995–2002." *Virus Genes* 27: 197–202; Poon LL, Y Guan, JM Nicholls, KY Yuen, and JS Peiris (2004). "The aetiology, origins, and diagnosis of severe acute respiratory syndrome." *Lancet Infectious Diseases* 4: 663–71.
160. Tseng W and H Zebregs (2003). "Foreign direct investment in China: Some lessons for other countries." In W Tseng and M Rodlauer (eds), *China, Competing in the Global Economy,* 68–88. International Monetary Fund, Washington DC.
161. Perkins FC (1997). "Export performance and enterprise reform in China's coastal provinces." *Economic Development and Cultural Change* 45: 501–39.

162. Rozelle S, C Pray, and J Huang (1999). "Importing the means of production: Foreign capital and technologies flows in China's agriculture." Paper presented at the 1999 IATRC Conference San Francisco, CA, 25–26 June. Available online at http://www.agecon.ucdavis.edu/people/faculty/facultydocs/Sumner/iatrc/rozelle.pdf.

163. Hertel TW, A Nin-Pratt, AN Rae, and S Ehui (1999). "Productivity growth and catching-up: Implications for China's trade in livestock products." Paper presented at the International Agricultural Trade Research Consortium meeting on China's Agricultural Trade and Policy, San Francisco, CA, 25–26 June. Available online at http://www.agecon.ucdavis.edu/people/faculty/facultydocs/Sumner/iatrc/hertel.pdf.

164. Carter CA and X Li (1999). "Economic reform and the changing pattern of China's agricultural trade." Paper presented at International Agricultural Trade Research Consortium San Francisco, 25–26 June. Available online at http://www.agecon.ucdavis.edu/people/faculty/facultydocs/Sumner/iatrc/colin.pdf.

165. Tseng W and H Zebregs (2003). "Foreign direct investment in China: Some lessons for other countries."

166. Tan KS and HE Khor (2006). "China's changing economic structure and implications for regional patterns of trade, protection and integration." *China & World Economy* 14: 1–19.

167. Whalley J and X Xin (2006). "China's FDI and non-FDI economies and the sustainability of future high Chinese growth." Working paper no. 12249. National Bureau of Economic Research, Cambridge, MA. Available online at http://unpan1.un.org/intradoc/groups/public/documents/APCITY/UNPAN026113.pdf.

168. Yeung F (2008). "Goldman Sachs pays US$300m for poultry farms." *South China Morning Post*, 4 August.

169. Wong E (2008). "Hints of discord on China land reform." *New York Times*. 16 October.

170. Harvey D (2006). *Spaces of Global Capitalism: A Theory of Uneven Geographical Development*. Verso, London.

171. Johnson G (1992). "The political economy of Chinese urbanization: Guangdong and the Pearl River Delta region." In GE Guldin (ed), *Urbanizing China*, 185–220. Greenwood Press, Westport, CT; Xueqiang X, R Yin-Wang Kwok, L Li, and X Yan (1995). "Production change in Guangdong." In R Yin-Wang and AY So (eds), *The Hong Kong-Guangdong Link: Partnership in Flux*, 135–62. ME Sharpe, New York; Zweig D (1991). "Internationalizing China's countryside: The political economy of exports from rural industry." *China Quarterly* 128: 716–41.

172. Heartfield J (2005). "China's comprador capitalism is coming home."

Review of Radical Political Economics 37: 196–214; Sit VFS (2004). "China's WTO accession and its impact on Hong Kong-Guangdong cooperation." *Asian Survey* 44: 815–35.

173. Heartfield J (2005). "China's comprador capitalism is coming home."
174. Rozelle S, C Pray and J Huang (1999). "Importing the means of production: Foreign capital and technologies flows in China's agriculture."
175. Heartfield J (2005). "China's comprador capitalism is coming home"; Gu C, J Shen, W Kwan-Yiu, and F Zhen (2001). "Regional polarization under the socialist market system since 1978: A case study of Guangdong province in south China." *Environment and Planning A* 33: 97–119.
176. Haley G, CT Tan, and U Haley (1998). *The New Asian Emperors: The Chinese Overseas, Their Strategies and Competitive Advantages.* Butterworth Heinemann, London.
177. Gu C, J Shen, W Kwan-Yiu, and F Zhen (2001). "Regional polarization under the socialist market system since 1978: A case study of Guangdong province in south China"; Lin GCS (2000). "State, capital, and space in China in an age of volatile globalization." *Environment and Planning A* 32: 455–71.
178. Perkins FC (1997). "Export performance and enterprise reform in China's coastal provinces."
179. Organisation for Economic Co-operation and Development (1998). *Agricultural Polices in Non-Member Countries.* Centre for Cooperation with Economies in Transition, Organization for Economic Co-operation and Development, Paris.
180. Simpson JR, Y Shi, O Li, W Chen, and S Liu (1999). "Pig, broiler and laying hen farm structure in China, 1996." Paper presented at IARTC International Symposium, 25–26 June. Available online at http://sumner.ucdavis.edu/facultydocs/Sumner/iatrc/simpson.pdf.
181. Rozelle S, C Pray and J Huang (1999). "Importing the means of production: Foreign capital and technologies flows in China's agriculture."
182. Zweig D (1991). "Internationalizing China's countryside: The political economy of exports from rural industry."
183. Tan KS and HE Khor (2006). "China's changing economic structure and implications for regional patterns of trade, protection and integration."
184. Hart-Landsberg M and P Burkett (2005). *China and Socialism: Market Reforms and Class Struggle.* Monthly Review Press, New York.
185. Li M (2008). "An age of transition: The United States, China, Peak Oil, and the demise of neoliberalism." *Monthly Review* 59: 20–34.
186. Hart-Landsberg M and P Burkett (2005). "China and socialism: Engaging the issues." *Critical Asian Studies* 37: 597–628.
187. Heartfield J (2005). "China's comprador capitalism is coming home."

188. Hart-Landsberg M and P Burkett (2005). *China and Socialism: Market Reforms and Class Struggle.*

189. Fan CC (2001). "Migration and labor-market returns in urban China: Results from a recent survey in Guangzhou." *Environment and Planning A* 33: 479–508.

190. Davis M (2006). *Planet of Slums.* Verso, London.

191. Seto KC, RK Kaurmann, and CE Woodcock (2000). "Landsat reveals China's farmland reserves, but they are vanishing fast." *Nature* 406: 121.

192. Lin GCS (1997). *Red Capitalism in South China: Growth and Development of the Pearl River Delta.* UBC Press, Vancouver.

193. Shi L (1993). "Health care in China: A rural–urban comparison after the socioeconomic reforms." *Bulletin of the World Health Organization* 71:7 23–36.

194. French HW (2006). "Wealth grows, but health care withers in China." *New York Times.* 14 January.

195. Tucker JD, GE Henderson, TF Wang, YY Huang, W Parish, SM Pan, XS Chen, and MS Cohen (2005). "Surplus men, sex work, and the spread of HIV in China." *AIDS* 19: 539–47.

196. Breitung W (2002). "Transformation of a boundary regime: The Hong Kong and Mainland China case." *Environment and Planning A* 34: 1749–62.

197. Carter CA and X Li (1999). "Economic reform and the changing pattern of China's agricultural trade."

198. Ibid; US Trade Representative (1998). "National trade estimate report on foreign trade barriers: China." Washington, DC. Available online at http://www.ustr.gov/assets/Document_Library/ Reports_Publications/1998/1998_National_Trade_Estimate/asset_ upload_file20_2798.pdf.

199. Lin GCS (2000). "State, capital, and space in China in an age of volatile globalization."

200. Hart-Landsberg M and P Burkett (2005). *China and Socialism: Market Reforms and Class Struggle.*

201. Tan KS and HE Khor (2006). "China's changing economic structure and implications for regional patterns of trade, protection and integration"; Hart-Landsberg M and P Burkett (2005). *China and Socialism: Market Reforms and Class Struggle.*

202. Hertel TW, K Anderson, JF Francois, and W Martin (2000). *Agriculture and Nonagricultural Liberalization in the Millennium Round.* Policy Discussion Paper No. 0016, Centre for International Economic Studies. University of Adelaide, Adelaide, Australia. Available online at https:// www.gtap.agecon.purdue.edu/resources/download/689.pdf.

203. Rweyemamu M, R Paskin, A Benkirane, V Martin, P Roeder, and K

Wojciechowski (2000). "Emerging diseases of Africa and the Middle East."

204. Kilpatrick AM, AA Chmura, DW Gibbons, RC Fleischer, PP Marra, and P Daszak (2006). "Predicting the global spread of H5N1 avian influenza." *Proceedings of the National Academy of Sciences USA* 103: 19368–73.

205. Duffy G, OA Lyncha, and C Cagneya (2008). "Tracking emerging zoonotic pathogens from farm to fork. Symposium on meat safety: From abattoir to consumer." *Meat Science* 78: 34–42.

206. Graham JP, JH Leibler, LB Price, JM Otte, DU Pfeiffer, T Tiensin, and EK Silbergeld (2008). "The animal–human interface and infectious disease in industrial food animal production: Rethinking biosecurity and biocontainment."

207. Gilbert M, P Chaitaweesub, T Parakamawongsa, S Premashthira, T Tiensin, W Kalpravidh, H Wagner and J Slingenbergh (2006). "Free-grazing ducks and highly pathogenic avian influenza, Thailand."*Emerging Infectious Diseases* 12: 227–234; Gilbert M et al. (2008). "Mapping H5N1 highly pathogenic avian influenza risk in Southeast Asia." *Proceedings of the National Academy of Sciences USA* 105: 4769–74.

208. Leff B, N Ramankutty, and JA Foley (2004). "Geographic distribution of major crops across the world." *Global Biogeochemical Cycles* 18. Available online at http://www.sage.wisc.edu/pubs/articles/F-L/Leff/Leff2004GBC.pdf.

209. Songserm T, R Jam-on, N Sae-Heng, N Meemak, DJ Hulse-Post, KM Sturm-Ramirez, and RG Webster (2006). "Domestic ducks and H5N1 influenza epidemic, Thailand." *Emerging Infectious Diseases* 12: 575–81.

210. Weis T (2007). *The Global Food Economy: The Battle for the Future of Farming.* Zed Books, London.

211. Manning L and RN Baines (2004). "Globalisation: A study of the poultry-meat supply chain"; Lewontin R and R Levins (2007). "The maturing of capitalist agriculture: Farmer as proletarian." In *Biology Under the Influence: Dialectical Essays on Ecology, Agriculture, and Health.* Monthly Review Press, New York.

212. McMichael P (2006). "Feeding the world: Agriculture, development and ecology."

213. Delforge I (2007). *Contract Farming in Thailand: A View from the Farm.*

214. Phongpaichit P and C Baker (1995). *Thailand, Economy and Politics.* Oxford University Press, Oxford.

215. Molle F (2007). "Scales and power in river basin management: The Chao Phraya River in Thailand." *The Geographical Journal* 173: 358–73.

216. Lemly AD, RT Kingsford, and JR Thompson (2000). "Irrigated

agriculture and wildlife conservation: conflict on a global scale." *Environmental Management* 25: 485–512.

217. Jeffries RL, RF Rockwell, and KF Abraham (2004). "The embarrassment of riches: Agricultural food subsidies, high goose numbers, and loss of Arctic wetlands—a continuing saga." *Environmental Reviews* 11: 193–232; Van Eerden MR, RH Drent, J Stahl, and JP Bakker (2005). "Connecting seas: Western Palearctic continental flyway for water birds in the perspective of changing land use and climate." *Global Change Biology* 11: 894–908.

218. Wallace RG (2007). "The great bird flu name game." *H5N1* blog. Available online at http://crofsblogs.typepad.com/h5n1/2007/12/should-we-play.html.

219. Hammond E (2007). "Flu virus sharing summit: Wrap-up." *Effect Measure* blog. http://scienceblogs.com/effectmeasure/2007/11/flu_virus_sharing_summit_wrap_1.php; Hammond E (2008). "Material transfer agreement hypocrisy." *Immunocompetent* blog. http://immunocompetent.com/index.php?op=ViewArticle&articleId=4&blogId=1.

220. Kilpatrick AM, AA Chmura, DW Gibbons, RC Fleischer, PP Marra, and P Daszak (2006). "Predicting the global spread of H5N1 avian influenza." Capua I and Alexander DJ (2006). "The challenge of avian influenza to the veterinary community." *Avian Pathology* 35: 189–205; Wallace RG and Fitch WM (2008). "Influenza A H5N1 immigration is filtered out at some international borders." *PLoS ONE* 3(2): e1697.

221. Cristalli A and I Capua (2007). "Practical problems in controlling H5N1 high pathogenicity avian influenza at village level in Vietnam and introduction of biosecurity measures." Graham JP, JH Leibler, LB Price, JM Otte, DU Pfeiffer, T Tiensin, and EK Silbergeld (2008). "The animal-human interface and infectious disease in industrial food animal production: Rethinking biosecurity and biocontainment." Ferguson N (2007). "Poverty, death, and a future influenza pandemic." *Lancet* 368: 2187–88.

222. Harvey D (1982/2006). *The Limits to Capital.*

223. Brown S and C Getz (2008). "Towards domestic fair trade? Farm labor, food localism, and the 'family scale' form." *GeoJournal* 73: 11–22; Levins R (1993). "The ecological transformation of Cuba." *Agriculture and Human Values* 10: 52–60; Lewontin R and R Levins (2007). "How Cuba is going ecological." In *Biology Under the Influence: Dialectical Essays on Ecology, Agriculture, and Health.* Monthly Review Press, New York.

224. Van Asseldonk MAPM, MPM Meuwissen, MCM Mourits and RBM Huirne (2005). "Economics of controlling avian influenza epidemics."

In RS Schrijver and G Koch (eds), *Avian Influenza: Prevention and Control*, 139–48. Springer, Dordrecht.

225 Lewontin R and R Levins (2007). "The maturing of capitalist agriculture: Farmer as proletarian."

226. Garrett L (2001). *Betrayal of Trust: The Collapse of Global Public Health*. Oxford University Press, Oxford.

227. Farmer P (2004). *Pathologies of Power: Health, Human Rights, and the New War on the Poor*. University of California Press, Berkeley; Kim JY, JV Millen, A Irwin, and J Gershman (eds) (2000). *Dying for Growth: Global Inequality and the Health of the Poor*. Common Courage Press, Boston.

228. Davis M (2005). *The Monster at Our Door: The Global Threat of Avian Flu*.

229. Wallace R and RG Wallace (2004). "Adaptive chronic infection, structured stress, and medical magic bullets: Do reductionist cures select for holistic diseases?" *BioSystems* 77: 93–108.

Do Pathogens Time Travel?

230. Haldane JBS (1957). "The cost of natural selection." *Journal of Genetics* 55: 511-24; Haldane JBS (1960). "More precise expressions for the cost of natural selection." *Journal of Genetics* 57: 351–360; Crow J (1970). "Genetic loads and the cost of natural selection." In K Kojima (ed), *Mathematical Topics in Population Genetics*, 128–77. Springer, Heidelberg; Bell G (2013). "Evolutionary rescue and the limits of adaptation." *Phil. Trans. R. Soc. B* 368: 0120080. Available online at http://dx.doi.org/10.1098/rstb.2012.0080.

231. Beatty J (1995). "The evolutionary contingency thesis." In G Wolters, JG Lennox (eds), *Concepts, Theories and Rationality in the Biological Sciences*, 45–81. University of Pittsburgh Press, Pittsburgh.

232. Turing AM (1936). "On computable numbers, with an application to the Entscheidungs problem." *Proceedings of the London Mathematical Society* 42: 230–65. doi:10.1112/plms/s2-42.1.230. Available online at http://plms.oxfordjournals.org/content/s2-42/1/230.extract .

233. Gould SJ (2002). *The Structure of Evolutionary Theory*. Harvard University Press, Cambridge, MA.

234. Gödel K (1930/1992). *On Formally Undecidable Propositions of Principia Mathematica and Related Systems*. Dover Books on Mathematics. Dover Publications.

235. Wallace RG (2010). "The axis of viral." *Farming Pathogens*. 14 September 2010. Available online at https://farmingpathogens.wordpress.com/2010/09/14/the-axis-of-viral/; Novak RM et al. (2005). "Prevalence of antiretroviral drug resistance mutations in chronically

HIV-infected, treatment-naive patients: Implications for routine resistance screening before initiation of antiretroviral therapy." *Clin Infect Dis.* 40(3): 468-74; Fourati S et al. (2012). "E138K and M184I mutations in HIV-1 reverse transcriptase coemerge as a result of APOBEC3 editing in the absence of drug exposure." *AIDS* 26(13): 1619–24. doi: 10.1097/QAD.0b013e3283560703; Houck P et al. (1995). "Amantadine-resistant Influenza A in nursing homes: Identification of a resistant virus prior to drug use." *Arch Intern Med.* 155: 533–37.

236. Wright S (1932). "The roles of mutation, inbreeding, crossbreeding, and selection in evolution." *Proceedings of the Sixth International Congress on Genetics.* 1:356-66. 355–66.

PART TWO
We Can Think Ourselves into a Plague

1. Goodman A and S Žižek (2010). "Slavoj Žižek: Far right and anti-immigrant politicians on the rise in Europe." *Democracy Now!* 18 October 2010. Available online at http://www.democracynow.org/2010/10/18/slavoj_zizek_far_right_and_anti.

2. Wallace R, D Wallace, and RG Wallace (2009). *Farming Human Pathogens: Ecological Resilience and Evolutionary Process.* Springer, Dordrecht.

3. Wallace R and RG Wallace (2004). "Adaptive chronic infection, structured stress, and medical magic bullets: do reductionist cures select for holistic diseases?" *BioSystems* 77: 93–108.

4. Wallace RG (2004). "Projecting the impact of HAART on the evolution of HIV's life history." *Ecological Modelling* 176: 227–53; Shim E and Galvani AP (2009). "Evolutionary repercussions of avian culling on host resistance and influenza virulence." *PLoS ONE* 4(5): e5503.

5. Wallace RG and H Stern. "By protease uracil load Qinghai-like and southern Chinese influenza A (H5N1) appear closest to evolving human-to-human infection." Unpublished ms.

6. Rabadan R, AJ Levine, and H Robins (2006). "Comparison of Avian and Human Influenza A Viruses Reveals a Mutational Bias on the Viral Genomes." *J Virol.* 80(23): 11887–91.

7. Levins R (1998). "The internal and external in explanatory theories." *Science as Culture* 7 :557–82.

Influenza's Historical Present

8. Xiao X, V Martin, Scott Newman, and B Yan (organizers) (2010). Second International Workshop on Community-Based Data Synthesis, Analysis and Modeling of Highly Pathogenic Avian Influenza H5N1 in Asia. Available online at http://www.eomf.ou.edu/workshop/2nd-birdflu/.

9. Wallace RG, L Bergmann, L Hogerwerf, and M Gilbert (2010). "Are influenzas in southern China byproducts of the region's globalising historical present?" In S Craddock, T Giles-Vernick, and J Gunn (eds), *Influenza and Public Health: Learning from Past Pandemics*. EarthScan Press, London.

10. Hogerwerf L, RG Wallace, D Ottaviani, J Slingenbergh, D Prosser, L Bergmann, and M Gilbert (2010). "Persistence of highly pathogenic influenza A (H5N1) defined by agro-ecological niche." *EcoHealth*. DOI: 10.1007/s10393-010-0324-z.

11. BBC News(2000). "Duck patrol advances on China's locusts." 12 July. Available online at http://news.bbc.co.uk/2/hi/asia-pacific/830435.stm.

12. Simoons FJ (1991). *Food in China: A Cultural and Historical Inquiry*. CRC Press, Boca Raton, FL.

13. Wallace RG (2009). "Breeding influenza: the political virology of off-shore farming." *Antipode* 41: 916–51.

14. Wang J, et al. (2008). "Identification of the progenitors of Indonesian and Vietnamese avian influenza A (H5N1) viruses from southern China." *Journal of Virology* 82: 3405–14.

15. Weng Q (2002). "Land use change analysis in the Zhujiang Delta of China using satellite remote sensing, GIS and stochastic modeling." *Journal of Environmental Management* 64: 273–84.

16. Seto KC and M Fragkias (2005). "Quantifying spatiotemporal patterns of urban land-use change in four cities of China with time series landscape metrics." *Landscape Ecology* 20: 871–88.

17. Wallace RG (2009). "Bird flu's Industrial Revolution." *Farming Pathogens*, 5 April 2009. Available online at https://farmingpathogens. wordpress.com/2009/04/05/bird-flus-industrial-revolution/.

18. Harvey D (1982/2006). *The Limits to Capital*. Verso, New York.

Does Influenza Evolve in Multiple Tenses?

19. Wallace RG, L Bergmann, L Hogerwerf, and M Gilbert (2010). "Are influenzas in southern China byproducts of the region's globalising historical present?" In S Craddock, T Giles-Vernick, and J Gunn (eds), *Influenza and Public Health: Learning from Past Pandemics*. EarthScan Press, London.

20. Wallace RG and L Bergmann (2010). "Influenza's historical present." *Farming Pathogens*, 11 June 2010. Available online at https://farming-pathogens.wordpress.com/2010/06/11/influenzas-historical-present.; Althusser L and E Balibar (1968/2009). *Reading Capital*. Verso, London.

21. Itoh Y et al. (2009). "*In vitro* and *in vivo* characterization of new swine-origin H1N1 influenza viruses." *Nature* 460: 1021–25.

22. Wallace R, D Wallace, and RG Wallace (2009.) *Farming Human*

Pathogens: Ecological Resilience and Evolutionary Process. Springer, Dordrecht.

23. Waddington CH (1952). "Genetic assimilation of an acquired character." *Evolution* 7: 118–26.
24. Gibson G and I Dworkin (2004). "Uncovering cryptic genetic variation." *Nature Reviews Genetics* 5: 681–90.
25. Wallace RG, HM HoDac, R Lathrop, and WM Fitch (2007). "A statistical phylogeography of influenza A H5N1." *Proceedings of the National Academy of Sciences* 104: 4473–78.
26. Rimmelzwaan G et al. (2005). "Full restoration of viral fitness by multiple compensatory co-mutations in the nucleoprotein of influenza A virus cytotoxic T-lymphocyte escape mutants." *J Gen Virol* 86: 1801–05.
27. Gilbert S (2003). "The reactive genome." In GB Muller and SA Newman (eds), *Origination of Organismal Form: Beyond the Gene in Developmental and Evolutionary Biology.* MIT Press, Cambridge, MA.
28. Ancel LW (1999). "A quantitative model of the Simpson–Baldwin Effect." *Theoretical Biology* 196: 197–209.
29. Shortridge KF and Stuart-Harris CH (1982). "An influenza epicentre?" *Lancet* 2: 812–13; Wallace RG (2009). "Breeding influenza: The political virology of offshore farming." *Antipode* 41: 916–51.

Virus Dumping

30. Flaccavento A (2010). "Walmart and the end of the local food movement." *Huff Post Food*, 26 October. Available online at http://www.huffingtonpost.com/anthony-flaccavento/walmart-and-the-end-of-th_b_774350.html.
31. Wise TA (2010). *Agricultural Dumping under NAFTA: Estimating the Costs of U.S. Agricultural Policies to Mexican Producers.* Mexican Rural Development Research Report No. 7, Woodrow Wilson International Center for Scholars. Available online at http://www.ase.tufts.edu/gdae/policy_research/AgNAFTA.html.
32. Wallace RG (2009). "NAFTA flu." *Farming Pathogens*, 28 April. Available online at https://farmingpathogens.wordpress.com/2009/04/28/the-nafta-flu/; Wallace RG (2009). "The hog industry strikes back." *Farming Pathogens*, 1 June. Available online at https://farmingpathogens.wordpress.com/2009/06/01/the-hog-industry -strikes-back/.
33. Wise TA (2010) *Agricultural Dumping under NAFTA: Estimating the Costs of U.S. Agricultural Policies to Mexican Producers.*
34. Saviano R (2007). *Gomorra.* Farrar, Straus and Giroux, New York.
35. Burch D (2005). "Production, consumption and trade in poultry: Corporate linkages and North–South supply chains." In N Fold and W Pritchard (eds), *Cross-Continental Food Chains,* 166–78. Routledge, London.

36. Davis M (2005). *"The Monster at Our Door: The Global Threat of Avian Flu."* New Press, New York.

37. Hayes S (2009). "Tag, we're it." *New York Times*, 10 March. Available online at http://www.nytimes.com/2009/03/11/opinion/11hayes.html?_r=1&scp=1&sq=farm+animals&st=nyt.

That's the Thicke

38. Neuman W (2010). "Small cheesemaker defies F.D.A. over recall." *New York Times*, 19 November. Available online at http://www.nytimes.com/2010/11/20/business/20artisan.html?_r=2&ref=william_neuman.

39. Miller L (2010). "What food says about class in America." *Newsweek*, 22 November. Available online at http://www.newsweek.com/what-food-says-about-class-america-69951.

40. Against the Grain (2010). *Harvey on Left Organization; Coyle on Cutting the Work Week*. 15 November. Available online at http://www.againstthegrain.org/program/368/id/461234/mon-11-15-10-harvey-left-organization-coyle-cutting-work-week; Hari J (2010). "How Goldman gambled on starvation." *The Independent*. 2 July. Available online at http://www.independent.co.uk/voices/commentators/johann-hari/johann-hari-how-goldman-gambled-on-starvation-2016088.html.

41. Fassler J (2010). "Conventional vs. organic: An Ag Secretary race to watch." *The Atlantic*, 27 October. Available online at http://www.theatlantic.com/health/archive/2010/10/conventional-vs-organic-an-ag-secretary-race-to-watch/65144/.

42. Malkin E (2010). "Growing a forest, and harvesting jobs." *New York Times*. 22 November. Available online at http://www.nytimes.com/2010/11/23/world/americas/23mexico.html.

43. Levins R (2007). "How Cuba is going ecological." In R Lewontin and R Levins, *Biology under the Influence: Dialectical Essays on Ecology, Agriculture, and Health*. Monthly Review Press, New York.

44. Pretty J (2009). "Can ecological agriculture feed nine billion people?" *Monthly Review* 61(6): 46–58. Available online at http://monthlyreview.org/2009/11/01/can-ecological-agriculture-feed-nine-billion-people.

45   Imhoff D (ed) (2010). *The CAFO Reader: The Tragedy of Industrial Animal Factories*. University of California Press, Berkeley; Kirby D (2010). *Animal Factory: The Looming Threat of Industrial Pig, Dairy, and Poultry to Humans and the Environment*. St Martin's Press, New York; Magdoff F and B Tokar (eds) (2010). *Agriculture and Food in Crisis: Conflict, Resistance and Renewal*. Monthly Review Press, New York.

46. Wallace RG (2010). "Grainmorrah." *Farming Pathogens*, 6

December. Available online at https://farmingpathogens.wordpress. com/2010/12/06/grainmorrah/.

47. Blum D (2010). "Arsenic and Tom Turkey." *Los Angeles Times*. 24 November. Available online at http://articles.latimes.com/2010/nov/24/ opinion/la-oe-blum-turkey-arsenic-20101124.

48. Philpott T (2010). "The FDA finally reveals how many antibiotics factory farms use—and it's a shitload." *Grist*. 11 December. Available online at http://grist.org/article/food-2010-12-10-fda-reveals-amount-of-antibiotic-use-on-factory-farms/.

49. Wallace RG (2010). "Grainmorrah."

50. Chrisman S (2010). "Looking back at a year of ag industry consolidation workshops, ahead of finale this week." *Civil Eats*. 6 December. Available online at http://civileats.com/2010/12/06/looking-back-at-a-year-of-ag-industry-consolidation-workshops-ahead-of-finale-this-week/.

PART THREE
Alien vs. Predator

1. Ehrenberg R (2008). "NASA unveils arsenic life form." *WIRED*. 2 December. Available online at http://www.wired.com/2010/12/nasa-finds -arsenic-life-form/.

2. Wolfe-Simon F et al. (2010). "A bacterium that can grow by using arsenic instead of phosphorus." *Science* 332: 1163–66.

3. Redfield R (2010). "Arsenic-associated bacteria (NASA's claims)." *RRResearch* blog. 4 December. Available online at http://rrresearch. fieldofscience.com/2010/12/arsenic-associated-bacteria-nasas.html; Redfield R (2010). "Comments on Dr. Wolfe-Simon's response." *RRResearch* blog. 16 December. Available online at http://rrresearch. fieldofscience.com/2010/12/text.html; Danchin A (2010). "Science and arsenic fool's gold: A toxic broth." *Journal of Cosmology* 13: 3617–20.

4. Marshall M (2010). "Life is found in deepest layer of Earth's crust." *New Scientist*, 18 November. Available online at http://www. newscientist.com/article/mg20827874.800-life-is-found-in-deepest-layer-of-earths-crust.html.

5. Wallace RG (2009). "'Biosecure' farms not so biosecure." *Farming Pathogens*. 26 August. Available online at https://farmingpathogens. wordpress.com/2009/08/26/biosecure-farms-not-so-biosecure/.

6. Wallace RG (2010). "Grainmorrah." *Farming Pathogens*. 6 December. Available online at https://farmingpathogens.wordpress. com/2010/12/06/grainmorrah/.

7. Wallace RG (2010). "Do pathogens time travel?" *Farming Pathogens*. 12 January. Available online at https://farmingpathogens.wordpress. com/2010/01/12/do-pathogens-time-travel/.

8. Nobusawa E and K Sato (2006). "Comparison of the mutation rates of human influenza A and B viruses." *Journal of Virology* 80: 3675–78.

9. Torrence PF (ed) (2007). *Combating the Threat of Pandemic Influenza: Drug Discovery Approaches.* Wiley, New York; Webster RG (2001). "A molecular whodunit." *Science* 293: 1773–75; Cinatl J, M Michaelis, and HW Doerr (2007). "The threat of avian influenza A (H5N1), Part 1: Epidemiologic concerns and virulence determinants." *Medical Microbiology and Immunology* 196(4): 181–90.

10. Wallace RG (2010). "Virus dumping." *Farming Pathogens.* 11 November. Available online at https://farmingpathogens.wordpress. com/2010/11/11/virus-dumping/.

11. Sankaranarayanan K, MN Timofeeff, R Spathis, TK Lowenstein, and JK Lum (2011). "Ancient Microbes from Halite Fluid Inclusions: Optimized Surface Sterilization and DNA Extraction." *PLoS ONE* 6(6): e20683. doi:10.1371/journal.pone.0020683; Lowenstein T (2011). "Bacteria back from the brink." *Earth* magazine. April. Available online at http://jahren-lab.com/storage/EARTH%20Magazine%202011.pdf.

12. Koribanics NM et al. (2015). "Spatial distribution of an uranium-respiring betaproteobacterium at the Rifle, CO Field Research Site." *PLoS ONE* 10(4): e0123378. doi:10.1371/journal.pone.0123378.

13. Reid C (2015). "Scientists find bacteria that 'breathe' uranium." *IFL Science!* 15 June. Available online at http://www.iflscience.com/ environment/scientists-find-bacteria-thrive-uranium.

The Scientific American

14. Le Rouzic A, JM Álvarez-Castro, and Ö Carlborg (2008). 'Dissection of the genetic architecture of body weight in chicken reveals the impact of epistasis on domestication traits." *Genetics* 179: 1591–99; Groeneveld LF et al. (2010). "Genetic diversity in farm animals—a review." *Animal Genetics* 41(S1): 6–31.

15. Lyall J et al. (2011). "Suppression of avian influenza transmission in genetically modified chickens." *Science* 331: 223–26.

16. Hughes V (2011). "Transgenic chickens curb bird flu transmission." *Nature.* 13 January. Available online at http://www.nature. com/news/2011/110113/full/news.2011.16.html; Wallace RG (2010). "Alien vs. Predator." *Farming Pathogens.* 21 December 2010. Available online at https://farmingpathogens.wordpress.com/2010/12/31/alien -vs-predator/.

17. Branswell H (2011). "Flu factories." *Scientific American.* January. Available online at http://www.scientificamerican.com/article/pan-demic-flu-factories/.

18. Meyers KP et al. (2006). "Are swine workers in the United States at

increased risk of infection with zoonotic influenza virus?" *Clin Infect Dis.* 42(1): 14–20.

19. Wallace RG (2009). "NAFTA flu." *Farming Pathogens.* 28 April. Available online at https://farmingpathogens.wordpress.com/2009/04/ 28/the-nafta-flu/; Wallace RG (2009). "The hog industry strikes back." *Farming Pathogens.* 1 June. Available online at https://farmingpathogens.wordpress.com/2009/06/01/the-hog-industry-strikes-back/; Wallace RG (2010). "Virus dumping." *Farming Pathogens.* 11 November. Available online at https://farmingpathogens.wordpress.com/2010/11/11/virus-dumping/; Wallace RG (2009). "Breeding influenza: The political virology of offshore farming." *Antipode* 41: 916–51.

20. Wallace RG (2009). "NAFTA flu."

21. Mirsky S and H Branswell (2010). "How you gonna keep flu down on the farm? Pig farms and public health." *Scientific American,* 22 December. Available online at http://www.scientificamerican.com/podcast/episode/how-you-gonna-keep-flu-down-on-the-10-12-22/.

22. Yowell E and FG Estrow (2011). "Farm Bill 1.01: An introduction and brief history of the Farm Bill." Food Systems Network NYC. Available online at http://www.foodsystemsnyc.org/articles/farm-bill-jan-2011.

23. Mészáros I (2010). *Social Structure and Forms of Consciousness,* vol. 1: *The Social Determination of Method.* Monthly Review Press, New York.

24. Žižek S (2011). "Good manners in the age of WikiLeaks." *London Review of Books* 33: 9–10.

Axis of Viral

25. Grmek MD (1990). *History of AIDS: Emergence and Origin of a Modern Pandemic.* Princeton University Press, Princeton.

26. Lacoste V et al. (2000). "Virology: KSHV-like herpesviruses in chimps and gorillas." *Nature* 407: 151–52.

27. Malaspina A et al. (2002). "Human Immunodeficiency Virus Type 1 bound to B Cells: Relationship to virus replicating in CD4+ T cells and circulating in plasma." *J Virol.* 76(17): 8855–63.

28. Nikolovska S et al. (1999). "In vitro inhibition of KSHV/HHV-8 infected endothelial cell growth by neutralizing monoclonal antibodies to human VEGFR-2 (KDR)." *JAIDS* 21: A28.

29. Marcelin A-G et al. (2004). "Quantification of Kaposi's Sarcoma-Associated Herpesvirus in blood, oral mucosa, and saliva in patients with Kaposi's Sarcoma." *AIDS Research and Human Retroviruses* 20(7): 704–8, doi:10.1089/0889222041524689.

30. Henke-Gendo C and TF Schulz (2004). "Transmission and disease association of Kaposi's sarcoma-associated herpesvirus: recent developments." *Current Opinion in Infectious Diseases.* 17(1): 53–57.

31. Huang L-M et al. (2001). "Reciprocal regulatory interaction between Human Herpesvirus 8 and Human Immunodeficiency Virus Type 1." *Journal of Biological Chemistry* 276: 13427–32.

32. Sun Q, S Zachariah, and PM Chaudhary (2003). "The human herpes virus 8-encoded viral FLICE-inhibitory protein induces cellular transformation via NF-kappaB activation." *J Biol Chem* 278(52): 52437–45; Sun Q, H Matta, PM Chaudhary (2005). "Kaposi's sarcoma associated herpes virus-encoded viral FLICE inhibitory protein activates transcription from HIV-1 Long Terminal Repeat via the classical NF-kappaB pathway and functionally cooperates with Tat." *Retrovirology* 2: 9.

33. Guo HG, S Pati, M Sadowska, M Charurat, and M Reitz (2004). "Tumorigenesis by human herpesvirus 8 vGPCR is accelerated by human immunodeficiency virus type 1 Tat." *J Virol.* 78(17): 9336–42.

34. Gage JR, EC Breen, A Echeverri, L Magpantay, T Kishimoto, S Miles, and O Martínez-Maza (1999). "Human herpesvirus 8-encoded interleukin 6 activates HIV-1 in the U1 monocytic cell line." *AIDS* 13(14):1851–55; Song J, T Ohkura, M Sugimoto, Y Mori, R Inagi, K Yamanishi, K Yoshizaki, and N Nishimoto (2002). "Human interleukin-6 induces human herpesvirus-8 replication in a body cavity-based lymphoma cell line." *J Med Virol.* 68(3): 404–11.

35. Lehrnbecher TL et al. (2000). "Variant genotypes of FcgammaRIIIA influence the development of Kaposi's sarcoma in HIV-infected men." *Blood.* 95(7): 2386–90.

36. Gandhi M et al. (2004). "Prevalence of human herpesvirus-8 salivary shedding in HIV increases with CD4 count." *J Dent Res.* 83(8): 639–43.

37. Wallace RG (2004). "Projecting the impact of HAART on the evolution of HIV's life history." *Ecological Modelling* 176: 227–53.

38. Jacobson LP et al. (2000). "Interaction of human immunodeficiency virus type 1 and human herpesvirus type 8 infections on the incidence of Kaposi's sarcoma." *J Infect Dis.* 181(6): 1940–49.

39. Krishnan HH, PP Naranatt, MS Smith, L Zeng, C Bloomer, and B Chandran (2004). "Concurrent expression of latent and a limited number of lytic genes with immune modulation and antiapoptotic function by Kaposi's sarcoma-associated herpesvirus early during infection of primary endothelial and fibroblast cells and subsequent decline of lytic gene expression." *J Virol.* 78(7): 3601–20.

40. Cohen MS (2000). "Preventing sexual transmission of HIV—new ideas from Sub-Saharan Africa." *N Engl J Med* 342: 970–72.

41. Kalipeni E, S Craddock, JR Oppong, J Ghosh (eds) (2003). *HIV and AIDS in Africa: Beyond Epidemiology.* Wiley-Blackwell, Hoboken.

42. Lawn SD (2004). "AIDS in Africa: the impact of coinfections on the pathogenesis of HIV-1 infection." *Journal of Infection* 48: 1–12.

Are Our Microbiomes Racial?

43. Zimmer C (2008). *Microcosm: E. coli and the New Science of Life.* Pantheon Books, New York; Zimmer C (2011). "Just 3 types of bacteria found in human gut." *New York Times.* 21 April. Available online at http://www.nytimes.com/2011/04/21/science/21gut.html; Yong E (2016). "You're probably not mostly microbes." *The Atlantic.* 8 January. Available online at http://www.theatlantic.com/science/archive/2016/01/youre-probably-not-mostly-microbes/423228/.

44. Wallace RG (2004). "Projecting the impact of HAART on the evolution of HIV's life history." *Ecological Modelling* 176: 227–53.

45. Wallace RG (2010). "The axis of viral." *Farming Pathogens,* 14 September. Available online at http://farmingpathogens.wordpress.com/2010/09/14/the-axis-of-viral/.

46. Arumugam M, J Raes, E Pelletier, D Le Paslier, T Yamada et al. (2011). "Enterotypes of the human gut microbiome." *Nature* 473: 174–80.

47. Ley RE, PJ Turnbaugh, S Klein and JI Gordon (2006). "Microbial ecology: Human gut microbes associated with obesity." *Nature* 444: 1022–23.

48. Smillie CS, MB Smith, J Friedman, OX Cordero, LA David, and EJ Alm (2011). "Ecology drives a global network of gene exchange connecting the human microbiome." *Nature* 480: 241–44.

49. Gould SJ (2002). *The Structure of Evolutionary Theory.* Harvard University Press, Cambridge, MA.

50. Human Microbiome Project Consortium (2012). "Structure, function and diversity of the healthy human microbiome." *Nature* 486(7402): 207–14; Human Microbiome Project Consortium (2012). "A framework for human microbiome research." *Nature* 486(7402): 215–21, doi: 10.1038/nature11209; Human Microbiome Project recent publications are available online at http://www.hmpdacc.org/pubs/publications.php.

51. Duster T (2003). "Medicine and People of Color: Unlikely Mix—Race, Biology, and Drugs." *San Francisco Chronicle.* 17 March.

52. Leroi AM (2005). "A family tree in every tree." *New York Times.* 14 April. Available online at http://www.nytimes.com/2005/03/14/opinion/a-family-tree-in-every-gene.html; Wallace RG (2005). "A racialized medical genomics: Shiny, bright and wrong." *RACE: The Power of an Illusion.* Available online at http://www.pbs.org/race/000_About/002_04-background-01-13.htm.

53. Saletan W (2008). "Unfinished race: Race, genes, and the future of medicine." *Slate.* 27 August. Available online at http://www.slate.com/articles/health_and_science/human_nature/2008/08/unfinished_race.html.

54. Pollack A (2010). "His corporate strategy: The scientific method." *New York Times.* 4 September. Available online at http://www.nytimes. com/2010/09/05/business/05venter.html.

55. Kahn J (2007). "Race in a bottle: Drugmakers are eager to develop medicines targeted at ethnic groups, but so far they have made poor choices based on unsound science." *Scientific American* 297(2): 40–45.

56. Duster T (2003). "Medicine and People of Color: Unlikely Mix—Race, Biology, and Drugs."

57. Ackerman J (2012). "How bacteria in our bodies protect our health." *Scientific American* 306(6): 36.

58. Miller GE, Engen PA, Gillevet PM, Shaikh M, Sikaroodi M, Forsyth CB et al. (2016). "Lower neighborhood socioeconomic status associated with reduced diversity of the colonic microbiota in healthy adults." *PLoS ONE* 11(2): e0148952, doi:10.1371/journal.pone.0148952.

The X-Men

59. Pond SL and SD Frost SD (2005). "A simple hierarchical approach to modeling distributions of substitution rates." *Mol Biol Evol.* 22(2): 223–34.

60. Plotkin JB and and J Dushoff (2003). "Codon bias and frequency-dependent selection on the hemagglutinin epitopes of influenza A virus." *PNAS* 100: 7152–57.

61. Taleb NN (2007). *The Black Swan: The Impact of the Highly Improbable.* Random House, New York.

62. Wallace RG (2010). "Does influenza evolve in multiple tenses?" *Farming Pathogens.* 20 June. Available online at https://farmingpathogens.word-press.com/2010/06/20/does-influenza-evolve-in-multiple-tenses/.

63. Stoltzfus A (2012). "Constructive neutral evolution: Exploring evolutionary theory's curious disconnect." *Biology Direct* 7: 35. doi:10.1186/1745-6150-7-35; Stoltzfus, A and K Cable (2014). "Mendelian-Mutationism: The forgotten evolutionary synthesis." *Journal of the History of Biology* 47: 501–46.

64. Force A, Lynch M, Pickett FB, Amores A, Yan YL et al. (1999). "Preservation of duplicate genes by complementary, degenerate mutations." *Genetics* 151: 1531–45; Orr HA (2002). "The population genetics of adaptation: the adaptation of DNA sequences." *Evolution* 56: 1317–30.

PART FOUR
Two Gentlemen of Verona

1. FAO/OIE/WHO Joint Scientific Consultation Writing Committee (2011). *Influenza and Other Emerging Zoonotic Diseases at the*

Human-Animal Interface. Proceedings of the FAO/OIE/WHO Joint Scientific Consultation, 27–29 April 2010, Verona, Italy; FAO Animal Production and Health Proceedings, No. 13. Rome, Italy. Available online at http://www.who.int/influenza/human_animal_interface/I1963E_lowres.pdf.

2. Enserlink M (2006). "As H5N1 keeps spreading, a call to release more data." *Science* 311: 1224.

3. Quammen D (2012). *Spillover: Animal Infections and the Next Human Pandemic.* W. W. Norton, New York.

4. 1st International One Health Congress Abstracts (2011). "Plenary abstracts." *EcoHealth* 7(1): 8–170.

5. One Health Platform. Available online at http://onehealthplatform.com/.

6. International Conference on One Medicine One Science. Available online at http://www.cvm.umn.edu/events/icomos/index.htm.

7. Han E (2016). "Colgate-Palmolive, Johnson & Johnson, and PepsiCo fail to keep palm oil promises." *Sydney Morning Herald.* 3 March. Available online at http://www.smh.com.au/business/retail/colgatepalmolive-johnsonjohnson-and-pepsico-fail-to-keep-palm-oil-promises-20160302-gn87r4.html; EcoHealth Alliance (2016) "EcoHealth Alliance Selects Colgate-Palmolive to Honor at Annual Benefit." 23 March. Available online at http://www.prnewswire.com/news-releases/ecohealth-alliance-selects-colgate-palmolive-to-honor-at-annual-benefit-300239930.html.

Food and Pharm WikiLeaks

8. Harris P (2011). "WikiLeaks has caused little lasting damage, says US State Department." *The Guardian.* 19 January. Available at http://www.guardian.co.uk/media/2011/jan/19/wikileaks-white-house-state-department; Elliot J (2010). "How the U.S. can now extradite Assange." *Salon.* 7 December. Available online at http://www.salon.com/2010/12/07/julian_assange_extradition/.

9. Keller B (2011). "Dealing with Assange and the WikiLeaks secrets." *New York Times Magazine.* 26 January. Available online at http://www.nytimes.com/2011/01/30/magazine/30Wikileaks-t.html?pagewanted=all.; Rees P (2011). "Unfiltered leaks." Available online at http://philrees.tv/index.php/2011/09/22/slider-pix-1/.

10. Žižek S (2011). "Good manners in the Age of WikiLeaks." *London Review of Books.* 20 January. Available online at http://www.lrb.co.uk/v33/n02/slavoj-zizek/good-manners-in-the-age-of-wikileaks.

11. Embassy Wellington (n.d.). "New Zealand Minister Hosts Mike Moore's 'Fahrenheit' 9/11" Fundraiser (almost)." Partial cable available online at

http://www.cablegatesearch.net/cable.php?id=04WELLINGTON647 &q=michael-moore%20new-zealand.

12. Embassy Abuja (2009). "Nigeria: Pfizer Reaches Preliminary Agreement For A \$75 Million Settlement." Dated 20 April 2009. Available online at http://cablegatesearch.net/cable.php?id=09ABUJA671&q=pfizer; Boseley S (2010). "WikiLeaks cables: Pfizer 'used dirty tricks to avoid clinical trial payout.'" *The Guardian*. 9 December. Available online at http://www.guardian.co.uk/business/2010/dec/09/wikileaks-cables -pfizer-nigeria.

13. Embassy Warsaw (2009). "Biotechnology Corn Event Demarche." 23 February. Available online at http://cablegatesearch.net/cable. php?id=09WARSAW199&q=gmo .

14. Page G (2008). *Speech: Trusting Photosynthesis.* Chautauqua Institute. 12 August. Available online at http://www.cargill.com/news/speeches-presentations/trusting-photosynthesis/index.jsp.

15. Embassy Paris (2006). "Judicial Decisions Favorable to Biotech Cultivation." 31 July. Available online at http://cablegatesearch.net/ cable.php?id=06PARIS5154&q=france%20gmo%20greenpeace%20 spain.

16. Embassy Paris (2007). "French Biotech Farmers Face Multiple Problems and Challenges." 13 August. Available online at http://cable-gatesearch.net/cable.php?id=07PARIS3399&q=france%20gmo%20 greenpeace%20spain.

17. Embassy Madrid (2009). "Spain's Biotech Crop under Threat." Dated 19 May. Available online at http://cablegatesearch.net/cable. php?id=09MADRID482&q=france%20gmo%20greenpeace%20spain.

18. Breckling B and R Verhoeven (eds). (2010). *Large-Area Effects of GM-Crop Cultivation: Proceedings of the Second Gmls-Conference 2010 in Bremen.* Peter Lang GmbH Internationaler Verlag der Wissenschaften, Frankfurt. Available online at http://www.peterlang. com/index.cfm?event=cmp.ccc.seitenstruktur.detailseiten&seitentyp= produkt&pk=57904.

19. Embassy Vatican (2009). "Pope Turns Up the Heat on Environmental Protection." 19 November. Available online at http://cablegatesearch. net/cable.php?id=09VATICAN119&q=gmos%20ideological%20 vatican.

20. Embassy Nairobi (2009). "Cautious Kenya Finally Enacts Long Awaited Biosafety Act Of 2009." 11 March. Available online at http:// cablegatesearch.net/cable.php?id=09NAIROBI496&q=genetically%20 kenya%20modified.

21. Wallace RG and RA Kock (2012). "Whose food footprint? Capitalism, agriculture and the environment." *Human Geography* 5(1): 63–83.

Available online at http://farmingpathogens.files.wordpress.com/2012 /05/hg-12-5-wallace-2.pdf.

22. Wallace RG (2010). "Virus dumping." *Farming Pathogens.* 11 November. Available online at http://farmingpathogens.wordpress. com/2010/11/11/virus-dumping/.

23. Embassy Nairobi (2009). "Cautious Kenya Finally Enacts Long Awaited Biosafety Act Of 2009."

24. Aarhus P (2012). "Africa's Frankenfoods." *The Indypendent.* 2 May. Available online at http://indypendent.org/africas-frankenfoods.

25. Embassy Nairobi (2009). "Cautious Kenya Finally Enacts Long Awaited Biosafety Act Of 2009."

26. Aarhus P (2012). "Africa's Frankenfoods."

27. Greenwald G (2012). "UN top torture official denounces Bradley Manning's detention." *Salon.* 7 March. Available online at http://www. salon.com/2012/03/07/un_top_torture_official_denounces_bradley _mannings_detention.

28. Embassy Brussels (2004). "Dining With Chris: Random Thoughts from Relex Commissioner Patten." 28 April. Available online at http://cablegatesearch.net/cable.php?id=04BRUSSELS1868&q=dinner.

Synchronize Your Barns

29. Webster RG (2001). "A molecular whodunit." *Science* 293: 1773–75; Cinatl J Jr, M Michaelis, and HW Doerr (2007). "The threat of avian influenza A (H5N1). Part I: Epidemiologic concerns and virulence determinants." *Med Microbiol Immunol* 196(4): 181–90.

30. Atkins K, RG Wallace, L Hogerwerf, M Gilbert, J Slingenbergh, J Otte, and AP Galvani (2010). *Livestock Landscapes and the Evolution of Virulence in Influenza.* Pro-Poor Livestock Policy Initiative. Food and Agriculture Organization, Rome.

31. Frank SA (1996). "Models of parasite virulence." *Quarterly Review of Biology* 71: 37–78.

32. Wallace RG (2009). "Breeding influenza: The political virology of offshore farming." *Antipode* 41: 16–51; Delgado C, M Rosegrant, H Steinfeld, S Ehui, and C Courbois (1999). "The Coming Livestock Revolution." *Choices: Choices at the Millennium, A Special Issue.* Fourth Quarter 1999. 40–44.

33. Atkins K et al. (2010). *Livestock Landscapes and the Evolution of Virulence in Influenza.*

34. Vijaykrishna D, J Bahl, S Riley, L Duan, JX Zhang, H Chen, JS Peiris, GJ Smith, and Y Guan (2008). "Evolutionary dynamics and emergence of panzootic H5N1 influenza viruses." *PLoS Pathogens* 4(9): e1000161.

35. Capua I and DJ Alexander (2004). "Avian influenza: recent developments." *Avian Pathology* 33: 393–404.
36. Wang M, C-X Fu and B-J Zheng (2009). "Antibodies against H5 and H9 avian influenza among poultry workers in China." *New England Journal of Medicine* 360: 2583–84.
37. Zhang P, Y Tang, X Liu, D Peng, W Liu, H Liu, S Lu, and X Lin (2008). "Characterization of H9N2 influenza viruses isolated from vaccinated flocks in an integrated broiler chicken operation in eastern China during a 5-year period (1998–2002)." *Journal of General Virology* 89: 3102–12.
38. Graham JP, JH Leibler, LB Price, JM Otte, DU Pfeiffer, T Tiensin, and EK Silbergeld (2008). "The animal-human interface and infectious disease in industrial food animal production: rethinking biosecurity and biocontainment." *Public Health Reports* 123: 282–99.
39. Otte J, D Roland-Holst, DU Pfeiffer, R Soares-Magalhaes, J Rushton, J Graham, and E Silbergeld (2007). *Industrial Livestock Production and Global Health Risks.* Pro-Poor Livestock Policy Initiative, Food and Agriculture Organization. Available online at http://www.fao.org/ag/againfo/programmes/en/pplpi/docarc/rep-hpai_industrialisationrisks.pdf.
40. Read A (1994). "Evolution of virulence." *Trends in Microbiology* 2: 73–76.
41. Atkins K et al. (2010). *Livestock Landscapes and the Evolution of Virulence in Influenza*; Alizon S, A Hurford, N Mideo, and M van Baalen (2009). "Virulence evolution and the trade-off hypothesis: History, current state of affairs and the future." *Journal of Evolutionary Biology* 22: 245–59.
42. Atkins K et al. (2010), *Livestock Landscapes and the Evolution of Virulence in Influenza.*
43. Atkins K et al. (2010). *Livestock Landscapes and the Evolution of Virulence in Influenza*; Van Baalen M and MW Sabelis (1995). "The dynamics of multiple infection and the evolution of virulence." *American Naturalist* 146: 881–910.
44. Lipsitch M and MA Nowak (1995). "The evolution of virulence in sexually transmitted HIV/AIDS." *Journal of Theoretical Biology* 174: 427–440.
45. Shim E and AP Galvani (2009). "Evolutionary repercussions of avian culling on host resistance and influenza virulence." *PLoS ONE* 4(5): e5503.
46. Shim E and AP Galvani (2009). "Evolutionary repercussions of avian culling on host resistance and influenza virulence." Tiensin TP, Chaitaweesub, T Songserm, A Chaisingh, W Hoonsuwan, C Buranathai,

T Parakamawongsa, S Premashthira, A Amonsin, M Gilbert, M Nielen, and A Stegeman (2005). "Highly pathogenic avian influenza H5N1, Thailand, 2004." *Emerging Infectious Diseases* 11: 1664–72; Tiensin TP, M Nielen, H Vernooij, T Songserm, W Kalpravidh, S Chotiprasatintara, A Chaisingh, S Wongkasemjit, K Chanachai, W Thanapongtham, T Srisuvan, and A Stegeman (2007). "Transmission of the highly pathogenic avian influenza Virus H5N1 within flocks during the 2004 epidemic in Thailand." *Journal of Infectious Diseases* 196: 1679–84.

47. As would be the case for the 2015 outbreak of H5N2 in the United States. The disease wasn't apparent until late in the infection, and often just before death.

48. Messinger SM and A Ostling (2009). "The consequences of spatial structure for the evolution of pathogen transmission rate and virulence." *American Naturalist* 174: 441–54.

49. Soares Magalhães RJ, A Ortiz-Pelaez, K Lan Lai Thi, Q Hoang Dinh, J Otte, and DU Pfeiffer (2010). "Associations between attributes of live poultry trade and HPAI H5N1 outbreaks: A descriptive and network analysis study in northern Vietnam." *BMC Veterinary Research* 6/10: doi:10.1186/1746-6148-6-10.

The Dirty Dozen

50. MSNBC.com (2010). "Which came first, the chicken or the egg?" 14 July. Available online at http://www.msnbc.msn.com/id/38238685/ns/technology_and_science-science/.

51. Meyes PZ (2010). "Chickens, eggs, this is no way to report on science." *Pharyngula* blog. Available online at http://scienceblogs.com/pharyngula/2010/07/chickens_eggs_this_is_no_way_t.php.

52. Zelensky AN and JE Gready (2005). "The C-type lectin-like domain superfamily." *FEBS Journal* 272: 6179–217.

53. CNN.com (2010). "Chicken and egg debate unscrambled." 26 May. Available online at http://articles.cnn.com/2006-05-26/tech/chicken.egg_1_chicken-eggs-first-egg-first-chicken?.

54. Bugos GE (1992). "Intellectual property protection in the American chicken-breeding industry." *Business History Review* 66: 127–68; Hy-Line International (2011). "Celebrating 75 years!—the early years." *Hy-Line Innovations* newsletter. Available online at http://www.hyline.com/UserDocs/news/Hyline_newsletter_LO-RES.pdf.

55. Knowles TG, Kestin SC, Haslam SM, Brown SN, Green LE et al. (2008). "Leg Disorders in broiler chickens: Prevalence, risk factors and prevention." *PLoS ONE* 3(2): e1545, doi:10.1371/journal.pone.0001545; Rubin CJ et al. (2010). "Whole-genome resequencing reveals loci under selection during chicken domestication." *Nature* 464(7288): 587–91.

56. Gura S (2007). *Livestock Genetics Companies. Concentration and Proprietary Strategies of an Emerging Power in the Global Food Economy.* League for Pastoral Peoples and Endogenous Livestock Development, Ober-Ramstadt, Germany. Available online at http://www.pastoralpeoples.org/docs/livestock_genetics_en.pdf.

57. Bugos GE (1992). "Intellectual property protection in the American chicken-breeding industry."; Koehler-Rollefson I (2006). "Concentration in the poultry sector." Presentation at "The Future of Animal Genetic Resources: Under Corporate Control or in the Hands of Farmers and Pastoralists?" International workshop, Bonn, Germany, 16 October. Available online at http://www.pastoralpeoples.org/docs/03Koehler-RollefsonLPP.pdf.

58. Associated Press (2009). "Video shows chicks ground up alive at Iowa egg hatchery." 1 September. Available online at http://articles.nydailynews.com/2009-09-01/news/17932028_1_egg-farmers-united-egg-producers-hy-line-north-america.

59. Koehler-Rollefson I (2006). "Concentration in the poultry sector."

60. Arthur JA and GAA Albers (2003). "Industrial perspective on problems and issues associated with poultry breeding." In WM Muir and SE Aggrey (eds), *Poultry Genetics, Breeding and Biotechnology.* CABI Publishing, UK.

61. Fulton JE (2006). "Avian Genetic Stock Preservation: An Industry Perspective." Paper for the Poultry Science Association Ancillary Scientists Symposium on "Conservation of Avian Genetic Resources: Current Opportunities and Challenges," July 31, 2005, Auburn, AL, organized and chaired by Dr. Muquarrab Qureshi. *Poultry Science* 85(2): 227–31.

62. Layton L (2010). "Salmonella-tainted eggs linked to U.S. government's failure to act." *Washington Post.* 11 December. Available online at http://www.washingtonpost.com/wp-dyn/content/article/2010/12/10/AR2010121007485.html.

63. Cornucopia Institute (2010). *Family Farmers Face Unfair Competition from "Organic" Factory Farms.* 26 September. Available online at http://www.cornucopia.org/2010/09/scrambled-eggs-report-spotlights-systemic-abuses-in-organic-egg-production/.

64. Neuman W (2010). "Clean living in the henhouse." *New York Times.* 6 October. Available online at http://www.nytimes.com/2010/10/07/business/07eggfarm.html; Kirby D (2010). *Animal Factory.* St. Martin's Press, New York.

65. Neuman W (2010). "An Iowa egg farmer and a history of salmonella." *New York Times.* 21 September. Available online at: http://www.nytimes.com/2010/09/22/business/22eggs.html.

66. Walsh P and M Hughlett (2012). "Listeria risk spurs Michael Foods to widen egg recall." *Star Tribune*. 2 February. Available online at http://www.startribune.com/local/138562219.html.

67. Wallace RG (2009). "Breeding influenza: The political virology of offshore farming." *Antipode* 41: 916–51.

68. Fulton JE (2006). "Avian Genetic Stock Preservation: An Industry Perspective."

69. Neuman W (2010). "Fried, scrambled, infected." *New York Times*. 25 September. Available online at http://www.nytimes.com/2010/09/26/weekinreview/26eggs.html.

70. Permin A and G Pedersen (2002). "The need for a holistic view on disease problems in free-range chickens." In *Characteristics and Parameters of Family Poultry Production in Africa*. FAO and International Atomic Energy Agency, Vienna. Available online at http://www-naweb.iaea.org/nafa/aph/public/1-the-need-permin.pdf; Riise JC, A Permin, and KN Kryger (2005). "Strategies for developing family poultry production at village level—Experiences from West Africa and Asia." *World's Poultry Science Journal* 61: 15–22.

71. Office of Public Affairs (2014). "Iowa Company and Top Executives Plead Guilty in Connection with Distribution of Adulterated Eggs." Department of Justice. 3 June. Available online at http://www.justice.gov/opa/pr/iowa-company-and-top-executives-plead-guilty-connection-distribution-adulterated-eggs.

72. Cone T (2012). "Federal bill would give nation's hens bigger cages." Associated Press. 2 June. Available online at http://news.yahoo.com/federal-bill-nations-hens-bigger-cages-181439436.html.

73. Associated Press (2014). "U.S. judge dismisses 6-state suit over California egg law." 4 October. Available online at http://www.nytimes.com/2014/10/04/business/us-judge-dismisses-6-state-suit-over-california-egg-law.html.

74. Centers for Disease Control and Prevention (2015). *Safer Food Saves Lives*. 3 November. Available online at http://www.cdc.gov/vitalsigns/foodsafety-2015/index.html.

75. Sun LH (2015). "Big and deadly: Major foodborne outbreaks spike sharply." *Washington Post*. 3 November. Available online at https://www.washingtonpost.com/news/to-your-health/wp/2015/11/03/major-foodborne-outbreaks-in-u-s-have-tripled-in-last-20-years/.

76. Stobbe M (2015). "CDC: More food poisoning outbreaks cross state lines." Associated Press. 3 November. Available online at http://bigstory.ap.org/article/150391c4ebd349cf8aee811aa2258b56/cdc-more-food-poisoning-outbreaks-cross-state-lines.

77. Centers for Disease Control and Prevention (2015). *Safer Food Saves Lives*.

The Red Swan

78. Wallace RG (2013). "The Red Swan: A political economy of Nassim Nicholas Taleb." *Farming Pathogens.* 28 January. Available online at http://farmingpathogens.wordpress.com/2013/01/28/the-red-swan/.

79. Taleb NN (2007). *The Black Swan: The Impact of the Highly Improbable.* Random House, New York; Taleb NN (2012). *Antifragile: Things That Gain from Disorder.* Random House, New York.

80. Fukuyama F (1992/2006). *The End of History and the Last Man.* Free Press, New York.

81. Popper K (1934/2005). *The Logic of Scientific Discovery.* Routledge, London and New York.

82. Lowenstein R (2000). *When Genius Failed: the Rise and Fall of Long-Term Capital Management.* Random House, New York.

83. Mayr E (1982/2003). *The Growth of Biological Thought: Diversity, Evolution and Inheritance.* Harvard University Press, Cambridge, MA.

84. Biggs R. et al. (2009). "Turning back from the brink: Detecting an impending regime shift in time to avert it." *P Natl Acad Sci USA* 106: 826–31.

85. Wallace R and R Fullilove R (1999). "Why simple regression models work so well describing 'risk behaviors' in the USA." *Environment and Planning A* 31(4):719–34.

86. Gould SJ and N Eldredge, Niles (1977). "Punctuated equilibria: The tempo and mode of evolution reconsidered." *Paleobiology* 3(2): 115–51.

87. Eknoyan G (2008). "Adolphe Quetelet (1796–1874): The average man and indices of obesity." *Nephrol. Dial. Transplant.* 23(1); 47–51; Gini C (1936). *On the Measure of Concentration with Special Reference to Income and Statistics.* Colorado College Publication, General Series No. 208, 73–79; Wilkinson R and K Pickett (2009). *The Spirit Level: Why More Equal Societies Almost Always Do Better.* Allen Lane, London.

88. Taleb NN (2007). *The Black Swan: The Impact of the Highly Improbable*; Taleb NN (2008). "The Fourth Quadrant: A map of the limits of statistics." *Edge.* 15 September. Available online at http://www.edge.org/3rd_culture/taleb08/taleb08_index.html.

89. Mandelbrot BB. (1982). *The Fractal Geometry of Nature.* W. H. Freeman, New York.

90. Levin SA (1992). "The problem of pattern and scale in ecology." *Ecology* 73: 1943–67.

91. Berg BA (2004). *Markov Chain Monte Carlo Simulations and Their Statistical Analysis.* World Scientific, New York.

92. Corder GW and DI Foreman (2009). *Nonparametric Statistics for Non-Statisticians.* John Wiley & Sons, Hoboken; Anderson MJ (2001). "A new method for non-parametric multivariate analysis of

variance." *Austral Ecology* 26: 32–46; Takezawa K (2006). *Introduction to Nonparametric Regression.* John Wiley & Sons, Hoboken; McDonald JH (2014). *Handbook of Biological Statistics,* 3rd ed.. Sparky House Publishing, Baltimore.

93. Gelman A, JB Carlin, H Stern, DB Dunson, A Vehtari, DB Rubin (2013). *Bayesian Data Analysis,* 3rd ed. Chapman and Hall/CRC, London.

94. Wallace R and R Fullilove (1999). "Why simple regression models work so well describing 'risk behaviors' in the USA."

95. Ginsberg A (1956/2006). *Howl and Other Poems.* City Lights Books, San Francisco.

96. Leibler JN et al. (2009). "Industrial food animal production and global health risks: Exploring the ecosystems and economics of avian influenza." *EcoHealth* 6(1): 58–70; Wallace RG (2011). "The Scientific American." *Farming Pathogens.* 18 January. Available online at https://farmingpathogens.wordpress.com/2011/01/18/the-scientific -american/.

97. Henwood D (1997). *Wall Street.* Verso, New York.

98. Leff HS and AF Rex (eds). (2003). *Maxwell's Demon 2: Entropy, Classical and Quantum Information, Computing.* Institute of Physics, London.

99. Campbell J (1949; 2008). *The Hero with a Thousand Faces.* New World Library, Novato, CA; Spengler O (1918; 1991). *The Decline of the West.* Oxford University Press, Oxford.

100. Lewis M (2010). *The Big Short: Inside the Doomsday Machine.* W. W. Norton, New York.

101. Sobel R (1988). *Panic on Wall Street: A Classic History of America's Financial Disasters—With a New Exploration of the Crash of 1987.* E. P. Dutton, New York.

102. Gibson W (2003). *Pattern Recognition.* Viking Press, New York.

103. Dewan S (2012). "Popular wrench fights a Chinese rival." *New York Times.* 8 November. Available online at http://www.nytimes.com/2012/11/09/business/popular-wrench-fights-a-chinese-rival.html.

104. Arrighi G (2009). "The winding paths of capital: Interview by David Harvey." *New Left Review* 56: 61–94.

105. Harvey D (2010). *The Enigma of Capital: And the Crises of Capitalism.* Profile Books, London.

106. Leeson N and E Whitley (1996). *Rogue Trader: How I Brought Down Barings Bank and Shook the Financial World.* Little Brown, Boston; Chellel K and P Hurtado (2012). "Ex-Credit Suisse CDO boss says he will fight for deal." Bloomberg Business. 28 September. Available online at http://www.bloomberg.com/news/articles/2012-09-26/ex-credit-suisse-cdo-chief-serageldin-said-to-be-arrested; McLean B and P Elkind (2003). *The Smartest Guys in the Room: The Amazing*

Rise and Scandalous Fall of Enron. Penguin Group, New York; Protess B (2012). "House report says Corzine's risky bets aids MF Global's fall." *New York Times*. 14 November. Available online at http://dealbook.nytimes.com/2012/11/14/congressional-report-blames-corzine-for-mf-globals-collapse/; Treasury Committee (2012). *Fixing LIBOR: Some Preliminary Findings, Second Report of Session 2012–13*. House of Commons, Parliament. Stationery Office Ltd., UK; Keoun B and P Kuntz (2011). "Wall Street aristocracy got $1.2 trillion in secret loans." Bloomberg Business. 21 August. Available online at http://www.bloomberg.com/news/articles/2011-08-21/wall-street-aristocracy-got-1-2-trillion-in-fed-s-secret-loans.

107. Taleb NN (2007). *The Black Swan: The Impact of the Highly Improbable*; Wallace RG (2012). "We need a Structural One Health." *Farming Pathogens*. Available at http://farmingpathogens.wordpress.com/2012/08/03/we-need-a-structural-one-health/.

108. Taleb NN (2007). *The Black Swan: The Impact of the Highly Improbable*.

109. Levine Y (2012). "Malcolm Gladwell unmasked: A look into the life & work of America's most successful propagandist." *S.H.A.M.E.* 31 May. Available online at http://shameproject.com/report/malcolm-gladwell-unmasked-life-work-of-americas-most-successful-propagandist/; Gladwell M (2002). "Blowing up." *The New Yorker*, 22 April. Available online at http://www.newyorker.com/magazine/2002/04/22/blowing-up.

110. Lewontin R and R Levins (2007). *Biology under the Influence: Dialectical Essays on Ecology, Agriculture and Health*. Monthly Review Press, New York.

111. Ibid.

Social Meadicine

112. Cipolla CM (1981). *Fighting the Plague in Seventeenth-Century Italy*. University of Wisconsin Press, Madison.

113. Watts S (1997). *Epidemics and History: Disease, Power and Imperialism*. Bath Press, Bath UK.

PART FIVE
Pale Mushy Wing

1. Wallace RG (2012). "The Dirty Dozen." Published for the first time in this volume.

2. Graham JP, Leibler JH, Price L B, Otte JM, Pfeiffer DU, Tiensin T, and Silbergeld EK (2008). "The animal–human interface and infectious disease in industrial food animal production: Rethinking biosecurity and biocontainment." *Public Health Reports* 123: 282–99.

Whose **Food Footprint?**

3. Solomon S et al. (eds) (2007). *Contribution of Working Group I to the Fourth Assessment Report of the Intergovernmental Panel on Climate Change, 2007.* Cambridge University Press, Cambridge and New York. Available online at http://www.ipcc.ch/publications_and_data/ar4/wg1/en/contents.html; Field CB et al. (eds) (2011). IPCC Workshop on Impacts of Ocean Acidification on Marine Biology and Ecosystems. Okinawa, Japan, 17–19 January 2011. IPCC Working Group II Technical Support Unit, Carnegie Institution, Stanford, CA, and the IPCC Working Group I Technical Support Unit, University of Bern, Switzerland. Available online at http://www.ipcc.ch/pdf/supporting-material/IPCC_IAOMBE_WorkshopReport_Japan.pdf; Hansen J (2009). *Storms of My Grandchildren: The Truth About the Coming Climate Catastrophe and Our Last Chance to Save Humanity.* Bloomsbury, New York; Foster JB, B Clark, and R York (2010). *The Ecological Rift: Capitalism's War on the Earth.* Monthly Review Press, New York.

4. Food and Agriculture Organization (2011). *The State of Food and Agriculture, 2010–2011.* FAO Economic and Social Development Department, Rome, Italy. Available online at http://www.fao.org/docrep/013/i2050e/i2050e00.htm.

5. Kaufman F (2011). "How Goldman Sachs created the food crisis." *Foreign Policy.* 27 April. Available online at http://www.foreignpolicy.com/articles/2011/04/27/how_goldman_sachs_created_the_food_crisis; Suppan S (2011). Excessive Speculation in Agriculture Commodities. Institute for Agriculture and Trade Policy report. Available online at http://www.iatp.org/documents/excessive-speculation-in-agriculture-commodities.

6. Clay J (2011). "Freeze the footprint of food." *Nature* 475: 287–89.

7. Foley JA et al. (2011). "Solutions for a cultivated planet." *Nature* 478: 337–42; Foley JA (2011). "Can we feed the world and sustain the planet?" *Scientific American* 305(5): 60–65; Holmes G (2011). "Conservation's friends in high places: Neoliberalism, networks, and the transnational conservation elite." *Global Environmental Politics* 11: 1–21.

8. Clay J (2010). "How big brands can help save biodiversity." TED Talks. 16 August. Available online at http://www.youtube.com/watch?v=jcp5vvxtEaU.

9. Food and Agriculture Organization (2011). *The State of Food and Agriculture, 2010–2011.* FAO Economic and Social Development Department, Rome, Italy. Available online at http://www.fao.org/docrep/013/i2050e/i2050e00.htm; Baird V (2011). "Why population

hysteria is more damaging than it seems." *The Guardian*. 24 October. Available online at http://www.guardian.co.uk/environment/2011/oct/24/population-hysteria-damaging?newsfeed=true.

10. Clay J (2010). "How big brands can help save biodiversity."

11. Ibid.

12. World Rainforest Movement (2010). "The 'greening' of a shady business—Roundtable for Sustainable Palm Oil." *GRAIN*. October 2010. Available online at http://www.grain.org/article/entries/4046-the-greening-of-a-shady-business-roundtable-for-sustainable-palm-oil#_ref.

13. Clay J (2010). "How big brands can help save biodiversity."

14. Pason Center for International Development and Technology Transfer (2011). *Oversight of Public and Private Initiatives to Eliminate the Worst Forms of Child Labor in the Cocoa Sector in Côte d'Ivoire and Ghana*. Tulane University. Available online at http://www.childlabor-payson.org/Tulane%20Final%20Report.pdf; Burke L (2012). "Ivory Coast's child labor behind chocolate." *Global Post*. Available online at http://www.globalpost.com/dispatch/news/regions/africa/120116/ivory-coast-child-labor-chocolate-cocoa-industry.

15. Foster JB, B Clark, and R York (2010). *The Ecological Rift: Capitalism's War on the Earth*; Jevons WS (1865). *The Coal Question: An Inquiry Concerning the Progress of the Nation, and the Probable Exhaustion of Our Coal Mines*. Macmillan, London.

16. Giampietro M (1994). "Sustainability and technological development in agriculture: A critical appraisal of genetic engineering." *BioScience* 44(10): 677–89.

17. Haas R, M Canavari, B Slee, T Chen, and B Anurugsa (2010). "Organic and quality food marketing in Asia and Europe: A double-sided perspective on marketing of quality food products." In R Haas, M Canavari, B Slee, T Chen, and B Anurugsa (eds). *Looking East, Looking West: Organic and Quality Food Marketing in Asia and Europe*. Wageningen Academic Publishers, The Netherlands; Smith MD et al. (2010). "Sustainability and global seafood." *Science* 327: 784–86.

18. Bergmann LR (2012). "Beyond imagining local causes/solutions to a global problem: Mapping carbon footprints of global capitalism." Conference presentation, Association of American Geographers Annual Meeting, New York, 25 February 2012. Abstract available online at http://meridian.aag.org/callforpapers/program/AbstractDetail.cfm?AbstractID=43259.

19. Mansfield B, DK Munroe, and K McSweeny (2010). "Does economic growth cause environmental recovery? Geographical explanations of forest regrowth." *Geography Compass* 4: 416–27.

20. Moore JW (2012). "Cheap food and bad money: Food, frontiers, and

financialization in the rise and demise of neoliberalism." *Review: A Journal of the Fernand Braudel Center* 33(2–3): 225-261.

21. Clay J (2011). "Freeze the footprint of food."

22. Ibid.

23. Bryceson DF (2010). "Sub-Saharan Africa's vanishing peasantries and the specter of a global food crisis." In F Magdoff and B Tokar (eds). *Agriculture and Food in Crisis: Conflict, Resistance and Renewal.* Monthly Review Press, New York.

24. Allina–Pisano J (2008). *The Post–Soviet Potemkin Village: Politics and Property Rights in the Black Earth.* Cambridge University Press, New York; Wallace RG, L Bergmann, L Hogerwerf, and M Gilbert (2010). "Are influenzas in southern China byproducts of the region's globalising historical present?" In S Craddock, T Giles–Vernick, and J Gunn (eds), *Influenza and Public Health: Learning from Past Pandemics.* EarthScan Press, London.

25. Mortimore M, S Anderson, L Cotula, J Davies, K Faccer, C Hesse, J Morton, W Nyangena, J Skinner, and C Wolfangel (2009). *Dryland Opportunities: A New Paradigm for People, Ecosystems and Development.* IUCN, Gland, Switzerland; IIED, London, and UNDP/DDC, Nairobi, Kenya; Glew L, MD Hudson, and PE Osborne (2010). *Evaluating the Effectiveness of Community Conservation in Northern Kenya.* A report to the Nature Conservancy. University of Southampton. Available online at https://www.iucn.org/knowledge/focus/previous_focus_topics/saving_our_drylands/publications/?uPubsID=3920.

26. Kinzig AP, Perrings C, Chapin III FS, Polasky S. Smith VK, Tilman D, and BL Turner II (2011). "Paying for ecosystem services—Promise and peril." *Science* 334: 603–4; Tanuro D (2010). *L'Impossible Capitalisme Vert.* La Découverte, Paris; Castree N (2008). "Neoliberalising nature: The logics of deregulation and reregulation." *Environment and Planning A* 40: 131–52.

27. Reinhardt N and P Barlett (1989). "The persistence of family farms in United States agriculture." *Sociologia Ruralis* 29: 203–25.

28. Foster JB, B Clark, and R York (2010). *The Ecological Rift: Capitalism's War on the Earth*; Weiss T (2007). *The Global Food Economy: The Battle for the Future of Farming.* Zed Books, London.

29. Mészáros I (2010). *Social Structure and Forms of Consciousness. vol. 1: The Social Determination of Method.* Monthly Review Press, New York.

30. Borras Jr SM and JC Franco (2012). "Global land grabbing and trajectories of agrarian change: A preliminary analysis." *Journal of Agrarian Change* 12(1): 34–59.

31. Holmes G (2011). "Conservation's friends in high places: Neoliberalism, networks, and the transnational conservation elite."

32. Singer P (2005). "Who pays for bird flu?" Available online at http://www.project-1151 syndicate.org/commentary/singer5; Wallace RG (2009). "Breeding influenza: The political virology of offshore farming." *Antipode* 41: 916–51.

33. Brenner R (2009). *What Is Good for Goldman Sachs Is Good for America. The Origins of the Present Crisis.* Center for Social Theory and Comparative History, UCLA. Available online at http://escholarship.org/uc/item/0sg0782h.

34. Foster JB, B Clark, and R York (2010). *The Ecological Rift: Capitalism's War on the Earth*; Lauderdale JM (1804). *An Inquiry into the Nature and Origin of Public Wealth and into the Means and Causes of Its Increase.* Arch. Constable and Co., Edinburgh.

35. Li TM (2009). "Exit from agriculture: A step forward or a step backward for the rural poor?" *Journal of Peasant Studies.* 365: 629–36; Harvey D (2010). *The Enigma of Capital and the Crises of Capitalism.* Oxford University Press, New York.

36. Henshaw C (2010). "Private sector interest grows in African farming." *Wall Street Journal.* 28 October. Available online at http://www.wsj.com/articles/SB10001424052702303467004575574152965709226.

37. Oakland Institute (2011). *Special Investigation: Understanding Land Investment Deals in Africa.* Available online at http://media.oaklandinstitute.org/special-investigation-understanding-land-investment-deals-africa.

38. Vidal J and C Provost (2011). "US universities in Africa 'land grab.'" *The Guardian.* 8 June. Available online at http://www.guardian.co.uk/world/2011/jun/08/us- universities- africa- land- grab.

39. Henshaw C (2010). "Private sector interest grows in African farming."

40. Oakland Institute (2011). *Land Deal Brief: AgriSol Energy and Pharos Global Agriculture Fund's Land Deal in Tanzania.* Available online at http://media.oaklandinstitute.org/land-deal-brief-agrisol-energy-and-pharos-global-agriculture-fund%E2%80%99s-land-deal-tanzania.

41. Vidal J and C Provost (2011). "US universities in Africa 'land grab.'"

42. Ibid.

43. Behnke R and C Kerven (2011). *Replacing Pastoralism with Irrigated Agriculture in the Awash Valley, North-Eastern Ethiopia: Counting the Costs.* Paper presented at the International Conference on Future of Pastoralism, 21–23 March 2011. Organized by the Future Agricultures Consortium at the Institute of Development Studies, University of Sussex and the Feinstein International Center, Tufts University.

44. Oakland Institute (2011). *Land Deal Brief: Nile Trading and Development, Inc. in South Sudan.* Available online at http://www.oaklandinstitute.org/land-deal-brief-nile-trading-and-development-inc-south-sudan.

45. Vidal J (2010). "Why is the Gates foundation investing in GM giant Monsanto?" *The Guardian*. Poverty Matters blog. 29 September. Available online at http://www.guardian.co.uk/global- development/ poverty- matters/2010/sep/29/gates- foundation- gm- monsanto.

46. Anson A (2011). "The 'bitter fruit' of a new agrarian model: Large-scale land deals and local livelihoods in Rwanda." Paper presented at the International Conference on Global Land Grabbing, 6-8 April 2011, Institute of Development Studies, University of Sussex.

47. Oakland Institute (2011). *Special Investigation: Understanding Land Investment Deals in Africa*. Available online at http://media. oaklandinstitute.org/special-investigation-understanding-land -investment-deals-africa.

48. Arrighi G (1966). "The political economy of Rhodesia." *New Left Review* 1/39: 35-65.

49. Arrighi G (2009). "The winding paths of capital." *New Left Review* 56: 61-94.

50. Amisi B, P Bond, N Cele, and T Ngwane (2009). "Xenophobia and Civil Society: Durban's Structured Social Divisions." *Politikon* 38: 59-83; Baird IG (2011). "Turning land into capital, turning people into labour: Primitive accumulation and the arrival of large-scale economic land concessions in the Lao People's Democratic Republic." *New Proposals: Journal of Marxism and Interdisciplinary Inquiry* 5: 10-26.

51. Bryceson DF (2010). "Sub-Saharan Africa's vanishing peasantries and the specter of a global food crisis."

52. Boyce JK (2007). "Is inequality bad for the environment?" PERI Working Paper 135. University of Massachusetts, Amherst. Available online at http://scholarworks.umass.edu/peri_workingpapers/121/.

53. Wallace RG (2011). "Egypt's food pyramid." *Farming Pathogens*. 16 February. Available online at http://farmingpathogens.wordpress. com/2011/02/16/egypts-food-pyramids/.

54. Wallace RG (2009). "Breeding influenza: The political virology of off-shore farming."

55. Davis DK (2006). "Neoliberalism, environmentalism, and agricultural restructuring in Morocco." *The Geographical Journal* 172: 88-105.

56. Hardin G (1968). "The tragedy of the commons." *Science* 162: 1243-48.

57. Ostrom E (1990). *Governing the Commons: The Evolution of Institutions for Collective Action*. Cambridge University Press, Cambridge; McCarthy J (2009). "Commons." In N Castree, D Demeritt, D Liverman, and B Rhoads (eds), *A Companion to Environmental Geography*. Wiley-Blackwell, West Sussex, UK.

58. Tierney J (2009). "The non-tragedy of the commons." *New York*

Times. 15 October. Available online at http://tierneylab.blogs.nytimes. com/2009/10/15/the-non-tragedy-of-the-commons/; Baaker K (2007). "The Commons versus the Commodity: Alter-globalization, anti-privatization and the human right to water in the global South." *Antipode* 39: 430–55.

59. Monsivais P, A Aggarwal, and A Drewnowski (2011). "Following federal guidelines to increase nutrient consumption may lead to higher food costs for consumers." *Health Affairs* 30(8): doi: 10.1377/hlthaff.2010.1273; Guthman J (2011). *Weighing In: Obesity, Food Justice, and the Limits of Capitalism.* University of California Press, Berkeley.

60. Leibler JN et al. (2009). "Industrial food animal production and global health risks: Exploring the ecosystems and economics of avian influenza." *EcoHealth* 6(1): 58–70.

61. Philpott T (2011). "Monsanto (still) denies superinsect problem despite evidence." *Mother Jones.* 8 December. Available online at http://motherjones.com/tom-philpott/2011/12/superinsects-monsanto-corn-epa.

62. Chee-Sanford JC et al. (2009). "Fate and transport of antibiotic residues and antibiotic resistance genes following land application of manure waste." *Journal of Environmental Quality* 38(3): 1086–1108. Available online at http://agdb.nal.usda.gov/bitstream/10113/29182/1/IND44197785.pdf; Gadd JB, LA Tremblay, and GL Northcott (2010). "Steroid estrogens, conjugated estrogens and estrogenic activity in farm dairy shed effluents." *Environmental Pollution* 158(3): 730–36.

63. Xua J, L Wub, and AC Chang (2009). "Degradation and adsorption of selected pharmaceuticals and personal care products (PPCPs) in agricultural soils." *Chemosphere* 77(10): 1299–1305.

64. Monath TP (2011). "Classical live viral vaccines." In PR Dormitzer et al. (eds). *Replicating Vaccines.* Birkhäuser Advances in Infectious Diseases, Part 1, 47–69. Springer, Basel. doi: 10.1007/978-3-0346-0277-8_3.

65. Kuchenmüller T, S Hird, C Stein, P Kramarz, A Nanda, and AH Havelaar (2009). "Estimating the global burden of foodborne diseases—a collaborative effort." *Euro Surveill.* 14(18). Available online at http://www.eurosurveillance.org/ViewArticle.aspx?ArticleId=19195.

66. Vogel G (2011). "Egyptian fenugreek seeds blamed for deadly E. coli outbreak; European authorities issue recall." *ScienceInsider.* 5 July. Available online at http://news.sciencemag.org/scienceinsider/2011/07/egyptian-fenugreek-seeds-blamed.html.

67. Siembieda JL, RA Kock, TA McCracken, and SH Newman (2011). "The role of wildlife in transboundary animal diseases." *Animal Health Research Reviews* 12 : 95–111.

68. Singer P (2005). "Who pays for bird flu?"; Wallace RG (2009).

"Breeding influenza: The political virology of offshore farming.";
Wallace RG (2010). "Virus dumping." *Farming Pathogens.* 11 November.
Available online at http://farmingpathogens.wordpress.com/2010/11/11/
virus–dumping/.

69. Clay J (2010). *"How big brands can help save biodiversity.";* Bello W
and M Baviera (2010). "Food wars." In F Magdoff and B Toker (eds),
Agriculture and Food in Crisis: Conflict, Resistance, and Renewal.
Monthly Review Press, New York.

70. Weiss T (2007). *The Global Food Economy: The Battle for the Future
of Farming;* Perfecto I and J Vandermeer (2010). "The agroecological
matrix as alternative to the land–sparing/agriculture intensification
model." *Proceedings of the National Academy of Sciences* 107(13): 5786–
91; Holt-Giménez E, R Patel, and A Shattuck (2009). *Food Rebellions!
Crisis and the Hunger for Justice.* Food First Books, Oakland, CA.

71. Badgley C, J Moghtader, E Quintero, E Zakem, MJ Chappell, K Aviles-
Vazquez, A Samulon, and I Perfecto (2007). "Organic agriculture and
the global food supply." *Renewable Agriculture and Food Systems* 22(2):
86–108; Pretty J, C Toulmin, and S Williams (2011). "Sustainable intensification in Africa." *International Journal of Agricultural Sustainability*
9(1): 5–24.

72. Pretty J (2009). "Can ecological agriculture feed nine billion people?"
Monthly Review 61(6): 46–58. Available online at http://monthlyreview.
org/2009/11/01/can-ecological-agriculture-feed-nine-billion-people.

73. Malkin E (2010). "Zapotec Indians grow trees, and jobs, in Oaxaca,
Mexico." *New York Times.* 22 November. Available online at http://
www.nytimes.com/2010/11/23/world/americas/23mexico.html.

74. Bennegouch N and M Hassane (2010). "MOORIBEN: the experience of a system of integrated services for Nigerien farmers." *Farming
Dynamics.* SOS Faim newsletter, September 2010. Available online
at   http://www.sosfaim.be/pdf/publications_en/farming_dynamics/
mooriben–for–nigerien–farmers–farming–dynamics23.pdf.

75. Mortimore M et al. (2009). *Dryland Opportunities: A New Paradigm for
People, Ecosystems and Development;* Kock RA (2010). "The newly proposed Laikipia disease control fence in Kenya." In K Ferguson and J Hanks
(eds). *Fencing Impacts: A Review of the Environmental, Social and Economic
Impacts of Game and Veterinary Fencing in Africa with Particular Reference
to the Great Limpopo and Kavango–Zambezi Transfrontier Conservation
Areas,* 71–75. Pretoria Mammal Research Institute.

76. Scherr SJ and JA McNeely (2008). "Biodiversity conservation and agricultural sustainability: Towards a new paradigm of 'ecoagriculture'
landscapes." *Phil. Trans. R. Soc. B* 363: 477–94.

77. Osbahr H, C Twyman, WN Adger, and DSG Thomas (2010). "Evaluating successful livelihood adaptation to climate variability and change in Southern Africa." *Ecology and Society* 15(2): 27. Available online at http://www.ecologyandsociety.org/vol15/iss2/art27/.

78. Dillon T (2011). *Factoring Culture and Discourse into an Appraisal of the Neoliberal Synthesis of Wildlife Conservation and Rural Development in Sub-Saharan Africa.* Master's thesis, Durham University. Available at Durham E-Theses Online: http://etheses.dur.ac.uk/912/.

79. Morton DC, RS DeFries, YE Shimabukuro, LO Anderson, E Arai, F del Bon Espirito–Santo, R Freitas, R and J Morisette (2006). "Cropland expansion changes deforestation dynamics in the southern Brazilian Amazon." *Proc Natl Acad Sci U S A* 103: 14637–41; Müller R, D Müller, F Schierhorn, G Gerold, and P Pacheco (2011). "Proximate causes of deforestation in the Bolivian lowlands: an analysis of spatial dynamics." *Regional Environmental Change.* doi: 10.1007/s10113–011–0259–0

80. Foster JB, B Clark, and R York (2010). *The Ecological Rift: Capitalism's War on the Earth.*

81. Levins R (2007). "How Cuba is going ecological." In R Lewontin and R Levins. *Biology under the Influence: Dialectical Essays on Ecology, Agriculture, and Health.* Monthly Review Press, New York.

82. Daly HE and J Farley (2011). *Ecological Economics: Principles and Applications.* 2nd ed. Island Press, Washington DC; Coker R, J Rushton, S Mounier–Jack, E Karimuribo, P Lutumba, D Kambarage, DU Pfeiffer, K Stärk, and M Rweyemamu (2011). "Towards a conceptual framework to support one-health research for policy on emerging zoonoses." *Lancet Infect Dis.* 11(4): 326–31.

83. Kenny C (2011). "Got cheap milk? Why ditching your fancy, organic, locavore lifestyle is good for the world's poor." *Foreign Policy.* The Optimist blog. 12 September. Available online at http://www.foreign-policy.com/articles/2011/09/12/got_cheap_milk?page=0,1.

84. Clapp J and DA Fuchs (eds). (2009). *Corporate Power in Global Agrifood Governance.* MIT Press, Cambridge, MA.

85. Lagi M, KZ Bertrand, and Y Bar–Yam (2011). "The food crises and political instability in North Africa and the Middle East." Available online at http://arxiv.org/PS_cache/arxiv/pdf/1108/1108.2455v1.pdf.

86. Kock RA, RG Wallace, and R Alders (2011). "Wildlife, wild food, food security and human society." OIE Global Conference on Wildlife: Animal Health and Biodiversity—Preparing for the Future. Conference presentation. Paris, 24 February 2011.

87. Weiss T (2007). *The Global Food Economy: The Battle for the Future of Farming.*

A Probiotic Ecology

88. Wittgenstein L (1960). *The Blue and Brown Book: Preliminary Studies for the 'Philosophical Investigations'*. Harper–Perennial. New York.

89. Keesing F, Belden LK, Daszak P, Dobson A, Harvell CD, Holt RD, Hudson P, Jolles A, Jones KE, Mitchell CE, Myers SS, Bogich T, and Ostfeld RS (2010). "Impacts of biodiversity on the emergence and transmission of infectious diseases." *Nature* 468: 647–52.

90. Hogerwerf L, R Houben, K Hall, M Gilbert, J Slingenbergh, and RG Wallace (2010). *Agroecological Resilience and Protopandemic Influenza*. Food and Agriculture Organization of the United Nations. Available upon request.

91. Wallace RG (2011). "Two gentlemen of Verona." Published for the first time in this volume.

92. Wallace RG (2009). "Breeding influenza: The political virology of offshore farming." *Antipode* 41: 916–51.

93. Mulder IE et al. (2009). "Environmentally–acquired bacteria influence diversity and natural innate immune responses at gut surfaces." *BMC Biology* 7, doi: 10.1186/1741–7007–7–79.

94. Atkins K, RG Wallace, L Hogerwerf, M Gilbert, J Slingenbergh, J Otte, and AP Galvani (2010). *Livestock Landscapes and the Evolution of Influenza Virulence*. Food and Agriculture Organization of the United Nations. Available upon request; Wallace RG and K Atkins (2011). "Synchronize your barns." Published for the first time in this volume.

95. Food and Agriculture Organization of the United Nations (2011). *Plant Production and Protection Division: Integrated Pest Management*. Available online at http://www.fao.org/agriculture/crops/core–themes/theme/pests/ipm/en/; Silici L (2010). *Conservation Agriculture and Sustainable Crop Intensification in Lesotho*. Integrated Crop Management Vol.10, 2010. Food and Agriculture Organization. Available online at http://www.fao.org/docrep/012/i1650e/i1650e00.pdf.

96. Berthouly C, G Leroy, TN Van, HH Thanh, B Bed'Hom, BT Nguyen, CC Vu, F Monicat, M Tixier–Boichard, E Verrier, JC Maillard, X Rognon (2009). "Genetic analysis of local Vietnamese chickens provides evidence of gene flow from wild to domestic populations." *BMC Genetics*. Jan 8, 2010: 1. Available online at https://www.ncbi.nlm.nih.gov/pmc/articles/PMC2628941/.

Strange Cotton

97. Wallace RG and L Bergmann (2010). "Influenza's historical present." *Farming Pathogens*. 11 June. Available online at https://farmingpathogens.wordpress.com/2010/06/11/influenzas–historical–present/.

98. New Hampshire Geological Survey and the Old Man of the Mountain

Legacy Fund (n.d.). *The Geologic Story of the Old Man of the Mountain.* Available online at http://des.nh.gov/organization/commissioner/gsu/documents/oldmanmtdisplay.pdf.

99. McClain C (2012). "How presidential elections are impacted by a 100 million year old coastline." *Deep Sea News.* 27 June. Available online at http://deepseanews.com/2012/06/how–presidential–elections–are–impacted–by–a–100–million–year–old–coastline/.

100. Johnson W (2013). *River of Dark Dreams: Slavery and Empire in the Cotton Kingdom.* Harvard University Press, Cambridge, MA.

101. Johnson W (2013). *River of Dark Dreams: Slavery and Empire in the Cotton Kingdom.*

102. Charney I (2010). "Spatial fix." In B Warf (ed). *Encyclopedia of Geography.* SAGE Publications, Thousand Oaks, CA.

103. Johnson W (2013). *River of Dark Dreams: Slavery and Empire in the Cotton Kingdom.*

104. Markusen AR (1987). *Regions: The Economics and Politics of Territory.* Rowman & Littlefield, New York.

105. Philpott T (2011). "Some arsenic with that supermarket chicken?" *Mother Jones.* 11 June. Available online at http://www.motherjones.com/tom–philpott/2011/06/arsenic–chicken–fda–roxarsone–pfizer; Thompson JM, R Polkinghorne, M Porter, HM Burrow, RA Hunter, GJ McCrabb, and R Watson (2008). "Effect of repeated implants of oestradiol–17 on beef palatability in Brahman and Braham cross steers finished to different market end points." *Aust. J. Exp. Agr.* 48(11): 1434–41.

106. Johnson W (2013). *River of Dark Dreams: Slavery and Empire in the Cotton Kingdom.*

107. Carlowicz M (2011). "Morganza floodway after five days of flow." *Visible Earth.* NASA. Available online at http://visibleearth.nasa.gov/view.php?id=50659. See farms upper right on the Mississippi River at http://eoimages.gsfc.nasa.gov/images/imagerecords/50000/50659/morganza_ast_2011138_lrg.jpg.

108. Allina-Pisano J (2007). *The Post–Soviet Potemkin Village: Politics and Property Rights in the Black Earth.* Cambridge University Press, Cambridge; Wong E (2008). "Hints of discord on land reform in China." *New York Times.* 15 October. Available online at http://www.nytimes.com/2008/10/16/world/asia/16china.html.

109. Wallace RG (2011). "The Scientific American." *Farming Pathogens.* 18 January. Available online at https://farmingpathogens.wordpress.com/2011/01/18/the–scientific–american/.

110. Johnson W (2013). *River of Dark Dreams: Slavery and Empire in the Cotton Kingdom.*

111. Ibid.; Northup S (1853; 2012). *Twelve Years a Slave.* Penguin Classics, New York.

112. Johnson W (2013). *River of Dark Dreams: Slavery and Empire in the Cotton Kingdom.*

113. Genoways T (2013). "Gagged by Big Ag." *Mother Jones.* July/August. Available online at http://www.motherjones.com/environment/2013/06/ag-gag-laws-mowmar-farms?page=2.

114. Fassler J (2010). "Conventional vs. organic: An Ag Secretary race to watch." *The Atlantic.* 27 October. Available online at http://www.theatlantic.com/health/archive/2010/10/conventional-vs-organic-an-ag-secretary-race-to-watch/65144/.

115. Foster JB, B Clark and R York (2010). *The Ecological Rift: Capitalism's War on the Earth.* Monthly Review Press, New York.

116. Johnson W (2013). *River of Dark Dreams: Slavery and Empire in the Cotton Kingdom.*

117. Ibid.; Wallace RG (2013). "The virus and the virus: David Quammen's 'Spillover.'" *CounterPunch,* Weekend edition June 14–16. Available online at http://www.counterpunch.org/2013/06/14/the-virus-and-the-virus/.

118. Johnson W (2013). *River of Dark Dreams: Slavery and Empire in the Cotton Kingdom.*

119. Tepper R (2013). "Paula Deen racist comments, use of N-word allegedly caught on video." *Huffington Post.* 21 June. Available online at http://www.huffingtonpost.com/2013/06/19/paula-deen-racist-comments-n-word-caught-on-video_n_3467287.html; Twitty MW (2013). "An open letter to Paula Deen." *Afroculinaria.* 25 June. Available online at http://afroculinaria.com/2013/06/25/an-open-letter-to-paula-deen/.

120. Johnson W (2013). *River of Dark Dreams: Slavery and Empire in the Cotton Kingdom.*

121. Ibid.; Macalister T (2010). "Revealed: Goldman Sachs 'made fortune betting against clients.'" *The Guardian.* 24 April. Available online at http://www.theguardian.com/world/2010/apr/25/goldman-sachs-senator-carl-levin.

122. Smithfield Foods (2013). "Shuanghui International and Smithfield Foods Agree to Strategic Combination, Creating a Leading Global Pork Enterprise." 29 May. Available online at http://investors.smithfieldfoods.com/releasedetail.cfm?ReleaseID=767743.

123. Food and Water Watch (2013). "Coalition of Farm, Consumer and Rural Organizations Urge Rejection of Smithfield Takeover." 9 June. Available online at http://www.foodandwaterwatch.org/pressreleases/coalition-of-farm-consumer-and-rural-organizations-urge-rejection-of-smithfield-takeover/.

124. Prashad V (2013). "The case of Smithfield pork." *CounterPunch.* 3

June. Available online at http://www.counterpunch.org/2013/06/03/the–case–of–smithfield–pork/.

125. Bottemiller H (2013). "Big pork deal comes amid friction over livestock drug." *Food & Environment Reporting Network*. 31 May. Available online at http://thefern.org/2013/05/big– pork– deal– comes– amid– friction– over– livestock– drug/.

126. Philpott T (2013). "Is the US about to become one big factory farm for China?" *Mother Jones*. 29 May. Available online at http://www.motherjones.com/tom–philpott/2013/05/chinas-biggest-meat-c-swallows–us–pork–giant–smithfield.

127. Sharma S (2013). "'Two converging rivers': Understanding Shuanghui's acquisition of Smithfield." *Think Forward* blog. Institute for Agriculture and Trade Policy. Available online at http://www.iatp.org/blog/201306/%E2%80%9Ctwo–converging–rivers%E2%80%9D–understanding–shuanghui%E2%80%99s–acquisition–of–smithfield.

128. Wallace RG (2012). "Food and pharm WikiLeaks." *Jacobin*. 5 September. Available online at https://www.jacobinmag.com/2012/09/food–and–pharm–wikileaks/.

129. Schaeffer A (2012). "Cargill's not so secret expansion plans in Indonesia." *The Contributor*. 10 August. Available online at http://thecontributor.com/environment/cargill%E2%80%99s–not–so–secret–expansion–plans–indonesia.

130. Wallace RG (2009). "The hog industry strikes back." *Farming Pathogens*. 1 June. Available online at https://farmingpathogens.wordpress.com/2009/06/01/the-hog-industry-strikes-back/.

131. Richardson J (2012). "How the US sold Africa to multinationals like Monsanto, Cargill, DuPont, PepsiCo and others." *AlterNet*. 23 May. Available online at http://www.alternet.org/story/155559/how_the_us_sold_africa_to_multinationals_like_monsanto,_cargill,_dupont,_pepsico_and_others.

132. Burke L (2012). "Ivory Coast's child labor behind chocolate." *Global Post*. 28 January. Available online at http://www.globalpost.com/dispatch/news/regions/africa/120116/ivory–coast–child–labor–chocolate–cocoa–industry.

133. Harvey D (2004). "The 'new' imperialism: accumulation by dispossession." *Socialist Register* 40: 63–87.

134. Johnson W (2013). *River of Dark Dreams: Slavery and Empire in the Cotton Kingdom;* Williams E (1944). *Capitalism and Slavery*. University of North Carolina Press, Chapel Hill.

135. Johnson W (2013). *River of Dark Dreams: Slavery and Empire in the Cotton Kingdom;* Vidal J (2010). "Why is the Gates foundation investing in GM giant Monsanto?" *The Guardian*. 29 September.

Available online at http://www.theguardian.com/global–development/poverty–matters/2010/sep/29/gates–foundation–gm–monsanto.

136. Johnson W (2013). *River of Dark Dreams: Slavery and Empire in the Cotton Kingdom.*
137. Wallace RG (2012). "Food and pharm WikiLeaks."
138. Markusen AR (1987); Lenin VI (1915; 1964). "Capitalism and agriculture in the United States of America." In *Collected Works.* Progress Publishers, Moscow.
139. Gisolfi MR (2006). "From crop lien to contract farming: The roots of agribusiness in the American South, 1929–1939." *Agricultural History* 80(2): 167–89.
140. Riffel BE (2014). "Poultry industry." In *The Encyclopedia of Arkansas History & Culture.* Available online at http://www.encyclopediaofarkansas.net/encyclopedia/entry–detail.aspx?entryID=2102.
141. Gisolfi MR (2006). "From crop lien to contract farming: The roots of agribusiness in the American South, 1929–1939."
142. Wallace RG (2010). "Virus dumping." *Farming Pathogens.* 11 November. Available online at https://farmingpathogens.wordpress.com/2010/11/11/virus–dumping/.
143. Johnston K (2013). "The messy link between slave owners and modern management." *Forbes.* 16 January. Available online at http://www.forbes.com/sites/hbsworkingknowledge/2013/01/16/the-messy-link-between-slave-owners-and-modern-management/;   Rosenthal   C (2013). "Plantations practiced modern management." *Harvard Business Review.* September 2013. Available online at https://hbr.org/2013/09/plantations-practiced-modern-management.
144. Johnson W (2013). *River of Dark Dreams: Slavery and Empire in the Cotton Kingdom*
145. Johnston K (2013). "The messy link between slave owners and modern management."
146. Ibid.

Cave/Man

147. Bhullar K et al. (2012). "Antibiotic resistance is prevalent in an isolated cave microbiome." *PLoS ONE* 7(4): e34953. doi: 10.1371/journal.pone.0034953.
148. Wallace RG (2010). "Does influenza evolve in multiple tenses?" *Farming Pathogens.* 20 June. Available online at https://farmingpathogens.wordpress.com/2010/06/20/does–influenza–evolve–in–multiple–tenses/; Wallace RG (2010). "We can think ourselves into a plague." *Farming Pathogens.* 25 October. Available online at https://farmingpathogens.wordpress.com/2010/10/25/we–can–think–ourselves–into–a–plague/.

149. Wallace RG and L Bergmann (2010). "Influenza's historical present." *Farming Pathogens*. 11 June. Available online at https://farmingpathogens.wordpress.com/2010/06/11/influenzas-historical-present/.

150. Voice of America (2012). "Naturally drug-resistant cave bacteria possible key to new antibiotics." 13 April. Available online at http://www.voanews.com/content/naturally-drug-resistant-cave-bacteria-possible-key-to-new-antibiotics-147430005/180318.html.

PART SIX
The Virus and the Virus

1. Quammen D (2012). *Spillover: Animal Infections and the Next Human Pandemic*. W. W. Norton, New York.

2. Rainforest Action Network (2010). *Cargill's Problems with Palm Oil*. May. Available online at http://d3n8a8pro7vhmx.cloudfront.net/rainforestactionnetwork/legacy_url/530/cargills_problems_with_palm_oil_low.pdf?1402698255.

3. Quammen D (2012). *Spillover: Animal Infections and the Next Human Pandemic*.

4. Wallace RG, HM HoDac, R Lathrop, and WM Fitch (2007). "A statistical phylogeography of influenza A H5N1." *Proceedings of the National Academy of Sciences* 104: 4473–78.

5. Wallace RG (2009). "Breeding influenza: The political virology of offshore farming." *Antipode* 41: 916–51.

6. Quammen D (2012). *Spillover: Animal Infections and the Next Human Pandemic*.

7. Wallace RG (2010). "King Leopold's pandemic." *Farming Pathogens*. 2 March. Available online at https://farmingpathogens.wordpress.com/2010/03/02/king-leopolds-pandemic/.

8. Rodney W (1972; 1982). *How Europe Underdeveloped Africa*. Howard University Press, Washington, DC.

9. Kalipeni E, S Craddock, JR Oppong, J Ghosh (eds) (2003). *HIV and AIDS in Africa: Beyond Epidemiology*. Wiley-Blackwell, Hoboken.

10. Wolfe ND, P Daszak, AM Kilpatrick, DS Burke (2005). "Bushmeat hunting, deforestation, and prediction of zoonoses emergence." *Emerg Infect Dis.* 11(12): 1822–27; Courgnaud V et al. (2004). "Simian T-Cell Leukemia Virus (STLV) Infection in Wild Primate Populations in Cameroon: Evidence for Dual STLV Type 1 and Type 3 Infection in Agile Mangabeys (*Cercocebus agilis*)." *J Virol.* 78(9): 4700–709.

11. Timberg C and D Halperin (2012). *Tinderbox: How the West Sparked the AIDS Epidemic and How the World Can Finally Overcome It*. Penguin Press, New York.

12. Gould P (1993). *The Slow Plague: A Geography of the AIDS Pandemic.* Blackwell Publishers, Cambridge, MA.

13. Quammen D (2012). *Spillover: Animal Infections and the Next Human Pandemic.*

14. Wallace RG (2012). "We need a Structural One Health." *Farming Pathogens.* 12 August. Available online at http://farmingpathogens. wordpress.com/2012/08/03/we-need-a-structural-one-health/.

15. Quammen D (2014). "Ebola virus: A grim, African reality." *New York Times.* 9 April. Available online at http://www.nytimes.com/2014/04/10/ opinion/ebola-virus-a-grim-african-reality.html; Wallace RG (2014). "Neoliberal Ebola?" *Farming Pathogens.* 23 April. Available online at https://farmingpathogens.wordpress.com/2014/04/23/neoliberal-ebola/.

Coffee Filter

16. Kapur R and MD Smith (2009). "Treatment of cardiovascular collapse from caffeine overdose with lidocaine, phenylephrine, and hemodialysis." *American Journal of Emergency Medicine* 27: 253.e3-253.e6.

17. Burns D (2001). *Growth in the Global Coffee Industry.* First International. International Coffee Organization World Coffee Conference. 18 May. Available online at http://dev.ico.org/event_pdfs/burns.pdf; Ponte S (2002). "The 'Latte Revolution'? Regulation, markets and consumption in the global coffee chain." *World Development* 30: 1099–1122.

18. Frischknecht PM, J Ulmer-Dukek, and TW Baumann (1986). "Purine alkaloid formation in buds and developing leaflets of *Coffea arabica*: Expression of an optimal defence strategy?" *Phytochemistry* 25: 613–16; Nathanson JA (1984). "Caffeine and related methylxanthines: possible naturally occurring pesticides." *Science* 226: 184–87.

19. Weinberg BA and BK Bealer (2002). *The World of Caffeine: The Science and Culture of the World's Most Popular Drug.* Routledge, New York; USDA (2014). *Coffee: World Markets and Trade.* Office of Global Analysis, Foreign Agricultural Service. Available online at http://apps. fas.usda.gov/psdonline/circulars/coffee.pdf; Goldschein E (2011). "11 incredible facts about the global coffee industry." *Business Insider.* 14 November. Available online at http://www.businessinsider.com/facts-about-the-coffee-industry-2011-11?op=1; Wild A (2004). *Coffee: A Dark History.* W. W. Norton, New York.

20. Wintgens JN (ed) (2012). *Coffee: Growing, Processing, Sustainable Production* (Second ed.). Wiley-VCH VerlangGmbH & Co. KGaA.

21. Marcone MF (2004). "Composition and properties of Indonesian palm civet coffee (Kopi Luwak) and Ethiopian civet coffee." *Food Research International* 37: 901–12.

22. Vandermeer J, I Perfecto, and S Philpott (2010). "Ecological complexity

and pest control in organic coffee production: Uncovering an autonomous ecosystem service." *BioScience* 60: 527–37.

23. Easwaramoorthy S and S Jayaraj (1978). "Effectiveness of the white halo fungus, *Cephalosporium lecanii*, against field populations of coffee green bug, *Coccus viridis.*" *Journal of Invertebrate Pathology* 32: 88–96.

24. Perfecto I, JH Vandermeer, GL Bautista, GI Nunez, R Greenberg, P Bichier, and S Langridge (2004). "Greater predation in shaded coffee farms: The role of resident neotropical birds." *Ecology* 85(10): 2677–81.

25. Williams-Guillen K, I Perfecto, and J Vandermeer (2008). "Bats limit insects in a neotropical agroforestry system." *Science* 320: 70.

26. Williams-Guillen K and I Perfecto (2011). "Ensemble composition and activity levels of insectivorous bats in response to management intensification in coffee agroforestry systems." *PLoS ONE* 6(1): e16502. doi: 10.1371/journal.pone.0016502.

27. Williams-Guillen K (2010). "Investigating trophic interactions with molecular methods: Insectivory by bats in the coffee agroecosystem." Presentation at 95th ESA Annual Meeting, 1–6 August 2010.

28. Perfecto I and J Vandermeer (2010). "The agroecological matrix as alternative to the land-sparing/agriculture intensification model." *Proceedings of the National Academy of Sciences USA* 107: 5786–91.

29. Morton DC, RS DeFries, YE Shimabukuro, LO Anderson, E Arai, F del Bon Espirito-Santo, R Freitas, and J Morisette (2006). "Cropland expansion changes deforestation dynamics in the southern Brazilian Amazon." *Proceedings of the National Academy of Sciences USA* 103(39): 14637–41; Etter A, C McAlpine, K Wilson, S Phinn, and H Possingham (2006). "Regional patterns of agricultural land use and deforestation in Colombia." *Agriculture, Ecosystems and Environment* 114: 369–86.

30. Craves J (2006). "The problems with sun coffee." *Coffee and Conservation.* 5 February. Available online at http://www.coffeehabitat.com/2006/02/the_problems_wi/.

31. Page GR (2008). *Trusting Photosynthesis: Thoughts on the Future of Global Food Production.* Chautuaqua Institute, August 2008. Available online at http://www.cargill.com/news/speeches-presentations/trusting-photosynthesis/index.jsp.

Homeland

32. Van Boeckel TP, MJ Tildesley, C Linard, J Halloy, MJ Keeling, and M Gilbert. "The Nosoi commute: A spatial perspective on the rise of BSL-4 laboratories in cities." Available online at http://arxiv.org/abs/1312.3283.

33. Rhodes K (2007). *High-Containment Biosafety Laboratories: Preliminary Observations on the Oversight of the Proliferation of BSL-3 and BSL-4*

Laboratories in the United States. Testimony Before the Subcommittee on Oversight and Investigations, Committee on Energy and Commerce, House of Representatives. U.S. Government Accountability Office. GAO-08-108T. Available online at http://www.gao.gov/new.items/d08108t.pdf; Wallace RG (2011). "A Dangerous Method." *Farming Pathogens.* 28 December. Available online at https://farmingpathogens.wordpress.com/2011/12/28/a-dangerous-method/.

34. Garrett L (2011). "The bioterrorist next door." *Foreign Policy.* 15 December. Available online at http://foreignpolicy.com/2011/12/15/the-bioterrorist-next-door/#sthash.FbHXLDbC.dpbs.

35. Lewontin R and R Levins (2007). *Biology Under the Influence: Dialectical Essays on Ecology, Agriculture and Health.* Monthly Review Press, New York.

36. O'Hara J (1934/2003). *Appointment in Samarra.* Harcourt Brace, San Diego, CA; Geltzer JA (2010). *US Counter-Terrorism Strategy and al-Qaeda: Signalling and the Terrorist World-View.* Routledge, Oxon, UK.

37. Begley S and J Steenhuysen (2012). "How secure are labs handling world's deadliest pathogens?" Reuters. 15 February. Available online at http://www.reuters.com/article/2012/02/15/us-health-biosecurity-idUSTRE81E0R420120215.

Disease's Circuits of Capital

38. Wallace RG, L Bergmann, R Kock, M Gilbert, L Hogerwerf, R Wallace, and M Holmberg (2015). "The dawn of Structural One Health: A new science tracking disease emergence along circuits of capital." *Social Science & Medicine* 129: 68–77.

39. Zinsstag J (2012). "Convergence of EcoHealth and One Health." *Ecohealth* 9(4): 371–73; Van Helden PD, LS van Helden, and EG Hoal (2013). "One world, one health." *EMBO reports* 14: 497–501. doi: 10.1038/embor.2013.61; Barrett MA and SA Osofsky (2013). "One Health: Interdependence of People, Other Species, and the Planet." In DL Katz, JG Elmore, DMG Wild and SC Lucan (eds). *Jekel's Epidemiology, Biostatistics, Preventive Medicine, and Public Health,* 4th ed. Elsevier/Saunders, Philadelphia.

40. Hueston W, J Appert, T Denny, L King, J Umber, and L Valeri (2013). "Assessing global adoption of One Health approaches." *Ecohealth* 10: 228–33.

41. Schwabe CW (1984). *Veterinary Medicine and Human Health.* Williams & Wilkins, Baltimore; Wilson ME, R Levins and A Spielman (eds). (1994). *Disease in Evolution: Global Changes and Emergence of Infectious Diseases.* Annals of the New York Academy of Sciences, New York; Saunders LZ (2000). "Virchow's contributions to veterinary

medicine: Celebrated then, forgotten now." *Vet Pathol.* 37: 199–207; Morens DM (2003). "Characterizing a 'new' disease: Epizootic and epidemic anthrax, 1769–1780." *Am J Public Health* 93: 886–93.

42. Webb JC, D Mergler, MW Parkes, J Saint-Charles, J Spiegel, D Waltner-Toews, A Yassi, A and RF Woollard (2010). "Tools for thoughtful action: The role of ecosystem approaches to health in enhancing public health." *Can J Public Health* 101: 439–41; Carpenter SR, HA Mooney, J Agard, D Capistrano, RS Defries, S Díaz, T Dietz, AK Duraiappah, A Oteng-Yeboah, HM Pereira, C Perrings, WV Reid, J Sarukhan, RJ Scholes, and A Whyte (2009). "Science for managing ecosystem services: Beyond the Millennium Ecosystem Assessment." *Proc Natl Acad Sci U S A.* 106: 1305–12.

43. Anderson T, I Capua, G Dauphin, R Donis, R Fouchier, E Mumford, M Peiris, D Swayne, and A Thiermann (2010). "FAO-OIE-WHO joint technical consultation on avian influenza at the human-animal interface." *Influenza Other Respi Viruses* 4(S1): 1–29.

44. Kahn LH, TP Monath, BH Bokma, EP Gibbs. and AA Aguirre (2012). "One Health, One Medicine." In AA Aguirre, R Ostfeld, and P Daszak (eds). *New Directions in Conservation Medicine: Applied Cases of Ecological Health.* Oxford University Press, New York.

45. McNeill WH (1977; 2010). *Plagues and Peoples.* Anchor Books, New York.

46. Pearce-Duvet JMC (2006). "The origin of human pathogens: evaluating the role of agriculture and domestic animals in the evolution of human disease." *Biological Reviews of the Cambridge Philosophical Society* 81(3): 369–82; Wolfe ND, CP Dunavan, and J Diamond (2007). "Origins of major human infectious diseases." *Nature* 447: 279–83.

47. Watts S (1997). *Epidemics and History: Disease, Power, and Imperialism.* Yale University Press, New Haven; Colgrove J (2002). "The McKeown Thesis: A historical controversy and its enduring influence." *Am J Public Health.* 92: 725–29.

48. Kock RA, R Alders, and RG Wallace (2012). "Wildlife, wild food, food security and human society." In *Animal Health and Biodiversity— Preparing for the Future: Illustrating Contributions to Public Health,* 71–79. Compendium of the OIE Global Conference on Wildlife 23–25 February 2011, Paris.

49. Ding Y, L Mearns, and P Wadhams (eds). (2013). *Working Group 1 Contribution to the IPCC Fifth Assessment Report (AR5), Climate Change 2013: The Physical Science Basis.* Intergovernmental Panel on Climate Change. Available online at http://www.ipcc.ch/report/ar5/wg1/#.UmcTwRAekVw.

50. McMichael P (2009). "Contradictions in the global development

project: geo-politics, global ecology and the 'development climate'" *Third World Quarterly* 30: 251–66; Foster JB, B Clark, and R York (2010). *The Ecological Rift: Capitalism's War on Earth.* Monthly Review Press, New York.

51. Jones BA, D Grace, R Kock, S Alonso, J Rushton, MY Said, D McKeever, F Mutua, J Young, J McDermott, and DU Pfeiffer (2013). "Zoonosis emergence linked to agricultural intensification and environmental change." *PNAS* 110: 8399–8404.

52. Liverani M, J Waage, T Barnett, DU Pfeiffer, J Rushton, JW Rudge, ME Loevinsohn, I Scoones, RD Smith, BS Cooper, LJ White, S Goh, P Horby, B Wren, O Gundogdu, A Woods, and RJ Coker (2013). "Understanding and managing zoonotic risk in the new livestock industries." *Environ Health Perspect.* 121: 873–877. doi: 10.1289/ehp.1206001.

53. Jones BA et al. (2013). "Zoonosis emergence linked to agricultural intensification and environmental change"; Liverani M et al. (2013). "Understanding and managing zoonotic risk in the new livestock industries."

54. De Haan C, P Gerber, and C Opio (2010). "Structural change in the livestock sector." In H Steinfeld, HA Mooney, F Schneider and LE Neville (eds). *Livestock in a Changing Landscape Drivers, Consequences, and Responses,* vol. 1. Island Press, Washington DC; McMichael P (2012). "The land grab and corporate food regime restructuring." *Journal of Peasant Studies* 39: 681–701.

55. Davis DK (2007). *Resurrecting the Granary of Rome: Environmental History and French Colonial Expansion in North Africa.* Ohio University Press, Athens, Ohio; Wallace RG and RA Kock (2012). "Whose food footprint? Capitalism, agriculture and the environment." *Human Geography* 5(1): 63–83; Sparke M (2014). "Health." In R Lee, N Castree, R Kitchin, V Lawson, A Paasi, S Radcliffe, C Philo, SM Roberts, and C Withers (eds), *The SAGE Handbook of Progress in Human Geography.* Sage, Thousand Oaks, CA.

56. Goldberg TL, SB Paige, and CA Chapman (2012). "The Kibale Ecohealth Project: Exploring connections among human health, animal health and landscape dynamics in Western Uganda." In AA Aguirre, R Ostfeld, and P Daszak (eds). *New Directions in Conservation Medicine: Applied Cases of Ecological Health.* Oxford University Press, New York.

57. Paul M, V Baritaux, S Wongnarkpet, C Poolkhet, W Thanapongtharm, F Roger, P Bonnet, and C Ducrot (2013). "Practices associated with Highly Pathogenic Avian Influenza spread in traditional poultry marketing chains: Social and economic perspectives." *Acta Tropica* 126: 43–53.

58. Giles-Vernick T, S Craddock, and J Gunn (eds). (2010). *Influenza and Public Health: Learning from Past Pandemics.* EarthScan Press, London.

59. Sparke M and D Anguelov (2012). "H1N1, globalization and the epidemiology of inequality." *Health & Place* 18: 726–36.

60. Forster P and O Charnoz (2013). "Producing knowledge in times of health crises: Insights from the international response to avian influenza in Indonesia." *Revue d'anthropologie des connaissances* 7(1).

61. Keck F (2010). "Une sentinelle sanitaire aux frontières du vivant. Les experts de la grippe aviaire à Hong Kong." *Terrain* 54: 26–41.

62. Kleinman AM, BR Bloom, A Saich, KA Mason, and F Aulino (2008). "Asian flus in ethnographic and political context: A biosocial approach." *Anthropology and Medicine* 15: 1–5; Lowe C (2010). "Preparing Indonesia: H5N1 influenza through the lens of global health." *Indonesia* 90: 147–70; Krieger N (2001). "Theories for social epidemiology in the 21st century: An ecosocial perspective." *Int J Epidemiol* 30: 668–77; Braun B (2007). "Biopolitics and the molecularization of life." *Cultural Geographies* 14: 6–28; Rayner G and T Lang (2012). *Ecological Public Health: Shaping the Conditions for Good Health.* Routledge, New York.

63. Krieger N (2001). "Theories for social epidemiology in the 21st century: An ecosocial perspective"; Bond P (2012). "Climate debt owed to Africa: What to demand and how to collect?" In M Muchie and A Baskaran (eds), *Innovation for Sustainability: African and European Perspectives.* Africa Institute of South Africa, Pretoria; Collard R-C and J Dempsey (2013). "Life for sale? The politics of lively commodities." *Environment and Planning A* 45(11): 2682–99; Hinchliffe S, J Allen, S Lavau, N Bingham, and S Carter (2013). "Biosecurity and the topologies of infected life: From borderlines to borderlands." *Transactions of the Institute of British Geographers* 38(4): 531–43.

64. Rabinowitz PM., R Kock, M Kachani, R Kunkel, J Thomas, J Gilbert, RG Wallace, C Blackmore, D Wong, W Karesh, B Natterson, R Dugas, C Rubin, for the Stone Mountain One Health Proof of Concept Working Group (2013). "Toward proof of concept of a 'One Health' approach to disease prediction and control." *Emerg Infect Dis.* Available online at http://dx.doi.org/10.3201/eid1912.130265.

65. De Vreese L (2009). "Epidemiology and causation." *Medicine, Health Care and Philosophy* 12: 345–53.

66. Preston ND, P Daszak, and RR Colwell (2013). "The human environment interface: Applying ecosystem concepts to health." *Curr Top Microbiol Immunol.* 365: 83–100.

67. Wallace RG (2013). "The virus and the virus: David Quammen's 'Spillover.'" *Counterpunch,* Weekend edition June 14–16, 2013. Available online at http://www.counterpunch.org/2013/06/14/the-virus-and-the-virus/.

68. Yeung HW (2005). "Rethinking relational economic geography." *Transactions of the Institute of British Geographers* 30: 37–51. doi: 10.1111/j.1475-5661.2005.00150.x

69. Robinson TP, GRW Wint, G Conchedda, TP Van Boeckel, V Ercoli, E Palamara, G Cinardi, L D'Aietti, SI Hay, and M Gilbert (2014). "Mapping the global distribution of livestock." *PLoS One* 9(5): e96084 doi: 10.1371/journal.pone.0096084.

70. Tilley H (2004). "Ecologies of complexity: Tropical environments, African trypanosomiasis, and the science of disease control in British colonial Africa, 1900–1940." *Osiris* 19: 21–38; Connell R (2007). *Southern Theory: The Global Dynamics of Knowledge in Social Science.* Polity Press, Unwin.

71. Foster JB, B Clark, and R York (2010). *The Ecological Rift: Capitalism's War on Earth*; Gindin S and L Panitch (2012). *The Making of Global Capitalism: The Political Economy of American Empire.* Verso Books, New York.

72. Mansfield B, DK Munroe, and K McSweeny (2010). "Does economic growth cause environmental recovery? Geographical explanations of forest regrowth." *Geography Compass* 4: 416–27; Liberti S (2011; 2013). *Land Grabbing: Journeys in the New Colonialism.* Verso Books, New York; Pearce F (2012). *The Land Grabbers: The New Fight Over Who Owns the Earth.* Beacon Press, Boston.

73. Kaufman F (2011). "How Goldman Sachs created the food crisis." *Foreign Policy.* 27 April. Available online at http://www.foreignpolicy.com/articles/2011/04/27/how_goldman_sachs_created_the_food_crisis; Daniel S (2012). "Situating private equity capital in the land grab debate." *Journal of Peasant Studies* 39: 703–29; Wohns S (2014). *Harvard in Iberá: Investigating Harvard University's Timber Plantations in the Iberá Wetlands of Argentina.* Oakland Institute and the Responsible Investment at Harvard Coalition. Available online at http://www.oaklandinstitute.org/sites/oaklandinstitute.org/files/OI_Report_Harvard_Ibera_0.pdf

74. Land Matrix Observatory (2014). *Global Map of Investments.* Available online at http://landmatrix.org/en/get-the-idea/global-map-investments/.

75. Oakland Institute (2011). *Special Investigation: Understanding Land Investment Deals in Africa.* Available online at http://media.oaklandinstitute.org/special-investigationunderstanding-land-investment-deals-africa.

76. Kahn LH, TP Monath, BH Bokma, EP Gibbs, and AA Aguirre (2012). "One Health, One Medicine." In AA Aguirre, R Ostfeld and P Daszak (eds), *New Directions in Conservation Medicine: Applied Cases of Ecological Health.* Oxford University Press, New York.

77. Pulliam JR, JH Epstein, J Dushoff, SA Rahman, M Bunning, AA Jamaluddin, AD Hyatt, HE Field, AP Dobson, P Daszak, and the Henipavirus Ecology Research Group (HERG) (2012). "Agricultural intensification, priming for persistence and the emergence of Nipah virus: A lethal bat-borne zoonosis." *J R Soc Interface.* 9: 89–101. doi: 10.1098/rsif.2011.0223. Epub 2011 Jun 1; Otte J and D Grace (2013). "Human health risks from the human-animal interface in Asia." In V Ahuja (ed.), *Asian Livestock: Challenges, Opportunities and the Response,* 121–60. Proceedings of an International Policy Forum held in Bangkok, Thailand, 16–17 August 2012, Animal Production and Health Commission for Asia and the Pacific, International Research Institute and Food and Agriculture Organization of the United Nations.

78. Zinsstag J, JS Mackenzie, M Jeggo, DL Heymann, JA Patz, and P Daszak (2012). "Mainstreaming one health." *Ecohealth* 9(2): 107–10.

79. Gould P (1993). *The Slow Plague: A Geography of the AIDS Pandemic.* Blackwell Publishers, Cambridge, MA.

80. Hosseini P, SH Sokolow, KJ Vandegrift, AM Kilpatrick, and P Daszak (2010). "Predictive power of air travel and socio-economic data for early pandemic spread." *PLoS ONE* 5(9): e12763. doi: 10.1371/journal. pone.0012763.

81. Mészáros I (2010). *Social Structure and Forms of Consciousness,* vol. 1: *The Social Determination of Method.* Monthly Review Press, New York.

82. Wallace RG and RA Kock (2012). "Whose food footprint? Capitalism, agriculture and the environment." *Human Geography* 5(1): 63–83.

83. Wallace RG (2012). "We need a Structural One Health." *Farming Pathogens.* Available online at http://farmingpathogens.wordpress. com/2012/08/03/we-need-a-structural-one-health/.

84. Smith JW, F le Gall, S Stephenson, and C de Haan (2012). *People, Pathogens and Our Planet.* vol. 2: *The Economics of One Health.* World Bank Report No. 69145-GLB. Available online at http://www-wds. worldbank.org/external/default/WDSContentServer/WDSP/IB/2012/ 06/12/000333038_20120612014653/Rendered/PDF/691450ESW0whit 0D0ESW120PPPvol120web.pdf.

85. Stine NW and DA Chokshi (2012). "Opportunity in austerity: A common agenda for medicine and public health." *N Engl J Med* 366: 395–97.

86. Jones BA et al. (2013). "Zoonosis emergence linked to agricultural intensification and environmental change"; Otte J, D Roland-Holst, DU Pfeiffer, R Soares-Magalhaes, J Rushton, J Graham, and E Silbergeld (2007). *Industrial Livestock Production and Global Health Risks.* Pro-Poor Livestock Policy Initiative, Food and Agriculture Organization of the United Nations. A Living from Livestock Research Report.

Available online at http://r4d.dfid.gov.uk/PDF/Outputs/Livestock/
PPLPIrep-hpai_industrialisationrisks.pdf; Graham JP, JH Leibler,
LB Price, JM Otte, DU Pfeiffer, T Tiensin, and EK Silbergeld (2008).
"The animal–human interface and infectious disease in industrial
food animal production: Rethinking biosecurity and biocontainment."
Public Health Reports 123: 282–99; Leibler JH, J Otte, D Roland-
Holst, DU Pfeiffer, R Soars Magalhaes, J Rushton, JP Graham, and EK
Silbergeld (2009). "Industrial food animal production and global health
risks: Exploring the ecosystems and economics of Avian Influenza."
EcoHealth 6: 58–70; Wallace RG (2009). "Breeding influenza: The
political virology of offshore farming." *Antipode* 41: 916–51; Drew TW
(2011). "The emergence and evolution of swine viral diseases: To what
extent have husbandry systems and global trade contributed to their
distribution and diversity?" *Rev Sci Tech* 30: 95–106.

87.   Moore J (2011). "Transcending the metabolic rift: A theory of crises in
the capitalist world-ecology." *Journal of Peasant Studies* 38: 1–46.

88.   Wallace RG and RA Kock (2012). "Whose food footprint? Capitalism,
agriculture and the environment"; Davis DK (2006). "Neoliberalism,
environmentalism, and agricultural restructuring in Morocco." *The
Geographical Journal* 172: 88–105.

89.   Liverani M et al. (2013). "Understanding and managing zoonotic risk
in the new livestock industries"; Wallace RG (2009). "Breeding influenza: The political virology of offshore farming"; Myers KP, CW Olsen,
SF Setterquist, AW Capuano, KJ Donham, EL Thacker, JA Merchant,
and GC Gray (2006). "Are swine workers in the United States at
increased risk of infection with zoonotic influenza virus?" *Clin Infect
Dis.* 42(1): 14–20; Gilchrist MJ, C Greko, DB Wallinga, GW Beran,
DG Riley, and PS Thorne (2007). "The potential role of concentrated
animal feeding operations in infectious disease epidemics and antibiotic resistance." *Environ Health Perspect.* 115: 313–16; Evans CM, GF
Medley, and LE Green (2008). "Porcine reproductive and respiratory
syndrome virus (PRRSV) in GB pig herds: Farm characteristics associated with heterogeneity in seroprevalence." *BMC Veterinary Research* 4:
48 doi: 10.1186/1746-6148-4-48; Mennerat A, F Nilsen, D Ebert, and
A Skorping (2010). "Intensive farming: evolutionary implications for
parasites and pathogens." *Evol Biol.* 37: 59–67; Leibler JH, M Carone,
and EK Silbergeld (2010). "Contribution of company affiliation and
social contacts to risk estimates of between-farm transmission of avian
influenza." *PLoS ONE* 5(3): e9888. doi: 10.1371/journal.pone.0009888;
Van Boeckel TP, W Thanapongtharm, T Robinson, L D'Aietti, and M
Gilbert (2012). "Predicting the distribution of intensive poultry farming
in Thailand." *Agriculture, Ecosystems & Environment* 149: 144–53; Smit

LAM, F van der Sman-de Beer, AWJ Opstal-van Winden, M Hooiveld, J Beekhuizen et al.. (2012). "Q Fever and pneumonia in an area with a high livestock density: A large population-based study." *PLoS ONE* 7: e38843. doi: 10.1371/journal.pone.0038843; Ercsey-Ravasz M, Z Toroczkai, Z Lakner, and J Baranyi (2012). "Complexity of the international agro-food trade network and its impact on food safety." *PLoS ONE* 7(5): e37810. doi: 10.1371/journal.pone.0037810; Bausch D and L Schwarz (2014). "Outbreak of Ebola virus disease in Guinea: Where ecology meets economy." *PLoS Neglected Tropical Diseases* 8: e3056.

90. Engering A, L Hogerwerf, and J Slingenbergh (2013). "Pathogen–host-environment interplay and disease emergence." *Emerging Microbes and Infections* 2: e5 doi: 10.1038/emi.2013.5 DOI: 10.1080/17530350. 2014.904243.

91. Alsan MM, M Westerhaus, M Herce, K Nakashima, and PE Farmer (2011). "Poverty, global health and infectious disease: Lessons from Haiti and Rwanda." *Infect Dis Clin North Am.* 25: 611–22. doi: 10.1016/j. idc.2011.05.004.

92. Jones BA et al. (2013). "Zoonosis emergence linked to agricultural intensification and environmental change."

93. Blackwell PJ (2010). "East Africa's pastoralist emergency: Is climate change the straw that breaks the camel's back?" *Third World Q.* 31: 1321–38; Brückner GK (2012). "Ensuring safe international trade: how are the roles and responsibilities evolving and what will the situation be in ten years' time?" *Rev Sci Tech.* 30: 317–24.

94. Zhu YG, TA Johnson, JQ Su, M Qiao, GX Guo, RD Stedtfeld, SA Hashsham, and JM Tiedje (2013). "Diverse and abundant antibiotic resistance genes in Chinese swine farms." *Proc Natl Acad Sci USA* 110(9): 3435–40.

95. Wallace RG, L Bergmann, L Hogerwerf, and M Gilbert (2010). "Are influenzas in southern China byproducts of the region's globalizing historical present?" In T Giles-Vernick, S Craddock and J Gunn (eds). *Influenza and Public Health: Learning from Past Pandemics*. EarthScan Press, London.

96. Paul M et al. (2013). "Practices associated with Highly Pathogenic Avian Influenza spread in traditional poultry marketing chains: Social and economic perspectives"; Van Boeckel TP et al. (2012). "Predicting the distribution of intensive poultry farming in Thailand."; Gilbert M, X Xiao, DU Pfeiffer, M Epprecht, S Boles, C Czarnecki, P Chaitaweesub, W Kalpravidh, PQ Minh, MJ Otte, V Martin, J Slingenbergh (2008). "Mapping H5N1 highly pathogenic avian influenza risk in Southeast Asia." *Proc Natl Acad Sci U S A.* 105: 4769–74; Gilbert M, X Xiao, P Chaitaweesub, W Kalpravidh, S Premashthira, S

Boles, and J Slingenbergh (2007). "Avian influenza, domestic ducks and rice agriculture in Thailand." *Agriculture, Ecosystems and Environment* 119: 409–15; Walker P, S Cauchemez, N Hartemink, T Tiensin, and AC Ghani (2012). "Outbreaks of H5N1 in poultry in Thailand: The relative role of poultry production types in sustaining transmission and the impact of active surveillance in control." *J. R. Soc. Interface.* Available online at doi: 10.1098/rsif.2012.0022; Amonsin A., C Choatrakol, J Lapkuntod, R Tantilertcharoen, R Thanawongnuwech, S Suradhat, K Suwannakarn, A Theamboonlers, and Y Poovorawan (2008). "Influenza virus (H5N1). in live bird markets and food markets, Thailand." *Emerging Infectious Diseases* 14: 1739–42.

97.   Allen J and S Lavau (2014). "'Just-in-Time' Disease: Biosecurity, poultry and power." *Journal of Cultural Economy.* doi: 10.1080/17530350.2014.904243.

98.   Boni MF, AP Galvani, L Abraham, AL Wickelgrend, and A Malani (2013). "Economic epidemiology of avian influenza on smallholder poultry farms." *Theoretical Population Biology* 90: 135–44.

99.   Mészáros I (2012). "Structural crisis needs structural change." *Monthly Review* 63(10): 19–32. Available online at http://monthlyreview.org/2012/03/01/structural-crisis-needs-structural-change/.

100. Armitage DR and D Johnson (2006). "Can resilience be reconciled with globalization and the increasingly complex conditions of resource degradation in Asian coastal regions?" *Ecology and Society* 11(1): 2. Available online at http://www.ecologyandsociety.org/vol11/iss1/art2/; Hornborg A (2009). "Zero-sum world: Challenges in conceptualizing environmental load displacement and ecologically unequal exchange in the world-system." *International Journal of Comparative Sociology* 50: 237–62.

101. Levins R (1998). "The internal and external in explanatory theories." *Science as Culture* 7(4): 557–82; Leach M and I Scoones (2013). "The social and political lives of zoonotic disease models: Narratives, science and policy." *Social Science & Medicine* 88: 10–17.

102. Gibson-Graham JK, E Erdem, and C Özselçuk (2013). "Thinking with Marx for a feminist postcapitalist politics." In R Jaeggi and D Loick (eds). *Marx' Kritik der Gesellschaft.* Akademie Verlag, Berlin.

103. Fearnley L (2013). "The birds of Poyang Lake: Sentinels at the interface of wild and domestic." *Limn* 3. Available online at http://limn.it/the-birds-of-poyang-lake-sentinels-at-the-interface-of-wild-and-domestic/.

104. Takekawa JY, SH Newman, X Xiao, DJ Prosser, KA Spragens, EC Palm, B Yan, T Li, F Lei, D Zhao, DC Douglas, SB Muzaffar, and W Ji (2010). "Migration of waterfowl in the East Asian flyway and spatial relationship to HPAI H5N1 outbreaks." *Avian Dis.* 54(S1): 466–76; Takekawa

JY, DJ Prosser, SH Newman, SB Muzaffar, NJ Hill, B Yan, X Xiao, F Lei, T Li, SE Schwarzbach, and JA Howell (2010). "Victims and vectors: Highly pathogenic avian influenza H5N1 and the ecology of wild birds." *Avian Biology Research* 3(2): 51–73.

105. Hoffman SG (2011). "The new tools of the science trade: Contested knowledge production and the conceptual vocabularies of academic capitalism." *Social Anthropology* 19: 439–62.

106. Lewontin R and R Levins (2007). *Biology Under the Influence: Dialectical Essays on Ecology, Agriculture and Health.* Monthly Review Press, New York.

107. Leibler JH et al. (2009). "Industrial food animal production and global health risks: Exploring the ecosystems and economics of Avian Influenza."

108. Wallace RG (2013). "Flu the farmer." *Farming Pathogens.* 17 April. Available online at http://farmingpathogens.wordpress.com/2013/04/17/farmer-flu/.

109. Harvey D (1982; 2006). *The Limits to Capital.* Verso, New York.

110. Marx K (1885; 1993). *Capital: A Critique of Political Economy.* Vol. 2, Penguin Classics, London; Sheppard E and T Barnes (1990). *The Capitalist Space Economy: Geographical Analysis After Ricardo, Marx and Sraffa.* Routledge, Oxford; Magdoff F and JB Foster (2014). "Stagnation and financialization: The nature of the contradiction." *Monthly Review,* 66(1). Available online at http://monthlyreview.org/2014/05/01/stagnation-and-financialization/.

111. Harvey D (1982; 2006). *The Limits to Capital*; Leonard C (2014). *The Meat Racket: The Secret Takeover of America's Food Business.* Simon & Schuster, New York.

112. Narayanan GB and TL Walmsley (eds). (2008). *Global Trade, Assistance, and Production: The GTAP 7 Data Base.* Center for Global Trade Analysis, Purdue University. Available online at: http://www.gtap.agecon.purdue.edu/databases/v7/v7_doco.asp.

113. Bergmann L and M Holmberg (in press). "Land in motion."*Annals of the American Association of Geographers*; Bergmann LR (2013). "Beyond the Anthropocene: Toward modest mathematical narratives for more-than-human global communities." Paper accepted to session: "Re-evaluating the Anthropocene, Resituating 'Anthropos,'" Annual Meeting of the Association of American Geographers, Los Angeles; Bergmann LR (2013). "Bound by chains of carbon: Ecological–economic geographies of globalization." *Annals of the Association of American Geographers,* 103: 1348–70. doi: 10.1080/00045608.2013.779547.

114. Bergmann LR (2013). "Bound by chains of carbon: Ecological–economic geographies of globalization."

115. Ibid.
116. Robinson TP et al. (2014). "Mapping the global distribution of livestock."
117. Elith J, SJ Phillips, T Hastie, M Dudík, YE Chee, and CJ Yates (2011). "A statistical explanation of MaxEnt for ecologists." *Diversity and Distributions* 17: 43–57; Van Boeckel TP, W Thanapongtharm, T Robinson, CM Biradar, X Xiao, and M Gilbert (2012). "Improving risk models for avian influenza: The role of intensive poultry farming and flooded land during the 2004 Thailand epidemic." *PLoS One* 7(11): e49528. doi: 10.1371/journal.pone.0049528.
118. Martin V, DU Pfeiffer, X Zhou, X Xiao, DJ Prosser, F Guo, and M Gilbert (2011). "Spatial distribution and risk factors of highly pathogenic avian influenza (HPAI) H5N1 in China." *PLoS Pathog.* 7(3): e1001308. doi: 10.1371/journal.ppat.1001308.

Flu the Farmer

119. Wallace RG (2013). "Broiler explosion." *Farming Pathogens.* 14 April. Available online at https://farmingpathogens.wordpress.com/2013/04/14/broiler-explosion/.
120. Dibner JJ, CD Knight, ML Kitchell, CA Atwell, AC Downs, and FJ Ivey (1998). "Early feeding and development of the immune system in neonatal poultry." *Journal of Applied Poultry Research* 7: 425–36.
121. Harris DL (1970). "Breeding for efficiency in livestock production: Defining the economic objectives." *Journal of Animal Science* 30(6): 860–865. doi: 10.2134/jas1970.306860x.
122. Black I (2013). "NSA spying scandal: What we have learned." *The Guardian.* 10 June. Available online at http://www.theguardian.com/world/2013/jun/10/nsa-spying-scandal-what-we-have-learned.
123. Jackson D (2013). "Obama defends surveillance programs." *USA Today.* 7 June. Available online at http://www.usatoday.com/story/news/politics/2013/06/07/obama-clapper-national-security-agency-leaks/2400405/.
124. Butler D (2008). "Politically correct names given to flu viruses." *Nature* 452: 923.
125. Branswell H (2011). "Flu factories." *Scientific American.* Available online at http://www.scientificamerican.com/article/pandemic-flu-factories/; USDA (2015). National Animal Health Laboratory Network (NAHLN). 23 March. Available online at http://www.aphis.usda.gov/animal_health/nahln/images/all_labs_disease_designations.gif; USDA (2015). All NAHLN Lab List. March 2015. Available online at http://www.aphis.usda.gov/animal_health/nahln/downloads/all_nahln_lab_list.pdf.
126. Branswell H (2011). "Flu factories."

127. Wallace RG (2009). "The hog industry strikes back." *Farming Pathogens*. 1 June. Available online at https://farmingpathogens.wordpress.com/2009/06/01/the-hog-industry-strikes-back/.

128. Nelson MI, P Lemey, Y Tan, A Vincent, TT-Y Lam et al. (2011). "Spatial dynamics of Human-Origin H1 Influenza A Virus in North American swine." *PLoS Pathog* 7(6): e1002077. doi: 10.1371/journal. ppat.1002077; Scotch M and C Mei (2013). "Phylogeography of swine influenza H3N2 in the United States: Translational public health for zoonotic disease surveillance." *Infection, Genetics and Evolution* 13: 224-229.

129. Webster RG and EJ Walker (2004). "Influenza." *American Scientist* 91: 122–29.

130. Greenwald G and E MacAskill (2013). "Boundless Informant: The NSA's secret tool to track global surveillance data." *The Guardian*. 11 June. Available online at http://www.theguardian.com/world/2013/jun/08/nsa-boundless-informant-global-datamining; Greenwald G and E MacAskill (2013). "NSA Prism program taps in to user data of Apple, Google and others." *The Guardian*. 7 June. Available online at http://www.theguardian.com/world/2013/jun/06/us-tech-giants-nsa-data.

131. Cohen R (2012). "Dept. of Homeland Security Forced to Release List of Keywords Used to Monitor Social Networking Sites." *Forbes*. 26 May. Available online at http://www.forbes.com/sites/reuvencohen/2012/05/26/department-of-homeland-security-forced-to-release-list-of-keywords-used-to-monitor-social-networking-sites/.

132. Spencer J (2014). "Livestock farmers battle information release." *Star Tribune* 8 July. Available online at http://www.startribune.com/business/214695181.html.

Distress of Columbia

133. McHugh J and PA Mackowiak (2014). "What really killed William Henry Harrison?" *New York Times*. 31 March. Available online at http://www.nytimes.com/2014/04/01/science/what-really-killed-william-henry -harrison.html; The White House Historical Association (n.d.). White House History Timelines. African Americans: 1790s–1840s. Available online at http://www.whitehousehistory.org/history/white-house-timelines/african-americans-1790s-1840s.html.

134. CNN (2008). "Slaves helped build White House, U.S. Capitol." 2 December. Available online at http://www.cnn.com/2008/US/12/02/slaves.white.house/index.html?_s=PM: US.

135. McHugh J and PA Mackowiak (2014). "What really killed William Henry Harrison?"

PART SEVEN
Did Neoliberalizing West African Forests Produce a New Niche for Ebola?

1. Wallace RG, R Kock, L Bergmann, M Gilbert, L Hogerwerf, C Pittiglio, R Mattioli, and R Wallace (2016). "Did neoliberalizing West African forests produce a new niche for Ebola?" *International Journal of Health Services.* 46(1): 149–65.

2. Henao-Restrepo A et al. (2015). "Efficacy and effectiveness of an rVSV-vectored vaccine expressing Ebola surface glycoprotein: Interim results from the Guinea ring vaccination cluster-randomised trial." *Lancet.* pii: S0140-6736(15)61117-5. doi: 10.1016/S0140-6736(15)61117-5.

3. Roush SW et al.(2007). "Historical comparisons of morbidity and mortality for vaccine-preventable diseases in the United States." *Journal of the American Medical Association* 298: 2155–63; Antona D et al. (2013). "Measles elimination efforts and 2008–2011 outbreak, France." *Emerging Infectious Diseases* 19: 357–64.

4. McNeil DG (2015). "New meningitis strain in Africa brings call for more vaccines." *New York Times.* 31 July. Available online at http://www.nytimes.com/2015/08/01/health/new-meningitis-strain-in-africa-brings-call-for-more-vaccines.html.

5. Pedrique B et al. (2013). "The drug and vaccine landscape for neglected diseases (2000–11): A systematic assessment." *Lancet Glob Health* 1(6): e371-9. doi: 10.1016/S2214-109X(13)70078-0; MacLennan CA and A Saul (2014). "Vaccines against poverty." *Proc Natl Acad Sci USA* 111(34): 12307–12. doi: 10.1073/pnas.1400473111; Barocchi MA and R Rappuoli R (2015). "Delivering vaccines to the people who need them most." *Philos Trans R Soc Lond B Biol Sci.* 370(1671): pii: 20140150. doi: 10.1098/rstb.2014.0150.

6. Wallace R (2002). "Immune cognition and vaccine strategy: Pathogenic challenge and ecological resilience." *Open Syst. Inf. Dyn.* 9: 51. doi: 10.1023/A: 1014282912635; Van Regenmortel MHV (2004). "Reductionism and complexity in molecular biology." *EMBO Rep.* 5(11): 1016–1020. doi: 10.1038/sj.embor.7400284.

7. Possas CA (2001). "Social ecosystem health: Confronting the complexity and emergence of infectious diseases." *Cad Saude Publica* 17(1): 31–41; King NB (2002). "Security, disease, commerce: Ideologies of postcolonial global health." *Social Studies of Science* 32/5–6: 763–89; Leach M and I Scoones (2013). "The social and political lives of zoonotic disease models: narratives, science and policy." *Soc. Sci. Med.* 88: 10e17; Degeling C, J Johnson, and C Mayes (2015). "Impure politics and pure science: Efficacious Ebola medications are only a palliation and not a cure for structural disadvantage." *American Journal of Bioethics* 15: 43–45.

8.   Editors (2015). "Trial and triumph." *Nature* 524(7563): 5.

9.   Wallace R and RG Wallace (2004). "Adaptive chronic infection, structured stress, and medical magic bullets: Do reductionist cures select for holistic diseases?" *BioSystems* 77: 93–108.

10.   Gilbert M and DU Pfeiffer (2012). "Risk factor modelling of the spatio-temporal patterns of highly pathogenic avian influenza (HPAIV). H5N1: A review." *Spatiotemporal Epidemiol.* 3(3): 173–83. doi: 10.1016/j.sste.2012.01.002; Wallace RG, L Bergmann, R Kock, M Gilbert, L Hogerwerf, R Wallace, and M Holmberg (2015). "The dawn of Structural One Health: A new science tracking disease emergence along circuits of capital." *Social Science & Medicine* 129: 68–77.

11.   Levins R (2006). "Strategies of abstraction." *Biol Philos* 21: 741–55; Schizas D (2012). "Systems ecology reloaded: A critical assessment focusing on the relations between science and ideology." In GP Stamou (ed). *Populations, Biocommunities, Ecosystems: A Review of Controversies in Ecological Thinking.* Bentham Science Publishers, Sharjah, U.A.E.

12.   Wallace RG (2004). "Projecting the impact of HAART on the evolution of HIV's life history." *Ecological Modelling.* 176: 227–53.

13.   WHO Ebola Response Team (2014). "Ebola virus disease in West Africa: The first 9 months of the epidemic and forward projections." *N Engl J Med* 371: 1481–95.

14.   Schoepp RJ, CA Rossi, SH Khan, A Goba, and JN Fair (2014). "Undiagnosed acute viral febrile illnesses, Sierra Leone." *Emerging Infectious Diseases* 20: 1176–82.

15.   Dudas G and A Rambaut (2014). "Phylogenetic analysis of Guinea 2014 EBOV Ebolavirus outbreak." *PLOS Currents Outbreaks* Edition 1, 2014. doi: 10.1371/currents.outbreaks.84eefe5ce43ec9dc0bf0670f7b 8b417d; Gire SK, A Goba and KG Andersen (2014). "Genomic surveillance elucidates Ebola virus origin and transmission during the 2014 outbreak." *Science* 345: 1369–72.

16.   Hoenen, T. et al. (2015). "Mutation rate and genotype variation of Ebola virus from Mali case sequences." *Science.* 348(6230): 117–19. doi: 10.1126/science.aaa5646; Simon-Loriere E et al. (2015). "Distinct lineages of Ebola virus in Guinea during the 2014 West African epidemic." *Nature* 524(7563): 102–4 doi: 10.1038/nature14612; Carroll MW et al. (2015). "Temporal and spatial analysis of the 2014-2015 Ebola virus outbreak in West Africa." *Nature.* 524(7563): 97–101. doi: 10.1038/ nature14594; Jun SR et al. (2015). "Ebola virus comparative genomics." *FEMS Microbiol Rev.* July 14. pii: fuv031. [Epub].

17.   Wallace RG, M Gilbert, R Wallace, C Pittiglio, R Mattioli and R Kock (2014). "Did Ebola emerge in West Africa by a policy-driven phase

change in agroecology?" *Environment and Planning A* 46(11). 2533–42; WHO *Ebola Situation Report*. 12 August 2015. Available online at http://apps.who.int/iris/bitstream/10665/182071/1/ebolasitrep_12Aug2015_eng.pdf?ua=1&ua=1.

18. Clark DV et al. (2015). "Long-term sequelae after Ebola virus disease in Bundibugyo, Uganda: a retrospective cohort study." *Lancet Infect Dis.* 15(8): 905–12; Qureshi AI et al. (2015). "Study of Ebola Virus Disease survivors in Guinea." *Clin Infect Dis.* pii: civ453. doi: 10.1371/currents.outbreaks.84eefe5ce43ec9dc0bf0670f7b8b417d; Christie A et al. (2015). "Possible sexual transmission of Ebola virus—Liberia, 2015." *MMWR Morb Mortal Wkly Rep.* 64(17): 479–81; Reardon S (2015). "Ebola's mental-health wounds linger in Africa." *Nature* 519: 13–14.

19. Kentikelenis A, L King, M McKee, and D Stuckler (2015). "The International Monetary Fund and the Ebola outbreak." *Lancet Glob Health* 3(2): e69-70. doi: 10.1016/S2214-109X(14)70377-70378; Fallah M, LA Skrip, E d'Harcourt, and AP Galvani (2015). "Strategies to prevent future Ebola epidemics." *Lancet* 386(9993): 131.

20. Gatherer D (2015). "The unprecedented scale of the West African Ebola virus disease outbreak is due to environmental and sociological factors, not special attributes of the currently circulating strain of the virus." *Evid Based Med.* 20(1): 28. doi: 10.1136/ebmed-2014-110127.

21. Bausch D and L Schwarz (2014). "Outbreak of Ebola virus disease in Guinea: where ecology meets economy." *PLOS Neglected Tropical Diseases* 8: e3056.

22. Morris ML, HP Binswanger-Mikhize, and D Byerlee (2009). *Awakening Africa's Sleeping Giant: Prospects for Commercial Agriculture in the Guinea Savannah Zone and Beyond.* World Bank Publications, Washington, DC.

23. Land Matrix Observatory (2015). *Global Map of Investments.* Available online at http://landmatrix.org/en/get-the-idea/global-map-investments/.

24. Farm Lands of Guinea (2011). "Farm Lands of Guinea completes reverse merger and investment valuing the company at USD$45 million." PR Newswire. Available online at http://www.bloomberg.com/apps/news?pid=newsarchive&sid=a9cwc86wQ3zQ.

25. Wallace RG et al. (2014). "Did Ebola emerge in West Africa by a policy-driven phase change in agroecology?"

26. Delarue J and H Cochet (2013). "Systemic impact evaluation: A methodology for complex agricultural development projects. The case of a contract farming project in Guinea." *European Journal of Development Research* 25: 778–96; Madelaine C, E Malezieux, N Sibelet, and RJ Manlay (2008). "Semi-wild palm groves reveal agricultural change in

the forest region of Guinea." *Agroforest Systems* 73: 189–204.

27. Madelaine C et al. (2008). "Semi-wild palm groves reveal agricultural change in the forest region of Guinea"; Fairhead J and M Leach (1999). *Misreading the African Landscape: Society and Ecology in a Forest– Savanna Mosaic.* Cambridge University Press, Cambridge.

28. Delarue J and H Cochet (2013). "Systemic impact evaluation: A methodology for complex agricultural development projects. The case of a contract farming project in Guinea."

29. Saouromou K (2015). "Guinée Forestière: De nouvelles réticences à la lutte contre Ebola à Yomou." *L'Express Guinee.* Available online at http://lexpressguinee.com/fichiers/videos5.php?langue=fr&idc=fr_ Guinee_Forestiere__De_nouvelles_reticences_a_la_lutte_contre_.

30. Lomas J (1998). "Social capital and health: Implications for public health and epidemiology." *Soc. Sci. Med.* 47: 1181–88.

31. Carrere R (2010). *Oil Palm in Africa: Past, Present and Future Scenarios.* World Rainforest Movement, Montevideo.

32. Carrere R (2010). *Oil Palm in Africa: Past, Present and Future Scenarios*; Madelaine C (2005). *Analyse du fonctionnement et de la dynamique de la palmeraie sub-spontanée en Guinée forestière. Cas du village de Nienh,* MSc thesis, ENGREF, AgroParisTech, Montpellier.

33. Wallace RG et al. (2014). "Did Ebola emerge in West Africa by a policy-driven phase change in agroecology?"

34. Pulliam JR et al. (2012). "Agricultural intensification, priming for persistence and the emergence of Nipah virus: a lethal bat-borne zoonosis." *J R Soc Interface* 9(66): 89-101, 2012 doi: 10.1098/rsif.2011.0223; Olival KJ and DT Hayman (2014). "Filoviruses in bats: Current knowledge and future directions." *Viruses* 6(4): 1759–88. doi: 10.3390/v6041759; Plowright RK et al. (2015). "Ecological dynamics of emerging bat virus spillover." *Proc Biol Sci.* 282(1798): 20142124. doi: 10.1098/rspb.2014.2124.

35. Shafie NJ et al. (2011). "Diversity pattern of bats at two contrasting habitat types along Kerian River, Perak, Malaysia." *Tropical Life Sciences Research* 22(2): 13–22.

36. Anti P et al. (2015). "Human-bat interactions in rural West Africa." *Emerg Infect Dis.* 21(8): 1418–21. doi: 10.3201/eid2108.142015.

37. Plowright RK et al. (2015). "Ecological dynamics of emerging bat virus spillover."

38. Luby SP, ES Gurley, and M Jahangir Hossain (2009). "Transmission of human infection with Nipah Virus." *Clinical Infectious Diseases* 49: 1743–48.

39. Leroy EM et al. (2009). "Human Ebola outbreak resulting from direct exposure to fruit bats in Luebo, Democratic Republic of Congo, 2007."

Vector Borne Zoonotic Dis. 9(6): 723–28. doi: 10.1089/vbz.2008.0167.

40. Saéz AM et al. (2014). "Investigating the zoonotic origin of the West African Ebola epidemic." *EMBO Molecular Medicine* 7(1): 17–23. doi 10.15252/emmm.201404792. Available online at http://embomolmed.embopress.org/content/embomm/early/2014/12/29/emmm.201404792.full.pdf.

41. Wallace R, L Bergmann, L Hogerwerf, R Kock, and RG Wallace (in press). "Ebola in the hog sector: Modeling pandemic emergence in commodity livestock." In RG Wallace (ed.), *Neoliberal Ebola: Modeling Disease Emergence from Finance to Forest and Farm.* Springer, New York.

42. Noer CL, T Dabelsteen, K Bohmann and A Monadjem (2012). "Molossid bats in an African agro-ecosystem select sugarcane fields as foraging habitat." *African Zoology* 47(1): 1–11; Taylor PJ, A Monadjem, and JN Steyn (2013). "Seasonal patterns of habitat use by insectivorous bats in a subtropical African agro-ecosystem dominated by macadamia orchards." *African Journal of Ecology* 51(4): 552–61; Stechert C et al. (2014). "Insecticide residues in bats along a land use-gradient dominated by cotton cultivation in northern Benin, West Africa." *Environ Sci Pollut Res Int.* 21(14): 8812–21. doi: 10.1007/s11356-014-2817-8.

43. WHO/International Study Team (1978). "Ebola haemorrhagic fever in Sudan, 1976." *Bull World Health Organ.* 56(2): 247–70; Bertherat E. et al. (1999). "Leptospirosis and Ebola virus infection in five gold-panning villages in northeastern Gabon." *Am J Trop Med Hyg.* 60(4): 610–15; Morvan JM, E Nakoun, V Deubel, and M Colyn (2000). "Forest ecosystems and Ebola virus." *Bull Soc Pathol Exot.* 93(3): 172–75. [in French]; Groseth A, H Feldmann, and JE Strong (2007). "The ecology of Ebola virus." *Trends Microbiol.* 15(9): 408–416.

44. Roden D (1974). "Regional inequality and rebellion in the Sudan." *Geographical Review* 64(4): 498–516; Smith DH, DP Francis, DIH Simpson and RB Highton (1978). "The Nzara outbreak of viral haemorrhagic fever." In S.R. Pattyn (ed.), *Ebola Virus Haemorrhagic Fever Proceedings of an International Colloquium on Ebola Virus Infection and Other Haemorrhagic Fevers held in Antwerp, Belgium, 6-8 December, 1977.* Elsevier, Amsterdam.

45. Wallace RG et al. (2015). "The dawn of Structural One Health: A new science tracking disease emergence along circuits of capital."

46. Bergmann L and M Holmberg (in press). "Land in motion." *Annals of the American Association of Geographers*; Bergmann LR (2013). "Bound by chains of carbon: Ecological–economic geographies of globalization." *Annals of the Association of American Geographers*, 103: 1348–70. doi: 10.1080/00045608.2013.779547.

47. Robinson TP et al. (2014). "Mapping the global distribution of livestock." *PLoS One* 9(5): e96084. http://dx.doi.org/10.1371/ journal. pone.0096084.

48. Wallace RG et al. (2015). "The dawn of Structural One Health: A new science tracking disease emergence along circuits of capital."

49. Sheppard E (2008). "Geographic dialectics?" *Environment and Planning A* 40: 2603–2612; Wallace RG, L Bergmann, L Hogerwerf, and M Gilbert (2010). "Are influenzas in southern China byproducts of the region's globalising historical present?" In T Giles-Vernick, S Craddock, and J Gunn (eds). *Influenza and Public Health: Learning from Past Pandemics.* EarthScan Press, London.

50. Osterholm MT, KA Moore, and LO Gostin (2015). "Public health in the age of Ebola in West Africa." *JAMA Intern Med.* 175(1): 7–8. doi: 10.1001/jamainternmed.2014.6235.

51. Mészáros I (2012). "Structural crisis needs structural change." *Monthly Review* 63(10): 19–32.

52. Schar D and P Daszak (2014). "Ebola economics: The case for an upstream approach to disease emergence." *EcoHealth* 11(4): 451–52.

53. Wallace RG et al. (2014) "Did Ebola emerge in West Africa by a policy-driven phase change in agroecology?"; Wallace R and RG Wallace (2014). "Blowback: New formal perspectives on agriculturally-driven pathogen evolution and spread." *Epidemiology and Infection.* doi: 10.1017/S0950268814000077.

54. Hogerwerf L, R Houben, K Hall, M Gilbert, J Slingenbergh, and RG Wallace (2010). *Agroecological Resilience and Protopandemic Influenza.* Animal Health and Production Division, Food and Agriculture Organization, Rome.

55. Barbarossa MV et al. (2015). "Transmission dynamics and final epidemic size of Ebola Virus Disease outbreaks with varying interventions." *PLoS One* 10(7): e0131398. doi: 10.1371/journal.pone.0131398.

56. Wallace R, L Bergmann, L Hogerwerf, R Kock, and RG Wallace (in press). "Ebola in the hog sector: Modeling pandemic emergence in commodity livestock."

57. Black F and M Scholes (1973). "The pricing of options and corporate liabilities." *Journal of Political Economy* 81: 637–54.

58. Bartsch SM. K Gorham and BY Lee (2015). "The cost of an Ebola case." *Pathog Glob Health* 109(1): 4–9.

59. Degeling C, J Johnson and C Mayes (2015). "Impure politics and pure science: Efficacious Ebola medications are only a palliation and not a cure for structural disadvantage."

60. Van Regenmortel MHV (2004). "Reductionism and complexity in molecular biology"; Wallace R and RG Wallace (2004). "Adaptive

chronic infection, structured stress, and medical magic bullets: Do reductionist cures select for holistic diseases?"; Wallace RG (2008). "Book review: Combating the Threat of Pandemic Influenza: Drug Discovery Approaches." *Quarterly Review of Biology* 83: 327–28.

Collateralized Farmers

61. Leonard C (2014). *The Meat Racket: The Secret Takeover of America's Food Business*. Simon & Schuster, New York.
62. Wallace RG (2010). "Grainmorrah." *Farming Pathogens*. 6 December. Available online at https://farmingpathogens.wordpress.com/2010/12/06/grainmorrah/.
63. Leonard C (2014). *The Meat Racket: The Secret Takeover of America's Food Business*.
64. Jenner A (2014). "Chicken farming and its discontents." *Modern Farmer*. 24 February. Available online at http://modernfarmer.com/2014/02/chicken-farming-discontents/.
65. Leonard C (2014). *The Meat Racket: The Secret Takeover of America's Food Business*.
66. Wallace RG (2013). "Flu the farmer." *Farming Pathogens*. 17 April. Available online at https://farmingpathogens.wordpress.com/2013/04/17/farmer-flu/.
67. Jones BA, D Grace, R Kock, S Alonso, J Rushton, MY Said, D McKeever, F Mutua, J Young, J McDermott, and DU Pfeiffer (2013). "Zoonosis emergence linked to agricultural intensification and environmental change." *PNAS*, 110: 8399–8404; Stephenson W (2013). "Indian farmers and suicide: How big is the problem?" BBC News. 23 January. Available online at http://www.bbc.com/news/magazine-21077458.
68. Kutner M (2014). "Death on the farm." *Newsweek*. 10 April. Available online at http://www.newsweek.com/death-farm-248127.

Mickey the Measles

69. Xia R (2015). "Measles outbreak: At least 95 cases in eight states and Mexico." *Los Angeles Times*. 28 January. Available online at http://www.latimes.com/local/lanow/la-me-ln-measles-outbreak-20150128-story.html.
70. CBS/AP (2015). "Arizona monitoring 1,000 people for measles." 28 January. Available online at http://www.cbsnews.com/news/arizona-monitoring-1000-people-for-measles-linked-to-disneyland/.
71. Canon G (2015). "Mickey Mouse still stricken with measles, thanks to the anti-vaxxers." 8 January. Available online at http://www.motherjones.com/blue-marble/2015/01/measles-outbreak-disneyland-anti-vaxxers.
72. CDC (2015). "Measles cases and outbreaks." Available online at http://www.cdc.gov/measles/cases-outbreaks.html; Zipprich J, K Winter, J

Hacker, D Xia, J Watt, and L Harriman L (2015). "Measles outbreak—California, December 2014-February 2015." *MMWR*. 64: 1–2.

73. Wallace RG and K Hall (2009). *It's a Small World: Preparing for a Pandemic Outbreak at and around Disneyland, 2010 and Beyond.* A report commissioned by UNITE HERE Local 11. November 2009. Available online at https://farmingpathogens.files.wordpress.com/2015/01/wallace-and-hall-its-a-small-world-final-report.pdf.

74. Higgins M (2009). "Theme parks confront flu jitters." *New York Times.* 3 November. Available online at http://www.nytimes.com/2009/11/08/travel/8pracflu.html.

75. Ebrahim SH, ZA Memish, TM Uyeki, TAM Khoja, N Marano, and SJN McNabb (2009). "Pandemic H1N1 and the 2009 Hajj." *Science* 326: 938–40.

76. Center for Responsive Politics (2014). *Walt Disney Co. Client Profile: Summary, 2014.* Available online at http://www.opensecrets.org/lobby/clientsum.php?id=d000000128.

77. California Department of Public Health (2015). "California Department of Public Health Confirms 59 Cases of Measles." 21 January. Available online at http://www.cdph.ca.gov/Pages/NR15-008.aspx.

78. Staff (2015). "Disneyland measles: 'Ideal' incubator for major outbreak." *Los Angeles Times.* 14 January. Available online at http://www.latimes.com/local/lanow/la-me-ln-measles-outbreak-at-disneyland-worst-in-15-years-20150114-story.html.

79. Chandler J (2015). "Five Disneyland Resort workers confirmed with measles." *Orange County Register.* 21 January. Available online at http://www.ocregister.com/articles/disneyland-648693-workers-measles.html.

80. Coker M (2015). "Chairman Bob Iger says measles outbreak is not Infecting Disneyland attendance." *OC Weekly.* 5 February. Available online at http://blogs.ocweekly.com/navelgazing/2015/02/bob_iger_disneyland_measles_attendance.php.

81. Allday E (2015). "Failure to vaccinate fueled state's measles epidemic." *San Francisco Chronicle.* 7 March. Available online at http://www.sfchronicle.com/bayarea/article/Failure-to-vaccinate-fueled-state-s-measles-6121401.php.

Made in Minnesota

82. Ip HS et al. (2015). "Novel Eurasian Highly Pathogenic Avian Influenza A H5 Viruses in Wild Birds, Washington, USA, 2014." *Emerg Infect Dis.* 21(5): 886–90.

83. Hughlett M (2015). "About 40 countries ban imports of Minnesota turkeys after avian flu outbreak." *Star Tribune.* 6 March. Available online at http://www.startribune.com/about-40-countries-ban-imports-of-

minnesota-turkeys-after-avian-flu-outbreak/295356371/;   Hargarten
J (2015). "Tracking the spread of avian influenza in Minnesota." *Star
Tribune.* 5 June. Available online at http://www.startribune.
com/interactive-track-the-spread-of-avian-flu-in-minnesota/299362711/.

84.   Hughlett M (2015). "Bird flu hits 5.3 million Iowa chickens; Hormel
      says turkey production down." *Star Tribune.* 21 April. Available online
      at http://www.startribune.com/5-3-million-hens-to-be-destroyed-as-
      bird-flu-spreads-to-nw-iowa-chicken-farm/300714491/; Hughlett M
      (2015). "Wisconsin chicken farm hit by bird flu afflicting Minnesota
      turkeys." *Star Tribune.* 13 April. Available online at http://www.
      startribune.com/wisconsin-chicken-farm-hit-by-bird-flu-afflicting-
      minnesota-turkeys/299580401/; Hughlett M (2015). "Cargill affected
      by spread of bird flu." *Star Tribune.* 11 March. Available online at
      http://www.startribune.com/cargill-affected-by-spread-of-bird-
      flu/295988321/; USDA (2015). "USDA Confirms Highly Pathogenic
      H5N2 Avian Influenza in Commercial Turkey Flock in Arkansas."
      Stakeholder Announcement. 11 March. Available online at http://www.
      aphis.usda.gov/stakeholders/downloads/2015/sa_hpai_arkansas.pdf.

85.   Hughlett M (2015). "Twin Cities grocers have temporary egg short-
      ages because of bird flu." *Star Tribune.* 8 May. Available online at http://
      www.startribune.com/twin-cities-grocers-have-temporary-egg-short-
      ages-because-of-bird-flu/302951231/.

86.   Hughlett M (2015). "Rembrandt Foods egg farm could be single larg-
      est operation hit by bird flu." *Star Tribune.* 30 April. Available online
      at http://www.startribune.com/rembrandt-foods-egg-farm-could-be-
      largest-hit-by-bird-flu/301842401/.

87.   Hughlett M (2015). "Minnesota turkey farmers could take devastating
      financial hit because of bird flu." *Star Tribune.* 12 April. Available online
      at http://www.startribune.com/minnesota-turkey-farmers-could-take-
      devastating-hit-from-bird-flu/299463631/.

88.   Minnesota Department of Agriculture and USDA (2013). *2012
      Minnesota Agricultural Statistics.* Available online at http://www.
      nass.usda.gov/Statistics_by_State/Minnesota/Publications/Annual_
      Statistical_Bulletin/2012/Whole%20Book.pdf.

89.   Hughlett M (2015). "About 40 countries ban imports of Minnesota tur-
      keys after avian flu outbreak."

90.   Pitt D and S Karnowski (2015). "A primer on the bird flu affecting Midwest
      poultry flocks." Associated Press. 21 April. Available online at http://news.
      yahoo.com/bird-flu-takes-biggest-toll-yet-virus-hits-055236427-finance.
      html.

91.   Hughlett M (2015). "Federal scientists working on bird flu vaccines."
      Star Tribune. 22 April. Available online at http://www.startribune.com/

federal-scientists-working-on-bird-flu-vaccines/300949201/; Wallace RG (2009). "Pigs do fly! Implications for influenza." *Farming Pathogens.* 3 December. Available online at https://farmingpathogens.wordpress. com/2009/12/03/pigs-do-fly-implications-for-influenza-2/.

92. Associated Press (2015). "Lawmakers drawing up contingency funding plans for bird flu." Available online at http://minnesota.cbslocal. com/2015/04/24/lawmakers-drawing-up-contingency-funding-plans -for-bird-flu/.
93. Hughlett M (2015). "Minnesota turkey farmers could take devastating financial hit because of bird flu."
94. Hughlett M (2015). "About 40 countries ban imports of Minnesota turkeys after avian flu outbreak."
95. Hughlett M (2015). "Bird flu may persist for several years in Minnesota, rest of U.S." *Star Tribune.* 16 April. Available online at http://www. startribune.com/bird-flu-may-persist-for-several-years-in-minnesota-rest-of-u-s/300151221/.
96. Hughlett M (2015). "Rembrandt Foods egg farm could be single largest operation hit by bird flu."
97. Karnowski S (2015). "CDC eyeing bird flu vaccine for humans, though risk is low." Associated Press. 22 April. Available online at http://www. salon.com/2015/04/22/cdc_eyeing_bird_flu_vaccine_for_humans _though_risk_is_low/.
98. Pitt D (2015). "No. 1 egg-producing state aims to keep bird flu out." Associated Press. 17 April. Available online at http://www.salon. com/2015/04/17/no_1_egg_producing_state_aims_to_keep_bird _flu_out/.
99. Neuman W (2010). "An Iowa egg farmer and a history of Salmonella." *New York Times.* 21 September. Available online at http://www.nytimes. com/2010/09/22/business/22eggs.html; Roos R (2015). "Michigan finds H5N2 in wild geese; Iowa hit again." CIDRAP News. 8 June. Available online at http://www.cidrap.umn.edu/news-perspective/2015/06/ michigan-finds-h5n2-wild-geese-iowa-hit-again.
100. Pitt D (2015). "No. 1 egg-producing state aims to keep bird flu out."
101. Hughlett M (2015). "About 40 countries ban imports of Minnesota turkeys after avian flu outbreak."
102. White R (2015). "What if all poultry flocks were raised cage-free?" *Star Tribune.* 10 April. Available online at http://www.startribune.com/ what-if-all-poultry-flocks-were-raised-cage-free/299263931/.
103. Meersman T (2015). "Free-range turkey debate could be reignited because of bird flu." *Star Tribune.* 25 May. Available online at www. startribune.com/free-range-turkey-debate-could-be-reignited-because-of-bird-flu/304873361/.

104. Vijaykrishna D et al. (2008). "Evolutionary dynamics and emergence of panzootic H5N1 influenza viruses." *PLoS Pathogens* 4(9): e1000161. doi: 10.1371/journal.ppat.1000161.
105. Marcotty J (2015). "Scientists race to decode secrets of deadly bird flu." *Star Tribune.* 8 June. http://www.startribune.com/scientists-race-to-decode-secrets-of-deadly-avian-flu-strain/306436121/.
106. Wallace RG (2013). "Protecting H3N2v's privacy." *Farming Pathogens.* 10 June. Available online at https://farmingpathogens.wordpress.com/2013/06/10/protecting-h3n2vs-privacy/.
107. Shiffer J (2015). "Location of infected livestock farms remains secret." *Star Tribune.* 15 April. Available online at http://www.startribune.com/location-of-infected-livestock-farms-remains-secret/299853641/.
108. Hughlett M (2015). "Bird flu hits 5.3 million Iowa chickens; Hormel says turkey production down." *Star Tribune.* 21 April. Available online at http://www.startribune.com/5-3-million-hens-to-be-destroyed-as-bird-flu-spreads-to-nw-iowa-chicken-farm/300714491/; Hughlett M (2015). "Latest bird flu outbreak brings total Minnesota turkeys affected to 1.4 million." *Star Tribune.* 15 April. http://www.startribune.com/bird-flu-has-become-epidemic-with-1-4m-minn-turkeys-affected/299732091/.
109. Shiffer J (2015). "Location of infected livestock farms remains secret."
110. Pitt D (2015). "Bird flu confirmed at Iowa farm with 5.3 million chickens." Associated Press. 20 April. Available online at http://news.yahoo.com/bird-flu-confirmed-iowa-farm-5-3-million-214705641--finance.html; Roos R and L Schnirring (2015). "Avian flu hits more farms in Iowa, Minnesota." CIDRAP News. 27 April. Available online at http://www.cidrap.umn.edu/news-perspective/2015/04/avian-flu-hits-more-farms-iowa-minnesota.
111. Roos R (2015). "Change in pattern of H5N2 spread raises questions." CIDRAP News. 7 May. Available online at http://www.cidrap.umn.edu/news-perspective/2015/05/change-pattern-h5n2-spread-raises-questions.
112. Wallace RG (2013). "Protecting H3N2v's privacy"; Butler D (2008). "Politically correct names given to flu viruses." *Nature* 452: 923.
113. Eller D (2015). "Iowa searching for help with millions of dead chickens." *Des Moines Register.* 18 May. Available online at www.usatoday.com/story/news/nation/2015/05/18/iowa-help-disposal-dead-chickens/27533993/.
114. Hughlett M (2015). "Minnesota turkey farmers could take devastating financial hit because of bird flu.".
115. Wallace RG (2009). "The agro-industrial roots of swine flu H1N1." *Farming Pathogens.* 26 April. Available online at https://

farmingpathogens.wordpress.com/2009/04/26/the-agro-industrial-roots -of-swine-flu-h1n1/.

116. Hughlett M (2015). "Minnesota turkey farmers could take devastating financial hit because of bird flu."

117. Wallace RG (2013). "Bird flew." *Farming Pathogens*. 26 March. Available online at https://farmingpathogens.wordpress.com/2013/03/26/bird-flew/.

118. Cooke F, RF Rockwell, and DB Lank (1995). *The Snow Geese of La Pérouse Bay: Natural Selection in the Wild*. Oxford University Press, Oxford.

119. Cox C and S Rundquist (2013). *Going, Going, Gone: Millions of Acres of Wetlands and Fragile Land Go Under the Plow*. Environmental Working Group. Available online at http://static.ewg.org/pdf/going_gone_cropland_hotspots_final.pdf; Wright CK and MC Wimberly (2013). "Recent land use change in the Western Corn Belt threatens grasslands and wetlands." *PNAS* 110: 4134–39. Available online at http://www.pnas.org/content/110/10/4134.full.pdf.

120. Environmental Working Group (2013). "Wetlands and wetland buffer converted to cropland, 2008–2012." Available online at http://a.tiles.mapbox.com/v3/ewg.WET_Hotspots.html#5/40.480/-98.525.

121. Hughlett M (2015). "Rembrandt Foods egg farm could be single largest operation hit by bird flu."

122. Ibid.; Associated Press (2015). "Bird flu found in hawk in western Minnesota." 30 April. Available online at minnesota.cbslocal.com/2015/04/30/bird-flu-found-in-hawk-in-western-minnesota/.

123. Hughlett M (2015). "Rembrandt Foods egg farm could be single largest operation hit by bird flu."

124. Leonard C (2014). *The Meat Racket: The Secret Takeover of America's Food Business*. Simon & Schuster, New York.

125. Wallace RG (2014). "Collateralized farmers." *Farming Pathogens*. 8 May. Available online at https://farmingpathogens.wordpress.com/2014/05/08/collateralized-farmers/.

126. Hughlett M and P Condon (2015). "Minnesota turkey deaths to top 2 million with new bird flu outbreaks." *Star Tribune*. 24 April. Available online at www.startribune.com/minn-turkey-deaths-to-top-2m-with-new -outbreaks/300852521/.

127. Hughlett M (2015). "Egg shortage from bird flu trickling down to consumers." *Star Tribune*. 30 May. Available online at http://www.startribune.com/egg-shortage-from-bird-flu-trickling-down-to-consumers/305580361/.

128. Sawyer L (2015). "Bird flu threat eases, but layoffs announced at Rembrandt Enterprises." *Star Tribune*. 21 May. Available online at http://www.startribune.com/bird-flu-threat-eases-but-layoffs-announced -at-rembrandt-enterprises/304643681/; Reuters (2015). "Bird flu leads

to Hormel layoffs, extra $330 million in government funds." 21 May. Available online at www.nydailynews.com/life-style/health/bird-flu-leads-hormel-layoffs-extra-330-million-gove-article-1.2212325.

129. Hughlett M (2015). "Hormel CEO sees fall as 'wild card' because of bird flu." *Star Tribune*. 20 May. Available online at www.startribune.com/hormel-ceo-sees-fall-as-wild-card-because-of-bird-flu/304416271/.

130. Hughlett M (2015). "Hormel operation in Meeker County becomes ninth Minnesota farm hit with bird flu." *Star Tribune*. 9 April. Available online at www.startribune.com/hormel-farm-in-meeker-county-is-latest-in-minnesota-with-bird-flu/299086071/.

131. Hughlett M (2015). "Hormel CEO sees fall as 'wild card' because of bird flu."

132. Wallace RG (2009). "Breeding influenza: the political virology of off-shore farming." *Antipode*. 41: 916–51.

133. Hughlett M (2016). "University of Minnesota study says farmers may have aided bird flu's spread." *Star Tribune*. 28 January. Available online at http://www.startribune.com/farmers-tilling-nearby-fields-might-have-contributed-to-bird-flu-epidemic/366919751/; Center for Animal and Food Safety (2016). *Epidemiologic Study of Highly Pathogenic Avian Influenza H5N1 among Turkey Farms 2015*. University of Minnesota. Summary report. Available online at https://www.cahfs.umn.edu/sites/cahfs.umn.edu/files/hpai_h5n2_2015_summary_report.pdf.

134. Center for Animal and Food Safety (2016). *Epidemiologic Study of Highly Pathogenic Avian Influenza H5N1 among Turkey Farms 2015*.

Missed Anthropy

135. Quammen D (2012). *Spillover: Animal Infections and the Next Human Pandemic*. W W Norton. 26 September. Available online at https://www.youtube.com/watch?v=qgsqfGssMF4; Quammen D (2012). *Spillover: Animal Infections and the Next Human Pandemic*. W. W. Norton, New York.

136. Robertson T (2012). *The Malthusian Moment: Global Population Growth and the Birth of American Environmentalism*. Rutgers University Press, Piscataway, NJ; Taylor PJ and R Garcia-Barrios (1999). "The dynamics of socio-environmental change and the limits of neo-Malthusian environmentalism," 139–67. In T Mount, H Shue and M Dore (eds). *Global Environmental Economics: Equity and the Limits to Markets*. Oxford Blackwell, Oxford.

137. Wallace RG (2012). "We need a Structural One Health." *Farming Pathogens*. 3 August. Available online at http://farmingpathogens. wordpress.com/2012/08/03/we-need-a-structural-one-health/.

138. Wallace RG and RA Kock (2012). "Whose food footprint? Capitalism,

agriculture and the environment." *Human Geography* 5(1): 68–83. Available online at http://farmingpathogens.files.wordpress.com/2012 /05/hg-12-5-wallace-2.pdf.

139. Cockburn A (1996). *The Golden Age Is In Us: Journeys and Encounters 1987–1994*. Verso, New York.

Index

CPSIA information can be obtained
at www.ICGtesting.com
Printed in the USA
JSHW021149020720
6463JS00003B/7